RACE AND RACE RELATIONS

Race and Race Relations

A CHRISTIAN VIEW OF HUMAN CONTACTS

By
ROBERT E. SPEER

NEGRO UNIVERSITIES PRESS
NEW YORK

Preface

TWO problems to which men have never yet found for themselves satisfactory answers are the problem of Church and State and the problem of race relations. This volume is an attempt to set forth the Christian conception and the Christian solution of the second of these problems. There is no pretence of approaching the problem without presuppositions. I do not believe that any one ever has approached or ever will approach the race problem with an absolutely neutral and colourless mind. Certainly no Christian can do so. He seeks to view it and every other subject with what he conceives to be the mind of Christ. That is assuredly the approach attempted in this study. It is an effort to set forth the way of Christ in race relationships.

This does not mean, however, that facts are evaded or bent in any way. Our only hope of ever solving any human problem is by finding and following the truth. And this is a sincere and earnest endeavour to find and state the truth about race and race relations. The best way to arrive at this truth is surely to go out among the races of the world and to associate with them in good will and friendship, to think of other races and to feel and act toward them as we should wish them to think of us and to feel and act toward us, and to seek to behave toward men of all races as one conceives Christ would approve. I have written as one who counts men of a score of different races as personal friends, as truly known as friends of his own race.

The effort has been made to supply in this volume a source book of material on the race question as well as a consistent and constructive statement of the Christian view. A friend of another race has criticised it on the ground that it should have been more partisan in some of its positions. I think there is no indefiniteness of conviction anywhere, but the writer's purpose has been to state fairly any divergent views in order that the reader may have the material for his own conclusions.

5

An abbreviated edition of this book was issued in the spring as a mission study text book by the Missionary Education Movement and the Council of Women for Home Missions. These agencies have cordially consented to the use of the material that was in the smaller book. That is less than half, however, of the present volume. The chapter by Sir Narayan Chandavarkar, of Bombay, did not appear at all in the smaller study book.

The author desires to acknowledge gratefully his obligation to Professor William Adams Brown, Professor Edward G. Conklin, the Rev. Andrew Thakar Das, Professor D. J. Fleming, Dr. George E. Haynes, Mr. Bruno Lasker, Professor F. W. Williams, Mornay Williams, Esq., and other friends, some of whom have read the manuscript, or part of it, and all of whom have helped with contributions or criticisms. No one of them, however, is in any way responsible for the views set forth.

I desire to call attention to the books of two of my most valued friends, J. H. Oldham's *Christianity and the Race Problem,* and Basil Matthews' *Clash of Colour.* All three of these books were written quite independently but, at the same time, with the same purpose and under the same conditions.

The race problem is capable of solution because so many men of different races in their own relationships have proved that it is. And Christ is the supreme proof.

R. E. S.

New York.

Contents

CHAPTER I

THE ORIGIN AND NATURE OF RACE

CHAPTER II

THE IDEA OF RACE SUPERIORITY

8 CONTENTS

CHAPTER III

The Good and Gain of Race and Race Distinction

CHAPTER IV

The Evils and Abuses of Race

CHAPTER V

ASPECTS AND RELATIONS OF RACE

CHAPTER VI

AN INDIAN STATESMAN'S VIEW OF RACE

CHAPTER VII

THE SOLUTION OF THE RACE PROBLEM

CHAPTER VIII

SOME SPECIFIC RACE PROBLEMS OF TODAY

I

THE ORIGIN AND NATURE OF RACE

THE questions of race and race relationships are the most insistent questions of the modern world, but there is no agreement as to what race is, as to how races originated, as to the character of racial differences, as to the meaning of race distinctions in human history, as to the solution of the problems of the relations of race to race, or as to the ultimate destiny of the present races of mankind.

The thesis of this book is simply the Christian view of these questions. It holds that God made of one blood all races of men and that all races are but parts of one human race. Mankind is one great kindred of all men. That is what the word " mankind " means. In this view races are not conceived as biological fixtures but simply as enlarged family groups which are subject to moulding and transforming influences just as families are. Furthermore, the life of each race and of all races, that is of humanity, is not explicable on any mechanistic or materialistic basis. God is at work in human life and organic and personal energies which represent freedom and spiritual purpose are the determining forces in unfolding human history. This is not an arbitrary pre-judgment. It is the reasonable conclusion from the actual facts of race and race relationships.

The study of the race problem should begin with the kindly and humane recognition of a race as simply an enlarged family. This is the origin of race according to the Bible and in the view of all the Semitic peoples.

" The antique conception of kinship is participation in one blood, which passes from parent to child and circulates in the

11

veins of every member of the family. The unity of the family or clan is viewed as a physical unity, for the blood is the life,—an idea familiar to us from the Old Testament,—and it is the same blood and therefore the same life that is shared by every descendant of the common ancestor. The idea that the race has a life of its own, of which individual lives are only parts, is expressed even more clearly by picturing the race as a tree, of which the ancestor is the root or stem and the descendants the branches. This figure is used by all the Semites, and is very common both in the Old Testament and in the Arabian poets." [1]

And the Semitic view is the view which is universally true. Bagehot saw the patria potestas at the root of all race- and nation-building: "First, the nation must possess the patria potestas in some form so marked as to give family life distinctness and precision, and to make a home education and a home discipline probable and possible. While descent is traced only through the mother, and while the family is therefore a vague entity, no progress to a high polity is possible. Secondly, that polity would seem to have been created very gradually; by the aggregation of families into clans or gentes, and of clans into nations, and then again by the widening of nations so as to include circumjacent outsiders, as well as the first compact and sacred group." [2] The racial sense of family unity has been the great cohesive force in China. There " the permanency of birth privileges (has been) allowed to the Royal Family not because it fulfills the functions of an autocracy, but because it embodies the conception of the nation as one family with a permanent relation to the will of Heaven, which so ordained the social nature of man." [3] This family tie, however, has never been exclusively the tie of blood relationship. " The mere tie of blood-relationship was of no account among the Romans. . . . The tie of family was not the tie of blood; it was not the tie produced by marriage and by generation but a bond created by civil law—a bond of power." [4] In other words

---

[1] W. Robertson Smith, *The Religion of the Semites*, p. 40 f.
[2] Bagehot, *Physics and Politics*, p. 184.
[3] Quoted in Curtis's *The Commonwealth of Nations*, p. 5.
[4] Ortolan, History of Roman Law, quoted in Storrs's, *The Divine Origin of Christianity*, p. 462.

the family, just like the race, is a social rather than a physiological institution.[5]

Because each race is in reality only an enlarged family group it is right to conceive of its growth as governed, in the main, by the same processes which shape the character and growth of a family. Common experiences accentuate family consciousness and character. Common memories and traditions which store up bits of common experience bind a family together and give it a temper and note of its own. The weight of such communities of interest and life in a race is immeasurably great. " The cementing force of contests waged against natural dangers, threatening the entire community and binding them together for a common defence," " all common needs which draw men out of barren isolation," common hopes and ideals and undertakings, bind the expanded family into a race personality. " In the low lying districts on the coast of the North Sea, in Germany and Holland, the common danger from broken dykes and inundation by reason of furious storms and high tides has evoked a feeling of union which has had important results. There is a deep meaning in the myths which intimately connect the fight against these forces of Nature, these hundred-headed hydras, or sea-monsters crawling on to the land, with the extortion of the highest benefits for races in the foundation of states and the acquisition of culture. No race shows this more than the Chinese." [6] The Chinese illustrate also the truth that race cohesion is more powerful than race consciousness. In old days, China had little sense of racial unity. Citizens of different provinces looked on one another more aversely than different nations in the West. But the fact of racial unity is more powerful than the sense, and to-day China's politicians are deliberately preparing to break China up into provincial nations with the confidence that ultimately these can be united under the pressure of Chinese race cohesion.

No present race, of course, represents the purity of a single

---

[5] LeRoy, *The Religion of the Primitives,* Chap. III. See Gulick's argument that the differences between the Eastern and the Western races are more sociological than biological. *Evolution of the Japanese,* pp. 424-428.

[6] Ratzel, *The History of Mankind,* Vol. I, p. 140.

family and its descendants. The intermingling of centuries has been too confusing. But innumerable family relationships are evident within and between the races. The Jews are still the seed of Abraham, with obvious and tenacious family resemblance. And the Welsh are the same stock as the Basques and the Britons, before the Britons were mixed with the conquering races. Some of the Latin American peoples differ from one another in racial character by reason of clearly traceable differences of family genealogy on both sides of their mixed inheritance, such as the Quichua-Galician stock of Bolivia, the Araucanian-Andalusian stock of Chile, and the Guarany-Portuguese stock of Brazil.

The truth about race character is well stated by Bruno Lasker:

" Many anthropologists discuss race as though what kept it together were purely a biological kinship. This is not so; in a sense the terms race and nation are interchangeable; in both the element of common memories, traditions, experiences, is present as well as common blood; only the relative weight of these two factors differs. In the family, properly speaking, the biological factor also is only one of the ties of union. For instance, in some of the greatest dynasties the proportion of the founder's blood in those who after several centuries still adhere to his patronymic and pride themselves on their descent is almost non-existent, so small. The clan, the tribe, indeed any large family in a primitive community, is composed not only of blood relatives but also the relatives by marriage and their offspring. What makes it a clan, a tribe, or a family is exactly the spiritual bond."

In the family life there are prenatal and transmitted characteristics, but each family as we know it, and likewise each race, is the product not only of these inherited tendencies, but also of its environment and education. Changed conditions can undo family and race inferiorities or dissimilarities. It is held by some that this statement is not true of inherited traits. But how did such racial traits come into existence? Surely they are not eternal. And if by some process they were produced, as they certainly were, the same or kindred processes can modify or transform them. We see this happening before our eyes in the case of families. In a generation two families may completely exchange their character and conditions as a result of outward circumstances or of the actions of individuals who rise above and reverse the family inheritance. With a far slower movement and by a far more intricate process races may change, and are not debarred from change by any deterministic racial prohibition. At the Universal Races Congress in London, in 1911, Dr. Myers, of the University of Cambridge, read a paper on " The Permanence of Racial Mental Differences," in which he laid down the four following propositions:

I. That the mental characters of the majority of the peasant class throughout Europe are essentially the same as those of primitive communities.

II. That such differences between them as exist are the result of differences in environment and in individual variability.

III. That the relation between the organism and its environment (considered in its broadest sense) is the ultimate cause of variation, bodily and mental.

IV. That this being admitted, the possibility of the progressive development of all primitive peoples must be conceded, if only the environment can be appropriately changed.

And he closed his paper with the assertion " that if only the environment can be gradually changed, perhaps with sufficient slowness and certainly in the appropriate direction, both the mental and the physical characters of the lowest races may ultimately attain those of the highest, and vice versa. If we assume, as I think we must assume, that the white and negro races owe their respective characters ultimately to their environment, there is no *a priori* reason, it seems to me, for denying the possibility of a reversal of their differences, if the environment to which they are respectively exposed be gradually, in the course of many hundreds of thousands of years, reversed." [7]

We are introduced at once into the familiar issue over heredity and education. How do we know that part at least of what we call heredity in children may not be the influence of parental compan-

[7] Spiller, *Papers on Inter-racial Problems, Communicated to the First Universal Races Congress,* London, 1911, pp. 73, 78. This volume will hereafter be cited as *Universal Races Congress.* See footnote on p. 36.

ionship, and in race the influence of social environment? It is enough to note that whatever the force of heredity in racial character may be, it is not sovereign and unalterable. No race is doomed by its inheritance to incapacity for progress and change. Nor is any race secured by its inheritance against deterioration and ruin. Trotsky, in his pamphlet on *Terrorism and Communism,* saw clearly that the quality of industry on which alone human society could rest, was not hereditary. " It is created," he says, " by economic pressure and social education." The origin and history of a race assuredly shape its character.[8] And there are anthropologists who hold that race heredity is the determining power. " Undoubtedly good environment and good education are important factors in the development of good citizens, but of even greater importance is good heredity," says Professor Conklin. " Indeed it is not mere chance or accident that certain forms of civilisation have arisen among certain races and other forms among other races ; on the contrary, inherited characteristics have to a large extent determined the type of civilisation which any race manifests. The qualities and achievements of nations are due less to governments than to grandmothers. . . . It is the duty of biology to teach the nation that heredity is more potent than environment or education." [9] As some one else has put it : " Heredity does rule the destinies of men, with environment only such a factor as the chemical developer, capable of bringing out the image on the film, but incapable of creating it." " To know the worst as well as the best in heredity ; to foresee and to select the best—this is the most essential force in the future evolution of human society," says Professor Osborn.[10] Professor Mc-Dougall also argues that the chief influence in determining national characteristics is racial inheritance. " The circumstance and environment may modify, or even check for a time, the effects of the inherited racial characteristics ; but these will always come out

---

[8] Taine, *History of English Literature,* Vol. I, Introduction, Paragraph V.

[9] The *Yale Review,* April, 1917, " Biology and National Welfare," by Edward G. Conklin, p. 477.

[10] *Eugenics, Genetics and the Family,* Vol. I, p. 4.

again and make themselves felt, and being thus the most persistent element in man's mental make-up, they will appear as the dominant influence in the development of the character and point of view of the group." [11] Mr. Lothrop Stoddard represents the extremest form of this view of the rigid determination of race inheritance. He holds that racial momentum is more powerful than ideas or institutions.[12] He even believes that heredity is responsible for race decay; "The whole weight of scientific evidence shows that degeneracy is caused not by environment but by heredity; that the degeneracy with which we have to deal is an old degeneracy due to taints which have been carried along in the germ plasm for generations." [13] But how did these taints get in? Why may not good come in through the same door which admitted evil? And why may not heredity take up and carry forward good as well as bad? Some answer that the door that was once open is shut, or that at any rate the differences which have developed in the past are "relatively permanent and uninfluenced by external conditions." [14] Others hold that inborn intelligence is static and that all differences "are attainments which are handed down." [15]

Mr. Stoddard is speaking of the one race which he considers superior. If that race is bad with hereditary degeneracy, and if race inheritance is the absolutely dominating force, it is a dark outlook for all that race and for all races. And Mr. Stoddard goes over bodily to the most rigid racial determinism. He rejects John Stuart Mill's statement: "Of all vulgar modes of escaping from the consideration of the effect of social and moral influences on the human mind, the most vulgar is that of attributing the diversity of conduct and character to inherent natural differences." [16] He accepts Woods's deliverance: "Experimentally and

[11] *The Hibbert Journal*, Jan., 1923, "The Influence of Race in History and Politics," by G. C. Field, p. 288.
[12] Stoddard, *The New World of Islam*, p. 35.
[13] Stoddard, *The Revolt Against Civilization*, p. 248.
[14] East, *Mankind at the Crossroads*, p. 131.
[15] See evidence in *Youth and the Race*, p. 307. The witness quoted sees no hope except in a control of the birth rate which will give the better classes with their better inheritance and their better opportunities a chance to outbreed the inferior classes.
[16] Stoddard, *The Revolt Against Civilization*, p. 39.

statistically, there is not a grain of proof that ordinary environment can alter the salient mental and moral traits in any measurable degree from what they were pre-determined to be through
innate influence." [17] And he sets forth as his own view that " it
has been conclusively proved that intelligence is pre-determined
by heredity; that individuals come into the world differing vastly
in mental capacities; that such differences remain virtually constant throughout life and cannot be lessened by environment or
education; that the present mental level of any individual can be
definitely ascertained, and even a child's future adult mental level
confidently predicted. These are surely discoveries whose practical importance can hardly be over-estimated. They enable us to
grade not merely individuals but whole nations and races according to their inborn capacities." [18]   Mr. Exline believes that the
time is at hand when every citizen will be listed according to his
ability and education, and will be educated according to his ability,
and assigned his own inferior or superior place according to the
tests which determine innate capacity; " a scientific classification
of citizens and an accurate destination of each to his proper
sphere, are indispensable alike to the freedom of the individual
and the welfare of society as a whole." [19]   This principle, good
for individuals, is held by many to be good also for races.

But this is a very subjective and passing view. Men who will
look at all the facts certainly can accept no such pessimistic theory.
They must recognise the power of education to modify or direct
inheritance. "There is no heredity without environment," says
Dr. Davenport, of the Carnegie Institution of Washington, " and
few environmental effects which are not dependent also upon
heredity." [20]   Professor East holds a stiff deterministic view but
believes that man's " actions are determined by the heredity he
receives and the environment in which he finds himself." [21]   " In
physical attributes," he holds, " it is found that heredity fixes the
potentiality of development within narrowly defined limits; en-

---

[17] *Ibid.*, p. 48.   [18] *Ibid.*, p. 56.
[19] New York *Times*, Book Review, January 7, 1923, on Exline's *Politics.*
[20] *Eugenics, Genetics and the Family*, Vol. I, p. 27.
[21] East, *Mankind at the Crossroads*, p. 3.

vironment determines matters definitely within these limits. If the parental gifts are right, the children will be tall; their exact height will depend upon their food, their work, their rest, and recreation. Similarly, mental attributes are inherited; whether these potential abilities are fully developed or remain partially dormant depends upon circumstances." [22] And Prof. Conklin writes,

" The quality of citizenship in this country, or in any other, depends not merely upon the stock or race but also upon the environmental conditions. Environment and education do not change heredity, but they do modify development. If there is one thing in biology more certain than another, it is that good environment cannot make good heredity out of that which is bad, but it can and does lead to the development in the individual of good potentialities, which are present in heredity, and to the suppression of bad ones. There are many alternative possibilities in each of us, and which ones will develop depends upon extrinsic conditions. A good citizen is one who has good social ideals and habits, and these are to a certain extent the result of his training and surroundings." [23]

Mr. Field goes much further in reviewing Prof. McDougall's *The Group Mind*. He admits that all influence of racial inheritance in explaining racial differences cannot be absolutely disproved, but he declares, " All attempts to isolate it and trace its working break down. It is not a measurable factor in the development of the national character and institutions, and cannot be taken into account for any practical purposes." [24] " Heredity," says Prof. Ross, " is a cheap offhand explanation of the characteristics of a people at a given moment, but how is it that continually characteristics change when there has been no change in heredity? The observed traits of French, Germans and English today are by no means the same as the traits they manifested about the middle of the last century. Many of the faults of contemporary South American character can easily be duplicated from the history of

[22] *Ibid.,* p. 31.
[23] *The Yale Review,* April, 1917, " Biology and National Welfare," p. 482.
[24] The *Hibbert Journal,* Jan., 1923, p. 299.

our own people. Today we succeed in making certain virtues fairly general among ourselves because gradually our society has equipped itself with the home training, the education, the religion, the ideals of life, the standards of conduct and the public opinion competent to produce these virtues. Societies that lack the right soul moulds will, of course, fail to obtain these virtues. But there is no reason why they may not borrow such moulds from the more experienced societies, just as we ourselves have sometimes done." [25]

Let us state the views of these two schools of opinion a little more fully. On the one hand, many believers in heredity believe also in its absolutism. Dr. David Starr Jordan declares:

"Nurture can do wonders with man, but it cannot alter the nature he is to transmit to his descendants. . . . The elements in the germ plasm are ancient and persistent, not affected by the vicissitudes of the individual life which bears them from generation to generation. . . . More permanent than climate or training or experience are the traits of heredity and in the long run it is always 'blood that tells.' . . . The claim is sometimes made on an assumed basis of science that all races are biologically equal and that the difference of capacity which appears is due to opportunity and education. But opportunity has come to no race as a gift. By effort it has created its own environment. Powerful strains make their own environment. The progress of each race has depended on its own inherent qualities. There has been no other leverage. Physical surroundings have played only a minor part." [26]

Others who deem heredity the stronger force, nevertheless balance their judgments with a large recognition of the place of education, especially of education by the social environment. "That physical environment is not to be disregarded in any historic study of a civilisation is obvious enough," says Goldenweiser, "but no physical environment can in itself be responsible for producing a definite type of civilisation, nor can any environment, barring extremes, prevent a civilisation from developing. 'Do not talk

---

[25] Ross, *South of Panama*, p. 249 f.
[26] Jordan, *War and the Breed*, pp. 13, 15, 16, 32 f.

to me about environmental determinants,' the philosopher Hegel is
reported to have said, ' Where the Greeks once lived, the Turks
live now. That settles the matter.' " But Goldenweiser also
writes, " Racial factors cannot be held responsible for the variety
of civilisational forms. For all we know or can convincingly assume, one generation receives nothing from its predecessor beyond
the psycho-physical inheritance of the race plus the accumulated
civilisational possessions acquired through education and other
channels of cultural transfer." [27] " On the whole," says Thorndike, " it seems certain that prevalent opinions much exaggerate
the influence of differences in circumstances and training in producing the intellectual and moral differences found in men of the
same nation and epoch. Certain nations seem to have been made
by certain environments when really the nation already made
selected the environment." But he adds, " To the real work of
man for man—the increase of achievement through the improvement of the environment—the influence of heredity offers no barrier," and he goes on, " Morality is more susceptible than intellect
to environmental influence." [28] Park and Burgess sum up the
matter as follows:

" The question remains still to what extent so-called racial characteristics are actually racial, *i. e.*, biological, and to what extent
they are the effect of environmental conditions. The thesis of this
paper, to state it again, is: (1) that fundamental temperamental
qualities, which are the basis of interest and attention, act as
selective agencies and as such determine what elements in the
cultural environment each race will select; in what region it will
seek and find its vocation in the larger social organisation; (2)
that, on the other hand, technique, science, machinery, tools, habits,
discipline, and all the intellectual and mechanical devices with
which the civilised man lives and works remain relatively external
to the inner core of significant attitudes and values which constitute what we may call the will of the group. This racial will is, to
be sure, largely social, that is, modified by social experience, but it
rests ultimately upon a complex of inherited characteristics, which
are racial.

---

[27] Goldenweiser, *Early Civilization*, pp. 292, 299 f., 397 f.
[28] *Educational Psychology*, Vol. III, pp. 311, 313.

" The individual man is the bearer of a double inheritance. As a member of a race, he transmits by interbreeding a biological inheritance. As a member of society, or a social group, on the other hand, he transmits by communication a social inheritance. The particular complex of inheritable characters which characterises the individuals of a racial group constitutes the racial temperament. The particular group of habits, accommodations, sentiments, attitudes, and ideals transmitted by communication and education constitutes a social tradition. Between this temperament and this tradition there is, as has been generally recognised, a very intimate relationship. My assumption is that temperament is the basis of the interests; that as such it determines in the long run the general run of attention, and this, eventually, determines the selection in the case of an individual of his vocation, in the case of the racial group of its culture. That is to say, temperament determines what things the individual and the group will be interested in; what elements of the general culture, to which they have access, they will assimilate; what, to state it pedagogically, they will learn.

" It will be evident at once that where individuals of the same race and hence the same temperament are associated, the temperamental interests will tend to reinforce one another, and the attention of members of the group will be more completely focused upon the specific objects and values that correspond to the racial temperament. In this way racial qualities become the basis for nationalities, a nationalistic group being merely a cultural and, eventually, a political society founded on the basis of racial inheritances." [29]

This estimate allows much to the power of social environment in race character. Others are willing to go further.

" The social inheritance of ideas and emotions to which the individual is submitted from infancy," says Bury, " is more important than the tendencies physically transmitted from parent to child. The power of education and government in moulding the members of a society has recently been illustrated on a large scale in the psychological transformation of the German people in the life of a generation. . . . Some thinkers are coming round to the opinion that enormous differences in capacity which seem fundamental

---

[29] *Introduction to the Science of Sociology*, by Robert E. Park and Ernest W. Burgess, Chapter II, "Human Nature," Section 4, "Temperament, Tradition and Nationality," pp. 137-138.

are a result of the differences in social inheritance, and that these are again due to a long sequence of historical circumstances; and consequently, that there is no people in the world doomed by nature to perpetual inferiority or irrevocably disqualified by race from playing a useful part in the future of civilisation." [30]

Even from the viewpoint of the mechanistic philosophy an argument is made out for the supremacy of education and environment over heredity. In *A Mechanistic View of War and Peace,* Dr. Crile, one of our leading surgeons, contends:

" The war reaction of a people is the final expression of its action patterns: their conduct is natural, inevitable. . . . War and peace can be comprehended only when they are considered as real effects of action patterns established by phylogeny and ontogeny. . . . Man should be considered as a mechanism, whose reactions under a given set of conditions are as inevitable as are the reactions of any other mechanism, such as a locomotive for example. . . . Subject races cannot be altered by force. . . . Force creates action patterns in opposition to, not in consonance with, that force. A people may be brutalised into formal submission, but brutal treatment results in creating in the brains of the children the strongest action patterns of opposition and of hatred. The conquering energy can never supplant the influence of the hating mother who plants action patterns in the brains of her children when the shades are drawn. . . . What limit can be set to the modification of the action patterns by education and training planned for the strengthening of the action patterns of peace? . . . The earliest predisposing cause of the present war of nations was the establishment of an action pattern of war in the first child who as a man is now concerned therein. *This event was a microscopic declaration of war.* Multiples of like action patterns made inevitable the final declaration of war between the nations. Therefore, like Prometheus, man is chained to the rock of fate, unless a new philosophy is introduced; unless the order of life of the majority of the inhabitants of the earth be so modified that in the next generation peace patterns shall be increased and war patterns lessened. . . . Man's action patterns reflect as in a mirror his environment. . . . The young of all animals are plastic. The child of man is most plastic. . . . If a child remains in a Christian portion of the web of life, Christian action

<hr>

[30] Bury, *The Idea of Progress,* p. 166 f.

patterns are formed; if in a pagan web he becomes pagan [note: not 'is,' but 'becomes']. . . . The action patterns thus formed in the plastic brain constitute the personality of the individual and make the reactions of the human mechanism as inevitable and as true as are the reactions of a man-made machine. . . . The environment therefore is the mould which predetermines the man. . . . The only way in which the action patterns of a people can be altered is by changing the mould—altering the environment. . . . In America, the plastic newborn of many races and nationalities are gathered and are so melted and moulded in our public schools that the second generations of European origin can scarcely be distinguished from those of *Mayflower* descent."

On the next page of his book, Dr. Crile speaks of man's comprehending "the dominating influence of his progenitors" and appreciating "the infinite possibilities of his training." [31]

Still more on the basis of spiritualistic philosophies, men believe in the freedom of race from the absolutism of heredity. "It is no longer doubtful," says Dr. W. H. Thompson in *Brain and Personality,* "that every race of man can be educated to know anything, from reading and writing to mathematics, philosophy and political economy. In other words, man is always and everywhere, man, and infinitely distant in mind from every ape." "The criminal," says Sir Basil Thomson, "is not born, but made." [32] Dr. Wiley sees the possibility of extirpating the liquor-thirst in thirty years, [33] and Kidd believes that the entire world could be remade by the mothers of any single generation. [34] A new school of sociologists is growing up which conceives human nature itself to be not a biological mechanism but a product of social relationships. "Human nature," says Professor Hartshorne, "is what human nature does—under certain conditions; namely, when it is in socially functioning relations." Professor Dunlap declares that human nature cannot be explained in terms of instincts or original tendencies, and that in the matter of ideals inherited capacity plays only a minor part. Professor Richardson holds that "instinctive

---

[31] *A Mechanistic View of War and Peace,* pp. 66, 58, 75, 77, 97, 100 f.
[32] New York *Times,* Dec. 23, 1922.
[33] New York *Times,* Jan. 26, 1923.
[34] Kidd, *The Science of Power.*

impulses never come to utterance, amorphously, as pure instinct. It is always as modified through conscious reactions to factors found in environment." Some even hold that education can change the center of personality and that it is justifiable for man to " envisage a new race." [35]

So much, at least, is clear: There is no fiat of fixed racial destiny. Races, like families and individuals, are free by right choices and under the influence of right forces to move on into a new and different character. As Finot says,

" All the condemnations of peoples and races in virtue of an innate superiority or inferiority have in reality failed. Life has taught us to be more circumspect in our judgments. A savant who presumes to pronounce a verdict of eternal barbarism against any people deserves to be laughed at.

" This possibility of developing the faculty of thinking implies at the same time the faculty of benefiting by its age-long conquests. It is thus that the peoples who approach tardily towards civilisation succeed in easily regaining the time lost throughout their period of barbarism. The complex world of culture opens out at once before a people who begin to draw from its source. Together with European thought they appropriate its social and political advantages, its discoveries and inventions. They enter thus abruptly within the space of a generation into the great civilised family, and benefit by its institutions which were formed after centuries of persevering toil.

" The Negroes, for example, whom it is desired to class among the most inferior races, astonish, as we shall see later on, all those who study their history without prejudice by their progress, which is altogether amazing. Fifty years ago those of the Southern States did not possess a hundred hectares of land. Today the number of negro landed proprietors exceeds 130,000 and represents a value of 1,500,000,000 francs, whereas they all are worth more than four thousand millions. The balance sheet of the last fifty years of this race's existence, which race was believed to be predestined to ' eternal servitude ' under men of ivory or brown colour, is a fact which should make the experts of human inequality pause and ponder." [36]

The truth about racial character and the possibility of racial

---

[35] See papers in *Religious Education*, Feb., 1923.
[36] Finot, *Race Prejudice*, p. 174 f.

progress is wisely put in a statement adapted from Marvin's *Progress and History:*

" We are not to conclude that physical heredity is of no importance to the social order; it must be obvious that the better the qualities of the individuals constituting a race, the more easily they will advance those traditions to a still higher point of excellence, and the more stoutly they would resist deterioration. The qualities upon which the social fabric calls must be there, and the more readily they are forthcoming, the more easily the social machine will work. Hence social progress necessarily implies a certain level of racial development, and its advance may always be checked by the limitations of the racial type. Nevertheless, if we look at human history as a whole, we are impressed with the stability of the great fundamental characteristics of human nature and the relatively sweeping character and often rapid development of social change.

" In view of this contrast we must hesitate to attribute any substantial share in human development to biological factors, and our hesitation is increased when we consider the factors on which social change depends. It is in the department of knowledge and industry that advance is more rapid and certain, and the reason is perfectly clear. It is that on this side each generation can build on the work of its predecessors. A man of very moderate mathematical capacity today can solve problems which puzzled Newton, because he has available the work of Newton and of many another since Newton's time. In the department of ethics the case is different. Each man's character has to be formed anew, and though teaching goes for much, it is not everything. The individual in the end works out his own salvation. Where there is true ethical progress it is in the advance of ethical conceptions and principles which can be handed on; of laws and institutions which can be built up, maintained, and improved. That is to say, there is progress just where the factor of social tradition comes into play and just so far as its influence extends. If the tradition is broken, the race begins again where it stood before the tradition was formed. We may infer that, while the race has been relatively stagnant, society has rapidly developed, and we must conclude that, whether for good or for evil, social changes are mainly determined, not by alterations of racial type, but by modifications of tradition due to the interactions of social causes. Progress is not racial but social." [37]

---

[37] Park and Burgess, *Introduction to the Science of Sociology*, p. 972.

The door of life and hope is open to all races.

But what is race? What are its fundamental criteria? The extreme biological view conceives that there is a fixed racial germ plasm which by heredity is absolutely determinative of racial character and of the character of individual members of each race.[38] But the races themselves are not fixtures. As Professor Dixon says: " A race is not a permanent entity, something static; on the contrary it is dynamic and is slowly developing and changing as the result of fresh increments of one or another of its original constituents or of some new one." And the difference in the germ plasm of different races cannot be found by the microscope nor can it be discovered by any chemical analysis. It is a biological hypothesis.[39] A more moderate view finds the racial dif-

---

[38] *Eugenics, Genetics and the Family,* Vol. I, pp. 65-75. Paper by C. E. McClung, " Evolution of the Chromosome Complex."

[39] A microscopic examination of the blood of Negro and white shows the same chromosomal composition, both in general form and in number of chromosomes. (*Eugenics, Genetics and the Family,* Vol. I, Plate I.) And so far as the surgeons now know, the blood of any race can be transfused into the veins of any other race. The qualities which make blood non-transferable are not racial but individual. The biologists hold, however, that even though the differences in racial germ plasm cannot be found by any tests, they are nevertheless there and are demonstrated by their effects. The sociologists reply that the effects may be due to other causes. It may be well to cite the views of the biologists. Prof. Conklin, of Princeton, writes:

" It is, of course, true that one cannot detect with the microscope any visible difference in the germ plasm of one human race as compared with that of another, but this would also be true if we were to compare the germ plasms of many different genera and even phyla of animals. The fact is that differences of an invisible nature may readily be detected by the results of development when they cannot be directly seen with the microscope. For example, there is no question that there is some difference in the germ plasm of a Negro and a white man, but this difference cannot be directly observed because our microscopes are too imperfect to see all the differences that actually exist in germ plasms. Of course, this method of detecting invisible differences is used in physics and chemistry, and in many other sciences.

" So far as I know there is no difference that is recognisable with the microscope between the blood of a Chinese and that of a white man. . . . But the point of real importance is that differences in germ plasm can be demonstrated to exist even though they cannot be seen directly, just as molecules and atoms can be demonstrated to exist though no one has ever seen a molecule or atom." (Letter E. G. Conklin, Feb. 25, 1924.)

Prof. Parshley, of Smith College, writes:

" Biologists are almost unanimously agreed that new hereditary types of animals and plants can appear only when the chromosomes of the germ

ferentia in various physiological measurements as to the size and shape of the head. Professor Dixon's definition and classification of races rest on three of these measurements, "the cranial or cephalic index, the altitudinal or length-height index and the nasal index." The old theories dealt crudely with long and narrow-headed races and with broad and flat-headed, but Prof. Dixon finds all kinds of heads in the same race, although certain of the twenty-seven possible combinations of his three indices predominate in the various races and sub-races. But Finot makes merry with these indices and with all brain measurements: "The truth

---

cells are modified; moreover, such new types do appear, both in nature (e. g., albino, deer, trout, etc.) and under domestication. Such new types are called 'mutations' for the very purpose of distinguishing them from 'fluctuating variations' (i. e., acquired characteristics) such as large size, due to good food; manual dexterity, due to practice; and any other peculiarity due to individual experience. It is, therefore, nonsensical for Kammerer to identify mutations and acquired characteristics. And it is even more nonsensical for him to pose as the sole refuge and support of Darwin, for the theory of natural selection stands as a fact of experience and of logic without regard to the mode of origin of mutations. In fact, if hereditary qualities could be improved in the mass—if the lower orders could be moved upward in a body under the influence, say, of education or prohibition (as Dr. Kammerer and the *New Republic* seem to think possible)—then the import of natural selection as a principle of evolution would, indeed, diminish towards the vanishing point and Darwin would soon be justly forgotten.

"One of the central problems of biology is, then, to discover the causes of these mutations. That is: what influences can so affect the chromosomes of the germ cells that the generation arising therefrom will be inherently different from its parents? This question is now under active investigation in a hundred biological laboratories; and the possible effects of the environment are being by no means neglected. It is thus premature to announce that the process works precisely thus and so; but modern biology is practically unanimous in certain beliefs: (1) hereditary qualities are extremely stable; (2) permanent true-breeding new races have never yet been produced by experimentally imposed environmental factors; (3) true mutations arise in single *individuals* only, even though thousands may be exposed to identical conditions; (4) the immediate causes of mutations— i. e., changes in hereditary factors (genes)—are unknown, but they are not considered 'inner,' 'supernatural,' or 'metaphysical'; on the contrary, they must be, in the last analysis, environmental; (5) human experience and experiment alike indicate that general circumstantial influences, such as education, training, starving, freezing, etc., do not ordinarily induce corresponding mutations, however much the individual may be modified by their action. This is a principle of practical value for human sociology no less than for commercial animal breeding; and it will not be disturbed, it is safe to say, by the ultimate discovery of just how chemical changes occur in the genes." (New York *Evening Post, Literary Review,* March 8, 1924, p. 586.)

is that the skull and the brain furnish no arguments in favour of organic inequality." [40]

Other teachers find the root of race difference in the glands and look for the principle of racial distinction and classification here. Professor Conklin, who believes racial heredity to be stronger than racial education, still thinks " that many characteristics which have hitherto been regarded as hereditary or racial may be due to environmental causes; it is probable, for example, that stature, long-headedness (dolichocephaly) or round-headedness (brachy-cephaly), etc., may sometimes be caused by higher or lower activity of the thyroid gland and that this may be influenced by food, particularly by the iodine intake." [41]   And now still other theories appear which go beyond the thyroid gland and the iodine intake to different activities of the pituitary body in different races.

" We are justified," Sir Arthur Keith says, " in regarding the pituitary gland as one of the principal pinions in the machinery which regulates the growth of the human body and is directly concerned in determining stature, cast of features, texture of skin and character of hair—all of them marks of race.   When we compare the chief racial types of humanity—Negro, the Mongol, and the Caucasian or European—we can recognise in the last-named a greater predominance of the pituitary than in the other two. The sharp and pronounced nasalisation of the face, the tendency to strong eyebrow ridges, the prominent chin, the tendency to bulk of body and height of stature in the majority of Europeans are best explained, so far as the present state of our knowledge goes, in terms of pituitary function." [42]

And what is the pituitary body?   The Century Dictionary defines it as " a small ovoid pale-reddish body, occupying the silla turcica and attached to the under surface of the cerebellum by the infundibulum."   This is a far more wonderful world than we have ever dreamed, if this is the explanation of the problem of race and of the human history which has grown out of it.

---

[40] Finot, *Race Prejudice,* Chap. VI, " The Divisions of Humanity from a Craniological Point of View."
[41] Conklin, *The Direction of Human Evolution,* p. 35.
[42] Thomson, *The Outline of Science,* Vol. IV, p. 1097.

These biological views regarding race-signs and race-heredity become of grave social significance when they are made the ground of theories of race determinism. It is not, however, of germ plasm, or cranial measure or thyroid or pituitary glands that men are thinking when they talk of race and race characteristics. It is quite other elements that they have in mind. As Prof. Dixon says in the opening paragraph of his great volume:

"We refer to the Negro or the Mongolian 'race' and in so doing have in mind primarily certain general physical character-istics of colour, hair and features, while linguistic, cultural, his-torical, and political factors play but a comparatively subordinate part in our conception. We also speak, however, of the Latin, the Anglo-Saxon, or the Celtic 'race,' but here, although physical characteristics are in some measure concerned, it is more on lan-guage and culture, and in considerable degree on historical and political unity that our mental picture rests. From the standpoint of the anthropologist this latter use of the word 'race' is inad-missible, for to him a race is a biological group, based on com-munity of physical characters. For groups characterised on the one hand by linguistic, or on the other hand by cultural, historical or political unity, he employs the terms 'stock' and 'nation.'" [43]

For us, however, in this study, the word race must bear this wider, human significance and it must mean the same thing in the case of Negro and Caucasian, of the Yellow and Brown peoples. It is not a matter of colour either of skin or of blood. Predominantly it is a matter of group culture and inheritance. There are different skin colours and we shall consider their sig-nificance later, and there are writers who speak of "white blood" and "black blood" and who believe presumably in brown and yellow blood, which shows how easy it is for men to fall under obsessions in their views of race. In strict scientific sense there is no sure racial classification, nor any sure theory of racial origin. There is only the possibility of a broad division of human groups marked with more or less vague general characteristics of colour and habitat and culture, of inheritance and social standards and ideals. We speak of the white, brown, yellow, black and red

---

[43] *The Racial History of Man*, p. 3.

races—Aryan or Caucasian, Hindu and Malay and Arab, Mongolian, Negro, Indian, but the terms are disputable or confused, and the groups overlap and are both deeply divided and commingled within. " All races are more or less mixed. There are no doubt four main groups, but each is a miscellany, and there are little groups that will not go into any of the four main divisions. Subject to these reservations, when it is clearly understood that when we speak of the main divisions we mean not simple and pure races, but groups of races, then they have a certain convenience in discussion." [44]   There are some anthropologists who in the face of the confusion deny the validity of the concept of race altogether. " Race," says Professor Ross, " is the cheap explanation tyros offer for any collective trait that they are too stupid or lazy to trace to its origin in the physical environment, the social environment or historical conditions." [45]   And Finot declares :

" The history of civilisation is only a continual come and go of peoples and races! All, without distinction of their biological characteristics, are summoned to this great struggle for life wherein we fight for human progress and happiness. All the ethnical elements can take part in it, all can contend for places of honour in it. Such is the general import of our biological and psychological equality, which remains intact underneath all our superficial divisions.

" In the present state of science it has become impossible for us to distinguish the ethnical origins of peoples. The constituent elements are so much intermingled that the most ardent partisans of inequality must admit the relationship of all the races. The purity of blood which we create at will, and which we find in the animal world, becomes impossible in the human *milieu*. The Negroes are related to the Whites, who are linked to the Yellows, as these last have common links both with Negroes and Whites. On the road which separates them we only meet with links which unite them.

" Nevertheless, we foresee an objection which certain minds who are satisfied with simple arguments are sure to make. ' Does the Negro ever cease in spite of everything to be a black, or the

[44] Wells, *The Outline of History*, Vol. I, p. 141.
[45] *Social Psychology*, p. 3.

Chinese a yellow? Would the author have us understand that between a Redskin, a Papuan, or a White there are no differences?' Far from wishing to hide them, we have done nothing but look for them. They exist, and we have laid stress on a considerable number of them, but they are only the passing products of the *milieu*. Having come about as the result of external circumstances, they disappear in the same way. As it is impossible to shut up human souls in dogmatic and eternal formulas, it is equally impossible to enclose human beings in immutable racial moulds. But more. As we have had the opportunity of proving, the word race cannot be used to determine the specific character of the floating distinctions between members of the human unity.

"In one word, the term race is only a product of our mental activities, the work of our intellect, and outside all reality. Science had need of races as hypothetical limits, and these ' products of art,' to use Lamarck's expression, have become concrete realities for the vulgar. Races as irreducible categories only exist as fictions in our brains." [46]

But it is not possible in this bold way to do away with the reality of race. We may not be able to formulate a scientific definition of race or to establish a clear classification of fixed races, but the broad fact of race is one of the surest realities in the world. The commonly accepted grouping of mankind recognises three rough general divisions. Thomson states the prevalent view as follows:

"More for convenience than with conviction, ethnologists are accustomed to recognise three primary groups of human races— the black, the yellow and the white. Each group has numerous subdivisions or races, each race may have its sub-race, each sub-race its breeds, each breed its stocks.

"1. The group of Black or Negroid races is typically characterised by darkly pigmented skin, frizzly hair, a broad flat nose, thick lips, prominent eyes, large teeth, a narrow hip-girdle, and long heads (dolichocephaly). But there is great variety within the group, which includes African negroes, South African bushmen, various Pygmy races, together with such divergent types as the Melanesians and the Australian blackfellows (who have not frizzly hair).

"2. The group of Yellow or Mongolian races is typically char-

---

[46] Finot, *Race Prejudice*, p. 316.

acterised by yellowish skin, black straight hair, broad face with prominent cheek bones, small nose, sunken narrow eyes, moderately sized teeth, and diverse types of skull. Here come in Chinese, Japanese, Tibetans, Siamese, Burmese, Malays, Brown Polynesians, Maoris, Esquimaux, and Red Indians; and most divergent of all, the Lapps and Finns, the Magyars and Turks.

"3. The group of White or Caucasian races is typically characterised by soft and straight hair, well-developed beard, retreating cheek bones, narrow and prominent nose, small teeth, and broad hip-girdle. But the group includes along with the fair-haired and white-skinned peoples of Northern Europe, the dark-haired and often dark-complexioned southerners. Thus in Europe we may distinguish the tall and blond Nordics, the stocky dark Alpines, and the small dark Mediterraneans, while in Asia there are the Indo-Aryan and other types. It hardly requires to be said, for the heterogeneity of our enumeration is so evident, that these three primary groups—Negroid, Mongolian and Caucasian —do not mean very much scientifically; yet every one will admit that a Persian is nearer to a Britisher than a Hottentot is, and we think we understand what an Arab is after, while a Chinaman remains a sphinx." [47]

Professor Thomson rejects as no longer tenable the former idea of an ancient trifurcation of the human species into these three, black, yellow and white, or any other primary races. His classification assigns the American Indians to the Yellow or Mongolian race, but Professor Dixon on the strength of head measurements maintains that our Indians represent a strong Negroid strain which came over from Asia by the Behring Straits. Dixon's theory " would regard the American Indian as not a single race, but as a complex of four main racial elements coming into the continent at different periods." [48] If they came across Asia, as they must have done, it is inconceivable that they did not leave their trace on the Asiatic races. And as Dixon maintains also, as will appear, that there is a strong Negroid element in the European races, it would seem impossible for any people to escape a black kinship. These various racial boundaries have been crossed

---

[47] Thomson, *The Outline of Science,* Vol. IV, p. 1095; *Encyclopedia Britannica,* art. " Ethnology."
[48] New York *Times,* Dec. 30, 1922.

and recrossed so that, as we shall see, there are no pure races. All are mixed and transfused. "If we regard mankind as a body ever in movement," says Ratzel, "we cannot, as once was usual, look upon it as a union of species, sub-species, groups, races, tribes, rigidly separate from each other. As soon as ever a portion of mankind had learnt to plow the dissociating ocean, the mark was set for ever progressing fusion." [49] Even a single race, as we regard it, is a composite. The great African race, the Bantu, is typical. "While the modern Bantu have much in common, they are not homogeneous either in culture or in physical appearance. This fact must be accounted for by the varying degrees of their mixture with the aboriginals and by the influence of diverse climatic conditions." [50] Of all these races, Professor Giddings thinks that the white group represents, more closely than any other, the primitive, undifferentiated type of humanity.[51]

How clearly unsatisfactory is our attempt to say what races there really are! We find that there are deeper divisions inside some of the accepted races of men than there are between these races and other races; secondly, that there are no pure and unmixed races unless among some of these ranked lowest; and thirdly, that the unity of man is unmistakably more real and conclusive than his racial diversification.

1. There are divisions intra-race more marked than the inter-race divisions. (a) In the classifications given above, the Jew belongs to the Caucasian or white group. The inaccuracy of the colour test is seen in the fact that there are Black Jews. If colour is the criterion of race, then the Jews are not a race. Perhaps, indeed, they are not. Later we shall consider this. Now it is enough to state that the Jews are counted a race within the Caucasic group, and yet the practical racial division, socially even if not biologically, between the Jews and the rest of this group is greater than the division between American and Chinese students in American universities. And Sir Charles Eliot holds that the Chinese as a race are more like Europeans than races much nearer

---

[49] *The History of Mankind,* Vol. I, p. 10.
[50] Smith, *The Religion of Lower Races,* p. 6.
[51] New York *Times,* April 17, 1923.

and more kindred to the European peoples.[52]   (b) The English and the Scotch-Irish are of one intimate race starting within the Caucasic group, but they have clashed with one another more than the Scotch-Irish have ever clashed with the French, a more distant stock, or with the Dutch.   Indeed so deep was the antagonism between Scotch-Irish and English at the time of the Revolutionary War that the issue of the war really turned upon it.   " The more one studies the details of the struggle, the more remarkable appears the successful issue.   It seemed little less than a miracle to Washington himself, when he calmly reviewed it in later days. The affair remains a mystery until we consider the effect of the Ulster migration " and of the deep antipathy of the Scotch-Irish immigrants due to the wrongs they had suffered from English landlords and English commercial policy.[53]   (c) Again and again in human history economic forces or other general influences have proved stronger than race cohesion.   We may not agree with the rather cynical judgment of a recent French writer in *Le Temps:*

" Above all, we must never forget that peoples are not linked together by racial ties, by resemblances, nor even by blood relationship.   All this is material for couplets about sister nations and academic speechifying at the Sorbonne or at the Capitol.   Racial resemblances mainly influence men of the same culture—the chosen few.   No, what brings peoples together and unites them is a solid network of common interests, common and tangible profits. These are the realities that bring themselves home to thousands of men—the workers, who are the strength and the population of a country." [54]

We do not yield to this extreme economic view.   But we must recognise the truth in it, namely, that many influences common to humanity are stronger than the solidarity of race.   " I am afraid I am not one of those happy, optimistic persons who confidently declare that war between Anglo-Saxons is impossible," said the Senior Counsel for Canada at the International Fisheries

---

[52] *Letters from the Far East,* p. 142.
[53] Ford, *The Scotch-Irish in America,* p. 526.
[54] *Le Temps,* April 19. 1923.   Article by Joseph Galtier, " Some Fascist Doctrines," quoted in *The Living Age,* May 26, 1923, p. 442.

arbitration, at the Hague in 1916. "On two occasions, Canada has supplied the battle ground for English and American soldiers. One hundred years have passed and I doubt if men have grown wiser." [55] Racial unity is by no means one of the strongest human forces. The most dreadful war in history, before the twentieth century, was fought between brothers of one race, and the occasion of the conflict was another race. Difference over the Negro was more powerful than White agreement.[56] And in the World War races were found allied with stranger races, warring against races to which they were kindred by blood. Dr. Patton, in his book *World Facts and America's Responsibility,* presents some of these instances of the transcendence of other forces over race. A chief of one of the Maori tribes, called upon to advise his young men as they were about to embark for the war, addressed them in these words:

"For the first time in the history of the Maori race, all tribes are united to fight together for the Empire. We have learned wisdom, and regret our former violence; and we are now at last united to fight for our white brethren. You soldiers, don't forget that we all originate from one common stock. We worship one God. Be truthful, be honourable. You carry the honour of the Maori race in your hands. Be brave; and remember the flag you will have flying over your tents. With reference to your religious beliefs, don't forget that you aim for one Heaven. Fear God, read and study your Bibles, and may the British reign over us forever."

Sarojini Naidu, the Hindu poetess, addressed to England a poem entitled: "The Gift of India," in which she sings of the loyalty of her country's soldiers in the great war.

"Gathered like pearls in their alien graves
Silent they sleep by the Persian waves;

---

[55] New York *Times,* Feb. 19, '21.
[56] *Report of Universal Races Congress,* 1911, p. 43. The full title of this volume, to be often quoted, is *Papers on Inter-racial Problems, communicated to the First Universal Races Congress, held at the University of London, July 26-29, 1911. Edited by G. Spiller.*

Scattered like shells on Egyptian sands,
They lie with pale brows and brave, broken hands;
They are strewn like blossoms mown down by chance
On the blood-brown meadows of Flanders and France."

Bishop Warne, of Lucknow, tells how his daughter at the outbreak of the war, hung a large map of the world in her study, on which she was accustomed to trace the progress of the armies on the various fronts, and how prominent natives from near and far would come in and ask to have her explain the latest news and indicate on the map where the Indian troops were engaged. One day an aged man from a city far in the North, arrived and enquired how things were going for the Allies. When all was explained, he expressed his gratitude, and then, on the supposition that she was English, he delivered himself on this wise: " I have come on a long journey to learn these things, and I want you to know that my heart is full. When you go back to England and see your king I want you to deliver this message from me. Say, ' My grandfather lived under the British raj; my father lived under the British raj; I have lived all my life under the British raj, and my children are living under the British raj today. In all these years we have had justice, protection, peace and plenty. Tell the King that we Indians are grateful for his rule over our land, and that we will stand by him to the very end.' "

When Djemal Pasha marched against Egypt in the ill-fated expedition of the spring of 1915, among the opposing troops lined up along the Suez Canal was a Moslem battalion from India. When the Turkish officers learned this fact, chuckling with glee, they passed the word around among the soldiers and reckoned upon an easy victory. They said " You will find the canal defended by Moslems. When ordered to charge you have but to shout, ' We are your brothers. We are fellow Moslems,' and they will throw down their arms and welcome you as brothers, and we shall march into Egypt as on a holiday excursion." The Turkish troops believed this word, and when the first charge was made and they shouted as they had been instructed, they were met by a blaze of rapid-fire guns and were mown down in heaps upon the desert

sands.[57] Race kinship is not the sovereign law. (d) Our broad
slashing race divisions according to colour, which dominate the
current alarmist propaganda, classify all the Indian people together as brown and treat them as a single element. But there is
no reality in such a fiction. The people of India are not all brown
and they are less tightly bound together than many of them are
bound to us. Here is the picture of India which Lord Dufferin
drew thirty-five years ago :

" This population is composed of a large number of distinct
nationalities, professing various religions, practising diverse rites,
speaking different languages, while many of them are still further
separated from one another by discordant prejudices, by conflicting source of usages, and even antagonistic material interests. But
perhaps the most patent characteristic of our Indian cosmos is its
division into two mighty political communities as distant from
each other as the poles asunder in their religious faith, their historical antecedents, their social organisation, and their natural
aptitudes ; on the one hand the Hindus numbering 190 millions,
with their polytheistic beliefs, their temples adorned with images
and idols, their venerations for the sacred cow, their elaborate
caste distinctions, and their habits of submission to successive
conquerors—on the other hand, the Mohammedans, a nation of
50 millions, with their monotheism, their iconoclastic fanaticism,
their animal sacrifices, their social equality, and their remem-
brance of the days when, enthroned at Delhi, they reigned supreme from the Himalayas to Cape Comorin. To these must be
added a host of minor nationalities—most of them numbering
millions—almost as widely differentiated from one another by
ethnological or political distinctions as are the Hindus from the
Mohammedans, such as the Sikhs, with their war-like habits and
traditions and their enthusiastic religious beliefs—the Robillas, the
Pathans, the Assamese—the Baluchees, and other wild and mar-
tial tribes on our frontiers—the hillmen dwelling in the folds of
the Himalayas—our subjects in Burma, Mongol in race and
Buddhist in religion—the Khonds, Mhairs, and Bheels, and other
non-Aryan peoples in the centre and south of India—and the enterprising Parsees, with their rapidly developing manufactures
and commercial interests. Again, amongst these numerous communities may be found at one and the same moment all the various

---

[57] Patton, *World Facts and America's Responsibility*, pp. 70-72.

stages of civilisation through which mankind has passed from the pre-historic ages to the present day. At one end of the scale we have the naked savage hillman, with his stone weapons, his head-hunting, his polyandrous habits, and his childish superstitions; and at the other, the Europeanised native gentleman, with his English costume, his advanced democratic ideas, his Western philosophy, and his literary culture; while between the two lie layer upon layer, or in close juxtaposition, wandering communities with their flocks of goats and moving tents; collections of undisciplined warriors, with their blood feuds, their clan organisations, and loose tribal government; feudal chiefs and barons with their retainers, their seignorial jurisdiction, and their mediæval notions; and modernised country gentlemen and enterprising merchants and manufacturers, with their well-managed estates and prosperous enterprises." [58]

Any race doctrines which assume the unity of the Indian people as one brown race deeply divided from us are fallacious. The people of India are many peoples and some of them are more akin in physiological and cultural qualities to us than they are to one another.

The general truth which needs to be understood is clearly stated by Professor Boas: " The differences between different types of man are on the whole small as compared to the range of variation in each type. . . . The differences between the different types of the white and of the Negro, that have a bearing upon vitality and mental ability, are much less than the individual variations in each case." [59] And Professor East says:

" There is definite evidence that thousands of differences now separate the primary races; though it is obvious that hereditary units, presumably much more numerous, are common property of all. . . . There are huge series of hereditary units possessed exclusively by each. Thus the white race has developed intellectual qualities superior to the black race, though the black race can resist malaria much better than the white. But though racial differences are such as to set average levels of performance for each, which may distinguish the one from the other, individual differences are broader still. In mental capacity, for example,

---

[58] *Report on Indian Constitutional Reforms,* 1918, p. 117.
[59] Boas, *The Mind of Primitive Man,* pp. 94, 269.

there is a much greater variation within the white race than between the mean levels of the white and the black." [60]

2. There are no pure or unmixed races unless they may be found among some of those ranked lowest.

" If in the past," says Professor Conklin, " God made of one blood all nations of men, it is certain that at present there is being made from all nations one blood. By the interbreeding of various races and breeds there has come to be a complicated intermixture of racial characters in almost every human stock, and this process is going on today more rapidly and extensively than ever before. Strictly speaking, there are no ' pure ' lines in any human group. If so-called ' pure ' English, Irish, Scotch, Dutch, German, Russian, French, Spanish, or Italian lines are traced back only a few generations they are found to include many foreign strains, and this is especially true of American families, even those of ' purest ' blood." [61]

And long ago Galton set forth the same view in words which recognised the changeability of human character and the mutability of race:

" Man is so educable an animal that it is difficult to distinguish between that part of his character which has been acquired through education and circumstance, and that which was in the original grain of his constitution. His character is exceedingly complex, even in members of the simplest and purest savage race; much more is it so in civilised races, who have long since been exempted from the full rigour of natural selection, and have become more mongrel in their breed than any other animal on the face of the earth." [62]

This conception of the composite character of race, even of races which have thought of themselves as pure races, is coming at last into our common American view.[63]

---

[60] East, *Mankind at the Crossroads*, p. 31.
[61] *The Direction of Human Evolution*, p. 47.
[62] *Inquiries into Human Faculty*, Chap. on " Nurture and Nature."
[63] " The Americans of purest lineage, for want of a better characterisation, derive their pride of ancestry from the very fact that their forefathers were roving emigrants whose stock became mixed with that of many other strains." Wichita, Kansas, *Beacon*, Oct. 15, 1923.

The fiction of race purity is greatest, perhaps, in the case of
the European peoples who represent in reality such an intermixture that no racial analysis is possible. Even the idea of a great
Nordic race, fair-haired, long-headed, of pure white blood, the
racial aristocrats of history, is now called in question. Prof.
Dixon finds the Nordic race to have been made up of a blending
of the Caspian and Mediterranean types " but with considerable
elements of the older Proto-Australoid and Proto-Negroid." [64]
Many students join in this idea of a Negroid strain in the European races, both Mediterranean and Nordic.[65]   That the Nordic
race is passing is true today as it has been true for thousands of
years. For good or ill all races are passing into the human race.

" That the Nordic race," says Dixon, " the result of the long
blending in the Baltic lands of the remnants of the older Palæo-
lithic folk with the Caspian and Mediterranean peoples during
Neolithic times, is gradually passing from the stage would seem,
from the evidence, to be only too true. But their passing is not a
recent matter—it has been going on for thousands of years, and
was already far advanced before the discovery of America. They
have played their part, and it has been a great part, in the world's
history. As a ' race,' as a complex of just these particular factors,
in just this combination, it seems doomed in the end to be absorbed in the wider complex which has been forming ever since
the Alpine peoples made their appearance in Europe. It is passing, just as the purer Mediterranean peoples are and for long have
been passing, in the sense of sinking into the greater racial entity
which has been so long in process of growth." [66]

It is often said that mixed as Europe or India may be, America
is more mixed still. Thus a writer in a British review writes:

---

[64] *The Racial History of Man,* p. 510.
[65] Du Bois, *The Negro,* p. 21.
[66] Dixon, *The Racial History of Man,* p. 520; See also Madison Grant,
The Passing of the Great Race; Gould, *America, a Family Matter;* and
New York *Times* editorial, " The Perfect Race," Nov. 12, 1922: " ' Historians,' says Mr. Madison Grant, ' have never considered race.'   Maybe that
is because nobody knows just what race is except these inspired Nordic
theologians. There is reason for their continual falling back on German
arguments.   The religion of a superior race was necessary to pan-
Germanism; outside of Germany it rather fails to convince.   There are
good arguments against unrestricted immigration, but this Nordic nonsense
is not one of them."

" To begin with, you must dispossess your mind of the idea that
there is an American people at all, as we understand a people in
Europe. . . . If you took the whole population of Europe,
mixed it roughly in a mortar, added a certain flavouring of
Africans, Asiatics, and the like, crushed it with your pestle and
scattered the result thinly over the Continent, you would have
something approximating to America. It would, however, more
closely approximate to a ' people ' than do the Americans at
present ; for instead of being properly mixed, they are divided into
ethnographic strata, which only touch at the edges. America tries
to forget this, and succeeds by vigourous newspaper propaganda
in making Europe forget it." [67]

But is this a true picture ? Far from it. The truth is that there
is more pure north European stock in the United States than there
is in Great Britain or in Germany. Mr. Rossiter, formerly of the
Federal Census office, demonstrates this. In 1910 the native
whites of native white parentage in the United States numbered
49,500,000, almost purely Anglo-Saxon. Adding the other Anglo-
Saxon and Teutonic elements, Mr. Rossiter finds that there are
" nearly 55,000,000 of men, women, and children of British ancestry, including the descendants in the second or later generations
of Irish, German, and other immigrants who came to America
sixty years ago, or earlier, and including also later Anglo-Saxon
arrivals and their children, welded into one vast and surprisingly
homogeneous element. The American native stock, with its assimilated early additions, is the greatest Anglo-Saxon element in
the world. In numbers it is greater than the entire combined
population of England, Scotland, Wales and Canada." [68] One of
the Nordic advocates, Mr. Burr, in *America's Race Heritage,*
maintains that four-fifths of our people are still pure Nordic.
This is his computation of our white population :

Nordic 80,984,319
Mediterranean (Iberian) 3,993,894
Alpine (Slav) 4,978,178

[67] Article by O. M. Hueffer in *National Review,* February, 1920, " Americans Mirrored in the English Mind."
[68] *Atlantic Monthly,* August, 1920. Art. " What Are Americans ? " p. 278.

Assyroid (Semite) 3,391,498
Unknown 323,729
                                   —————
Total "white" 93,671,618

We shall study later more in detail the composite character of
the American people. It is, of course, a fact that a great deal of
French, Irish and Dutch blood is mingled with this Anglo-Saxon
stock, but it remains true that the great body of the American
people constitutes among the races of the world, all of which are
mixed, as pure a race as any, and a purer race than any except
perhaps the Chinese or some of the African peoples.

3. The unity of man is unmistakably more real and conclusive
than his racial diversification. Race resemblances and kinships
are greater than race differences.[69] Beneath and above all the
races is the one human race, one in origin and one in essential
nature. This is the Biblical teaching and ethnology confirms it.
"Fair and dark races, long and short-headed, intelligent and
primitive," says von Luschan, "all come from one stock." [70]
"Systematists generally agree," says Conklin, "that there is at
present but one species of man, namely, *Homo Sapiens*, and that
all races and varieties have arisen in the first instance from a
common human stock." [71] "Man, then," says the writer of the
article on "Ethnology" in the *Encyclopedia Britannica*, "may be
regarded as specifically one, and thus he must have had an original cradle land, whence the peopling of the earth was brought
about by migration. The evidence goes to prove that the world
was peopled by a generalised proto-human form. Each division of
mankind would thus have had its pleistocene ancestors and would
have been differentiated into races by the influence of climatic and
other surroundings." [72] Men are many but man is one, with a
unity that is rich with the originality of God. As a Hebrew rabbi
remarked at a little race conference in New York: " When human
kings issued coinage they stamped their image on the coins and

[69] Okuma, *Fifty Years of New Japan*, Vol. II, pp. 461, 477-489.
[70] *Universal Races Congress*, 1921, p. 21.
[71] *The Direction of Human Evolution*, p. 34.
[72] *Encyclopedia Britannica*, Vol. IX, p. 850.

they all looked alike. When God stamped His image on men they all looked different."

The ethnologists can find no evidence for any doctrine which denies the unity of men. Our own human experience teaches us the same lesson. We are at variance with the human facts and with the reality of life until we come into the personal and social realisation of the solidarity of humanity. A life like Dr. Steiner's is a condensation of the whole process of human education in the fact of racial unity. He sums up his conclusions in the chapter on Tolstoy in *Against the Current:*

" ' Alles ist Rasse ' was the note which dominated the teaching of History in all its multitudinous divisions. I sometimes think that the opposite is true and that there is nothing in race; for I have experienced oneness with all sorts of people, both in the lower and the higher spheres of our nature.

" This latter theory Tolstoy dogmatically affirmed. ' You are a Jew, you say,' and he would grasp my arm so tightly that I could feel the pulsing blood in his sensitive hands. ' I am a Russian; yet I feel no difference in the touch of your hands, in the look of your eyes, and hear none as you speak to me. There are differences in the colour of the skin, the shape of the nose and eyes, but beneath the surface we are all alike.'

" So far as I know, Tolstoy has not changed these views, but I doubt that even the man who alters his viewpoint often has changed in that one fundamental belief. To me this oneness of all men has become a conviction, the one religious doctrine which I hold with a scientific dogmatism; for I know Chinamen, whose slanting eyes do not prevent them from seeing the world just as I see it; Hindus, who, removed from their imprisoning system of caste, take this human view of man. I have met Japanese the travail of whose soul is akin to mine, and Negroes whose souls are so white that one might envy them their purity.

" Knowing every shade of Slav, Teuton and Latin, the Aryan and Semitic peoples, I have found them all alike at their best and at their worst. Dissimilar they are in their various environments, reflecting all the differences of climate, food, religion and government; but let them climb the heights to which the soul aspires or let them sink to the level to which fleshly lust drags them, and they are brother angels or brother brutes." [73]

---

[73] Steiner, *Against the Current,* p. 211.

And this is just our problem, " the problem of dealing with men who seem to us somehow very widely different from ourselves, in physical constitution, in temperament, in all their deeper nature. so that we are tempted to think of them as natural strangers to our souls, while nevertheless we find that they are stubbornly there in our world and that they are men as much determined to live as we are and are men who in turn find us as incomprehensible as we find them." [74]   And yet, incomprehensible only when we conceive them as strangers and not as brothers, in truth just like ourselves.

When did the consciousness of race and of racial differences first come to men? What evidence of its presence do we find and what forms did it take among the ancient people? Mr. Marvin finds the feeling of race consciousness earliest among the ancient Greeks.

" They were the first," says he, " to distinguish between themselves, the city-founding, freedom-loving, philosophising Hellenes and the other races whom they met with, who did not possess these qualities and uttered a strange and unintelligible speech, and were hence called ' Barbaroi' or stammerers. The Romans, as they came into the same Greek system of city-states and civilised life, were admitted within the pale. We thus gain from the quick, questioning, analytic mind of Greece the first division between Western Races and the World. . . . Side by side with the birth of this consciousness of a superior civilisation, comes the first deliberate effort to train up each generation of fresh members of the community in the traditions, the habits, and the meaning of the civilisation which they had inherited." [75]

In differentiating themselves from other races the Greeks had in mind æsthetic and moral and intellectual differences. Mr. Bevan gathers various utterances of the Greek race-consciousness. " ' In the case of the barbarians all, except one man, are slaves,' says an oft-quoted line in Euripides. The poets, Aristotle observes, speak as if a ' slave' and a ' barbarian' were really the same thing, and he accepts such utterances as stating a serious

[74] *International Journal of Ethics*, April, 1906, pp. 47-50. Art. by Josiah Royce, " Race Questions and Race Prejudices."
[75] *Western Races and the World*, p. 20.

scientific fact. ' Persons with the natural faculty of command are wanting amongst the barbarians.' " [76] " The qualities in virtue of which mankind is superior to the other animals," wrote Plato's contemporary Isocrates, " are the same qualities in virtue of which the Hellenes, as a race, are superior to the barbarians, that is, they have minds better trained for intelligence and for the expression of thought in words." The Greeks had, therefore, a natural right to rule over barbarians, as Euripides wrote in Iphigenia:

> " It is meet
> That Greece should over Barbarians bear sway,
> Not that Barbarians lord it over Greece;
> Nature hath formed them slaves, the Grecians free."

As a matter of fact in the fourth century B. C. there were more Greeks ruled by Persians than there were barbarian subjects of Greece, but Isocrates was already preaching the doctrine of the duty of Greece to conquer Asia, not to establish any selfish despotism but to extend the blessings of a rational rule conceived in terms of guardianship over weaker peoples. Aristotle counselled Alexander in his conquests to keep the status of Greek and Asiatic quite distinct, but Alexander, says Mr. Bevan,

" adopted a policy definitely contrary to this advice. Whatever his ideas may have been when he first invaded Asia, by the time that he was secure in the seat of the Great King, he formed the design of a fusion between East and West. His idea was apparently to initiate a systematic mixing of races—a mode of unifying the inhabitants of his Empire in one Eurasian amalgam. . . . It does not, of course, follow from Alexander's desire to merge the Greeks in a racial amalgam that he wished their culture to be similarly merged in a nondescript syncretism. It is conceivable that while he wanted the races mixed, he wished Hellenism as a culture to be predominant. The indications rather point to this being in his mind. The cities of Greek type which he founded all over the empire were to be nurseries of Hellenic life. In a tract attributed to Plutarch and written at any rate many centuries after Alexander, he is lauded as the belligerent missionary of a higher

---

[76] *Western Races and the World*, p. 50.

culture in the backward East. . . . We must beware of con-
founding this cultural pride of the Greeks with racial intolerance.
The Greeks thought poorly of barbarian culture, but, provided a
barbarian took on the Hellenistic character, they do not seem to
have subjected him to any social exclusion on account of his blood.
There is an interesting protest recorded on the part of the great
Alexandrine geographer Eratosthenes (born 276 B. C.) against the
racial intolerance involved in Aristotle's advice to Alexander as to
his attitude to Greeks and barbarians respectively. The division
between men, he said, should not go by race but by moral character; there were many undesirable sorts of Greeks and many
civilised kinds of barbarians, such as the Indians and Persians.
Just so in the Plutarchian tract referred to above it is said that
the distinction of Hellene and barbarian was not to be taken as
depending on race or on fashion of dress, but upon virtue and
vice. There is, even so, a noteworthy assumption implicit in this
identification of virtue with Hellenism.

"The educated class all over Asia Minor, Mesopotamia, Syria
and Egypt during the centuries succeeding Alexander became
'Greeks.' There can have been no very clear line of demarcation
between the Greeks of barbarian origin and the Greeks of Hellenic blood." [77]

The Roman consciousness of race began with a sense of Rome's
indebtedness to the Greek race. The discerning Romans realised
that they had been themselves among the barbarians and in joke.
at least, they applied the word to their native culture and even
spoke of their own language as "a barbarous tongue." Cicero
writes to his brother who was Roman Governor of Asia in 60
B. C., ruling over Greeks:

"Seeing that we are set over a race of men who not only possess
the higher culture, but are held to be the source from which it has
spread to others, we are above all things bound to repay to them
that which we have received at their hands. For I am not
ashamed to confess—the more so, since my life and achievements
have been such as to place me above all suspicion of laziness and
frivolity—that whatever I have accomplished has been attained by
the principles and methods handed down to us by Greek teachers
and their works. And so, beside the general good faith which we

[77] *Western Races and the World*, pp. 57-60.

owe to all men, we are, I think, under a special obligation to that race." [78]

This racial respect for the Greeks was perhaps a mark of the more intelligent and rational feeling. Among the mass of the people and with the politicians who manipulated them the orthodox view was contempt for the Greeks. Cicero speaks of Crassus as seeking influence by affecting to despise the Greeks and of Antonius doing so by affecting ignorance of their culture. As the Roman conquests grew under Julius Cæsar it is clear that he cherished the idea of a cosmopolitan world state. He gave Roman citizenship indiscriminately to men of many races, but died with his full plans undeveloped. He took Africans and Asiatics to Gaul. What happened in the world war in France had happened two thousand years before. By the time of Augustus it had become clear that Rome must find some solution of the problem of relation to her subject races of varying degrees of culture. He did not repeat Cæsar's experiment of introducing Gauls into the Roman Senate which had offended Roman prejudice. He checked the infiltration of alien blood into the citizen stock and reimposed slavery restrictions which had been relaxed by Cæsar. " Under his rule, moreover, and that of his immediate successors, service in the legions, implying the full Roman citizenship (which was conferred upon those not already possessed thereof on enlistment) was in the main confined to Italians, or to members of the extra-Italian communities of Roman right, which were not as yet numerous. . . . But on the other hand Augustus was firm in his grasp of the sound principle that service should form the pathway to citizenship. This was shown by his reorganisation of the ' auxiliary ' regiments, formed by levies of unenfranchised provincials. . . . It is likely enough that those who served with distinction in the irregular corps passed into one or another branch of the regular army, and so were absorbed into the ruling race." [79]

The deliberate policy of the Roman Empire was unity by Romanisation. A system of municipal institutions was created

---

[78] *Western Races and the World*, p. 71.
[79] *Ibid.*, Chapter by H. Stuart Jones on " The Roman Empire," pp. 78, 83.

which reconciled the unity of the State with a measure of local freedom and promoted " the rise of the more backward races of the Empire to a higher plane of civilisation " in accordance with " a cardinal principle of Rome's policy to establish an ordered graduation of status and privilege by which her subjects might climb to an equality with the ruling race." [80] Little by little the successors of Augustus " substituted fresh bonds of union for the older cohesive forces of race and tribe " and " built up like some coral island of the Southern Seas a new Græco-Roman nationality."

Rome worked with a far clearer and surer recognition of the principle of human unity than characterised Greek thought. Aristotelian theory had declared the inequality of human nature. Cicero asserted its identity and equality. " There is no resemblance," he says, " in nature so great as that between man and man, there is no equality so complete, there is only one possible definition of mankind, for reason is common to all. Men differ indeed in learning, but are equal in the capacity for learning, there is no race which under the guidance of reason cannot attain to virtue." [81] Roman law and modern civilisation rested upon this ideal. Ulpian lays down the broad general principle that men are by the natural law equal and free. Florentinus treats slavery as an institution of the " jus gentium," which is contrary to nature. Tryphoninus says that liberty belongs to the natural law. [82]

And it was not Rome's theory and practice of human unity which led to her downfall. Her welcome to the new races brought her far more than they received from her. She lived on through them. It was not they which destroyed her. " The cause of decay," Mr. Stuart Jones holds, " lay deeper. The failure was a failure to solve the fundamental problem (with which we are still wrestling) of the relation of the individual to the State, especially the Great State." [83] The truth of human unity will destroy only those institutions which are built on false ideas of society and

[80] *Ibid.*, p. 93.
[81] *Ibid.*, Chap. by A. J. Carlyle on " The Influence of Christianity," p. 111.
[82] *Ibid.*, p. 112.
[83] *Ibid.*, p. 106.

politics. And indeed it is the falsehood of these ideas and not the truth of human unity which is the destructive force.

Here and there in the New Testament there are references to these race feelings of Romans and Greeks, to racial prejudices and to the absorption of Jewish elements into Roman citizenship.[84] We shall consider later the teaching of Christianity and the New Testament with regard to race. But we must turn here to the facts as to race feeling among the Hebrews in the centuries before the Romans and Greeks. It is significant to note that the word " race " is not found in the King James version except in the sense of a running contest. What does this mean? It would seem to mean that the conception of race was not a living conception at the time the King James version was made. The ancient racial problems had been solved or had dropped out of sight. The modern ones had not arisen. Hebrew and Greek words accordingly which we would now translate " race " were rendered " people," " nation," " heathen," " Gentiles." The Hebrews and the Old Testament used three main words which in our modern conception mean " race." In Anglicised forms these words were am, goi and leom. The first word is from the root " to collect " or " gather together," hence, a people. It is used of single races or tribes,[85] of the tribes of Israel,[86] of a man's race or family,[87] of the citizens as opposed to rulers,[88] of the whole human race.[89] The second word means a " confluence " or " body of men." It is used of the Hebrew nation,[90] but in the plural especially of the other nations besides Israel,[91] often with the added notion of their being foes or barbarians,[92] or of being strangers to the true religion.[93] The third word is from an unused root meaning " to agree," perhaps " to gather together." It is much less used than the two other words. It is found in Gen. XXV, 23; XXVII, 29; Psa. VII, 8; Prov. XXIV, 24; Isa. XVII, 12. Daniel uses a distinctive word of his own for nation, " umwah." [94] There are no clear distinc-

---

[84] Acts XVI; XVIII, 2; Col. III, 11.   [85] Judges V, 18.
[86] Gen. XLIX, 10.   [87] Lev. XXI, 1, 4.   [88] I Kings XII, 16.
[89] Isa. XL, 7.   [90] Isa. I, 4.   [91] Neh. V, 8.
[92] Psa. II, 1, 8; IX, 6, 16, 20, 21; X, 16; LIX, 6, 9.
[93] Jer. XXXI, 10; Ezek. XXIII, 30; XXX, 11; Psa. CXXXV, 15.
[94] Dan. III, 4, 7, 29; IV, 1; V, 19; VI, 25; VII, 14.

tions in Hebrew thought or language between race and nation. The Hebrews spoke of themselves as many nations and as many races, whereas they were, from our way of thinking, only one race and one nation. And they spoke of the peoples who were not Hebrews as peoples, or nations or races indiscriminately, and Daniel speaks of languages in the same order, "All peoples, nations and languages."

The education of the Hebrews was an education in the sense of race distinction and racial mission. It was begun distinctly as a process of racial and national differentiation,[95] and throughout the whole history the Old Testament writers make the purpose and meaning of the story as they understood it, perfectly clear. In Egypt and then in Canaan they were disciplined to a sense of segregated national and racial personality. The conquest of the Promised Land was left incomplete as part of this training.[96] And the long tragic story of the nation's alternating prosperity and suffering is one of the most instructive chapters in the history of the race problem, with unequaled light on its significance and solution.

Under this education the ancient Hebrews acquired the sense of race distinction in a unique measure. The phrase, "The Chosen People," which we apply to them, does not occur in the Old Testament, but the word "chosen" is used a few times and the idea, of course, was a dominant idea in the consciousness of Israel. The question which concerns us, however, is as to Israel's attitude to other races. A careful reading of the Old Testament does not support the view that the Hebrews held a narrow race view or disbelieved in the solidarity of humanity. Abraham's call was a call not to isolated racial privilege but to racial training for universal human service. Other races were conceded to have their own culture and worship. The Hebrews were warned against what was unworthy in these,[97] and their insufficiency was openly declared.[98] Adverse and hostile racial judgments occur,[99] but these

[95] Gen. XII, 1-3. [96] Judges II, 21-III, 4. [97] Deut. XII, 30, 31.
[98] II Kings XVII, 33; XIX, 12; II Chron. XXXII, 15, 17, 23; Isa. XXXVI, 18; XXXVII, 12; Jer. II, 11.
[99] Micah V, 15; II Chron. XXVIII, 3; XXXIII, 9.

are mild in comparison with the racial provocation which the moral condition of ancient culture afforded. And if we will compare the revised version of the Old Testament with the King James Version and will note the scores of passages where the Revised Version substitutes "nations" for "heathen" in the translation we will be surprised to see how much of the supposed warrant for the idea of Old Testament race prejudice fades away. There are, to be sure, harsh racial notes in some of the old characters and incidents, but the Spirit of God which was seeking to make the Jews pure and faithful was seeking also to make them just and brotherly, and was succeeding. They learned to speak in friendly terms of the other races.[100] They conceived Jehovah as the ruler of other nations as well as their own.[101] God purposed to fulfill the "desire of all nations,"[102] and peace was to be the law of the life of all peoples.[103]

If some Hebrews forgot all this and thought of themselves as the one superior race destined to rule the world and of the other races as "lesser breeds without the law," they did only what some men in other races have done ever since down until today, and what more men are doing now, probably, than ever before.

Indeed the race problem as we know it is a very modern problem. Take any dictionary of quotations and look for quotations on race and see if you can find one. Take up at random any dozen books on history and politics and look in the index for "race" and note the result. There is no article on "race" or the "race problem" in the Encyclopedia Britannica or any other representative encyclopedia. What little there is on the subject will be found under "ethnology" or "anthropology."

"Most of our race problems," says Professor Conklin, "are of relatively recent origin and are caused chiefly by the pressure of population within certain centres and its overflow into other lands as well as by the importation of cheap labour. The white man in particular has forced himself on other races, and the pressure of

---

[100] Psa. CII, 15; Zech. IX, 10; Ezek. XXXVIII, 23; XXXIX, 27; Mal. I, 11.
[101] Isa. XLV, 5; Jer. XXVII, 7, 8; Joel III, 12.
[102] Hag. II, 7.   [103] Micah IV, 3.

whites into the lands of coloured races has gone much farther than the reverse. Furthermore, the white man's demand for cheap labour is chiefly responsible for the importation of coloured races into the lands of the whites and for the general mixing up of all races of mankind. The present competition between races is a contest in the relative growth of populations and in economic progress rather than in military power." [104]

Even if this inevitable and progressive intermingling of the races were not occurring, the duty of reaching a right and true theory of race relations would remain, for there would still be a large measure of necessary inter-race communication. And if this were not true and each race were destined to live its own separated economic and social life, how each race would live would depend upon its principles of education and its individual and social ideals and its conception of what humanity is and what is to be its destiny. Each race must work out the true world theory and this will be found to be not racial but human.

But the considerations mentioned by Prof. Conklin are actual facts. The races are mingling in the tropics under necessities described by Mr. Kidd twenty-five years ago. He conceived that white invasion and domination of the tropics was inevitable and yet he recognised its difficulty. " In climatic conditions which are a burden to him; in the midst of races in a different and lower stage of development; divorced from the influences which have produced him, from the moral and political environment from which he sprang, the white man does not in the end, in such circumstances, tend so much to raise the level of the races amongst whom he has made his unnatural home, as he tends himself to sink slowly to the level around him." [105] Kidd's solution was the acceptance of the trust under a sense and acknowledgment of trusteeship. It seemed to him to be a permanent and enduring responsibility in which there was no room " for small-minded comparisons between the different merits of civilised races and peoples." He took for granted the reality of the inferiority of the uncivilised races and contended for " the holding of the tropics by

---

[104] Conklin, *The Direction of Human Evolution,* p. 40.
[105] Kidd, *The Control of the Tropics,* p. 50.

the English speaking peoples as a trust for civilisation." What the relation of temperate and tropical races shall be in this situation, is among the real race problems we must face.

And outside of the tropical and of the north and south race relations there are the race relationships which run east and west in the world and the relationships which are intra-national in Europe, and above all now in the United States. What is the fundamental element in these relationships? Is it racial, or social, or economic? Is it a sense of instinctive racial antipathy or is it the reaction of fear? We shall seek light on these questions. Meanwhile it is well to emphasise here, as a too often overlooked element in the growth of the race problem, two facts brought about by modern world developments, the fact of mass contacts of races, and the fact of contacts of individuals of those races with other races and with individuals of those other races. "A primary cause of race friction," says a thoughtful Southern writer, "is the vague, rather intangible but wholly real feeling of ‘ pressure ’ which comes to the white man almost instinctively in the presence of a mass of people of a different race. In a certain important sense all racial problems are distinctly problems of racial distribution. Certainly the definite action of the controlling race, particularly as expressed in laws, is determined by the factor of the numerical difference between its population and that of the inferior group." [106] The writer is speaking of the relations of the black and white races in the Southern States in America, but what he says is true in its measure elsewhere and of other races than "the white races" to whom he refers. All races everywhere to-day are being pressed against other races. The majority and minority elements in the association vary greatly. The contacts are both direct and personal and also indirect and economic or political. They are the most real and significant facts in modern history. However the races arose, whatever we may think of race and its nature and purpose, the race issues are here as a fact and we have the problem of a right and just and peace-making solution of the racial questions insistently confronting us.

---

[106] Stone, *The American Race Problem,* p. 217.

II

THE IDEA OF RACE SUPERIORITY

IT is an interesting fact that in behalf of each separate human race the claim of superiority has been made. We need not go beyond the list of present races as the colour ethnologists define them.

The red people when they first met the whites were compelled to recognise and gradually submit to their power. But they held the firm conviction of their own racial superiority. Jedediah Morse relates in the *American Universal Geography,* published in Boston in 1796, a story told in 1766 at a salt lick in Ohio to Col. G. Morgan by an old Indian chief, eighty-four years of age, who was the head of a party of Iroquois and Wyandot Indians.

" After the Great Spirit formed the world, he made the various birds and beasts which now inhabit it. He also made man, but having formed him white and very imperfect and ill-tempered he placed him on one side of it where he now inhabits and from whence he has lately found a passage across the water to be a plague to us. As the Great Spirit was not pleased with this, his work, he took of black clay and made what *you* call a Negro with a woolly head. This black man was made better than the white man, but still he did not answer the wish of the Great Spirit; that is, he was imperfect. At last, the Great Spirit, having procured a piece of pure red clay, formed from it the Red Man, perfectly to his mind, and he was so well pleased with him that he placed him on this great island, separate from the white and black men; and gave him rules for his conduct, promising happiness in proportion as they should be observed. He increased exceedingly and was perfectly happy for ages; but the foolish young people, at length forgetting his rules, became exceedingly ill-tempered and wicked. In consequence of this, the Great Spirit created the great buffaloes, the bones of which you now see before us; these made war upon the human species alone, and destroyed all but a few, who repented and promised the Great Spirit to live according to his laws if he would restrain the devouring enemy. Whereupon he sent lightning and thunder and destroyed the whole race in this spot, but excepted a male and female which he shut up in yonder mountain, ready to let loose again, should occasion require." [1]

The modern Indian does not speak so strongly but he does not in his heart accept the idea of his racial inferiority. In the Old Oregon Trail celebration at Meacham, Oregon, on President Harding's Alaskan trip, Chief Sumkin, an aged Indian of eighty-seven years, said to the President: " I know that friendship is one of the best things that can be known in this world, and I say the truth when I speak. The reason I say that is because I do not believe that my race is better than yours. I believe that all races in this world are just as good as one another. One of the best things we can do is to meet friends." " We ought to understand each other in friendship and peace," the President replied.[2]

How inferior is a race which produces such a tale as this?

" TAKES CAPTOR TO HOSPITAL.

" Indian Accused of Murder Mushes 100 Miles in Alaska with Officer.

" Anchorage, Alaska, April 18 (Associated Press)—While taking an Indian accused of murder from Fort Gibbon to Fairbanks recently Deputy United States Marshal E. B. Webster was stricken with appendicitis. The Marshal's prisoner placed him on the sled with which they had been travelling and mushed more than a hundred miles with him to a hospital where an operation was performed." [3]

The Chinese when they first met the white races were entirely assured of the unique and primary place of the yellow people and for generations treated the Western nations with pride and scorn. And who can deny the grounds of their judgment? They have been for ages the great center of light and civilisation in Central and Eastern Asia. They have given literature and religion to the millions of Korea and Japan. Even a generation of Western

---

[1] Morse, *The American Universal Geography*, Part I, p. 194, Boston, 1796.
[2] New York *Times*, July 5, 1923.
[3] New York *Times*, April 19, 1923.

civilisation has not shaken Chinese influence off the thought and
politics and ethics of Japan. Printing originated with the
Chinese, and was used by them hundreds of years before it was
known in the West. The magnetic needle, gunpowder, silk fab-
rics, chinaware and porcelain were old tales with the Chinese
before our civilisation began. Our latest ideas were wrought out
by the Chinese ages ago,—Civil Service examinations and assign-
ment of office for merit and tested capacity, trades unions and
organisations, the sense of local responsibility in municipal administration. It is not to be wondered at that China has always
looked down upon the other races and deemed them barbarians.
And even after contact with the Western races this conviction
remained. "Western nations, taken as a whole, do not impress
educated Chinese with a sense of the superiority of such nations
to China. This feeling was admirably exemplified in the reply of
His Excellency Kuo, former Chinese Minister to Great Britain.
when told, in answer to a question, that in Dr. Legge's opinion
the moral condition of England is higher than that of China.
After pausing to take in this judgment in all its bearings, His Excellency replied, with deep feeling, ' I am very much surprised.' " [4]
" China can do without foreigners, whilst foreigners are dependent
on us," said Hia Sieh.[5] " We say to the Western world," says a
Chinese writer, Lowe Chuan-hwa, " do not think we are fools,
for however you may cloak your policies of imperialism with
benevolent pretensions of altruism, your hypocrisy is glowingly
manifest to the intelligent people of Han. And surely a review of
history reveals that nations which are blind to cruelty and injustice, and deaf to the voice of reason and fairness can be taught
only with the whirring swish of the sword. You are teaching us
that force with or without Christianity is our only redeemer." [6]
And there are Westerners today who prefer the civilisation of the
yellow race to that of the white. " I am inclined to think," says
Bertrand Russell, " that Chinese life brings more happiness to the
Chinese than English life does to us. . . . The Chinese are

[4] Smith, *Chinese Characteristics*, p. 105.
[5] *Chinese Intercourse with Europe*, trans. by E. H. Parker, p. 55.
[6] *The Nation*, Feb. 7, 1923. Art. " The Christian Peril in China."

gentle, urbane, seeking only justice and freedom. They have a civilisation superior to ours in all that makes for human happiness." [7] This is not true, but most of the Chinese race have hitherto believed it.

And the other great branch of the yellow race, the Japanese, although they are clearly a mixture of the yellow and the brown races, swinging down through the Chosen peninsula and up from the Dravidian areas in the islands to the south, are even more sure of their racial ascendency. The Japanese race is heaven-descended. "The Emperors of our country," says Dr. Kakehi, "are persons equipped with qualities without parallel in the world; they are both the centers of (religious) faith and of temporal power. The center of this phenomenal world is the Mikado's land (Mi-kuni, *i. e.,* Japan). From this center we must expand this Great Spirit throughout the world." Kakehi declares with enthusiasm, "There are voices which cry, 'Great Japan is the Land of the Gods.' Nor is this to be wondered at. It is a true statement of fact. It is a matter of course. The expansion of Great Japan throughout the world and the elevation of the entire world into the Land of the Gods is the urgent business of the present, and again, it is our eternal and unchanging object." [8] "Just as our country possesses in the towering peak of Mt. Fuji," says Dr. Kato, "a natural beauty unsurpassed in all the world, so also this Orient land of virtuous men, with its historical record stretching across three thousand boundless years, with its Imperial House above reaching in unbroken lineage back to immemorial ages, with its subjects below looking up to this Line as it towers beyond mountains and stars, with its heroes and remarkable men, a country, indeed, not unworthy the name, 'The Land of the Gods,' this land has produced a national organisation that is peerless in the earth." [9] Dr. Uesugi Shinkichi boldly

---

[7] Russell, *The Problem of China*, pp. 73, 175; *Atlantic Monthly*, March, 1924. Art. by Upton Close, "Some Asian Views of White Culture;" see also two books by Englishmen posing as Chinese, *Letters from a Chinese Official*, and Lin Shao-Yang, *A Chinese Appeal Concerning Christian Missions*.

[8] Holtom, *The Political Philosophy of Modern Shinto*, p. 107.

[9] *Ibid.*, p. 119.

contrasts the wreckage of the West with the saving mission of
Japan:

> "It is now most clear that the salvation of the entire human
> race is the mission of our empire. Nations are now in a condition
> of disorder. There are classes within the nations, each class strug-
> gling for its own interests and each thinking the other an irrecon-
> cilable enemy. Radicalism is spreading abroad. The poison of
> the disease penetrates flesh and bones and threatens to overthrow
> the state. The idea of reliance upon the state is conspicuously
> weakened. The heart of man has lost its power to coöperate.
> Individuals do as they please, acting dissolutely without restric-
> tion. The capitalistic classes of England and America, flushed
> with the victory of the Great War, have become arrogant and
> domineering throughout the world and are giving rein to un-
> bounded greed. Behold the world is full of the struggle between
> capital and labour. They are fallen into the pit. The hell of
> fighting and bloodshed has appeared on earth. When we observe
> such conditions, there is not one of our people who does not
> believe that, if they only had our Emperor as theirs, they would
> not come to such extremity. . . . Our people, through the
> benevolent virtue of the Emperors, have attained a national con-
> stitution that is without parallel in the world. . . . Now, if all
> the human race should come to look up to the virtue of our Em-
> peror and should come to live under that influence, then there
> would be light for the future of humanity. Thus the world can
> be saved from destruction. Thus life can be lived within the
> realms of goodness and beauty. Of a truth, great is the mission
> of our nation." [10]

It is indeed great and the people of that nation are not to be set
down as a race biologically and socially inferior.[11] And the
Koreans from whom the Japanese received much of their art and
the Chinese from whom Japan took politics and philosophy deem
themselves superior to the Japanese.

[10] *Ibid.,* p. 126.
[11] Eliot, *Japanese Characteristics.* Some of the advocates of Japanese
exclusion from the United States frankly rest their case on the acknowledgment of elements of superiority in Japanese character. Mr. McClatchy
said that the reasons for special legislation regarding the Japanese were
"complimentary rather than otherwise," and Dr. Wheeler said, "Their
good taste, persistent industry, their excellent qualities and their virtues
render their presence amongst us a pitiful danger." *Racial Relations and
the Christian Ideal,* pp. 42, 48.

The brown race is, as we have seen, no single race at all, although one contemporary school of race theorists deals with it as a unity. The Indian leaders, however they approve or endure the preservation of race and caste distinction in India, do not concede for a moment the superiority of the white race or of white civilisation. The current tendency of thought in India is contempt for Western culture and the exaltation of the past of India. Rabindranath Tagore is only one, although he is in the West the best known, of the spokesmen of the mind of India. Read his description of the East:

" Take it in whatever spirit you like, here is India, of about fifty centuries at least, who tried to live peacefully and think deeply, the India devoid of all politics, whose one ambition has been to know this world as of soul, to live here every moment of her life in the meek spirit of adoration, in the glad consciousness of an eternal and personal relationship with it."

Then turn to his parallel description of the West:

" We have seen this great stream of civilisation choking itself from débris carried by its innumerable channels. We have seen that with all its vaunted love of humanity it has proved itself the greatest menace to man, far worse than the sudden outbursts of nomadic barbarism from which men suffered in the early ages of history. We have seen that, in spite of its boasted love of freedom, it has produced worse forms of slavery than ever were current in earlier societies—slavery whose chains are unbreakable, either because they are unseen or because they assume the names and appearance of freedom. We have seen, under the spell of its gigantic sordidness, man losing faith in all the heroic ideals of life which have made him great."

Finally, hear his injunction to his countrymen after he has summed up the horrors of modern civilisation:

" Be not ashamed, my brothers, to stand before the proud
        and the powerful
    With your white robe of simpleness.
    Let your crown be of humility, your freedom the freedom
        of the soul.

Build God's throne daily upon the ample bareness of your
poverty,
And know that what is huge is not great and pride is not
everlasting." [12]

And Mr. Gandhi, who has been a far greater force in India, has preached the same doctrine. " It behooves every lover of India to cling to the old Indian civilisation even as a child clings to its mother's breast." " In order to restore India to its pristine condition, we have to return to it." " Machinery is the chief symbol of modern civilisation. It represents a great sin." " We should only do what we can with our hands and feet." He appeals for the retention of " the same kind of cottages that we had in former times." " Railways accentuate the evil nature of man." They should be given up together with tram cars and electric lights. " Hand-made earthen saucers " should be used as lamps. " Where this cursed modern civilisation has not reached, India remains as it was before. The English do not rule over them. . . . I would certainly advise you to go into the interior that has not yet been polluted by the railways and to live there for six months. You might then be patriotic and speak of home rule. Now you see what I consider to be real civilisation." [13] He opposes modern education. " Tilak and Ram Mohun Roy," he has recently said, " would have been far greater men if they had not had the con-- tagion of English learning." And in his paper, *Young India,* Jan. 26, 1921, he wrote: " My conviction is deeper today than ever. I feel that if India would discard modern civilisation she can only gain by doing so." " The glitter of western civilisation, its institutions and its systems as such have no charm for India. Her children are not going to live a life individual or corporate that is set by this standard," says another Indian writer.[14]

And the black race, too, is human like the other races. It be-

---

[12] *The East and the West,* Jan., 1923, Art. by Lord Meston on " India at the Crossways," p. 68; see Tagore's paper, " India has her Renaissance," in the *Allahabad Leader,* Oct. 29, '22, with a poem on " Juzwat i Varma," in *Arya Samaj,* April, 1923.

[13] See Wellock, *India's Awakening,* p. 29 f.

[14] See *Bharat Sevak,* March, 1923, p. 9.

lieves in its superiority and sees no sublimity in the culture of the white race. One of their own writers, a French Negro, speaks for them with no pride but only with the desire to enable the white race to help Africa. " Civilisation," he says, " civilisation, pride of the Europeans and charnel house of innocents. . . . You have built your kingdom on corpses. Whatever you wish, whatever you do, you move in lies. At sight of you, gushing tears, shrieks of agony. You are might prevailing over right. You are not a torch, you are a conflagration. You devour whatever you touch. . . . If we knew of what vileness the great colonial life is composed, of what daily vileness, we should talk of it less, we should not talk of it at all." [15] And his book is a picture of the life the Africans whom he describes preferred to the life of the white people they knew and obeyed and despised. Du Bois denies the inferiority of the African. " When the European was still satisfied with rude stone tools, the Africans had invented or adopted the art of smelting iron," says Boas. " We are indebted to the Negro for the very keystone of our modern civilisation and we owe him the discovery of iron," says Torday.

" Long before cotton weaving was a British industry, West Africa and the Soudan were supplying a large part of the world with cotton cloth. . . . Viewing the Basuto National Assembly in South Africa, Lord Bryce recently wrote, ' The resemblance to the primary assemblies of the early peoples of Europe is close enough to add another to the arguments which discredit the theory that there is any such thing as an Aryan type of institutions.' . . . Perhaps no race has shown in its earlier development a more magnificent art impulse than the Negro. . . . In disposition the Negro is among the most lovable of men." [16]

And others think as highly of the Negro's claim to superiority. The old Indian chief who talked to Col. Morgan ranked the Negro above the white and next to the Indian. Park, too, says of him: " The Negro is, by natural disposition, neither an intellectual nor an idealist, like the Jew; nor a brooding introspective

[15] Rene Maran, *Batouala,* pp. 10, 13.
[16] Du Bois, *The Negro,* pp. 114, 115, 123, 137.

like the East Indian, nor pioneer and frontierman like the Anglo-Saxon. He is primarily an artist, living life for its own sake. His métier is expression rather than action. He is, so to speak, the lady among the races." [17]   Few would assent to such a racial judgment, but few would dissent from the statement of von Luschan regarding individuals, " I am still seriously convinced that certain white men may be on a lower intellectual and moral level than certain coloured Africans." [18]   And a noted French musical critic, Paul Landorwey, cannot speak too highly of the Negro tenor, Roland Hayes, whom no racial strain has disqualified. " I doubt," says he, " if we have in Paris a single tenor who knows as well his métier, and who handles his voice with such a mastery. . . . Roland Hayes is not at all a primitive in whom the instinct dominates. He would be incapable of singing as he has done the old pieces of Handel, of Caldara, of Paradies, of Mozart, which require a talent of execution subtle and reflective. . . . Let us remember this: Roland Hayes, ' the Negro singer,' is a very great artist." [19]   Our race theories must make room in the world for such gifts from one race to all races.[20] " A half-dozen financially fortunate ones go to Atlanta opera once every 365 days," says a Nashville paper.   " And Fisk University generously and artistically purveys choral art for all the rest of us ; that is, all the rest of us who have the taste and discrimination to avail ourselves of it when it is offered." [21]

The Latin American people, like the people of India, are a complex of races rather than a single race and, like the Indians, they are as convinced as any race of their right to deny any charges of racial inferiority.   And at the present time they are specially clear that our North American culture is not an enviable or desirable thing, and that in comparison with it, except for its energy and

[17] Park and Burgess, *Introduction to the Science of Sociology*, p. 136.
[18] *Universal Races Congress*, 1911, p. 22.
[19] Federal Council of the Churches, Research Department *Information Service*, Nov. 3, 1923, quoting from the *Musical Courier*.
[20] See also article in the Nashville *Banner*, April 27, 1923, expressing the obligation of Nashville to the Negro chorus of Fisk University which alone provides opera music for the city.
[21] Quoted in *Fisk University News*, May, 1923, pp. 5-8.

commercial efficiency, their own is better. " We Latin Americans," says José Enrique Rodo, " have an inheritance of race, a great ethnic tradition to maintain, a sacred bond which unites us to immortal pages of history and puts us on our honour to preserve this for the future." [22]

" Orphaned of the profound tradition that attended his birth, the North American has not yet replaced the inspiring ideality of his past with any high unselfish conception of the future. He lives for the immediate reality of the present, and for this subordinates all his activities in the egoism of material well-being, albeit both individual and collective. . . . Not even the selfishness of patriotism, for want of higher impulses, nor the pride of race, both of which transfigured and exalted in ancient days even the prosaic hardness of the life of Rome, can light a glimmer of ideality or beauty in a people where a cosmopolite confusion and the atomism of a badly understood democracy impede the formation of a veritable national conscience. . . . If one had to characterise his taste, in a word, it would be that which in itself involves the negation of great art; strained brutality of effect, insensibility to soft tones or an exquisite style, the cult of bigness, and that sensationalism which excludes all noble serenity as incompatible with the hurry of his hectic life. . . . Any casual observer of their political customs will tell you how the obsession of material interest tends steadily to enervate and eradicate the sentiment of law or right. . . . They lack that great gift of amiability—likeableness, in a lofty sense; that extraordinary power of sympathy with which those races endowed by Providence for the task of education know how to make of their culture a beauty, as did Greece, lovable, eternal, and yet always with something of their own." Against all this Rodo holds up the Latin American ideal: " Hospitable to things of the spirit, and not only to the immigrant throngs; thoughtful, without sacrificing its energy of action; serene and strong and withal full of generous enthusiasm; resplendent with the charm of morning calm like the smile of a waking infant, yet with the light of awakening thought." [23]

And Gabriella Mistral, the Chilean poetess, says that there are two things that must unite Spanish America, first, the beautiful Spanish language, and second, the pain caused by the United

---

[22] *Ariel*, p. 93.
[23] *Ariel*, pp. 106, 111, 116, 122, 137.

States, *e. g.,* in Panama, Haiti, Santo Domingo and Mexico. If we think these judgments unjust, are we sure that our own racial judgments are not so? [24] Are we as fair toward the South Americans as we wish them to be toward us? One of their number, Enrique Gil, sets us an example in his address before the Ateneo Hispano Americano, at Buenos Aires, May 19, 1922. He alludes to the common declaration of the Argentinos, " But, men, we are much more advanced than the Americans, we possess more culture," and out of his own personal experiences in the United States he speaks for us in the interest of a " real and effective understanding." [25]

Even so-called savage people have been convinced of the real superiority of their race culture to that of other people who supposed themselves to be advanced races. When the United States and Great Britain and Germany partitioned the Samoan Islands, Malietoa Tanu protested against such a disposition of his kingdom and also addressed a letter to the London *Times* in which he asserted that " the civilisation which had been introduced by the foreign governments into Polynesia was inferior to that which its inhabitants previously possessed." [26]

One of the most recent writers on the race question, Professor Josey, in *Race and National Solidarity,* sets forth the superiority of the white race as the basis of its right to dominate the world and argues for the frank rejection of all universalistic conceptions and of the weakness of the ideal of human brotherhood and for the bold acceptance of the mission of white world supremacy:

" Races differ greatly in their ability to impose their will on nature and on other men. The complexity of their mental processes, their initiative and ingenuity, their contributions to the

[24] See Calderon's criticism of North American culture and race character in *Latin America, Its Rise and Progress,* pp. 288 ff., 308, 311.

[25] *Inter-America,* Feb., 1923. Art. " An Argentine's Impressions of the United States." See also President Harding's address at the unveiling of the statue of Bolivar in New York City, April 19, 1921, in " International Conciliation," Inter American Division Bulletin, No. 25, p. 24.

[26] Foster, *American Diplomacy in the Orient,* p. 397. See account of the breaking down of old civilisation by the new, with evil moral results, in article by C. W. Abel, " Conflicting Forces in Papua," in *The Missionary Review of the World,* May, 1923.

welfare of mankind are by no means equal. In all these the white race excels. Just as we see man as a species dominating, excelling, and living on other forms of life, so we see the white race excelling the other races, acting as masters, and drawing to themselves a large part of the wealth of the world. The white races dominate mankind. They are the rulers *par excellence*. In the white man the evolutionary process seems to have reached its highest point. He is its culminating achievement." [27]

Other branches of the Aryan race cherish the same ideas.

" From the Avesta's time," writes Mirza Saeed Khan, of Teheran, " Persians have considered all Aryan things as best and have looked down upon all that is non-Aryan and have thought of their home land as ' the good abode ' given them by the Ahar Mazda. These prejudices have been perpetuated, and their ancient success has led the Persians to consider themselves mentally and physically superior to all other nations. And if opportunity is given to them certainly they prove themselves to be in mental capacity inferior to none. And their country which in most parts bears no trees to shelter from the sun in summer and to give fuel for the severe winters is considered the best of all countries." [28]

The conviction of human inequality, generalised into the sense of race or class superiority, appears to be universal. It surely is very ancient. No one race or class is left alone in the possession of the feeling of privilege and pride. It was and is an essential defect of the heathen temper in men that they disbelieve in equality in the interest of the assertion of their superiority of status or privilege over other races. The ancient world was under this curse and the spirit of race superiority in the modern world perpetuates it.

" Among the ancients the thought of Humanity, as a vital or-

[27] *Op. cit.*, p. 225. " No one will question that the Western nations have assumed a superior attitude towards the Eastern peoples, whose civilisation is centuries older than theirs, a civilisation which the peoples of the East still consider superior to that of the West. . . . This spirit of domination is not confined to governments. The individual European in his relation with the Eastern peoples sometimes manifests a contempt for their present feelings which can only produce deep-seated resentment." Rowell, *The British Empire and World Peace*, p. 95.
[28] Letter from Mirza Saeed Khan, M.D., Teheran, July 9, 1923.

ganism, each part related to every other, and all capable of being
pervaded by one supreme spirit,—this was not a thought of the
highest philosophy, or of the subtlest and most delicate song.   It
came by Him who surpassed philosophers, as far as He surpassed
the rigourous limitations of Hebrew sympathy.   The local religions had tended always to isolate states; while individual liberties
shrank, in each, in precise proportion to such isolation.   The individual existed for the interest of the state; and classes thus inevitably arose, with rights varying according to their fortunate
fitness to serve it.   So came the great number of the free poor at
Athens; who might hear Demosthenes from the Bema, or see
Pericles in the Pnyx, but who had no part in public affairs.   So
came the almost unending struggle between plebeians and patri-
cians at Rome, with the final practical disappearance from Italy
of the middle class of small proprietors.   And so came the sentiment, repeated by Plautus with brutal frankness, that 'a man is
a wolf to another man whom he does not know'; the more terrible
maxim of one nobler than Plautus—whose writings have given to
the name of Plato a lustre which neither Propylæ nor Parthenon
could equally give to that of Pericles—that the poor and hungry,
being condemned by their appeals for assistance, should be expelled from market-place and city, and 'the country be cleared of
that sort of animal.' " [29]

Some ethnologists today revive and reaffirm this old pre-
Christian doctrine of a pluralistic humanity.   They deride the
language of the American Declaration of Independence with its
assertion of human equality.   And it is obvious enough that all
men are not equal in height or weight or colour or wealth or intellectual capacity or in an hundred other ways.   But the broad
principle of human equality, of the solidarity of men, of the unity
of mankind remains nevertheless the true working principle.[30]
Any departure from it, when it is formulated or acted upon in
the interest of privilege and not of service, of isolation and not of
brotherhood, reduces itself to folly or to harm.   A writer at the
Universal Races Congress presented a paper on " The Intellectual
Standing of Different Races and their Respective Opportunities
for Culture," in which he determined the opportunities for culture
in any given people or race by the number of pupils and students

---

[29] Storrs's, *The Divine Origin of Christianity*, p. 164.
[30] Westcott, *The Gospel of the Resurrection*.   Notice to 2nd edition.

per unit of the population and the average intellectual standing of the same people by the number of university students per unit of the population, and then calculated the natural capacity of the people by dividing Intellectual Standing by Opportunity for Culture. By such calculation he ranks the United States first in intellectual standing, France fourth, Great Britain sixth, Spain seventh, Germany ninth, Japan eighteenth, Negroes in the United States twentieth, Mexico twenty-first, Russia twenty-third, India twenty-fourth. In natural capacity he ranks the United States first, Mexico sixth, Russia tenth, Japan eleventh, Germany twelfth, Great Britain fourteenth, India sixteenth. This writer says that " the Negro in Africa does not appear to be able to rise beyond the standard of elementary education, several attempts to impart secondary education having failed." [31] Other more fantastic judgments abound. Some are ready to arrange the races in a gradation of rank by head measurements, or facial angles, or aptitude for natural science or for metaphysics or for war. And some are interested in only one broad generalisation which exalts the white or more particularly the Nordic race and groups all the other races together in one " tide of colour." In his introduction to Mr. Stoddard's book, *The Rising Tide of Colour,* Mr. Madison Grant sets forth this thesis : [32]

" If this great race, (*i. e.,* the Nordic) with its capacity for leadership and fighting, should ultimately pass, with it would pass that which we call civilisation. It would be succeeded by an unstable and bastardised population, where worth and merit would have no inherent right to leadership and among which a new and darker age would blot out our racial inheritance.

" Such a catastrophe cannot threaten if the Nordic race will gather itself together in time, shake off the shackles of an inveterate altruism, discard the vain phantom of internationalism, and reassert the pride of race and the right of merit to rule.

" The Nordic race has been driven from many of its lands, but still grasps firmly the control of the world, and it is certainly not

[31] *Universal Races Congress,* 1911, p. 88.
[32] See a criticism of this view in New York *Times, Current History,* April, 1924. Art. by Johan J. Smertenks, " The Claim of ' Nordic ' Race Superiority," pp. 15-23.

at a greater numerical disadvantage than often before in contrast to the teeming population of eastern Asia.

" It has repeatedly been confronted with crises where the accident of battle, or the genius of a leader, saved a well-nigh hopeless day. It has survived defeat, it has survived the greater danger of victory, and, if it takes warning in time, it may face the future with assurance. Fight it must, but let that fight be not a civil war against its own blood kindred but against the dangerous foreign races, whether they advance sword in hand or in the more insidious guise of beggars at our gates, pleading for admittance to share our prosperity." [33]

Mr. Stoddard sees the decay of the white dominance over the other races which Mr. Grant appears to deem the racial right of the white people.

" The reader will remember," he says, " how west-central Asia, which in the dawn of history was predominantly white man's country, is today racially brown man's land in which white blood survives only as vestigial traces of vanishing significance. If this portion of Asia, the former seat of mighty white empires and possibly the very homeland of the white race itself, should have so entirely changed its ethnic character, what assurance can the most impressive political panorama give us that the present world-order may not swiftly and utterly pass away?

" The force of this query is exemplified when we turn from the political to the racial map of the globe. What a transformation! Instead of a world politically nine-tenths white, we see a world of which only four-tenths at the most can be considered predominantly white in blood, the rest of the world being inhabited mainly by the other primary races of mankind—yellows, browns, blacks, and reds. Speaking by continents, Europe, North America to the Rio Grande, the southern portion of South America, the Siberian part of Asia, and Australasia constitute the real white world; while the bulk of Asia, virtually the whole of Africa, and most of Central and South America form the world of colour. The respective areas of these two racially contrasted worlds are 22,-000,000 square miles for the whites and 31,000,000 square miles for the coloured races. Furthermore, it must be remembered that fully one-third of the white area (notably Australasia and Siberia) is very thinly inhabited and is thus held by a very slender

[33] Stoddard, *The Rising Tide of Colour*, p. 29 f.

racial tenure—the only tenure which counts in the long run." [34]
" One thing is certain: the white man will have to recognise that
the practically absolute world-dominion which he exercised during
the nineteenth century can no longer be maintained." [35]

This is deemed a lamentable prospect not because the principle
of the domination of the other races by the white race is a wrong
principle, but because the white race is no longer able as the
stronger race to dominate the rest, and the other races are no
longer willing as the inferior races to be dominated.

Over against the theories of this school our modern biologists
and sociologists alike reject the notion of prescriptive race superiority. " The old idea of absolute stability of human types,"
says Boas, " must evidently be given up and with it the belief of
the hereditary superiority of certain types over others." [36]   " In
vain," says Finot, " is the attempt to endow certain privileged
nations with every virtue by overwhelming their adversaries with
condemnation to eternal inferiority." [37]   East believes in white
race superiority, but he calls the " belief in the general superiority
of all the individuals of one race over all the individuals of another " indefensible.[38]

" It will materially help," says Kidd in *The Control of the
Tropics,* " towards the solution of this and other difficult problems,
if we are in a position, as it appears we shall be, to say with
greater clearness in the future, than we have been able to do in
the past, what it is constitutes superiority and inferiority of race.
We shall probably have to set aside many of our old ideas on the
subject.   Neither in respect alone of colour, nor of descent, nor
even of the possession of high intellectual capacity, can science
give us any warrant for speaking of one race as superior to
another.   The evolution which man is undergoing is, over and
above everything else, a social evolution.   There is, therefore,
but one absolute test of superiority.   It is only the race possessing

---

[34] *Ibid.,* p. 5 f.
[35] *Ibid.,* p. 228.
[36] *Universal Races Congress,* 1911, art. on " Instability of Human Types,"
by Franz Boas, p. 103.
[37] *Race Prejudice,* p. 316.
[38] East, *Mankind at the Crossroads,* p. 132.

in the highest degree the qualities contributing to social efficiency
that can be recognised as having any claim to superiority." [39]

" We have wasted an infinite amount of time," says Mr. Stone,

" in interminable controversies over the relative superiority and
inferiority of different races. Such discussions have a certain
value when conducted by scientific men in a purely scientific spirit.
But for the purpose of explaining or establishing any fixed principle of race relations they are little better than worthless. The
Japanese is doubtless quite well satisfied of the superiority of his
people over the mushroom growths of western civilisation, and
finds no difficulty in borrowing from the latter whatever is worth
reproducing, and improving on it in adapting it to his own racial
needs. The Chinese do not waste their time in idle chatter over
the relative status of their race as compared with the white barbarians who have intruded themselves upon them with their
grotesque customs, their heathenish ideas, and their childishly new
religion. The Hindu regards with veiled contempt the racial pretensions of his conqueror, and, while biding the time when the
darker races of the earth shall once more come into their own,
does not bother himself with such an idle question as to whether
his temporary overlord is his racial equal. Only the white man
writes volumes to establish on paper the fact of a superiority
which is either self-evident and not in need of demonstration, on
the one hand, or is not a fact and is not demonstrable, on the other.
The really important matter is one about which there need be little
dispute—the fact of racial differences. It is the practical question
of differences—the fundamental differences of physical appearance, of mental habit and thought, of social customs and religious
beliefs, of the thousand and one things keenly and clearly ap-
preciable, yet sometimes elusive and undefinable—these are the
things which at once create and find expression in what we call
race problems and race prejudices, for want of better terms. In
just so far as these differences are fixed and permanently associated characteristics of two groups of people will the antipathies
and problems between the two be permanent." [40]

But as a matter of fact the implication of inferiority and su-

---

[39] *The Control of the Tropics,* p. 97 f.
[40] Adapted by Park & Burgess, *Introduction to the Science of Sociology,*
p. 632, from Stone, " Is Race Friction between Blacks and Whites in the
United States Growing and Inevitable? " in the *American Journal of Sociology,* XIII, 1907-8, pp. 677-696.

periority is there and makes the difficulty. It is not simply difference. It is the judgment of inferiority. But biologically, Dr.
Kelsey denies the reality of inferiority; " at all events until some
one is able to put his fingers upon some physical difference which
can be shown to have some connection with the degree of culture
or the possibility thereof, we have no right to assume that one
group of human beings is either superior or inferior to any other.
Indeed some of our best anthropologists tell us that if we give a
fixed value to all the various parts of the body and then proceed
to measure the various races, we shall find one standing about as
high as the rest on our social scale." [41] Fresh scrutiny needs to
be given to all claims of racial superiority and all charges of inferiority against other races. The evidence often presented " appears to have been devised to sustain a condemnation already
determined." [42]

The removal of the antipathies and the solution of the problems just referred to is the task for all men of reason and good
will today, and especially of Christianity. It will help us on our
way to examine a little further the idea of race superiority in the
hope that hereafter we shall not waste such an " infinite amount
of time " over it.

There are two races whose relations to the other races invariably arise in every discussion of the idea of race superiority.
One is the Jew. The problem of the Jewish race will appear
later. Here it will suffice to view it in one aspect alone. Does the
Jew feel himself a superior race? Mr. Belloc's book, *The Jews*,
will be differently judged by different readers. To some it will
seem malicious. But probably his statement of the Jewish race-
mind is true:

" The Jew individually feels himself superior to his non-Jewish
contemporary and neighbour of whatever race, and particularly
of our race; the Jew feels his nation immeasurably superior to any
other human community, and particularly to our modern national
communities in Europe. . . . He reposes in the same confidence

---

[41] *The Physical Basis of Society*, p. 292.
[42] Weller, *Prejudice or Foreigners*, p. 5.

as was felt by Disraeli when he said: 'The Jew cannot be absorbed; it is not possible for a superior race to be absorbed by an inferior.' But unfortunately he does not only repose on that foundation; he also acts upon it, and that is intolerable. . . . There is one last thing to be said, which it is almost impossible to say without danger of giving pain and therefore of confusing the problem and making the solution more difficult. But it must be said, because, if we shirk it, the problem is confused the more. It is this: While it is undoubtedly true, and will always be true, that a Jew feels himself the superior of his hosts, it is also true that his hosts feel themselves immeasurably superior to the Jew. We can only arrive at a just and peaceable solution of our difficulties by remembering that the Jew, to whom we have given special and alien status in the Commonwealth, is all the while thinking of himself as our superior. But on his side the Jew must recognise, however unpalatable to him the recognition may be, that those among whom he is living and whose inferiority he takes for granted, on their side regard him as something much less than themselves." [43] " It is clear that in this conflict between the Jew and, let us say, the European (for it is between the Jew and the white Occidental race that our present problem lies, though the same problem arises with all other races among whom the Jew may find himself), both parties cannot be right." [44]

Belloc suggests that a being superior to the race of man looking down might decide which party is right, but that failing such a decision our human solution must simply accept the fact that each party believes itself to be superior and " in the settlement they arrive at, admit as a factor necessarily and permanently present what each still secretly regards as a folly, but an incurable folly, in the other." [45] A better solution and the only possible one is to eschew all ideas of superiority and to recognise different and supplementary equipment for a common life and service, after the example of Mayer Sulzberger, of whom a newspaper of his city said when he was gone:

" Philadelphia knew him as a learned lawyer, a judge of superior qualifications in jurisprudence, and an earnest, influential

[43] Belloc, *The Jews*, pp. 108, 112, 116.
[44] *Ibid.*, p. 119.
[45] *Ibid.*, p. 119.

and generous supporter of every form of philanthropy that contributed to the welfare and uplift of his race.

"A smaller group of scholars knew him for an erudite Orientalist, whose opinion on a Hebrew or Assyrian text was received with authority by savants in Europe and the United States.

"Furthermore, he stood out as a patriot, the spokesman and exemplar of the highest type of Americanism in his race. Few of his fellow-citizens in the past forty years would have suspected that Mayer Sulzberger was foreign born. For more than seventy of his four score years he was identified with Philadelphia, and, as a representative citizen, demonstrated the completeness of assimilation which leaves not even an invisible line between the 'one hundred per cent. Americanism' of the native born and the foreign born who come here in childhood." [46]

The other race over which the issue of superiority or inferiority is most frequently raised or regarding which it is commonly assumed to be a closed issue is the Negro race. As the issue is raised by Kidd in *The Control of the Tropics,* it relates both to the Latin American and the African people. Are these races to be set down as prescriptively inferior? We shall consider the problem of both these races later, but now we ask only regarding the Negro. Is he to be dogmatically condemned to a status of race inferiority? Those who know the Negro race best in Africa do not admit it. M. Allegret cites the opinion of African administrators,—of General Sir F. G. Guggisberg, Governor of the Gold Coast:

"If we provided natives with the means of getting a really first rate education, would they be capable of taking their place alongside Europeans? I emphatically reply: 'Yes, certainly.' The reason of my affirmation is that many Africans have already attained to this, and that by their own efforts. . . . The day will come when the black race will have developed to such an extent that an irresistible movement will push the élite towards the higher ranges of education. It will be impelled by an instinctive thirst for knowledge and also by a desire to share in the direction of the social and political life of the masses."

And General Mangin says,

---

[46] Philadelphia *Evening Bulletin,* April 21, 1923.

" The African is quite capable of standing on his own feet.
The steamers and trains are manned by natives who have been
trained with remarkable rapidity. All our telegraph stations are
in the hands of natives. The Negro is probably as competent as
the white man to handle the scientific instruments of civilisation.
. . . I do not deny that he still has to be educated. What I do
maintain is that he has qualities of head and heart which ought not
to be treated as negligible. He is by nature good and faithful and
endowed with a sense of honour, and if he is really given the
chance, he will reach a high level. There is an élite in the black
world capable of excelling in all regions of human intelligence.
On the other hand I do not in the least believe that, if the black
race is raised above its present position, there is any chance of its
entering into conflict with the white race. It will take its place in
the human family and will develop side by side and simultaneously
with us." [47]

And Dr. James Stewart, who knew the African as well as any
man, would not allow any judgment of fixed racial inferiority
against him:

" Even today educated Englishmen speak of him as an ' inferior
animal,' as a ' blend of child and beast,' or a ' useless and dangerous brute,' scarcely possessing human rights. To those who use
such language I would say, how badly we use the power and the
gifts that God has given us when we so regard the unfortunate
African! It is well that there is gradually growing a saner and
humaner belief, that there is a wide and possibly great future for
the African himself, as well as for his continent. By this it is not
meant that particular tribes or even separate races may not disappear as individual men do. Both come and go. Nor it is meant
that the African will suddenly reach a highly civilised condition,
and gain a position which other races have secured only after
centuries of strenuous effort. Yet there is some peculiarity in the
history of the African race, and some inherent vitality in it as a
whole, that affords a basis for a future entirely different from the
past. . . . The African race is certain to survive and increase.
It cannot be placed amongst those races that are dying or decaying. On the contrary, it possesses a wonderful vitality. Centuries
of subjugation, and all the suffering through which the African

---

[47] *International Review of Missions*, April, 1923, art. " The Present Crisis
in Africa," p. 165.

has come, have not quenched that vitality, nor destroyed a certain buoyancy of spirits, which has acted, no doubt, as a preservative."

Dr. Stewart rejected the view of those who deemed the African "different and inferior not merely in degree but in kind to the white race" and held that "as to the power of the African to take up or utilise what civilisation has to offer him, it may be again repeated there need also be no doubt." [48] Professor Boas sees no fixed barrier to the full development of the Negro race with other races:

"To this question anthropology can give the decided answer that the traits of African culture as observed in the aboriginal home of the Negro are those of a healthy primitive people, with a considerable degree of personal initiative, with a talent for organisation, and with imaginative power, with technical skill and thrift. Neither is a warlike spirit absent in the race, as proved by the mighty conquerors who overthrew states and founded new empires, and by the courage of the armies that follow the bidding of their leaders. There is nothing to prove that licentiousness, shiftless laziness, lack of initiative, are fundamental characteristics of the race. Everything points out that these qualities are the result of social conditions, rather than of hereditary traits."

Professor Boas finds that "no proof of the inferiority of the Negro type could be given except that it seemed quite possible that perhaps the race would not produce quite so many men of the highest genius as other races; while there was nothing at all that could be interpreted as suggesting any material difference in the mental capacity of the bulk of the Negro population as compared with the bulk of the white population." [49]

Let one of their own members, as capable as any member of any race of stating the cause of racial justice, set forth the case against the notion of Negro racial inferiority:

"It has often been assumed that the Negro is physically in-

---

[48] Stewart, *Dawn in the Dark Continent*, pp. 357, 364, 369.
[49] *The Mind of Primitive Man.*

ferior to other races and markedly distinguishable from them; modern science gives no authority for such an assumption. The supposed inferiority cannot rest on colour, for that is ' due to the combined influences of a great number of factors of environment working through physical processes,' and, ' however marked the contrasts may be, there is no corresponding difference in anatomical structure discoverable.' So, too, difference in texture of hair is a matter of degree, not kind, and is caused by heat, moisture, exposure, and the like.

" The bony skeleton presents no distinctly racial lines of variation. Prognathism ' presents too many individual varieties to be taken as a distinctive character of race.' Difference in physical measurements does not show the Negro to be a more primitive evolutionary form. Comparative ethnology today affords ' no support to the view which sees in the so-called lower races of mankind a transition stage from beast to man.'

" Much has been made of the supposed smaller brain of the Negro race; but this is as yet an unproved assumption, based on the uncritical measurement of less than a thousand Negro brains as compared with eleven thousand or more European brains. Even if future measurement prove the average Negro brain lighter, the vast majority of Negro brain weights fall within the same limits as the whites; and finally, ' neither size nor weight of the brain seems to be of importance' as an index of mental capacity. We may, therefore, say with Ratzel, ' There is only one species of man. The variations are numerous, but do not go deep.'

" To this we may add the word of the Secretary of the First Races Congress: ' We are, then, under the necessity of concluding that an impartial investigator would be inclined to look upon the various important peoples of the world as to all intents and purposes essentially equal in intellect, enterprise, morality, and physique.' . . .

" Let it therefore be said, once for all, that racial inferiority is not the cause of anti-Negro prejudice. Boas, the anthropologist, says: ' An unbiased estimate of the anthropological evidence so far brought forward does not permit us to countenance the belief in a racial inferiority which would unfit an individual of the Negro race to take his part in modern civilisation. We do not know of any demand made on the human body or mind in modern life that anatomical or ethnological evidence would prove to be beyond the powers of the Negro.'

" We have every reason to suppose that all races are capable, under proper guidance, of being fitted into the complex scheme of our modern civilisation, and the policy of artificially excluding them from its benefits is as unjustifiable scientifically as it is ethnically abhorrent." [50]

There are many errors which lie back of our ideas of race superiority.

1. One is to assume the validity and supremacy of our own standards and to condemn to inferiority all non-conformity with those standards. As Finot says:

"The science of inequality is emphatically a science of white people. It is they who have invented it and set it going, who have maintained, cherished, and propagated it, thanks to their observations and their deductions. Deeming themselves greater than men of other colours, they have elevated into superior qualities all the traits which are peculiar to themselves, commencing with the whiteness of the skin and the pliancy of the hair. But nothing proves that these vaunted traits are traits of real superiority.

"'If the Chinese and the Egyptians had judged our ancestors as we too often judge foreign races,' says Quatrefages, 'they would have found in them many traits of inferiority such as this white skin in which we take so much pride, and which they might have regarded as showing an irremediable etiolation.' This is what dogmatic anthropologists seem at all times to have forgotten. Human varieties have not been studied like those of animals and plants, that is to say, without conventional prejudices as to their respective values and as to those which are superior and inferior. Facts have often yielded to sentiments. We have been persuaded, with the help of our feelings, to accept our own preferences rather than impartial observations, and our own prejudices rather than scientific laws.

"In pursuing this course the elementary commandments of experimental science are transgressed. The majority of the anthropologists, faithful in this respect to the scholastic teachings, have begun by assuming the inequality of human beings as an axiom. On this preliminary basis they have built an imposing edifice, but really one of fictitious solidity." [51]

---

[50] Du Bois, *The Negro*, pp. 104 f., 139 f.; see also *The World Tomorrow*, March, 1922, Art. by H. A. Miller, "The Myth of Racial Inferiority": "If both the culturally superior and inferior races will accept the fact that inherent racial inferiority is a myth, the world may be saved some of the painful experiences it has suffered as other myths of privilege and prestige have been shattered."
[51] *Race Prejudice*, p. 310.

We regard with favour certain physical characteristics, white skin, fair hair, blue eyes, a certain type of features, our own odours. Another race will naturally have entirely different tastes. It is a matter not of superiority or inferiority but of variety. " Some men say that coloured people are ' ugly.' They should be reminded that beauty is very relative, and that our own idea of beauty is subject to changes of fashion. We know, too, that artists so refined as the Japanese find our large eyes and our high noses horrid." [52]   In moral qualities we exalt energy, promptitude, exactness, veracity, readiness for progress, etc. These are good qualities, but in the first place are we sure that we individually possess them in sufficient measure to be entitled to racial self-satisfaction, and in the second place how shall we weigh them against qualities of patience, long-suffering, considerateness, contentment, possessed by other races in a measure beyond us? If we were to judge each race by its possession of the qualities exalted by Jesus, especially in the Beatitudes, which races would rank highest?

Having in mind the error of reading our prejudices into our racial judgments we should do well to recollect the words of the Secretary of the Universal Races Congress in 1911, " We are under the necessity of concluding that an impartial investigator would be inclined to look upon the various important peoples of the world as, to all intents and purposes, essentially equals in intellect, enterprise, morality and physique. . . . We ought to combat the irreconcilable contentions prevalent among all the more important races of mankind that their customs, their civilisations, and their race are superior to those of other races. In explanation of existing differences we would refer to special needs arising from peculiar geographical and economic conditions, and to related divergences in national history; and, in explanation of the attitude assumed, we would refer to intimacy with one's own customs leading psychologically to a love of them and unfamiliarity with others' customs tending to lead psychologically to dislike and contempt of these

---

[52] *Universal Races Congress*, 1911, p. 14.

latter." [53] " No one," says Sir Charles Eliot, " possesses the necessary impartiality and cosmopolitan outlook to be able to decide whether the Asiatic or the European character is, as a whole, the better." [54] The problem of race prejudice is not so much a fundamental biological problem as it is a social problem of our own manufacture which grows out of our acceptance of our own preferences as absolute by giving them a name, and chiefly under the cultivating manipulation of scholars and teachers and political leaders. Race prejudice in the mass of common people is the product of accumulated social education. As Professor Royce says:

" Our so-called race problems are merely problems caused by our antipathies. Now the mental antipathies of men are very elemental, wide-spread and momentous mental phenomena. But they are also in their fundamental nature extremely capricious, and extremely suggestible mental phenomena. Let the individual man alone, and he will feel antipathies for certain other human beings very much as any young child does—namely, quite capriciously—just as he will also feel all kinds of capricious likings for people. But train a man first to give names to his antipathies, and then to regard the antipathies thus learned as sacred merely because they have a name, and then you get the phenomena of racial hatred, or class hatred, and so on indefinitely. Such trained hatreds are peculiarly pathetic and peculiarly deceitful, because they combine in such a subtle way the elemental vehemence of the hatred that a child may feel for a stranger, or a cat, or a dog, with the appearance of dignity and sobriety and sense of duty which a name gives." [55]

There is a further aspect of injustice in our condemning other races because they do not conform to our standard. It is revealed in our condemnation of these very races when they do conform to our standard and do the same things that we do. We condemn Japan and Turkey, for example, for attempting to vernacularise all schools, and yet twenty-one American states passed laws designed to prevent the teaching of foreign languages to pupils

---

[53] *Universal Races Congress,* 1911, pp. 35, 38.
[54] *Letters from the Far East,* p. 28.
[55] Royce, *Race Prejudice and Other American Questions,* p. 47.

below the eighth grade in public, private and parochial schools, which were enforced until declared unconstitutional by the Supreme Court. And Oregon passed laws designed apparently to force all children into the public schools. We protested against the possibility of such action on the part of Japan in Korea. We condemn Latin American countries for requiring examination in Spanish or Portuguese on the part of American doctors desiring to practise medicine, but in the Philippine Islands all business accounts are required to be kept in English, Spanish, or one of the dialects of the Philippine Islands. The Chinese merchants have protested in vain. Would American merchants submit to a corresponding law in China? In many ways we allow to ourselves what we condemn in others. But if we standardise our own ways we must be prepared to take all the consequences. If we do not allow Japanese to hold land in America, we must not object if they forbid our holding land in Japan. If we forbid brown and yellow people to become Americans, we cannot object if brown and yellow people deal likewise with us.

2. A second error is the assumption that backwardness and inferiority are synonymous. "Backward," says Ratzel, "does not necessarily mean inferior." The conception of child races is a familiar conception. We have worked with it as a pretext in politics in relation to "subject peoples" and to the questions involved,—"of responsibility to weaker races, of the relations of the governing power to great systems of native jurisprudence and religion, which take us back to the very childhood of the world, and in which the first principle of successful policy is that we are dealing, as it were, with children."[56] But we have not accepted this conception in its full application to race relationships. It is time that we should do so. A so-called inferior race is simply a race which has not yet enjoyed the education and felt the influences which would lift it to the level of its potential happiness and serviceableness. And in this sense all races are still inferior.[57]

---

[56] Kidd, *The Control of the Tropics*, p. 33 f.
[57] "Our western civilisation is perhaps not absolutely the glorious thing we like to imagine it." Seeley, *The Expansion of England*, p. 354.

3. A third error is the idea that the apparent inferiority of a race is due to its race-character and destiny and not, as is the fact, to its lack of motive and opportunity and inspiration, although this lack is an effect as well as a cause of race-character. And it is of equal importance that the race which needs these should receive them and that the race which has them to give should impart them. In dealing with the question of African character and the problem of labour in South Africa the South African Native Races Committee declared in its report in 1908:

" It is often said that the native is indolent and must be taught the 'dignity of labour.' Gradually, however, it is being recognised that the true cause of the difficulty is to be found, not in any inherent defect in the character of the natives, but in the absence of a sufficient motive to engage in continuous work. Uneducated natives can satisfy their primitive needs with little exertion; and if they are content with their present earnings, the difficulty of obtaining labour is not likely to disappear. But the progress of education tends inevitably to raise the standard of living, and by creating fresh needs supplies a powerful incentive to labour. And from the point of view of the white colonists there are other reasons of still greater weight for educating the natives. Nothing could be more unworthy, or in the long run more disastrous, than that the whites in South Africa should regard the natives as a mere ' labour asset.' If this view prevailed—and it is to be feared that it still has some advocates—it would inevitably result in the demoralisation of the white communities. ' We have to bear in mind,' writes Sir Marshal Clarke, ' that where two races on different planes of civilisation come into such close contact as do the whites and blacks in South Africa, they act and react on each other, and where the higher race neglects its duty to the lower it will itself suffer.' Neglect of this duty has many serious consequences, but perhaps none more disastrous than its effects on the white children. . . . As Mr. Barnett justly says, ' the mental and moral development of the white children is inextricably involved in that of the black.' " [58]

A superior race that does not seek to share its superiority with an inferior will inevitably be dragged down to share the lower race's inferiority.

---

[58] *The South African Natives*, p. 186 f.

4. A more radical error is the idea of the fixedness of race character, of the fiat of unalterable race status.[59] On the other hand the truth is that there is no static, inherent, abiding status of race superiority or inferiority. No race is assured of continued ascendency. The alarmist school realises this. Indeed this is the cry of alarm it is sounding abroad. Having cherished the idea of white ascendency it now sees that ascendency threatened, and unconvinced of the right solution of the race problem, it is appealing for the segregation and racial withdrawal and for the eugenic race-breeding of the white peoples in the interest of the preservation of their superiority of race character. This truth of race-growth and change is indeed a warning to all race-vanity and privilege, but it is also the hope of all races, superior or inferior. None of them is doomed to a fixed status. A true ethnological view is a confirmation of the promises of Christianity to the races and to the men who comprise them. Mr. Spiller maintains,

" The physical and mental characteristics observable in a particular race are not (1) permanent, (2) modifiable only through ages of environmental pressure; but (3) marked changes in popular education, in public sentiment, and in environment generally, may, apart from intermarriage, materially transform physical and especially mental characteristics in a generation or two. The status of a race at any particular moment of time offers no index to its innate or inherited capacities. It is of great importance in this respect to recognise that civilisations are meteoric in nature, bursting out of obscurity only to plunge back into it. . . .

" Differences in economic, hygienic, moral, and educational standards play a vital part in estranging races which come in contact with each other. These differences, like social differences generally, are in substance almost certainly due to passing social conditions and not to innate racial characteristics, and the aim should be, as in social differences, to remove these rather than to accentuate them by regarding them as fixed.

" The deepest cause of race misunderstandings is perhaps the tacit assumption that the present characteristics of a race are the expression of fixed and permanent racial characteristics. If so, anthropologists, sociologists, and scientific thinkers as a class, could powerfully assist the movement for a juster appreciation of

---

[59] Townsend's *Asia and Europe* sets forth this view persuasively.

races by persistently pointing out in their lectures and in their works the fundamental fallacy involved in taking a static instead of a dynamic, a momentary instead of a historic, a local instead of a general, point of view of race characteristics. And such dynamic teaching could be conveniently introduced into schools, more especially in the geography and history lessons; also into colleges for the training of teachers, diplomats, colonial administrators, and missionaries.

"The belief in racial superiority is largely due, as is suggested above, to unenlightened psychological repulsion and underestimation of the dynamic or environmental factors; there is no fair proof of some races being substantially superior to others in inborn capacity, and hence our moral standard need never be modified." [60]

The Chinese race which is often cited as the outstanding proof that a race may become static and fixed is a clear and convincing disproof of such a theory. In the museum in the old Forbidden Palace in Peking are gathered such remnants of Chinese art as the "superior" races have not stolen. They are arranged chronologically and they show that a race is not controlled by forces which move it gradually upward or downward. On the other hand, great artistic impulses which rose to magnificent expression in one dynasty die down and disappear only to break forth again with still richer power here or there centuries afterwards. These resurrections and increments of power, with results, in some forms, such as the "Nordic" race has never produced, are due to one or the other of two causes, both of which disprove the theory of racial immobility. Either they are due to the dying down and then the awakening again of latent racial capacity or they come from the impulse of some race amalgamation. In *Outlines of Chinese Art,* Dr. Ferguson lays the stress upon the distinctiveness of Chinese art effort and its independence of all outside influence. He says:

"It has been the genius of the Chinese to preserve unchanged the same art spirit from generation to generation, even though

---

[60] *Universal Races Congress,* 1911, paper by G. Spiller on "The Problem of Race Equality," p. 34.

early examples might perish. . . . It is safe to say that the same art motives which flourished in the Shan and Chow dynasties stirred the hearts of artists in the Ming and Manchu dynasties. . . . It is interesting to note that art motives became stabilised before China began to have much intercourse with outside nations. . . . We know that by this time (5th century B. C.) there had been developments of artistic creation in bronze. jade and ideographs which have continued to control the minds of artists down to the present time."

In contrast with this point of view, in *Epochs of Chinese and Japanese Art,* Fenollosa writes: " Medieval art in Japan and China is as much involved with Buddhism as is medieval European art with Christianity." He adds: " The writer wishes to break down the old fallacy of regarding Chinese civilisation as standing for thousands of years at a dead level by openly exhibiting the special environing culture and special structural beauties which render the art of each period unique." Further on, he writes: " At creative periods all forms of art will be found to interact," and he indicates in scheme his theory of the source of outside influences upon Chinese art.

It is interesting to note the similarity and parallelism between the development of literature in China and in Europe. The " Golden Age " of literature in China in the Chou dynasty corresponds somewhat in time to the Golden Age of the great Greek thinkers and writers; again there is a period of stagnation in China which resembles closely the Dark Ages in Europe; the Renaissance in the Sun Dynasty in China occurred just a short time before the Renaissance in Europe. A graph marking the rise and fall of the spirit and volume of literary production in China would correspond very closely to one which would indicate similar fluctuations in Europe, but the situation in China is a much more valid argument against the race determinists than that in Europe, because there has been on the whole a fairly homogeneous race development in China, without all the intermixture and blending of racial stock which is so apparent in Europe. The literary movement now in progress in China is evidence of vitality which as yet shows no sign of decay. Of course, one does not mean to say that there were not variations in the racial stream in China due to the influx of the Mongols and the Manchus, but the racial stock as a whole is fairly homogeneous, being chiefly the Sinitic race, to which in popular usage the rather loose term of Mongolian is generally applied.

I presented this question, of the proof by the Chinese race of the truth of racial vitality and expansion, to Prof. F. W. Williams, of Yale University, and he has stated his view of the case in the following suggestive letter:

" The question you put interests me greatly; it quite accords with an idea I have long cherished and applied to the histories of all culture groups. It is not only in China that you will find periods of convulsion, usually involving some foreign incursions, followed by surprising departures in intellectual achievement. Egypt in the IV-VI Dynasties, after the union of Upper and Lower Egypt, and again after the Hyksos; Babylonia under the First Dynasty; Persia under the Achamenids; India after several Tartar conquests and notably that of the Moguls, and plenty other instances seem to me to point to a law of race improvement that brings new vitality to an old nation following penetration or conquest by outsiders. All the great moments of Chinese history appear subsequent to long struggles with the Tartars and to be connected with a freshening of the population after the barbarians are incorporated with the older stock. The Chou, the Han, the Sui-T'ang, the Mongol, the Manchu Dynasties all involve a renascence after conflict with Tartars who become amalgamated with the Chinese and invigourate a decadent people. The greatness of the Sung period seems to be due to causes less obvious, but in this case I incline to the theory that its intellectual and artistic superiority might have been due to constant influxes of Toba Tartars preceding the Mongol advance. Conversely the law seems to involve decadence after the new vigour becomes thin. It is evident not only in art and letters but in decentralising political tendencies which destroy schools and coöperation everywhere and let loose reactionary elements. A country cannot remain at its best unless reinvigorated from time to time by foreign blood. China, which has ever been supercilious or jealous of outsiders, has been better able than Europe as a whole to defend its borders and has had relatively little voluntary immigration; having dammed the natural inflow it has suffered repeated inundations at intervals, but these have never become deluges and it has thus far managed to recover its losses and eventually improve its status by each mix-up. Unlike India, it has not been handicapped by deeply rooted religious prejudices or by physical barriers which kept its sections in great pockets; being fairly homogenous it has always recovered.

" As to decadence, no nation in history appears at its best in art or learning for many generations at a time. When we recall the fact that Greece was great for only two centuries and Rome for never more than two centuries at a time, with spasms of degeneracy between, China's record does not appear exceptional. One finds sudden culmination followed by imitation and loss of originality everywhere in recorded history. The details of this process are interesting and would be worth following, *e. g.,* why does architecture always precede sculpture and painting in a revival of the arts —to give place usually to poetry and criticism and philosophy? But this inquiry leads us away from our main thesis. I believe one will discover in any great museum in the world evidence that (as you put it) ' race capacity and achievement does not necessarily move along a slow and orderly gradient, either down or up, but is liable to great convulsions, to sudden collapses or to equally sudden resurrection.'

" One corollary suggests itself to me:—We are done, perhaps forever, with masses of nomadic barbarians in the world; is the new age of man to be fructified and quickened by rivulets of immigrants carried constantly over seas instead of occasional floods over lands? Of course the New World has thus far been peopled in this way, and equally, of course, the Old World has no room for people who do not fight their way in. Will our policy of stopping the rivulets here bring about presently a flood of civilised instead of barbarous invaders such as China has known for ages? " [61]

---

[61] Professor Thomas F. Carter, of the Department of Chinese in Columbia University, writes in comment on these references to Chinese history: " The whole course of Chinese History seems to have gone up and down like sea waves or perhaps more like the seasons of the year. There was the time of poetry and vigourous thinking of the Chou Dynasty that was distinctly a springtime of the race; there was the rather sultry but ripe scholarship of the Han Dynasty falling into general decay toward the end of the Han period; there was the long winter of the dark ages corresponding roughly to the Dark Ages of Europe; there was again a springtime of lyric poetry and vigourous art in the T'ang Dynasty, followed again by a period of ripe scholarship during the Sung period, and again by a period of decline under the Mongóls; and finally there has been a long winter under the Mings and Manchus. Whether we see signs of approaching spring, either in the present day Christian movement or in the intellectual renaissance, remains to be seen.
" Professor Williams's Theory of the origin in race amalgamation of each

5. It is an error also to identify races and civilisations and to condemn as inferior the peoples of inferior or backward culture. In the first place, our western civilisation is itself none too superior. To the extent that it embodies the truth which God has written upon nature and conforms to the mind of Christ it is true civilisation. But in neither of these respects has it advanced far enough, and it is seamed with evils which are now so patent to the world that in condemning them there is danger that we may lose the essential values to which they are clinging. In the second place, so far as it is good it is not ours. It is or is meant to be all men's universal possession. As Spiller said at the Universal Races Congress:

" So far at least as intellectual or moral aptitudes are concerned, we ought to speak of civilisations where we now speak of races; the stage or form of the civilisation of a people has no connection

---

of the periods of special vigour is very interesting and seems to be well founded. It would seem to me, however, that the theory could be carried further and that it might be shown that each of the great barbarian intrusions into China brought first disorganisation and a period of stagnation before the slow process of race amalgamation succeeded in bringing new vigour.

" The greatest resurrection of Chinese culture, the one that brought new vigour to all lines of Chinese endeavour, was the rather sudden revival under the T'angs after the period of the Dark Ages. It would seem that here we have something more than race amalgamation. It was new religion injected into the rather formal body of Chinese thought that combined with race amalgamation to bring about the new birth. It was a new culture, a Buddhist culture, a culture in which China's ancient formalism was combined with a vigourous culture from outside through religion that brought in the T'ang revival. The T'ang culture is almost as different from that which existed before the Dark Ages as the reviving culture of Mediæval Europe was different from that of Greece and Rome. And the difference, like that in Europe, was one caused by religion. It seems to me that we have here the reconciliation of the two theories of Chinese art which you quote; the theory of Ferguson and that of Fenollosa. Chinese Civilisation of T'ang times and especially Chinese art had its foundation in the art of the earlier period, but it was transformed and transfused by Buddhism almost as much as that of the Middle Ages in Europe was transformed by Christianity. I say 'almost' because the Dark Ages in China lasted a shorter time than in Europe and Buddhism made a less complete triumph, so that the classical influence was stronger and the influence of the new religion not as strong as in Europe, but the situation was analogous. A study of this period is instructive as illustrating how a rebirth of Chinese culture in the past has been directly due to the permeating influence of a religion from outside." Letter, T. F. Carter, Nov. 14, 1923.

with its special inborn physical characteristics; and even its physical characteristics are to no small extent the direct result of the environment, physical and social, under which it is living at the moment. To aid in clearing up the conceptions of race and civilisation, it would be of great value to define these.

" Each race might with advantage study the customs and civilisations of other races, even those it thinks the lowliest ones, for the definite purpose of improving its own customs and civilisation. Unostentatious conduct generally and respect for the customs of other races, provided these are not morally objectionable, should be recommended to all who come in passing or permanent contact with members of other races." [62]

And Ratzel declares:

" The gap which differences of civilisation create between two groups of human beings is in truth quite independent, whether in its depth or in its breadth, of the differences in their mental endowments. We need only observe what a mass of accidents has operated in all that determines the height of the stage of civilisation reached by a people, or in the total sum of their civilisation, to guard ourselves with the utmost care from drawing hasty conclusions as to their equipment either in body, intellect, or soul. Highly-gifted races can be poorly equipped with all that makes for civilisation, and so may produce the impression of holding a low position among mankind. . . . Race as such has nothing to do with the possession of civilisation. It would be silly to deny that in our own times the highest civilisation has been in the hands of the Caucasian, or white, races; but, on the other hand, it is an equally important fact that for thousands of years in all civilising movements there has been a dominant tendency to raise all races to the level of their burdens and duties, and therewith to make real earnest of the great conception of humanity—a conception which has been proclaimed as a specially distinguishing attribute of the modern world, but of which many still do not believe in the realisation. But let us only look outside the border of the brief and narrow course of events which we arrogantly call the history of the world, and we shall have to recognise that members of every race have borne their part in the history which lies beyond." [63]

We need to remember our racial debt. It is too often assumed that our claimed racial superiority is our racial achievement. It is not so. " I am a part of all that I have met " is more true of a race even than of a person. All generations and the races which preceded us and races which surround us helped to make and endow us. To any race conscious of its privilege, St. Paul puts his ancient question, "What hast thou that thou didst not receive?" "Our own civilisation," says General Mangin, who commanded the French African troops on the western front in the World War, "has its sources in Asia, which is yellow; in India which is bronzed; and in Egypt which is black. Greece and Rome are comparatively late-comers. We owe much to the Arabs. Our alphabets come from Asia, and our figures from Arabia, and long before Europe was settled there existed great civilisations. We, white men, are not the first, and we may not be the last, representatives of civilisation.. It is necessary to cultivate the world sense and to think in less limited periods of time." [64] " Our own civilisation," adds Leroy Beaulieu, " is not the monopoly of one race, but was constructed by the concurrence of many people. . . . The whole history of our civilisation, therefore, protests against its having ever been at any time monopolised by the Aryan branch of the white race. . . . The unity of race which has hitherto been imagined to exist among all Western peoples is now proved to be chimerical. . . . It seems impossible with the present facts to sustain a priori that one race cannot assimilate the civilisation of another." [65]

6. We err also in our sweeping race judgments when we fasten all individuals of a race within a racial inheritance as though the generalised character which we give to the race holds each member of the race in its determinism. Thank God, it does nothing of the kind. Men of the so-called inferior races, not in exceptional cases but by the thousand, can be cited who transcend in character, culture, power, influence, usefulness and humanity members of

---

[64] *London Observer*, quoted in *The Crisis*, March, 1922. See *Racial Relations and the Christian Ideal*, p. 8.
[65] Beaulieu, *The Awakening of the East*, p. 172; See Anesaki, *The Religious and Social Problems of the Orient*, Chap. III; Buckle, *History of Civilisation in England*, Vol. I, Chap. II, on "Influence Exercised by Physical Laws over the Organisation of Society and over the Character of Individuals."

the so-called superior races. Furthermore, as Professor H. A. Miller says: " Instead of drawing a line between races, psychological comparison demonstrates by the overlapping, similarity instead of difference. Divergences between the extremes of ' superior ' and ' inferior ' groups are almost exactly equal. It is manifestly absurd for the great mass of a race whom the lists classify as being of ' C ' grade, to claim, because there are one or two per cent. more of the ' A ' grade in this race, that therefore these ' C's ' have a God-given right to rule the other race which has also ' A's ' and ' B's ' in it." [66]

A few months ago the African Chief Khama finished his long career. He was over ninety years of age and he could remember meeting Livingstone on one of his earliest missionary journeys. He was elected as chief of the Bamangwato, one of the Bantu tribes of South Africa, in 1872, and had been their chief for fifty years. Mr. Harris, in his biography of Khama, writes: " Has there been in history a more dramatic figure than this son of a sorcerer, standing up in the kraal of his tribe, and bravely breaking with the heathen sanctions and standards of his race? . . . No Mendelism can explain how it is that this one man should have stood out against the inviolate traditions of the centuries and broken the tides of evil that for ages swept over his land. To that problem Khama himself would give but one answer—' it is the transforming power of the Grace of God.' " Referring to the widespread influence exerted by this Christian community, Mr. Harris says: " From that church, where the chief leads his people to prayer, and where true Christian characters have been formed, there spreads out into the wastes a stream of influence that makes for healing and light. For many years the Bamangwato have sustained their own mission work at Lake Mgami and numerous little stations in other lonely outposts." Khama's efforts to protect his people from the destructive influences of alcohol imported by European traders brought him into frequent collision with them. After his election as chief he summoned all the whites and informed them that intoxicating drinks were no longer to be sold to

---

[66] *The World Tomorrow*, March, 1922, p. 68.

his people. The whites might import brandy for their own use but they might not sell it to Africans. To this they professed to agree. A few days later he found several of the whites " roaring drunk." After waiting until they were sober he summoned them to his court. He asked no questions but simply stated the facts as he had seen them. " You think," said he, " you can despise my laws because I am a black man. Well, I am black, but I am chief of my own country. When you white men rule the country, then you may do as you like. At present I rule, and I shall maintain the laws you insult and despise." Then he went on, naming the offenders one by one, " Take everything you have, strip the iron off the roofs, gather all your possessions, and go! More, if there is any other white man here who does not like my laws, let him go, too. You ought to be ashamed of yourselves. I am trying to lead my people according to the Word of God, which we have received from you white people, and you show us an example of wickedness. You know that some of my brothers have learned to like the drink, and you tempt them with it. I make an end of it today. Go! Take your cattle, leave my town, and never come back."

Utter silence followed this speech. The men were smitten with shame and bewilderment. This decree meant blank ruin to many who were thus expelled, and some of them followed Khama to his house to plead for pity. " Pity!" said he, " when I had pity, and warned you, you despised me. Now I have pity for my own people." One pleaded that he had grown up in the country, and that Khama and he were old friends. " What!" said Khama, " you dare to speak, you who made me a promise, and then brought casks of drink to the river and smuggled them into the country? You call yourself my friend! You are my worst enemy!" So the canteen keepers and brandy smugglers had to load up their wagons and trek, and the Great Thirst Land " went dry." [67]

It was Khama who appealed to the British Government against the liquor deluge in Africa and who, when in England, met Queen Victoria with a dignity and capacity equal to her own. Any theory

---

[67] Adapted from *The East and the West*, Jan., 1923, review of *Khama, the Great African Chief*, by J. C. Harris; *The Missionary Review of the World*, May, 1923, Art. " Khama, a Christian Chief of Africa."

of race judgments which sets down Khama as a member of an inferior human caste to be judged by an arbitrary group judgment rather than by the truth is obviously foolish and false. It is not so much a matter of race and race as of man and man.

" I have always been made sad," said Booker Washington, " when I have heard members of any race claiming rights and privileges, or certain badges of distinction, on the ground simply that they were members of this or that race, regardless of their own individual worth or attainments. I have been made to feel sad for such persons because I am conscious of the fact that mere connection with what is known as a superior race will not permanently carry an individual forward unless he has individual worth, and mere connection with what is regarded as an inferior race will not finally hold an individual back if he possess intrinsic, individual merit. Every persecuted individual and race should get much consolation out of the great human law, which is universal and eternal, that merit, no matter under what skin found, is, in the long run, recognised and rewarded. This I have said here, not to call attention to myself as an individual, but to the race to which I am proud to belong." [68]

And fair and just men of all races are coming to realise this, even though more slowly than Booker Washington's hopeful words imply. And none are leading in this righteous and creative way of treating the race problems more wisely and efficiently than the best white men and women in the South. " The Negro is a human being," said Prof. Josiah Morse, of the University of South Carolina, at the Southern Sociological Congress in Atlanta in 1913,

" and modern anthropology has shown that the differences among human beings—anatomical, physiological, and mental—are insignificant as compared with their fundamental resemblances and identities. We shall certainly not need a Negro science of medicine. The things that breed disease among the whites—poverty, ignorance, overcrowding, immorality, alcoholism, unsanitary premises, neglect and malnutrition of children. etc.—will breed disease with equal facility among the Negroes. And we may rest assured that the measures and remedies that

[68] *Up from Slavery,* p. 40 f.

prevent and cure diseases among the whites will do the same for the blacks.

" And what is true of the body in this respect is also true of the mind. The conditions that make for morality or immorality, for happiness or unhappiness, for love and hate, sympathy and antipathy, kindness and cruelty, etc., among the whites accomplish the same results for the blacks. We shall not need a separate psychology for the Negroes, nor a separate logic, ethics, sociology, economics; not even a separate religion or art. The laws and facts of human nature discovered by these various sciences are equally true of the coloured races of man as of the white. Science knows no essential distinctions, because nature knows none. And that is why, in my opinion, our problem is not nearly so difficult as it might be, or as it appears to some. We know the essential facts and conditions; we know that everything human, from culture to disease, is intercommunicable among the races of men; we know that the foundation stones upon which this universe rests are righteousness and justice, and honesty, and love; we know that injustice cannot be done with impunity to the doer, that it must be paid for with compound interest and at an exorbitant rate; we know that no problem can be permanently solved unless it be solved fairly and in a generous spirit; we know that the Negro is here to stay, and that our welfare and happiness and health and progress are inextricably interwoven with his—then let us teach these truths honestly and fearlessly. . . . In this way, I believe, we shall most speedily and effectively rid our social system of the poisons of prejudice which are now causing so much suffering and loss to both races; and in this way we shall lay the foundation, at least, for the satisfactory solution of the problem in the future." [69]

This examination of the idea of race superiority has not been made under a presupposition of theoretical race equality of any kind, nor has it touched the nature, characteristics and limitations of the idea of racial equality which has emerged. Questions of political, economic or social equality are not as yet under discussion. Our review has had four things in mind: (1) the dissolution of the prejudice against any race, which may become its racial discouragement and which implies the assumption that it or its members are barred from any of the achievements or possessions

[69] *The South Mobilising for Social Service,* p. 403 f.

of humanity; (2) the affirmation of the truth of a general equality in racial capacity; (3) the emergence of the duty of service as the one real evidence and privilege of race superiority, and (4) the reassertion from a larger viewpoint of the truth of human unity. Let us note each of these points.

1. Some students of the race problem see an approach toward its solution in the recognition by the races deemed inferior, of their inferiority. Mr. Stone took this view:

" Open manifestations of race antipathy will be aggravated if each group feels its superiority over the other. They will be fewer and milder when one race accepts the position of inferiority outwardly or really feels the superiority of the other. In all cases the element of individual or racial self-assertiveness plays an important part. The white man on the Pacific coast may insist that he does not feel anything like the race prejudice toward the Chinaman that he does toward the Japanese. In truth the antipathy is equal in either case, but the Chinaman accepts the position and imputation of inferiority—no matter what or how he may really feel beneath his passive exterior. On the other hand, the Japanese neither accepts the position nor plays the rôle of an inferior—and when attacked he does not run. Aside from all question of the relative commendable traits of the two races, it is easy to see that the characteristics of one group are much more likely than those of the other to provoke outbreaks of antipathy when brought into contact with the white race. . . . The simpler the relations between diverse races, the less friction there will be; the more complex the relations, the greater the friction. The simplest relations possible are those in which the relative status of superior and inferior is mutually accepted as the historical, essential, and matter-of-fact basis of relationship between the two. The most complex relation possible between any two racial groups is that of a theoretical equality which one race denies and the other insists upon. The accepted relation of superior and inferior may exist not only without bitterness on one side or harsh feelings upon the other, but it may be characterised by a sentiment and affection wholly impossible between the same groups under conditions demanding a recognition of so-called equality." [70]

The difficulties in the way of this solution are probably insur-

---

[70] Stone, *The American Race Problem,* pp. 219, 223.

mountable. The acceptance of a status of inferiority is both good and bad for a man. It may be both better and worse for a race. Any development of a spirit of racial despair in any race would be a damage to the whole of humanity. India talks of the "slave mentality" which has been given to it by the subjection of the last century. Such talk is itself tragic. It is a dreadful thing when either individuals or races lose confidence in their capacity, and the whole world suffers the cost of their loss. The acceptance of a destined limit to progress is the surest deterrent to progress, and the abandonment of the hope of progress is death to man and races alike. Furthermore, individuals of the race which is invited to accept inferiority, who are themselves on a level with the superior individuals of the superior race, are psychologically incapable of submergence in the racial menialism proposed for them, and the interests of the society to which they and the superior race alike belong will not be likely to acquiesce in the situation that would be produced. The idea of individual superiority surrendering to the doom of indiscriminate racial condemnation is impossible.[71] Moreover, the world into which we have come or are coming is sure to be so convinced that human solidarity is a stronger principle than race, while both principles are recognised as essential and valid, that it is certain that some other racial adjustment than that of exclusive race aristocracy will have to be found. Later we must try to find it. If we miss it, it will be because we have no eyes to see what is near and no capacity to discern the real truth, which is simply this: that human beings are human beings

---

[71] "Might not the point be made that an admission of inferiority is not necessarily discouraging if it is felt to exist in regard to certain qualities only? For instance, Italians may admit that in the matter of height and physical strength they are, on an average, inferior to Anglo-Saxons. That would not discourage them. In the same way, Americans may admit that they are less artistic than the Japanese; Hindus that they are less musical than Italians; Russians that they are less logical than the French. A mutual recognition of specific racial or national superiorities and inferiorities, without attempts to formulate any general theory of superiority, might lead to greater admiration of all races towards each other, and to greater efforts on the part of each further to perfect itself in the qualities in which it already excels and to make good, in so far as that is possible, the felt failings or handicaps in racial or national character and abilities."—
BRUNO LASKER.

and are to be thought of and treated as human beings. A coloured woman uncovers the heart of the matter in some simple suggestions which she makes to white women in a paper on " Coöperation between White and Coloured Women "; "(1) Coloured women resent being called by their first names, except by intimate friends with whom such a privilege is an exchange. (2) Coloured women should be consulted about plans that include them. (3) There should be Christian frankness and open-mindedness in the approach to any problem. (4) The natural assumption that all white is superior and that all black is inferior must be eliminated before any really coöperative spirit can be fostered." [72]   What is this but to ask that human beings should be treated as human beings; that we should behave toward members of other races exactly as we would wish them to behave toward us? The Golden Rule was not given with any racial limitations upon its application.

It is desirable that we should try to put ourselves in the place of those individuals who are compelled to bear the weight of a judgment of inferiority against the race to which they belong. Such a judgment is an almost killing handicap. As Max Eastman says in the introduction to *Harlem Shadows:* " The children of the subjected race never have a chance. To be deprived at the very dawn of selfhood of a sense of possible superiority, is to be undernourished at the point of chief educative importance, and to be assailed in early childhood with a pervading intimation of inferiority is poison in the very centers of growth except for people of the very highest force of character; therefore, to be born into a subjected race is to grow up inferior, not only to the other races, but to one's own potential self." [73]   It is one evidence of the indestructible capacity for superiority in inferior races that so many individuals in them are able to conquer this handicap and demonstrate their ability to meet on equal terms the best of other races.

2. The present extent of our knowledge of ethnology leads students to minimise the difference in capacity between races. Professor John Dewey says: " Careful study has made it doubtful

---

[72] *The Missionary Review of the World,* June, 1922, p. 487.
[73] Quoted in *Racial Relations and the Christian Ideal,* p. 9.

whether their (savages') native capacities are appreciably inferior to those of civilised men. It has made it certain that native differences are not sufficient to account for the difference in culture."

Professor Robert E. Park, of the University of Chicago, says: " The difference between a savage and a civilised man is not due to any fundamental differences in their brain cells, but to the connections and mutual stimulations which are established by experience and education between those cells. In the savage those possibilities are not absent but latent. In the same way the difference between the civilisation of Central Africa and that of Western Europe is due, not to the difference in native abilities of the individuals and the peoples who have created them, but rather to the form which the association and interaction between those individuals and groups of individuals has taken."

Mr. H. G. Wells declares " that in Asia the average brain is not one whit inferior in quality to the average European brain; that history shows Asiatics to be as bold, as vigourous, as generous, as self-sacrificing and as capable of strong collective action as Europeans," and he adds, " that there are and must continue to be many more Asiatics than Europeans in the world." [74]

Professor Franz Boas, head of the Anthropological Department of Columbia University, writes:

" The differences between different types of man are, on the whole, small as compared to the range of variation in each type. . . . We are not inclined to consider the mental organisation of different races of man as differing in fundamental points. Although, therefore, the distribution of faculty among the races of man is far from being known, we can say this much: the average faculty of the white race is found to the same degree in a large proportion of individuals of all other races, and although it is probable that some of these races may not produce as large a proportion of great men as our own race, there is no reason to suppose that they are unable to reach the level of civilisation represented by the bulk of our own people." [75]

[74] Quoted in Kawakami, *The Real Japanese Question,* p. 224.
[75] Quoted by D. J. Fleming, *International Review of Missions,* Jan., 1923, Art. on " Relative Racial Capacity," p. 116.

The facts as we now know them, however, do not involve more than the idea of a general equality of racial capacity, and the doctrine of human solidarity implies no more.[76] The average ability of some races is below that of other races. These other races may have some compensating capacities which the stronger races lack, but the net balance may be heavy on the other side.[77] And yet in the fulfilment of the whole life of humanity the capacities of each race and of all may be equally essential.

There is much that we do not yet know. But we know enough to take home to ourselves some important lessons which Prof. Fleming draws out in his paper on " Relative Racial Capacity ": One is that we should not think of ourselves more highly than we ought to think. There should be a certain wholesome humility, such as there has never been in the past. As an English correspondent writes: " The whole of the British position in the East has been as de Gobineau pointed out long ago, built up by maintenance of a caste system far more rigourous than the Portuguese, Spanish, French, Dutch, or other famous colonisers ever attempted. Without this caste system, it is indeed difficult to imagine how we could possibly have obtained our success in India at all, or how a handful of whites could have maintained their dominance over so many millions. We selected good men, and they went East definitely as superior beings, to play the rôle of Providence to extremely helpless people. But the system that made our success is now outgrown. Our supreme self-assurance, our consciousness of other people's inferiority, has become a canker eating the Oriental heart." [78] This is a lesson that the Anglo-Saxon especially ought to take home. Professor Fleming says:

---

[76] See Ross's estimate of the capacity and general equality with us of the yellow race. *The Changing Chinese*, p. 63.

[77] The American Army psychological tests during the war resulted in a higher average for the white soldiers as compared with the Negroes, but many considerations need to be weighed in this connection, including educational advantages. See *National Academy of Science Memoirs*, Vol. XV, pp. 705-742. And Major Moton points out that in the first draft 75.60% of Negroes were accepted on the basis of physical fitness and only 69.71% of whites. *The Negro of Today*, p. 20.

[78] *Atlantic Monthly*, May, 1923, art. by Arthur Moore, " Bolshevism from an Eastern Angle."

" It is very easy for the white race to assume its superiority as a matter of course, and to do without thinking a multitude of little things which rankle harmfully in the hearts of another people. . . . Just as we have given up the idea of the divine right of kings, and are giving up the age-long conception of male superiority, we will very likely have to give up the flattering delusion of decided racial superiority. We can see, also, the right of each person to be treated as an individual and not classed in a group. . . . We forget that when we talk about the characteristics of a race as a whole, we are dealing with an abstraction that has no existence in nature. . . . If we were wishing to select a hundred people who are to be quite superior to another hundred, one of the most foolish ways would be to choose them by race. Selecting one hundred persons at random from one race supposedly superior, would by no means give you a group uniformly superior to another hundred chosen at random from a supposedly inferior race. . . . The selection of leadership by means of race alone would be a very inefficient method of procedure. . . . This discussion may make us more ready to see the good in another people. . . . Lastly, the present stage of psychological tests should give us great confidence that, given the right sort of training, we can find in any group the leadership it needs." [79]

If races are unequal, the right way to express the inequality is not by arbitrary and generalised discrimination, but by demonstration of individual superiority in fair rivalry. As the *Harvard Lampoon* remarked in an editorial endorsing the action of the Overseers of the University adverse to racial discriminations in the regulations for admission of students:

" It would indeed be a radical move for Harvard University to take definite measures toward the expulsion of Negroes and Jews, and the recent decision was by no means a surprise. There are very few undergraduates who have any feeling about the Negroes whatsoever.

" But it is fair to say that a great many who profess broadmindedness to their friends, secretly long for Harvard to be a college for the Christian races. Their wish will never be gratified so long as there are Jews who work more earnestly and with greater diligence than Christians, so long as there are Jews whose minds are

---

[79] *International Review of Missions,* Jan., 1923, art. on " Relative Racial Capacity," pp. 117-120.

quicker and keener, so long as there are Christians who scorn intellectual labour to the preference of idle hours wasted doing nothing.

" What is needed to ' solve ' the racial problem is hard work for its own sake. There will never be a struggle for supremacy in numbers. It will forever be a silent rivalry of race, a competition for intellectual superiority.

" Those who still want the Jews excluded can never do so by statutes and laws; they can only see to it that their own sons are keen enough to pass the entrance examinations with a higher mark than the sons of their Jewish classmates.

" Intellectual rivals need not be enemies; often they are the best of friends. Intellectual rivalry, such as one meets in entrance examinations, does not concern itself with proving that the ' other fellow,' whether he be Jew or Christian or ethical culturist, is dumber than you, but it consists in proving that you yourself are superior to all comers, whoever they may be. There are many lessons of diligence and perseverance to be learned from the Jews." [80]

3. There is one way in which it is open to any race to affirm and demonstrate its superiority, and that is in its humble and unselfish service of other races, by maintaining a character for moral rectitude and purity and by helping other races on their way, by accepting the principle " that racial greatness consists in service; that races are bound by the same code of honour that binds individuals to each other; that races are accountable to the same moral judgment bar before which individuals stand; that the relationships of races should be governed by the same Christian principle as that which obtains among all good men." " In the long run," as Prof. Conklin has said, " supremacy will pass in every community, nation or race to the more intelligent, the more capable, the more ethical. . . . In this struggle of races and peoples, there is reason to believe that success will ultimately rest with the intelligent, the capable, and the attention of all who love their race should be centered upon raising the standards of heredity, of education, and of social ideals." [81]

---

[80] *Harvard Lampoon*, May 8, 1923.
[81] *The Direction of Human Evolution*, p. 45 f. Guizot, *History of Civilisation*, chs. I, II.

"My only fear for white supremacy," writes a great-spirited Southern woman, "is that we should prove unworthy of it. If we fail, then we shall pass. Supremacy is for service. It is suicide to thrust other races back from the good we hold for humanity. For him who would be greatest the price is still that he should be servant of all." [82]

And the man or the race which truly is superior will find the whole world a brotherhood. In the *Analects* of Confucius we are told that Sze-me-Niu, full of anxiety said, "Other men all have brothers. I only have not." One of the leaders of the disciples of Confucius, Tsze-hsia by name, replied: "There is the following saying which I have heard: 'Death and life have their determined appointment; riches and honours depend upon heaven.' Let the superior man never fail reverentially to order his own conduct and let him be respectful to others and observant of propriety; then all within the four seas will be his brothers. Why should the superior man be distressed because he has no brothers?" [83] Either he will find men brothers or he will make them so. That is the one sure proof of his superiority.

"In a word," wrote Bishop Bashford, "the influence of each race and each civilisation will last so long as it deserves to last. The influence of the white races will pale before the influence of the yellow races if the latter surpass us in intellectual and moral power." [84]

4. Let us return again to the fundamental thought of the unity of all races in the one race. And let us end this chapter with two noble assertions of it.

One is an affirmation of faith in human unity based on the evidence of human speech and the intercommunication of men of the most diverse races. In an essay on "Language as a Link," Prof. Smith, Waynflete Professor of Mental and Moral Philosophy at Oxford, writes avowing his faith

"that mankind constitutes a real unity, that there is an identity

[82] Hammond, *In Black and White*, p. 89.
[83] Legge, *Analects of Confucius*, Book XII, chap. 5.
[84] *China, an Interpretation*, p. 444.

of nature running through and present in all mankind. This is not, or not merely, a natural unity. It does not lie in, or arise from, singleness of ancestry or kinship of blood; it is not merely the result of historic accident or physical causes. I cannot think of it as less than a spiritual unity which can neither be produced nor destroyed from without. All men can say ' We ' with a truth and significance incommunicable to other beings than men: they share in a complex but single type of experience. And with this goes a mutual or reciprocal communion in which no other beings participate; they are all literally one with one another." [85]

The other word is by Mr. F. S. Marvin:

" A dangerous frame of mind has often prevailed in the past, and is naturally feared by good people in the present, a consciousness of progress by those who share it, with pride of place, and a claim to overlordship in the interests of the overlord and the detriment of others. The danger is real; such ill-used strength has wrought devastation for centuries, but is by no means inherent in the enlightened consciousness of progress or power. It is power without enlightenment and without responsibility that works evil and may ruin a race as it has often ruined a family. The enlightenment needed here concerns the source of Western power; the responsibility arises from any fair consideration of its proper use. We are ready to say that the West must be trustee for the rest of mankind; this book, in fact, sets out to be a variation on that theme. But such sound and high doctrine needs for its full force the realisation of the social and historic truth on which it rests. The West should be the world-trustee, not because of any inherent right, still less because of its temporary power, but because the riches and resources which it holds, have come to it, directly or indirectly, at near or far remove, from the whole race of man. The gifts of Humanity, all Humanity must enjoy and thrive on them, or it will be impoverished and decay, including the vanguard which has, at the moment, the largest share.

" If this seems merely the language of exhortation, describing rather an ideal laid up in heaven than the possibilities of a sinful world, it will be well to consider how profound is the common basis of all human culture, how deep the debt of the most advanced sections of mankind to all their predecessors, perhaps most of all to the earliest and simplest. Art, numeration, all the most indispensable inventions, fire, the wheel, the loom, the bow, the

---

[85] *Western Races and the World,* p. 30 f.

knife, are due to races of mankind struggling against natural hardships which we soft Westerners can now barely imagine, and certainly with their equipment could never face. These men, were they now alive, would rank with the most backward of existing races.[86]

"Let us now look at our problem in the light of this historical perspective, which anthropology has opened up to us in recent years. Our first analogy was that of a family, and we shall find that we come back to that as the nearest and most helpful guide. All the races of mankind, in view of their common origin and common qualities, may be regarded as one family, with one home and one Father, however we may conceive that greatest and highest of Beings who embraces and sustains us.

"We, therefore, as one family, owe affection and service to one another, and all of us feel and recognise this tie according to our powers of sympathy and understanding. But, like all analogies, this one is not complete; there is something less on the one side, and something more on the other. The family of nations is far less united by love and constant association, and the various members in too many cases have never even heard of one another. But, on the other hand, there is something more in the wider relation which history and sociology have lately revealed to us.

"Every member in the great family, even the strongest and most advanced, owes the essentials of social life to races of men similar in civilisation to those whom we now regard as backward, and whom we are called upon, as our kindred, to help on their upward path." [87]

---

[86] "Every single one of the important plant foods was discovered and brought into cultivation by prehistoric man. Our bygone progenitors must have been pretty busy old fellows and just as keen as their descendants. . . . There is nothing to indicate the superiority of contemporary man over the Cro-Magnon man of some 30,000 years ago in inherent capacity." East, *Mankind at the Crossroads*, pp. 162, 19.

[87] *Western Races and the World*, pp. 14-16. All races succeed to and build upon other races. Okuma, *Fifty Years of New Japan*, p. 463.

III

THE GOOD AND GAIN OF RACE AND RACE DISTINCTION

IN the rich imagery of four of the Prophets, the Hebrew race is spoken of as " mother." [1] It is significant that in each passage where this noble metaphor is used the race is held up to reprobation and reproach for its shortcomings or transgressions. It is as though the Prophets sought to bring out in the degradation and misuse of race the fact of its honour and glory. A man's race was his mother. What more glorious tribute could be paid to its true nature and significance? A man should feel and act with regard to his race as he would with regard to his mother. He would defend her from any assault of word or deed. He would never endure from others and he would never tolerate from himself one word of slander or disrespect regarding her. He would never do or allow to be done in her name or in her alleged interest any mean or dishonourable thing. He would act toward the mothers of other men as he would wish them to act toward his own. The world and the world's history would be different if men had always spoken and acted with regard to all races, their own and others, in this conception of motherhood, and it would be a long step today toward the solution of the race problem if we would always speak of race as a man would speak of his own or of another man's mother.

Such a way of looking at race would dispose at once of all race shame, secrecy, disrespect or contempt. Mr. Belloc, in his book on *The Jews*, speaks of the convention so long maintained by Jews

" against alluding to Jewish nationality or Jewish interests in any form. Whether the Jews were wise or not to cherish that

---

[1] Isa. L, 1; Jer. L, 12; Ezek. XIX, 2, 10; Hos. II, 4; IV, 5.

105

convention, as they undoubtedly did, does not concern this part
of my argument. I am talking of our duty and not of theirs. But
I say that unless the convention is softened and at last dissolved,
nothing can be done. Both parties should know that it only does
harm. It renders stilted and absurd all our relations; it fosters
that suspicion of secrecy which I have insisted upon as the chief
irritant in those relations, and it creates a feeling of exception, of
oddity, which is the very worst service that could be rendered to
the Jews themselves.

"Some little time ago the convention went so far that even a
mention, a neutral—nay, a laudatory mention, of anything Jewish
in a general company led to an immediate awkwardness. Men
looked over their shoulders, women gave downward glances right
and left. A sort of hunt began, to see whether anyone present
could possibly in any remote connection be offended by the mon-
strous deed. If a man said, 'What a poet Heine was and how
thoroughly Jewish is his irony!' and said it in a room full of
people, the adjective 'Jewish' acted like a pistol shot—could anything be more absurd! Yet so it was.

"But the point I make is not against the absurdity of this convention but against its peril. It is an obstacle to all right handling
of what is becoming daily a more and more insistent and acute
difficulty." [2]

The Jews are not the only people who have maintained or endured this convention or who are now escaping from it. Many
Negroes and members of other races have at times felt, or shown
their fear of, a tone of race depreciation. The manly spirit of
self-respect, devoid of all boasting on one side and of all syco-
phancy on the other is more and more characterising each race
and ought to characterise it. It is or ought to be just as proud a
distinction for a Chinese to be a Chinese, or an African an African, as for a Frenchman to be a Frenchman or an American an
American. Each race has a work to do in the world for itself and
for all races which no other race can do. To be born into any
race, to be a worthy member of it, lifting it to its true character
and its true duty, is glory and honour for any man. "To admit
that racial distinctions actually exist," says Mr. Madison Grant,
"raises at once the presumption of the innate superiority of one

[2] Belloc, *The Jews*, p. 258.

race over another." [3]   But does it raise this presumption except
in the minds of those who see it everywhere and whose minds are
closed to any other presumption?   Distinctions in nature do not
all involve the presumption of inferiority.   They suggest instead
the richness of diversity and the contribution of differences to a
more comprehensive unity.

The existence of races gives richness and variety to humanity.
In any one section of mankind, race or family, it is a good thing
that the individuals are not all alike.   So also of all mankind.   St.
Paul wrote, nineteen centuries ago, a great statement on the unity
and variety of humanity.   It is a noble biological conception of
the ideal society pictured in the conception of the Church as an
organism:

" There are diversities of gifts, but the same Spirit.   And there
are diversities of ministrations, and the same Lord.   And there are
diversities of workings, but the same God, who worketh all things
in all.   But to each one is given the manifestation of the Spirit to
profit withal.   For to one is given through the Spirit the word of
wisdom; and to another the word of knowledge, according to the
same Spirit; to another faith, in the same Spirit; and to another
gifts of healings, in the one Spirit; and to another workings of
miracles; and to another prophecy; and to another discernings of
spirits; to another divers kinds of tongues; and to another the interpretation of tongues: but all these worketh the one and the
same Spirit, dividing to each one severally as he will.   For as the
body is one, and hath many members, and all the members of
the body, being many, are one body, so also is Christ.   For in one
Spirit were we all baptised into one body, whether Jews or Greeks,
whether bond or free; and were all made to drink of one Spirit.
For the body is not one member, but many.   If the foot shall say,
' Because I am not the hand, I am not of the body'; it is not
therefore not of the body.   And if the ear shall say, ' Because I
am not the eye, I am not of the body'; it is not therefore not of
the body.   If the whole body were an eye, where were the hearing?   If the whole were hearing, where were the smelling?   But
now hath God set the members each one of them in the body, even
as it pleased him.   And if they were all one member, where were
the body?   But now they are many members, but one body.   And

---

[3] New York *Times*, Book Review, Nov. 12, 1922, Grant's review of
Gould's *America, a Family Matter.*

the eye cannot say to the hand, 'I have no need of thee'; nor again the head to the feet, 'I have no need of you.' Nay, much rather, those members of the body which seem to be more feeble are necessary: and those parts of the body, which we think to be less honourable, upon these we bestow more abundant honour; and our uncomely parts have more abundant comeliness; whereas our comely parts have no need; but God tempered the body together, giving more abundant honour to that part which lacked; that there should be no schism in the body; but that the members should have the same care one for another. And whether one member suffereth, all the members suffer with it; or one member is honoured, all the members rejoice with it. Now ye are the body of Christ, and severally members thereof." [4]

This is the greatest utterance in all literature on the race problem. The diversity of humanity is essential to its health and life and glory. " As we see the value of the individual, of every individual, so we must see the value of each nation, that all are needed. . . . There is not room on this planet," says Miss Follett, " for a lot of similar nations, but only for a lot of different nations. A group of nations must create a group culture which shall be broader than the culture of one nation alone." [5] And the Southern white woman who has been already quoted and who is one of those seeking really to apply the Christian spirit to the race problem, writes: " Life does not develop towards uniformity, but towards richness of variety in a unity of beauty and service. Unless the Race of Man contradicts all known laws of life it will develop in the same way; and whether white, or yellow, or black, they who guard their own racial integrity, in a spirit of brotherhood free from all other-racial scorn, will most truly serve the Race to which all belong. What we white people need to lay aside is not our care for racial separateness, but our prejudice. The black race needs, in aspiring to the fullest possible development, to foster a fuller faith in its own blood, and in the world's need for some service which it, and it alone, can render in richest measure to the great Brotherhood of Man." [6] This is the Negro's desire

---

[4] I Cor. XII, 4-27.
[5] Follett, *The New State*, p. 344 ff.
[6] Hammond, *In Black and White*, p. 44.

for himself. " The Negro wants to be *himself in colour* and in distinguishing characteristics, to perfect all his possibilities, to have latitude for the unfolding of essential elements of character by which friction from individual and group contact is reduced. He wishes to contribute of the richness of his individuality, without having his claims to justice and equality questioned, ignored, abridged or denied. In other words, he claims the right to be different without being treated or necessarily considered an inferior." [7]

The effort of races to fulfill themselves, and to achieve what other races have achieved and to attain a rational self-adequacy, in a spirit of service and not of isolation, is a wholesome and enlarging moral discipline for men as individuals and for human society. It is beyond the scope of our study to consider the relation of the conception of the solidarity of the human race to such economic problems as the question of free trade and protection. Either theory is reconcilable with the unity of human interest if it is so conceived and followed, and if it is practiced in the ultimate interest of all mankind; although the theory of free trade may be held to be presumptively the truer theory for a really unified world. But in a world so imperfectly unified as ours, and compelled to operate by the device of distinct races and nationalities, and providentially subjected to the education of such operations for rich and justifying ends,—in such a world the duty of each race to perfect itself and to seek a full equipment for its racial task is a duty whose fulfilment is good for each race and for all races. A movement like the Swadeshi, or home-industry, movement of India, is at the bottom a wholesome movement. It springs from the realisation of the fact that the most injurious subjection of a race may be not its obvious political subjection, but its invisible economic subordination. As Mr. Ranade, one of India's greatest leaders, said twenty-five years ago: " The political domination of one country by another attracts far more attention than the more formidable though unfelt domination, which the capital,

---

[7] *The Missionary Review of the World*, June, 1922, art. by Nannie Helen Burroughs, " Legitimate Ambitions of the Negro."

enterprise and skill of one country exercise over the trade and manufactures of another. This latter domination has an insidious influence which paralyses the springs of all the various activities which together make up the life of a nation." [8] Mr. Montague and Lord Chelmsford recognised this and in their reform measures they approved the Indian demand for economic self-development:

" The people are poor, and their poverty raises the question whether the general level of well-being could not be materially raised by the development of industries. It is also clear that the lack of outlet for educated youth is a serious misfortune which has contributed not a little in the past to political unrest in Bengal. But perhaps an even greater mischief is the discontent aroused in the minds of those who are jealous for India by seeing that she is so largely dependent on foreign countries for manufactured goods. They noted that her foreign trade was always growing, but they also saw that its leading feature continued to be the barter of raw materials valued at relatively low prices for imported manufactures, which obviously afforded profits and prosperity to other countries industrially more advanced. Patriotic Indians might well ask themselves why these profits should not accrue to their country; and also why so large a portion of the industries which flourished in the country was financed by European capital and managed by European skill. . . . Economic discontents definitely merged in political agitation over the partition of Bengal. The Swadeshi movement was the positive, and the boycott the negative expression of the same purpose. The advanced politicians took up and tried to put in practice the ideas for new developments promoted by the newly-instituted industrial conference, while at the same time they encouraged or countenanced the boycott, which had been adopted in the hope of bringing pressure to bear on manufacturing opinion at home in favour of the annulment of the partition. These events synchronised with Japan's defeat of Russia, an event which dazzled the imagination of many young educated Indians. In Japanese progress and efficiency they thought they saw an example of what could be effected by an Asiatic nation free of foreign control. Many students helped by scholarships granted by patriotic persons or associations hurried to Japan for technical and industrial training. Many of them returned to take part in the Swadeshi movement of the years 1907

[8] *Report on Indian Constitutional Reforms*, p. 264.

to 1909. . . . On all grounds a forward policy in industrial development is urgently called for, not merely to give India economic stability; but in order to satisfy the aspirations of her people who desire to see her stand before the world as a well-poised, up-to-date country; in order to provide an outlet for the energies of her young men who are otherwise drawn exclusively to government service or a few overstocked professions; in order that money now lying unproductive may be applied to the benefit of the whole community; and in order that the too speculative and literary tendencies of Indian thought may be bent to more practical ends, and the people may be better qualified to shoulder the new responsibilities which the new constitution will lay upon them." [9]

It is a good thing for each race and for all the world that there has not been any dead level of racial attainment but that all have had to struggle together and with various measures of speed in their achievement and against various forms of difficulty and hindrance. What Mr. Gladstone wrote at the age of twenty-three is true of nations as of men: " In the future," said he, " I hope circumstances will bind me down to work with a rigour which my natural sluggishness will find it impossible to elude. Periods like these through which I have been passing, grievous generally in many of their results, are by no means unfavourable to the due growth and progress of individual character. I remember a very wise saying of Archidamus in Thucydides, that the being educated in the midst of difficulties brings strength and efficacy to the character." The passage to which Mr. Gladstone refers is where Archidamus says: " We should remember that man differs little from man except that he turns out best who is trained in the sharpest school." The richer and sterner each race's struggle for self-realisation has been, if its spirit is pure of hatred or false pride, the larger its contribution to the whole life of humanity.

Some modes of racial segregation have been brought about and are maintained in the interest of just forms of racial pride and self-expression. Mary White Ovington speaks of this in *Half a Man:*

---

[9] *Report on Indian Constitutional Reforms,* pp. 264-267.

"While the coloured people in New York started with segregated schools and attained to mixed schools, the movement in the churches was the reverse. At first the Negroes were attendants of white churches, sitting in the gallery or on the rear seats, and waiting until the white people were through before partaking of the communion; but as their number increased they chafed under their position. Why should they be placed apart to hear the doctrine of Christ, and why, too, should they not have full opportunity to preach that doctrine? The desire for self-expression was perhaps the greatest factor in leading them to separate from the white church." [10]

If the distinction of race was not to be forgotten in the Church, some such development as this was inevitable. But it may be objected that there is no more warrant for such separation of race in the interest of self-expression than for the separation of sex. If white and Negro churches are necessary, why not separate churches for men and women? The answer which some are making is that there may be some form of such separate churches, if the Church does not recognise equality of sex. Where race and sex cannot find adequate opportunity for full service and self-expression and fulfillment of function within any single association or institution, their separate organisation would seem to be reasonable and necessary, and essential to the development of the maximum social good.

In some American denominations Negroes are members on the same basis as whites, but have practically no part in the life or government of the Church. In others they are members sometimes in white local congregations and sometimes in separate congregations of their own with their own minister, participating fully in the administration and government of the denomination. In other cases they are organised with separate dioceses, with or without their own bishops. A fourth type of organisation is the wholly separate and independent Negro denomination. The overwhelming majority of the Negroes are in churches of this fourth type. An interesting discussion on this question occurred at the General Convention of the Protestant Episcopal Church in New

[10] Ovington, *Half a Man*, p. 19 f.

York in 1913, over the question of establishing a racial Negro diocese. The delegates from the South were divided. A lay delegate from South Carolina opposed the suggestion:

" ' From whom does this request come?' asked Mr. Bacot. ' I am reliably informed that the Negroes of the Seventh Missionary District have not asked the General Convention for a separate diocese. In Virginia and South Carolina they are against it, and in my own diocese I know they do not want it. It seems that only those communicants in North Carolina want it.

" ' Now, our position is this: We do not think that a race which is developing, or rather which has not developed to such extent that it is capable of self-administration, should be permitted to have the full power of a diocese. Personally I do not believe that the evolution of the Negro has gone far enough to justify the Church in granting to him the highest order. If the Negroes are allowed to have a separate missionary district, they will desire separate councils, and in the end they will want to have an entirely separate church. In that event we would have the Protestant Episcopal Church White and the Protestant Episcopal Church Black and probably the A. P. E. Church.'

" Speaking for the proposed plan, John C. Buxton, lay deputy from the Diocese of North Carolina, said: ' The gentleman from South Carolina has asserted that this matter was thrashed out and settled satisfactorily at the Boston Convention. I want to say that's not the first mistake that was ever made at Boston on the Negro question.'

" When the laughter of the House of Deputies had subsided he explained that a separate missionary district for the Negroes was favoured by his diocese because it was believed to be for the good of that race. Mr. Buxton recalled the allegiance the Negroes of the South had given to their masters during the Civil War, when they were left to take care of the wives and children of the Southern soldiers who had gone to the front. He said that every consideration should be given to the Negro communicants, and added that he did not desire a separate diocese for coloured people as a matter of race discrimination, because he would just as soon touch elbows with a Negro as with a white man when the time came to partake of the Holy Communion. He advised that the report of the majority be accepted if the Episcopal Church desired to be rid of the Negro.

" Opposing a racial missionary diocese, the Rev. George S. Whitney, of the Diocese of Georgia, said that the real friends of the Negro race did not desire to give them an excuse to get out of the Church and establish an ' A. P. E. Church.' Dr. Whitney said that he was born in the North and had been in the South for fifteen years. The Negro, he said, was not yet ready to undertake the great responsibility of an independent diocese. The race already had shown its inability to conduct an independent administration. Furthermore, Dr. Whitney said that white rectors, or priests, who had work among Negro communicants in all probability would be forced to give up their tasks if they were placed under the jurisdiction of a Negro bishop." [11]

Just as racial effort and economic self-dependence is a good thing for the world, so is the desire and struggle for racial self-determination. We were made very familiar with the idea of the self-determination of peoples by the discussions of the war time. But the conception did not come into being then for the first time. We must not wince today when reminded of its explicit avowal in the Declaration of Independence: " Governments derive their just powers from the consent of the governed. . . . Whenever any government becomes destructive of these ends (*i. e.*, the securing of the rights of equality, life, liberty and the pursuit of happiness), it is the right of the people to alter or to abolish it, and to institute a new government, laying its foundation on such principles and organising its powers in such form as to them shall seem most likely to effect their safety and happiness." If these were true principles for us in 1776, why are they not true principles for all men always?

Before the war made the phrase " race autonomy " cosmopolitan, a speaker at the Universal Races Congress dealt with the subject dispassionately with a view to pointing out the race-gain of the idea that no race is barred from freedom and power by any fiat of racial incapacity. The unrest of races subjected to domination from without, he conceived to be a good and inevitable thing.

"Unless," he argued, "it is alleged that a man confessedly fallible in dealing with the members of his own advanced race becomes infallible when dealing with men whose language, ideals,

---

[11] New York *Times,* Oct. 23, 1913.

and religion are alien to his, it follows that mistakes are made by all dominant races in their treatment of subject races.

"Is it to be desired, then, that the latter should be either too unintelligent to know when they are misruled or too apathetic to care? The avowal of either desire would obviously amount to a complete condemnation of the ideal or polity involving it. Every polity professes to aim at betterment. But where there exist no means of correction or protest on the part of those who suffer by errors of government, there must be generated either apathetic despair or a smoldering resentment. It would be gratuitously absurd to expect that the men of the 'backward' race should be positively more patiently forgiving or more cheerfully tolerant than their 'advanced' masters. If they can be so, they are the more 'advanced' race of the two, in some of the main points of capacity for self rule. . . . If the ruled are to progress, they must think and judge; and if they think and judge they must from time to time be dissatisfied. There is no escape from the dilemma; and if the ruling race is at all conscientious, at all sincere in its professed desire for the betterment of its subjects, it must desire to know when and why they are dissatisfied. The need for reciprocity holds no less, albeit with a difference, in the case of the ruler. To exercise an absolute control over a community or a congeries of communities in the belief that one is absolutely infallible, is to tread the path of insanity.

"To know that one is politically fallible, and yet never to care for the opinion of those whom one may be at any moment misgoverning, is to set conscience aside. Either way, demoralisation or deterioration follows as inevitably for the ruler as for the ruled.

"All history proclaims the lesson. Whether we take ancient despots ruling empires through satraps, or States playing the despot to other States, the sequence is infallibly evil. Never is there any continuity of sound life. In the absence of control from the governed, the despotisms invariably grew corrupt and feeble. . . . The contemporary problem may be put in a nutshell. Are the subject races of today progressing or not? If yes, they must be on the way, however slowly, to a measure of self-government. If not, the domination of the advanced races is a plain failure; and the talk of 'beneficent rule' becomes an idle hypocrisy. The only possible alternative thesis is that the subject races are incapable of progress; and this is actually affirmed by some imperialists who reason that only in 'temperate climates' do the natural conditions essential to self-government subsist. Their doctrine may be left to the acceptance of all who can find ground for exultation and magniloquence in the prospect of a perpetual dominion of white men over cowed coloured races who secretly and helplessly hate them. . . . The perpetual absence of every element of political self-determination from a people's life means a failure of civilisation. . . . It would seem that a first step towards a scientific or even a quasi-rational view of the problem must be to put aside the instinctive hypothesis that faculty for self-government is a matter of ' race.' " [12]

And the working out of this problem of reasonable and ethical and fiduciary autonomy by each race for itself, and by the "stronger" races for the "weaker," is a school of humanity wherein all men are meant to learn lessons of self-control, of kindness and of truth. The problem is infinitely difficult. Human races do not move collectively. There are always more progressive nations which cannot wait for the patient education of the mass, and there are always in every race men who seek their own interests or the supposed interests of their race above the interests of humanity, and back of all moral deficiencies lie our mutual incapacities, our want of sympathy and imagination of power to judge causes and forces and foresee consequences and effects. Men and races are simply unequal to the tasks they have to deal with. But the acknowledgment of this and the humble desire to work with God in the making of humanity are genuine benefits of the institution of race outweighing its evils. It is part of this education that "strong" races must surmount their appetite for dominion and "weak" races transcend their servility. Only this cannot be done, as many of the young men of India seem to think it can, by denouncing the "slave mentality" of their race and reproaching the influence of British rule in India which is alleged to have crushed out the freedom of the Indian soul. It can only be done by disproving that freedom has been crushed out and by displaying not a servile but a noble and human mind. Races rise to their own place not by making claims or bemoaning errors, but by achieving work and by rendering service. Other races cannot raise them or make them free. Each race must do these things for itself. No man can give another man his independence. The

---

[12] *Universal Races Congress*, 1911, paper by John M. Robertson, M.P., on "The Rationale of Autonomy," pp. 41-44.

first man can disclaim responsibility for the second, but if the second man is to be self-dependent, only he can achieve it. Mr. Stone states a universal truth about races and men when he says: " When the friend of the Negro masses would know the whole truth behind the forces which today most militate against the material progress of the race, he must go deep below the surface of troubles which the white man can remove or rectify." [13] The white race can do much, far more than it has yet done, to help other races, but in the same sense for races as for men, God bids us to work out our own salvation, and He made races that He might save men with a yet greater salvation.

Just as every man has a proper and righteous pride in his mother, so every man ought to have a just and ennobling pride in his race. There are brave spirits in some of the races to whom this love of race and loyalty of racial duty means a living sacrifice. Thus a clear seer of one of the South American races writes:

" I believe that the place that God has given one within the race, be that whatever it may, even the most despised, is His commandment, His will, and we must be absolutely faithful to that place even to the most extreme duty.

" I am of this race, weakened by its mixtures, filled with sores, menaced by its disgraceful bloody struggles, half asleep at the most important time in its destiny. I look and I measure the magnitude of its defects. I count its errors one by one. There is no other probably who has a more capable eye to see its negligence. I have at times been called an outcast because of the sane comparison I have made between it and other races which work for the world. But I am faithful to my own and I must remain with it even until the end. I have the greatest possible pain concerning its future. I have seen the many pages of criticism which I have read in the South concerning my country. Believing them unjust, yet without the hard-headedness of a person who does not care to think, I accept the harsh judgments which are made against my people. But I maintain absolutely my filial attitude toward them." [14]

It would be hard to find a more worthy illustration of such

[13] Stone, *The American Race Problem*, p. 147.
[14] Letter, Miss Gabriella Mistral to S. G. Inman, Jan., 1924.

pride, at once humble, modest and exalted, than Booker Washington's *Up from Slavery*. A manly race-spirit breathes from every page of that book from the first paragraph to the last.

This is the first paragraph:

"I was born a slave on a plantation in Franklin County, Virginia. I am not quite sure of the exact place or exact date of my birth, but at any rate I suspect I must have been born somewhere and at some time. As nearly as I have been able to learn, I was born near a cross-roads post office called Hale's Ford, and the year was 1858 or 1859. I do not know the month or the day. The earliest impressions I can now recall are of the plantation and the slave quarters—the latter being the part of the plantation where the slaves had their cabins."

And this is the last:

"This time I am in Richmond as the guest of the coloured people of the city; and came at their request to deliver an address last night to both races in the Academy of Music, the largest and finest audience room in the city. This was the first time that the coloured people have ever been permitted to use this hall. The day before I came, the City Council passed a vote to attend the meeting in a body to hear me speak. The state Legislature, including the House of Delegates and the Senate, also passed a unanimous vote to attend in a body. In the presence of hundreds of coloured people, many distinguished white citizens, the City Council, the state Legislature, and state officials, I delivered my message, which was one of hope and cheer; and from the bottom of my heart I thanked both races for this welcome back to the state that gave me birth."

Between these two paragraphs lie many others which reveal the right racial sense for every man:

"I have learned that success is to be measured not so much by the position that one has reached in life as by the obstacles which he has overcome while trying to succeed. Looked at from this standpoint, I almost reach the conclusion that often the Negro boy's birth and connection with an unpopular race is an advantage, so far as real life is concerned. With few exceptions, the Negro youth must work harder and must perform his tasks even better than a white youth in order to secure recognition. But out of the hard and unusual struggle through which he is compelled to pass, he gets a strength, a confidence, that one misses whose pathway is comparatively smooth by reason of birth and race. From any point of view, I had rather be what I am, a member of the Negro race, than be able to claim membership with the most favoured of any other race. . . .

" I believe that my race will succeed in proportion as it learns to do a common thing in an uncommon manner; learns to do a thing so thoroughly that no one can improve upon what it has done; learns to make its services of indispensable value. This was the spirit that inspired me in my first effort at Hampton, when I was given the opportunity to sweep and dust that schoolroom. In a degree I felt that my whole future life depended upon the thoroughness with which I cleaned that room, and I was determined to do it so well that no one could find any fault with the job. Few people ever stopped, I found, when looking at his pictures, to inquire whether Mr. Tanner was a Negro painter, a French painter, or a German painter. They simply knew that he was able to produce something which the world wanted—a great painting—and the matter of his colour did not enter into their minds. When a Negro girl learns to cook, to wash dishes, to sew, to write a book, or a Negro boy learns to groom horses, or to grow sweet potatoes, or to produce butter, or to build a house, or to be able to practise medicine, as well or better than some one else, they will be rewarded regardless of race or colour. In the long run, the world is going to have the best, and any difference in race, religion, or previous history will not long keep the world from what it wants.

" I think that the whole future of my race hinges on the question as to whether or not it can make itself of such indispensable value that the people in the town and state where we reside will feel that our presence is necessary to the happiness and well-being of the community. No man who continues to add something to the material, intellectual, and moral well-being of the place in which he lives is long left without proper reward. This is a great human law which cannot be permanently nullified." [15]

Such a man's pride in his race makes the race more worthy of pride. And often the proud spirit of a race will hold up a man who would have fallen if he had leaned on personal pride or self-respect, but whom his race consciousness made strong. There is

---

[15] *Up from Slavery*, pp. 1, 319, 39 f, 280 ff.

a striking poem by Sir Alfred Lyall entitled: " Theology in Ex-
tremis, or a soliloquy that may have been delivered in India, June,
1857." Prefixed to the poem is the statement: " ' They would
have spared life to any of their English prisoners who should consent to profess Mohammedanism, by repeating the usual short
formula: but only one half-caste cared to save himself in that
way.' "[16] The poem describes the thoughts of an Englishman
who had been taken prisoner by Mohammedan rebels in the
Indian Mutiny. He is face to face with a cruel death. They
offer him his life if he will repeat something from the Koran. If
he complies, no one is likely ever to hear of it, and he will be free
to return to England and to the woman he loves. Moreover, and
here is the real point, he is not a believer in Christianity, so that it
is no question of denying his Saviour. What ought he to do?
Deliverance is easy, and the relief and advantage would be un-
speakably great. But he does not really hesitate and every shadow
of doubt disappears when he hears his fellow prisoner, a half-
caste, pattering eagerly the words demanded. He himself has no
hope of heaven and he loves life—

> " Yet for the honour of English race
> May I not live or endure disgrace.
> Ay, but the word if I could have said it,
> I by no terrors of hell perplext,
> Hard to be silent and have no credit
> From men in this world, or reward in the next;
> None to bear witness and reckon the cost
> Of the name that is saved by the life that is lost.
> I must begone to the crowd untold
> Of men by the cause which they served unknown,
> Who moulder in myriad graves of old;
> Never a story and never a stone
> Tells of the martyrs who died like me
> Just for the pride of the old countree."

The motives which held this man are not of the highest, but
nevertheless they are high. The pride of loyalty to the best moral
ideals of one's race and of fidelity to its traditions is a worthy

[16] Extract from an Indian newspaper.

and uplifting pride. If better moral ideals than these appear and if the old traditions are found to be at variance with truth, it is a man's duty to abandon the racial grooves. This is only to say again that race is a great principle but that humanity is greater and that its parts only fulfill their mission as they come together in the whole. "I do not pin my dreams for the future to my country or even to my race," said Mr. Justice Holmes, of the United States Supreme Court. "Beyond the vision of battling races and the impoverished earth, I catch a dreaming glimpse of peace." [17] "And that dream belongs only to a true pride and a true humility. The intimation which we get from nature and from the history of man is that the meek are, after all, to inherit the earth, and that their inheritance is to be assured only through the complete communion of which the word heard around the world gives prophecy." [18]

The best white sentiment of the South is coming to realise that pride of race is an equal good for both the black and the white races and that the best solution of the problem of social equality is to develop in each race a sense of true race pride. As Dr. Weatherford says:

" So long as all honour lies in being associated with the white man, the Negro will want social intermingling. So long as there are none of his own race that can meet him on a high plane and can satisfy the longings of his soul, just so long will he be driven to seek fellowship with white men. But build him up, make him sufficient in himself, give him within his own race that life which will satisfy, and the social question will be solved. The cultivated Negro is less and less inclined to lose himself and his race in the sea of another race. As he develops, he is building a new race pride. He no longer objects to being called a Negro—it is becoming the badge of his race and the mark of his self-sufficiency. We have nothing, therefore, to fear from giving him a chance." [19]

And not only nothing to fear but everything to gain. New human

---

[17] New York *Times,* April 21, 1913.
[18] New York *Times,* editorial, " Fossils of Failure," Jan. 15, 1923.
[19] *Racial Relations and the Christian Ideal,* p. 58; Weatherford, *Race Relationships in the South,* Vol. I, p. 173.

values will be added to the national wealth.   And between two
races, each equally justified in cherishing a true racial pride, the
question of inter-race relationship will be lifted to an entirely
new plane.

It is a good thing for mankind to have the discipline of the
duty of rising from race prejudice and ignorance to a higher level
of interracial knowledge and sympathy.   There is, even in many
of the best men of the modern world, a strange insularity and
want of world view and race insight which needs this discipline.
" The Life and Letters of Walter H. Page " reveal what a large,
true, human spirit he was.   He was one of the first as a young
man " to take an open stand for the pitiably neglected black man :
he insisted that he should be taught to read and write, and instructed in agriculture and the manual trades.   A man who advocated such revolutionary things in those days was accused—and
Page was so accused—of attempting to promote the ' social equality ' of the two races." [20]

" The only acceptable measure of any civilisation, Page believed,
was the extent to which it improved the condition of the common
citizen.   A few cultured and university-trained men at the top ; a
few ancient families living in luxury ; a few painters and poets
and statesmen and generals ; these things, in Page's view, did not
constitute a satisfactory state of society ; the real test was the extent to which the masses participated in education, in the necessities and comforts of existence, in the right of self-evolution and
self-expression, in that ' equality of opportunity,' which, Page
never wearied of repeating, ' was the basis of social progress.'
The mere right to vote and to hold office was not democracy ;
parliamentary majorities and political caucuses were not democracy—at the best these things were only details and not the most
important ones ; democracy was the right to every man to enjoy,
in accordance with his aptitudes of character and mentality, the
material and spiritual opportunities that nature and science had
placed at the disposition of mankind.   This democratic creed had
now become the dominating interest of Page's life." [21]

In one of his letters to his brother he wrote of classes in

[20] *The Life and Letters of Walter H. Page,* Vol. I, p. 43.
[21] *Ibid.,* p. 71.

England words which might be applied to races: " To an American democrat the sad thing is the servile class. Before the law the chimney sweep and the peer have exactly the same standing. They have worked that out with absolute justice. But there it stops. The serving class is what we would call abject. It does not occur to them that they might ever become—or that their descendants might ever become—ladies and gentlemen." [22]

" In an address delivered in June, 1914, before the Royal Institution of Great Britain, Page gave what he regarded as the definition of the American ideal. ' The fundamental article in the creed of the American democracy—you may call it the fundamental dogma if you like—is the unchanging and unchangeable resolve that every human being shall have his opportunity for his utmost development—his chance to become and to do the best that he can.' Democracy is not only a system of government—' it is a scheme of society.' Every citizen must have not only the suffrage, he must likewise enjoy the same advantages as his neighbour for education, for social opportunity, for good health, for success in agriculture, manufacture, finance, and business and professional life. The country that most successfully opened all these avenues to every boy and girl, exclusively on individual merit, was in Page's view the most democratic." [23]

But these great principles do not seem to have been given in Mr. Page's biography the universal application which, if they are genuine principles, they must be given. If they are sound for white people, so are they sound for black and yellow people. If America ought to be democratic in the sense described, so also should the world. Page thought in noble terms of the British and American peoples, but his dream for them is the true dream for all peoples.

Part of the discipline of spirit which a true world-feeling involves is the conquest of race-partisanship. Men must learn how to have a true race-pride without contempt or effrontery or false assumption toward other races. An American writer says: " The superiority of a race cannot be preserved without pride of blood and an uncompromising attitude toward the lower races," and he

[22] Ibid., p. 155. [23] Ibid., p. 191.

proceeds to contrast the dedication of the United States and Canada to the highest type of civilisation with Latin America which " for centuries will drag the ball and chain of hybridism." [24] Another American writer applies these words with approval to the attitude of the white to the black race in the United States. Yet elsewhere he realises that no hopeful and happy solution of race problems or of human life is possible on the basis of such an attitude of mind. " The essence of the race problem is that of the peaceful common occupancy of the same territory by two widely differing people. Whatever builds up amicable relations between the tenants in common tends to minimise the problem of their tenancy. Whatever tends to create friction between them makes their problem more acute." [25] The race problem needs to be conceived in vastly broader outlines than these. It is not a question of common tenancy of America. It is a question of common tenancy of a world which is smaller and more interdependent than America once was. But the conditions of the solution are the same,—" amicable relations." There can be no amicable relations without mutual respect and common justice and a discontinuance of the practice of levelling individual persons down or up to a group mass, irrespective of personal character and capacity. The variety of races is provided, perhaps, to afford us all a school in which to grow this larger human view of man, and to achieve the great ends in a world society which Mr. Zimmern conceives in the case of the British Empire can only be attained " when the white populations have faced and conquered their hidden prejudices and disdains and thus made possible not merely the régime of external justice and fair-play which has been the distinctive feature of British rule among ' native peoples,' but a deeper sympathy and understanding, of which mutual respect must be the basis." [26]

A broader knowledge of men and of the wide and significant characteristics of race expands our minds and interprets life and

---

[24] E. A. Ross, quoted by Stone, *The American Race Problem*, p. 241.
[25] *Ibid.*, p. 251.
[26] *New York Evening Post, Literary Review*, March 8, 1924, art. on " Partnership vs. Domination."

history for us. Lyall points out " that India with its multiplicity of religions and its variety of political groups, is the best surviving specimen, on a large scale, of the ancient world of history, the Orbis veteribus notus." [27] And the political and administrative problems associated with the modern race relations of Asia reproduce many of the features of the Roman Empire. We understand those race mouldings and mergings in proportion as we understand our own today.

The discontent of single races and the general unrest of all races are signs of life. Mr. Putnam Weale, who is among the colour-terrorists, sees clearly the inevitableness and, on the whole, the good of all racial aspirations and expansions. He deplores the failure of the western peoples to realise the significance of the universal spread of knowledge.

" The world influence of this new growth," he says, " and its really vast significance are still so utterly unappreciated that the political and social unrest which this new knowledge necessarily brings in its train (in China and India, just as much as in Portugal and Spain) is attributed to the masses becoming infected with anarchistic ideas—that is, to their blind devotion to destructive and not to constructive principles—whereas, if the truth be known, so far from such being a true statement of the case, since masses no more than individuals do not willingly court destruction, this commotion is merely the sign that knowledge—with its accompanying conviction that political salvation lies within the grasp of all—is reaching the most widely-separated peoples.[28] . . . When Asia is as universally educated as Europe is today, it will be time to know that almost every old assumption regarding this great region will have been quietly bridged over night; and thus it will come about that dawn will find those who have not prepared themselves for such changes unable to adjust their views and still weakly talking of conspiracies and revolutions, when what they are witnessing will be nothing but the natural evolution of the human race." [29]

This is a necessary movement and a desirable goal. The whole race has a common interest in the success of the movement and

[27] Lyall, *Asiatic Studies,* First Series, p. ix.
[28] Weale, *The Conflict of Colour,* p. 14. [29] *Ibid.,* p. 18.

the attainment of the goal. In this movement race servility is ever more and more clearly seen as an evil. The spirit of self-respecting and self-forgetful service should control every race and the spirit of servility be found in none. President Harding, in a letter to the Young People's Commission of the Chicago Church Federation, expressed his disbelief in racial amalgamation as a solution of the race problem, but added, " Partnership of the races in developing the highest aims of all humanity there must be, if humanity, not only here but everywhere, is to achieve the ends we have set forth." [30]

The excesses to which some races carry the spirit of racial revolt and self-assertion must not lead us to condemn the sense of race self-respect and the desire for racial personality. Mr. Gandhi and the Nationalist Movement in India may have erred, but their error was a mixture with good, as illustrated in a letter of Mr. Gandhi to a friend:

"(1) There is no impassable barrier between East and West.

"(2) There is no such thing as Western or European civilisation, but there is a modern civilisation which is purely material.

"(3) The people of Europe, before they were touched by modern civilisation, had much in common with the people of the East; anyhow the people of India, and even today Europeans who are not touched by modern civilisation, are far better able to mix with Indians than the offspring of that civilisation.

"(4) It is not the British people who are ruling India, but it is modern civilisation, through its railways, telegraph, telephone, and almost every invention which has been claimed to be a triumph of civilisation.

"(5) Bombay, Calcutta, and the other chief cities of India are the real plague spots.

"(6) If British rule were replaced tomorrow by Indian rule based on modern methods, India would be no better, except that she would be able then to retain some of the money that is drained away to England; but then India would only become a second or fifth nation of Europe or America.

"(7) East and West can only really meet when the West has thrown overboard modern civilisation, almost in its entirety. They can also seemingly meet when East has also adopted modern

---

[30] Chicago *Church Federation Bulletin*, June, 1923.

civilisation, but that meeting would be an armed truce, even as it is between, say Germany and England, both of which nations are living in the Hall of Death in order to avoid being devoured the one by the other. . . .

"(12) India's salvation consists in unlearning what she has learnt during the past fifty years. The railways, telegraphs, hospitals, lawyers, doctors and such like have all to go, and the so-called upper classes have to learn to live consciously and religiously and deliberately the simple peasant life, knowing it to be a life giving true happiness. . . .

" If you agree with me, then it will be your duty to tell the revolutionaries and everybody else that the freedom they want, or think they want, is not to be obtained by killing people or doing violence, but by setting themselves right and by becoming and remaining truly Indian. Then the British rulers will be servants and not masters. They will be trustees, and not tyrants, and they will live in perfect peace with the whole of the inhabitants of India. The future, therefore, lies not with the British race, but with the Indians themselves, and if they have sufficient self-abnegation and abstemiousness, they can make themselves free this very moment, and when we have arrived in India at the simplicity which is still ours largely and which was ours entirely until a few years ago, it will still be possible for the best Indians and the best Europeans to see one another throughout the length and breadth of India, and act as the leaven." [31]

The impossibility of this program must not be allowed to hide the right spirit of longing for racial integrity and dignity. The whole world will be better for the peaceful effort of men to find a better balance between the forces of rest and the forces of change than we have thus far achieved.

Variety of production and freedom of interchange are the sources of the world's wealth and prosperity. The existence of a diversity of races adapted to the conditions and climates of all parts of the world and capable of producing all that can be produced is an indispensable means to the widest human welfare. No reasonable person is able any longer to dispute the economic unity and interdependence of mankind, or to question that one of the most important tasks in the world is to bring the races into such

---

[31] *Speeches and Writings of M. K. Gandhi*, pp. 134-137.

right thoughts and relationships to one another as shall lead them to realise their mutual dependence and to work out in the fullest measure the benefits which God meant mankind to derive from it. Sociologists and economists increasingly concern themselves with this subject. " It must be remembered," says Kidd, " that it is in an interchange of commodities between these regions (the Tropics) and those at present occupied by the European peoples that it is possible to have permanently operative, on the largest scale upon which it could be made operative in the world, the great natural principle underlying all trade, *i. e.,* that the interchange of products between peoples and regions possessing different natural capacities tends to be mutually advantageous." [32] Kidd was concerned to expound what he conceived to be the right principle of race relationships in the matter of the development of the undeveloped areas of the world. He deplored the gloomy spectacle of the nineteenth century, the domination by Europe under a wrong economic and social policy of a tropical area larger than Europe itself, a " railing off of immense regions in the tropics under the policy which has suggested their acquirement, regions tending, in the absence of white colonists, to simply revert to the type of States worked for gain, and slowly but surely surrounding themselves with a wall of laws and tariffs operating in favour of the European Power in possession, to the exclusion of the interests of

---

[32] *The Control of the Tropics,* p. 14. " The system of colonial exploitation has also failed to satisfy the large proportion of the dominant peoples, and the echoes of the discontent it produces among the dependent peoples ring from every colonised area of the earth. There is somewhere a remedy if there is a goal of succsss for society. It has not yet been found. It does not lie in the adoption of socialism or communism in dependent states, nor in the exclusion of foreign investments from countries where business organisation, exploiting skill, and economic initiative are not developed among the indigenes.

" The problem awaits solution in the growth of a new spirit among the exploiting peoples, a spirit which already shows signs of becoming dominant at no remote day, which shall provide for the dependent nation possessing great natural wealth its political and economic opportunity to the limit of its growing capacity, at the same time affording the more highly organised nation full opportunity—mutually profitable opportunity, to assist in the progressive labour of reducing the resources of the earth to the service of mankind."—(Priestley, *The Mexican Nation, A History,* p. xvii f.)

the rest of the world." [33] The impossibility of allowing great areas of the earth to lie fallow or unproductive was obvious to Kidd as it was obvious to every one in the days before the war when the consuming power of the nations seemed to threaten a great excess over their power of production and when the advantageous possibilities of world-wide trade seemed to be unlimited. These developments have been retarded by the war and by its colossal destruction of human power both to produce and to consume, but this retardation has been offset in its effects upon the increase of the intimacy of race relations by the unprecedented increase of that intimacy in the associations, both military and economic, which the war brought about.

We see far more clearly now than before the war the absolute indissolubleness of all human interests and the inevitable economic unity of the world. The world was aware of the fact before the war but it miscalculated both its strength and its weakness. It believed that the financial interdependence of the nations, "the peace of Dives," as Mr. Kipling described it, would hold the nations together. It was an empty faith. Not even certain financial ruin can prevent war, and by itself it ought not to. On the other hand men had no conception of the indissolubleness of the commercial solidarity of mankind. They did not realise that the economic life of the world had become an organic unity and that if any nation should fall, all must feel the downpull. Even yet many men will not believe it. They talk in the old language of "trade war," as though the ancient Shibboleths were any longer true. Trade war is trade suicide in a unified world. The nation that injures other nations in trade conflict simply injures itself. If a man gashes his leg with his hand, the hand shares in the loss and suffering. And it is so in humanity. In the development and distribution of raw material, in the interchange of goods, in the use of credits, the interest of one is the interest of all and the interest of all is the interest of each.[34] Any other doctrine and the prac-

---

[33] *The Control of the Tropics*, p. 31 f.
[34] "The pressing insistence by governments upon the selfish interests of their own nationals has not always proved the most beneficial policy. Reasonable nationalism as a basis for international relations ought surely to

tice of it will bring their own judgment with them. The male-
factors who are immediately guilty may figure up only profit but
time and facts will reckon with their children. The truth is the
only profitable economic theory and the truth is that the economic
interest of humanity is indivisible. The war, which was the
greatest economic schism ever known, has demonstrated this principle of unity.[35]

The white races need the products of the other races and they
need equally the markets which the other races afford for the
products of the white races. Originally it was the need of products which led to exploration and trade and conquest. But in later
years it became the need of markets, and Mr. Stoddard's case for
white supremacy includes its need and duty, if it can, to dominate
in industry.

" I have showed," he says, " the profound effect of the ' industrial revolution' in furthering white world-supremacy, and I
pointed out the tremendous advantages accruing to the white
world from exploitation of undeveloped coloured lands and from
exports of manufactured goods to coloured markets. The prodigious wealth thereby amassed has been a prime cause of white
prosperity, has buttressed the maintenance of white world-
hegemony, and has made possible much of the prodigious increase
of white population.

comprehend that sovereign states should be friendly equals in the peaceful
rivalry of expanding commerce; that developed communication and other
facilities of modern life render nations economically dependent upon one
another; that armed conflicts between great nations in modern times
destroy for long periods the economic life of the victor as well as the conquered; and that the foreign affairs of nations must be conducted with the
knowledge that these truths cannot be ignored. . . . Men in high stations and seeking high stations in public life too frequently resort to the
appeal to racial differences to secure a temporary personal advantage.
Perhaps we may be permitted to hope that as public opinion becomes informed in the field of international relations this method of seeking support
will not gain the approval unfortunately too frequently granted in the
past."—From the American Ambassador's address at the dinner in Tokyo,
given by the Japan-American Society of Tokyo in honour of the members
of the Japanese delegation to the Washington Disarmament Conference.
Printed in the *Korea Review*, July, 1922.

[35] The effect of the decay of economic trust and solidarity within any one
nation is a comprehensible picture of the equally certain and far most
costly effects of the want of economic trust and solidarity between nations
and races. (See *International Conciliation*, No. 185, April, 1923. " The
Evolution of Soviet Russia," p. 218 f.)

" We realise what the loss of these advantages would mean. As a matter of fact, it would mean throughout the white world diminished prosperity, lessened political and military strength, and such relative economic and social stagnation as would depress national vigour and check population. It is even possible to visualise a white world reverting to the condition of Europe in the fifteenth century—thrown back upon itself, on the defensive, and with a static rather than a progressive civilisation. Such conditions could, of course, occur only as the result of coloured military and industrial triumphs of the most sweeping character. But the possibility exists, nevertheless, as I shall endeavour to show." [36]

And he proceeds to describe the disaster of an awakened industrial life among the " coloured " races which would threaten the industrial supremacy of the white world.

In truth of course selling and buying are inseparable, for nations are able to purchase only as they can pay, and they can only pay not in money but in products or possessions of their own taken in exchange. A producing race selling for ever to non-producing races is an economic myth. The wealth of all races depends upon increased and continuous intercourse and exchange, from which all shall profit alike and in a real sense equally. To the extent that any race shares unequally, its power to continue the intercourse to the profit of itself and of the other races is impaired. The world is made up of many races because economically this is a gain to all.

Sometimes men dream that a national or world-society would be happier if it were simpler, more homogeneous and equalitarian, and free from the intricacies of economic organisation and interdependence which characterise our complicated world life with its diverse races and its delicate, highly organised, interlaced relationships. This dream may be examined and disproved by reason or it may be more easily dispelled by the test of life, both in individuals and in nations. What is the richest and happiest human life? Undoubtedly the life that is richest in its relationships and obligations and ministries, not the life withdrawn from the great flowing streams and returned to the primitive and unrelated. Which is the richer and happier nation, Siam or Canada? Canada is beset with

---

[36] *The Rising Tide of Colour*, p. 240 f.

all the problems of our modern world and is wrestling for freedom
and progress amid all the forces and relationships of our complex
modern life. Siam is free from all this. The Tolstoyan dream is
come true there. Every man raises his own sustenance. His own
paddy field yields rice enough for him and his family. A day or
two suffices to build his house. A few fruit trees supply his
luxuries. The genial sun and a simple garment clothe him in
comfort. He is delivered from all the highly wrought interdependence of life among us. And his reward is not happiness, but
inertia. We may be sure that a world of many races, striving
ceaselessly to realise themselves and their divinely appointed purposes and to work out a rich human life on the basis of their
diverse varieties, associated in a common human family under one
great father God, is a far nobler and more fruitful sort of world
than a world of simplified uniformity.

It is a further gain to humanity that in working out our inter-
racial problems the races are under the necessity of being always
on their guard morally lest they injure or retard each other. The
danger of this is one of the evils of race. The new strength and
virtue which come from overcoming this danger are among the
blessings which flow from race. The East has its well-grounded
fear of the spread of individualism with its evil features and of
the impoverishment and exploitation of the other races by the
white race. The white race can find in the most real temptation to
which it has been exposed in this regard, and to which it has
succumbed, a chance for the same kind of moral victory and enlargement which comes to the individual.

> " Why comes temptation
> But for man to meet and master
> And make crouch beneath his foot,
> And so be pedestaled
> In triumph? "

The supreme gain of the institution of race, however, and the
divine purpose in its establishment according to St. John's great
conception, is the development, through special racial experience
and achievement, of moral character-values which are to be the

race's contribution to the common human stock. Separation of race was certainly one of the conditions which made possible the development of religion among the Hebrews, of art among the Greeks and of law among the Romans. This religion, art and law are the common possession of humanity, even now. All the races are in a vast school. Out of it at the last they are to come into the one City of God bringing their treasures with them. This was St. John's sublime vision: "And the city hath no need of the sun, neither of the moon, to shine upon it: for the glory of God did lighten it, and the lamp thereof is the Lamb. And the races shall walk amidst the light thereof: and the kings of the earth bring their glory into it. And the gates thereof shall in no wise be shut by day (for there is no night there) ; and they shall bring the glory and the honour of the races into it: and there shall in no wise enter into it any thing unclean, or he that maketh an abomination and a lie; but only they that are written in the Lamb's book of life." [37]

Can we discern at all the values which God is working out for man in the experience and character of the races? The missionary movement has been studying this question with interest for a hundred years. It has approached it from two points of view. First, what are the qualities of character in the non-Christian races which can be welcomed and used in the universal Church of Christ which, as one body, is, in its ideal, the hope and promise and norm of a united humanity? Second, what values in Christianity are brought into clearer light or perhaps for the first time discovered by the application of the Gospel to the demands and capacities of the non-Christian peoples? What have they to add not to Christ but to our apprehension of the fulness which is in Christ and which no one race can apprehend alone?

1. The volume entitled *Mankind and the Church* is a collection of studies by missionary bishops of the Church of England, which they describe as "An Attempt to Estimate the Contribution of Great Races to the Fulness of the Church of God."

a. The Papuan race of the South Seas is dealt with as repre-

---

[37] Rev. XXI, 23-37.

sentative of the primitive races. Its weaknesses are described as impurity, untruthfulness and callousness, and its virtues as generosity, domestic affection, patience and sense of justice, and the contribution of this child-race is held to be (1) consciousness of the unseen, (2) simplicity of faith and life, (3) corporate spirit, (4) faithfulness.

" Is there not," concludes the Bishop of New Guinea, " a message from the Papuans to inform the white race? The world of modern life is a stern battleground of competition, and a ceaseless struggle for existence. The race tends to harden under its influence. Then as it extends beyond white lands and reaches the rich islands of the Pacific with their balmy air and soft zephyrs, it passes as it were from the place of business to the playground and the nursery, and the hard nature, the unimpassioned spirit comes into contact with native races simple in habits, unselfish in heart and unassertive in disposition. It is as though Christ takes, as of old, a little child, and sets him in the midst and draws out lessons for the grown-up disciples. The passive virtues are wonderfully revealed in the Papuan who is growing in grace. In his gentleness, unselfishness, patience, good temper, this bright child of nature displays many of the elements that make up the Perfect Life." [38]

b. The African race is considered for the most part in *Mankind and the Church* in its characteristics when Christianised, and rather in the African and West Indian habitat than in the United States, and the emphasis is on the race's contribution to the Church rather than to general social values.[39] Archbishop Nuttall, of the West Indies, concludes:

" The subjects, the habits of thought, and the modes of action in which the Christianity of the Negro race will, to a considerable degree, affect the sum-total of Christianity in the future, may be stated under the following heads:
"(1) Realising the personality of God and the objectivity of

[38] *Mankind and the Church*, p. 68.
[39] Sir H. H. Johnston declares, regarding the African race's contribution, that it will be " an important quota to the whole sum of humanity, an element of soundness and stability in physical development and certain mental qualities which the perfected man can not afford to do without."—Quoted in *Christ and Human Need*, p. 117.

divine manifestation. Cheerful acceptance of all providential arrangements as the acts of a wise and loving God. Old Testament religion in a Christian form.

"(2) The emotional element generally in the presentation of truth, and the experimental realising of it.

"(3) Musical tastes of a particular kind, and the emotional expression of religious ideas in music, in song, and in worship.

"(4) The social element. The sense of brotherhood in the Church. Taking an active personal share in the services of public worship, and in the actual work of the Church. Supporting the Church financially. Community in service and sympathy in affliction and in joy as well as sorrow.

"(5) A strong appreciation of the authority of the Church, and recognition of the value of its disciplinary arrangements." [40] The last point rests on the conviction that "the Negro has a strong appreciation of authority of law. This manifests itself in civil affairs. He not only makes a loyal subject, but readily admits his responsibility to obey the law of the land. Even in things in which he fails to obey, he does not dispute the authority, but makes the best excuses he can for his non-obedience." [41]

Archbishop Nuttall quotes letters from three correspondents who view the question of the possibility of any racial contribution by the African in different lights:

(a) " The African has given no evidence of originating power in his nature. Their very language, 'that storehouse of the accumulated experience of mankind,' is childish, inorganic, almost fluid. Their history, they have none, except what the child has: driven, directed, thought for by others, never able to take their faith into their own hands. If we apply the Socialist axiom, 'from him according to his capacity, to him according to his needs,' we shall very quickly reach the conclusion that so vigourous, hardy, well-developed a plant as Christianity has nothing to receive from so exiguous a source as Africa, and, after all, as there are the higher tribes that give, so may there not be those who only take?"

(b) " While it (i. e., the Negro's fatalistic trust in God) is soiled and obscured by ignorance, the very sense of the belief will at times put it right across the path of development; but as ignorance is replaced by knowledge, and as the belief is, so to speak,

[40] *Mankind and the Church,* p. 113.
[41] *Ibid.,* p. 110.

put into working order, we see more and more the advantage of its vital strength. Once let it cease to chain him down in fatalism, and it will be the noblest stay man can have.

"To Christian practice, I think the Negro will bring a distinctively strong ability and tendency to recognise and appreciate the common human brotherhood, more frankly, generously, and naturally than ever before. For this he is prepared by the development of the emotional in his character, which enables him to seize great ideas though standing, for the present, somewhat in the way of his ability to work these out in every detail. It seems to me almost that he has been prepared for the realisation of the human brotherhood by his history, which has brought him experiences tending to wean him from strong and definite national feeling, which, admirably as it helps men at certain stages, is certainly likely to stand in the way when the movement is begun towards that universal community of all human beings to which it seems to me that Christianity points as the highest development of human government."

(c) "I find it impossible to believe that the race has nothing to contribute. I believe it has something, and will make its contribution if helped to do so. . . . I have concluded that the Negro race is providentially intended to emphasise an intuitive apprehension of the supernatural, and the place of the emotional in the religious life. Individuals of the Negro race have been strong in reasoning out their faith in the verities of religion; but the supernatural is peculiarly immediate to the apprehension of the Negro mind. The supernatural is the atmosphere in which he lives, moves, and has his being. He has certainly the defect of his quality in a very marked degree—he believes too much, accepts too readily things and facts as supernatural which are not, and multiplies with a facile imagination beings to be adored and feared. He greatly needs to have this defect balanced by the reasonings of a more intellectual race, but not to be overdone; and the superior races need the Negro's intuitive apprehension of the supernatural to save them from the mere deductions of a cultured reason, whose tendency is in the direction of a pure materialism.

"On the second point, which I have named, I may briefly remark that as the intellectual, the emotional, and the practical in happy and harmonious combination are essential to a well-constructed and completed religious life, I see in no race whose characteristics I have studied the emotional lodged to anything like the degree in which it exists in the Negro. This, I am aware, has its drawbacks, its dangers. It often runs riot. It is often in religion regarded as an end in itself, and not the motive force to impel the right action. It needs to be checked, controlled, and combined with the intellectual and the practical. But it has a distinct religious value, and I think it is the Negro's special mission to contribute this element." [42]

c. The racial characteristics of the Japanese, as described by Bishop Awdry, are

" versatility and power of imitation; absence of habitual tension of the mind and will, leading to an easy acquiescence and giving up of effort in face of temporary difficulties; and in close connection with this an absence of despair, discontent or disgust at failure or disappointment, leading to a ready resumption of steady work at the old task as soon as the difficulty is past; an almost childish curiosity and love of prettiness and of romance; intense patriotism and loyalty and obedience to law and custom; patient, uncomplaining endurance, except where an injustice, or rather an inequality or irregularity of treatment, is supposed; not a little suspiciousness behind a childlike simplicity; very widespread natural eloquence, coupled with diplomatic power of keeping a secret by word and bearing; an apparent lack of sensitiveness to pain, which is surprising when considered with their acute observation, accurate imitation, vivacity of mind, and almost exaggerated sentiment for honour according to their national ideals, and love for beauty in flower, landscape, and feature. One would have supposed that these various forms of sensitiveness to pleasure could hardly have grown up without bringing a corresponding sensitiveness to pain of every kind, but perhaps the key may lie in the fact that their ideals are conventional rather than spontaneous, and their courtesy has its roots in ceremonious custom rather than in sympathy; while their remarkable kindness to children and to other living creatures, unless some definite occasion leads them to an opposite line of conduct, seems rather to arise from natural happiness and an easy-going and kindly disposition, which likes to live in a happy world and sees no reason to interfere with other people's whims and wishes, than to be connected in any way with the idea of duty. Some of these characteristics will appear contradictory. I can only say that they are national characteristics, and that they co-exist. . . . We in the West greatly overrate the importance of the individual as compared with the body of which he is a member; we encourage self-seeking, because it is the most powerful inducement to energy; we separate the man as a unit,

---

[42] *Ibid.,* pp. 130-133.

because that develops his power of will and helps him to stand alone. Must we not also add, we think so much of accumulation of wealth as a chief element of power, that the qualities which tend to win in the race for wealth come to have a wholly fictitious value in our estimate of character? But exactly the opposite is the case in the Oriental, and perhaps especially in the Japanese. Peacefulness of life, not energy, is what he both enjoys and admires. Self-assertion and pushing are to him the ugliest of vices. A profession of humility, of his own utter unimportance as compared with others, is the habit of his talk. Time is not regarded as money, and is unimportant in his eyes." [43]

These words were written before the Russo-Japanese War. Bishop Awdry added these qualifications after that war:

" The past ten years (since 1896), and especially the past three, have made a great change in this. The whole look of the common people is more alert than it was. They appear to be observing the things that pass before them with greater interest and more keenness. The lips, that used often to hang apart, are now generally closed. They began perceptibly to close in the early weeks of the Russian War. There is a far greater appearance both of decision and of sense of responsibility in face and bearing. Universal education has much to do with this, but the greatest educator has been the war." . . . " Since the above was written the change in the Japanese is amazing. I will not say the advance, for in some respects I do not think it is an advance. Energy in trade, the value set on wealth, the association of accumulating capital with patriotism, the economy of time, the development of a more expansive style of living, the wide extension of the sense of individual responsibility, and the dropping out from common talk of Shikata ga nai and Kamaimasen, are all conspicuous. Yet in these things, too, the lead is given to national thought by the emperor—the suggestion of what should be comes from above; and loyalty thus is part of the foundation of national money-making as well as of personal sacrifice." [44]

The change which has taken place in Japanese character [45] is itself an evidence of the inevitableness of the racial interchange

---

[43] *Ibid.*, pp. 141 f., 151 f.
[44] *Ibid.*, pp. 141, 154.
[45] See Gulick, *The Evolution of the Japanese.*

which is going on in the world and which is affecting the white races as much as any others. The old Japan also had been deeply affected by the Chinese and the Koreans but for some centuries before Perry came it had been isolated and at ease. Bishop Awdry comments on this: " This leisure, this self-contained condition, and this total absence of foreign competition, are elements in the development of a clever nation which have gone to make the Japanese what they are found in the present generation: in some ways better, in some ways worse, but in almost all ways different from other nations. Industrious, yet not strenuous; a nation of artists, yet not reaching after large or high ideals; remarkably obedient to law and authority, yet ready for every change; the pupils of the most stolid and immovable people of the world, yet themselves vivacious and volatile, romantic and fantastic in their ideas; they certainly offer a most interesting field for conjecture as to what they will become now that they travel in all countries, revel in every kind of new idea and invention, and enter with zest into every branch of that world-wide competition which is the most striking feature of our time." [46]

The contributions of the Japanese race, Bishop Awdry is convinced, are fundamental:

" Three broad characteristics stand out, distinct yet intimately connected with each other—characteristics which belong to the very foundations of Japanese ideals, and to the very ground tints of the characters of those who aim at following those ideals; characteristics, too, which put to shame the coarseness and selfishness and self-assertion, the ugliness and disproportions and even vices and vicious tendencies which, under the names of being practical, efficient, and self-respecting, seem to pose as part of the popular ideals of the West. These must be pruned and trained if the truth and the beauty and the goodness of Christ are to be fully exhibited in His Church on earth. They will not be pruned till the Anglo-Saxon learns to see, as the Eastern already sees, that they are blotches and deformities upon a grand ideal and a noble character.

" If, then, the Japanese, or those among them who exhibit the best features of the national type, will continue true through all

---

[46] *Ibid.,* p. 160 f.

changes to the highest traditions of the race, we think they may
contribute in three directions to that through which the Church as
a whole may attain to the measure of the stature of the fulness
of Christ—

" 1. Cheerful patience, neither fatalistic nor despairing.

" 2. A proper estimate of wealth in comparison with other
things.

" 3. The self-subordination of the individual to the interests of
the whole body." [47]

The danger of today is that the Japanese under the pressure of
race associations with the West will not contribute these qualities
to us and to all races, but will surrender instead to the very characteristics which they ought to help us to surmount. Likewise in
the appreciation and preservation of beauty Japan, and indeed all
of Asia, is in peril of surrendering to inferior ideals instead of
standing fast by racial artistic characteristics and guarding them
as a universal trust. We may recall two testimonies. Baron
Hubner says:

" The Japanese are wonderful lovers of nature. In Europe a
feeling for beauty has to be developed by education. Our peasants will talk to you of the fertility of the soil, of the abundance
of water so useful for their mills, of the value of their woods, but
not of the picturesque charms of the country. They are not perhaps entirely insensible to them, but if they do feel them it is in a
vague undefined sort of way for which they would be puzzled to
account. It is not so with the Japanese labourer. With him the
sense of beauty is innate." [48]

And a more recent writer points out the passion for perfection of
detail which exists together with the more general appreciation
of beauty:

" Coupled with an inherent æsthetic, which the Tokugawa influences fostered into exquisite taste, and linked with the Oriental
habit of patient industry, Japanese thoroughness has produced the
most minutely perfect specimens of art that have ever delighted

---

[47] *Ibid.,* p. 229.
[48] Quoted in Robinson, *The Character of Christ and Non-Christian
Races,* p. 181.

the world. An artist will chisel at a little block of ivory for years —not to reap pecuniary reward, but to satisfy his passion toward perfection—until at length you hold in your hands a tiny figure which is a microcosm in itself, and will yield to the microscope alone the completeness of its dainty perfections." [49]

The world cannot afford to lose these things which were committed to Japan's trust.

d. The essay on the Chinese by Bishop Hoare deals with the steadfastness, diligence, practical sense and solidarity of Chinese character and the evidence of the value of these qualities already afforded in the Christian Church in China, and its energy, its martyr-spirit, its will for unity. Commercially and intellectually the Chinese can hold their own with any race.

" No merchant in the East can afford to despise the Chinaman as a man of commerce. His industry, his ability, his reliability, all combine to make him a formidable rival to any European competitor; his power of combination for purposes of trade, and the manner in which he holds to his fellow-countrymen as against the foreigner, enables him, in his own land at any rate, to dictate terms to the European. And in other respects it is, I think, impossible to say that the Chinaman is inferior intellectually to the European. His method of education is different from ours, it has been very different for centuries, and it is the fashion to speak with contempt of his methods; but whether it be as the result of, or in spite of, his methods, the intellectual power of the present generation of Chinese is, without gainsaying, very remarkable. It would be interesting to hear how an advocate for the principle of heredity would explain the fact that a race whose educational training has been for centuries purely classical; whose standard of excellence, by which all candidates for office have been judged, consisted in the power of writing artificial themes in hieroglyphic characters, can at once turn to Western subjects and methods, and show themselves the equals of those whose ancestors have long given their minds to such subjects." [50]

Chinese character and race influence are still unsolved problems. Some of the ancient fundamental characteristics of the

---

[49] *Ibid.*, p. 182, quoted from *Young Japan*, by S. A. Scherer, p. 154.
[50] *Mankind and the Church*, p. 243.

Japanese were Chinese characteristics also. Indeed the models of Japan were borrowed from China. It remains to be seen whether China can swing through the transformation which is demanded of her as Japan has done. But if a race is to be credited with its ideals and the moral standards of its best men the Chinese race, as a race, has as much to give racially as any race not excluding the white races, for the Chinese gave Confucianism to Asia while Christianity was given to the white race. And it is hard to exaggerate the significance of Confucianism, which is to be truly considered not as a religion, but as a racial moral accumulation. Dr. Faber's summary of its points of contact with Christianity shows how far the Chinese race made its way:

1. Divine Providence over human affairs and visitation of human sins are acknowledged.
2. An invisible world above and around this material life is firmly believed in.
3. Moral law is positively set forth as binding equally on men and spirits.
4. Prayer is offered in public calamities as well as for private needs, in the belief that it is heard and answered by spiritual powers.
5. Sacrifices are regarded as necessary to come into closer contact with the spiritual world.
6. Miracles are believed in as the natural efficacy of spirits.
7. Moral duty is taught, and its obligations in the five human relations.
8. Cultivation of the moral character is regarded as the basis for the successful carrying out of the social duties.
9. Virtue is valued above riches and honour.
10. In case of failure in political and social life, moral self-culture and practice of humanity are to be attended to even more carefully than before.
11. Sincerity and truth are shown to be the only basis for self-culture and the reform of the world.
12. The Golden Rule is proclaimed as the principle of moral conduct among our fellow-men.
13. Every ruler should carry out a benevolent government for the benefit of the people.

That many of these points are fully practised need hardly be asserted. The remarkable thing is that they exist, for this differentiates the Chinese from every other race. They bring with them reverence for the rule of reason and respect for moral institutions, and an ideal of a world order of peace and concord.[51]

Indeed what race but the Chinese answers the description of Prof. Flinders Petrie in an article searching for some hope for modern civilisation:

"If we were able to mould the future, the reasonable course would be to look around for a race which would best counteract the deficiencies of ourselves, and to favour a mixture in isolation. We need to remedy the unrest and excitability of the present population by producing a more stolid and hard-working people; to counteract the lack of security by a sense of permanence and commercial morality; to hinder the prevalent waste by the development of a frugal and saving habit; to keep our knowledge to its right uses by a peace-loving people who do not glorify fighting; to turn our intellectual frivolity into a love of solid reading and literature. We need a race less sensitive in nerves, though not less perceptive in thought; and, above all, it must be a race which commands the respect and affection of those who have lived among it and know it best. I leave it to the reader to think what cultivated race of the present world would fulfill these conditions."[52]

e. The Mohammedan races with which Bishop Lefroy deals in *Mankind and the Church* are not cognate races at all, but nevertheless in a sense it is right to group the North Indian and West Asiatic peoples whose characteristics have found expression in Islam. The fundamental conviction of these races is the Power and Unity of God,

"the conviction that, amidst all the chaos and confusion and disorders of the world which so fearfully obscure it, there is, nevertheless, an ultimate Will, resistless, supreme, and that man is called to be a minister of that Will, to promulgate it, to compel —if necessary by very simple and elementary means indeed—

---

[51] See Millard's *Review of the Far East,* March 8, 1919, art. by Chen Huan-chang, "A Universal Government as the Confucian Ideal of Perfect Peace."
[52] *Yale Review,* Jan., 1922, art. on "The Outlook for Civilisation."

obedience to that Will—this it was which welded the Mohammedan hosts into so invincible an engine of conquest, which inspired them with a spirit of military subordination and discipline,
as well as with a contempt of death, such as has probably never
been surpassed in any system—this it is which, so far as it is still
in any true sense operative amongst Mohammedans, gives at once
that backbone of character, that firmness of determination and
strength of will, and also that uncomplaining patience and submission in the presence of the bitterest misfortune, which characterise and adorn the best adherents of the creed.

" That the Unity of God is a necessary ingredient in any such
conception of His reality and power as this—made necessary by
some of the most fundamental laws of human thought—is obvious, and this truth of unity is the one which has been most
clearly grasped in thought by Mohammedan theologians themselves, and most earnestly and continuously insisted on. But
deeper even than the unity, goes the reality of the existence of
God—of His presence and His power—and this I put unhesitat-
ingly as the fundamental truth of Mohammedanism.

" It can hardly be questioned that we ourselves urgently need
a clearer grasp of this truth at the present time. Thoughtful
minds in the West have been occupied with the discovery of those
secondary causes which are the methods of God's working in the
world. Their researches have been met with such marvelous
success that men have sometimes failed to retain the true sense of
proportion, and in the fascinating disclosures of the methods of
the operation of God's Will have been in danger of losing sight
of the presence and activity of that Will itself. We therefore
greatly need to be recalled to that deepest note of Mohammedan
teaching, and to hear again that ultimate declaration of the existence of God, ' I am that I am.' This, then, is the first contribution which I believe the Mohammedan races will bring to the
Christian Church as they are themselves gathered into its fold." [53]

A second contribution of these races is their insistence on the
theory, however they have misread it, that it is the knowledge of
God which lies at the base of human life and gives strength to
human society, that this strength is due to religious truth rather
than to any maxims of practical morality or any principles of
politics, and that there is a positive objective reality to this truth
and to all truth. Mohammedanism is one of the most terrible,

---

[53] *Mankind and the Church*, p. 284 f.

sterilising and destructive of all religions. Wherever it has gone it has either found a desert or in the long run made one.[54] But the races which begot this religion and which have borne it have some great truths and some qualities of life which they need to bring that they may be rectified and employed by man.

f. With regard to the Indian races, Mr. Lowes Dickinson has written a very discouraging essay in which, in the matter of art and æsthetic contributions, he groups China and Japan with India. He speaks of the effect of contact with the West on Indian arts and crafts and goes on from this to deeper things:

" There can be no doubt that these generally have declined, if not perished; and the immediate cause is the competition of Western wares. This is most evident in textiles, where factory-made goods, mainly imported, but partly also manufactured in India, are killing the old domestic industries. But the decline seems to be general; I, at any rate, saw nowhere any modern products, whether in brasswork, wood-carving, embroidery, or enamel, which seemed to me to have any merit. To attribute this decline, however, merely to the competition of Western wares is not to go to the bottom of the matter. For the question remains, Why are Western wares preferred? The answer that they are cheaper is sufficient, no doubt, in the case of goods used by the mass of the people; cheapness, if you are poor, will override, in the East as in the West, all other considerations. But there is something more than this. Some Indian arts, that of painting, for instance, that of architecture on a grand scale, and the arts allied to it, always depended in India on the patronage of princes. These princes still exist and are still wealthy. But they prefer to patronise bad Western art. Why? Obviously because they have no real taste, and the prestige of the West overrides everything else in their mind. They want to have houses and clothes as like as possible to those of Europeans. And this raises the general question, to me a very interesting one, whether taste in all Oriental countries has not been for generations merely a habit; whether people went on making and using beautiful things merely because their fathers and grandfathers had done so; and as soon as anything new is offered, run to that, not only for the sake of cheapness, but for the sake of novelty and snobbery. My observations in China and

---

[54] See the best apology for it in Bosworth Smith, *Mohammed and Mohammedanism,* and Ameer Ali, Syed, *The Spirit of Islam.*

in Japan, as well as in India, suggested to me very forcibly that this is the truth—that the arts of the East have long been dead, long before contact with the West, so far as active and intelligent taste is concerned, and that their collapse before the Western invasion is due not only to the cheapness of Western goods, but to an actual preference for them on other grounds, or, at any rate, an absence of preference for the more beautiful native products. Indians attribute the decline of their arts and crafts, as they attribute everything else, to the malign activities of the British Government. I believe they do not go deep enough. They should attribute it to the lack of effective and positive taste among their own leaders.

" To sum up, I find in India a peculiar civilisation, antithetical to that of the West. I find a religious consciousness which negates what is really the religious postulate of the West, that life in time is the real and important life; and a social institution, caste, which negates the implicit assumption of the West, that the desirable thing is equality of opportunity. I find also that in India the contact between East and West assumes a form peculiarly acute and irritating, owing to the fact that India has been conquered and is governed by a Western Power. But the contact, none the less, is having the same disintegrating effect it produces in other Eastern countries. And I do not doubt that sooner or later, whether or no British rule maintains itself, the religious consciousness of India will be transformed by the methods and results of positive science, and its institutions by the economic influences of industrialism. In this transformation something, of course, will be lost. But my own opinion is that India has more to gain and less to lose by contact with the West than any other Eastern country." [55]

Christians believe that the West has in Christianity not a racial possession but a universal trust for all men far transcending anything the other peoples have to give the West. Whether the other religions have anything to give to Christianity is the point still to be considered. But that the Indian races have something to contribute to the common life of man one can not doubt. Mr. Gokhale names the characteristics which he believes India still retains and " which once placed us in the van of the world's civilisation—the depth of our spirituality, our serene outlook on

[55] *An Essay on the Civilisations of India, China and Japan*, pp. 38-41.

life, our conception of domestic and social duty." Sir Richard Temple described Indian characteristics as he conceived them some years ago: " For the upper and middle classes, domestic affection, munificence, tenacious adherence to custom, veneration with awe leading to superstition, love of external nature, and inclination for abstract meditation, mental acuteness and subtlety, litigiousness, shrewdness of observation; for the humbler classes, temperance, patience, docility, charitableness to the indigent, endurance, fortitude under disaster, and industry." [56] But the outstanding characteristic of India is, no doubt, the religiousness of the whole of life. As Mr. Bernard Lucas says:

" In the West we are accustomed to speak of a certain phase of life as the religious life, and to draw sharp distinctions between what we call sacred and secular. In India, on the other hand, life is essentially religious, and in the strictest sense of the word there is nothing which can properly be called secular at all. Religion is all-pervading as the atmosphere itself; it penetrates into every nook and corner of life, so that the Hindu can never escape from its influence. It presides over his birth, fixes his name, determines his education, settles his calling, arranges his marriage, orders every detail of his family and social life, and controls his destiny through all time. Not only so, but it gives colour and shape to the external world in which he lives and moves. Animate and inanimate nature, rivers and hills, trees and plants, rocks and stones, everything in the animal and vegetable kingdom, are all alike existing in this all-pervading religious atmosphere, and present themselves to his mind through this all-embracing medium. It is this fact perhaps more than anything else which makes the Hindu an insoluble enigma to the man of the West. Its subtle influence is encountered at every turn, its tint is present in every landscape, its pungent essence can be detected everywhere. It has to be reckoned with in the India Office, in the Legislative Council, in the Government Office, in market and school, in the largest town as well as in the smallest hamlet." [57]

If only the Indian races might bring to the life of all men this ideal of the domination of the whole life by religion and if that religion were Christ!

[56] Quoted by Beach, *India and Christian Opportunity,* p. 81.
[57] Quoted by Sherwood Eddy, *India Awakening,* p. 28.

2. We have been considering the contribution which it may be hoped other races are to make to the fulness of human life and character. The Christian conviction, of course, is that all this is simply raw material awaiting the cleansing and unifying power of Christianity, whose mission it is to purify all that is unholy, to illumine all that is dark, to raise up all that is low, to redeem all life and to bind it to the uses of the Kingdom of Christ. History is full of the work which Christianity has wrought in this long and still continuing process. And the traces of it are written all over our common institutions. The names of the days of the week show the power of Christianity to take up and strip of their old unworthiness the very names of heathen gods and put them to use in Christian service. The Church even calls the most sacred and significant of all its celebrations, the celebration of the central fact of the Resurrection of Christ, by the name of a heathen goddess, Eastra. There are those who have deprecated the course of the Christian Church in this respect. The Friends decline to use the once heathen names of the days and months. And Mr. Bertrand Russell reverses the usual criticism of Christian missions as ruthlessly destructive, and reproaches the education given in mission schools in China because " it makes the students more conservative in purely Chinese matters than the young men and women who have had a modern education under Chinese auspices. Europeans in general," he adds, " are more conservative about China than the modern Chinese are and they tend to convey their conservatism to their pupils." [58] Apart from these students of mission colleges who were taught to revere their country and to be " conservative in purely Chinese matters," Mr. Russell met only socialists among the young students. " To a man they are socialists, as are most of the best among the Chinese teachers." [59] If Mr. Russell's criticism of the mission schools is accurate it is greatly to their credit. They are doing just what Christianity has always sought to do, to redeem and conserve. The white race will do its duty toward other races to the extent that it becomes Christian and seeks to

---

[58] Russell, *The Problem of China*, p. 263.
[59] *Ibid.*, p. 235.

help all races to " abhor that which is evil and to cleave to that which is good."

But our final question is not what Christianity or any race so far as it is Christian, can do to help other races to realise their true character and mission, but how will the contact of Christianity with other races bring out its latent fulness more clearly and richly? We need to consider the reaction of the contact of Christianity with the non-Christian religions and peoples, not upon Christianity, but upon our apprehension and conceptions of Christianity. No one of us believes that we have the whole of Christian truth. If we believed that we had the whole of this truth that would be the surrender of our conviction that Christianity is the final and absolute religion. How is it possible for us in a small fragment of the long corporate experience of humanity, a few races in a mere generation of time, to claim that we have gathered all the truth of the inexhaustible religion into our own personal comprehension and experience? We know that we have not, by reason of the primary and fundamental conviction we hold of the value of Christianity. We see this also as we lay Christianity over against the non-Christian religions of the world. We discover, as we do so, truths in Christianity which we had not discerned before, or truths in a glory, in a magnitude, that we had not imagined.[60] It is to be stated clearly that we look for nothing from the non-Christian religions to be added to the Christianity of the New Testament. Every truth in these religions is already in Christianity, and it is there proportioned and balanced as it is not in any of the other religions. But we have much to learn of our own religion. It reaches infinitely beyond our present comprehension of it. The thought and life of other peoples has much to teach us of the riches of our own faith; but not one single aspect of truth can be named which these other religions are able to contribute to the religion of the New Testament.

But it may be asked, is not the Oriental consciousness to enlarge and enrich our comparatively pinched and practical conceptions? But is there such a thing as an Oriental consciousness? A West-

---

[60] *Edinburgh Missionary Congress Report,* Vol. IV., p. 325.

ern woman has been until Gandhi arose, the chief preacher of such a consciousness in India, and the whole conception of such a consciousness as a great force to be dealt with in philosophy and religion has been produced and nourished in the West. There is doubtless a rough utility in thus setting the East off against the West, but both East and West are divided within themselves by differences of race and tradition as great as separate them from one another. The Chinese consciousness is nearer to Western materialism and the Hindu consciousness to Western idealism than the Chinese and Hindu consciousness are to each other. The phrase, the Oriental consciousness, serves a more or less useful purpose, but it does not define a source of new religious knowledge or promise a correction of Christianity.

Nevertheless, we have much to learn from others. Some think otherwise. Professor Ross says, " The Western culture now extends to so much of the human race that it can find no other equal culture to mate with," and he speaks of the demonstration of sociology of " the eccentric and barren character of the Oriental civilisation. Equipped with that incomparable instrument, *the scientific method,* the Western intellect will probably go its way with little heed to what the East offers it." [61] But others differ. " The West has yet much to learn in the school of Vedanta, so ancient and so meditative," says one Christian writer.[62] And Mr. Slater says: " The West has to learn from the East, and the East from the West. The questions raised by the Vedanta will have to pass into Christianity if the best minds of India are to embrace it; and the Church of the ' farther East ' will doubtless contribute something to the thought of Christendom of the science of the soul, and of the omnipentrativeness and immanence of Deity." [63] These are sober and true words. They speak of the inadequacy of our thought, not of the inadequacy of Christianity. It is not Christianity that needs help or enlargement. It is we. And it is only by their acceptance of Christianity that other races can give us their help. We do not primarily need a larger intellectual com-

[61] Ross, *Social Psychology,* p. 356.
[62] N. MacNicol, *Hibbert Journal,* October, 1908.
[63] Slater, *The Higher Hinduism,* p. 291.

prehension of the Gospel. Indeed, we cannot get it by mere speculation, by comparison of opinions, by new codifications of truth, or
new efforts to state the life and will of God and the nature and end
of our souls in words. We can only get it by more experience,
more life, by the actual occupation of humanity by God. It is in
the experience of Christianity that help is needed. It is in our
living it, in our getting the Gospel embodied in our life. It is thus
that the other races are to help us. And it is the races that are to
help us. It is the great racial qualities which are to be the contribution of these peoples to the Spirit of God for His use as the
materials of the Kingdom of God, the incarnation of the Gospel in
the life of mankind. The non-Christian peoples are far better
than the evils of their religions. Even the sanctification of error
and wrong in the non-Christian religions has not extirpated from
these peoples the likeness of God, which will not be effaced, and
that original capacity for Him, for the indwelling of His life, for
the execution of His will of righteousness, which is to be their
contribution to the universal Church. It is from these races that
the new goods of Christianity are to come. To the extent to which
the religions of the different races have really supported the strong
national qualities of these peoples, which they are to bring to the
enlargement of our interpretation of the Gospel by the enlargement of our experience of God in Christ, they have made
a contribution, but to the extent that they have weakened them
they have increased the measure of the encumbrance they have
been on the life of the world, or will be if they obstruct the
triumph of Christianity. But it is the character of the various
races which Christianity wants, to redeem and use them. And we
will cherish the hope, though as yet it is only a hope, which Dr.
Gibson sets forth in his *Mission Problems and Mission Methods
in South China,* that through the qualities which the races are to
bring into the Church, the Church may pass forward into the
Gospel which is perfect and complete and needing only to be understood and accepted in its divine fulness:

" A review of earlier Church history would show how the varying types of different races have contributed to the development of

Christian theology. The Greek mind contributed to it its speculative liberality, its profound philosophical insight, its sense of the
essential dignity of human nature. The Roman type of mental
development contributed, on the other hand, the strong sense of
law out of which has arisen the whole region of what is called
forensic theology. It also imposed on Christian thought definiteness, and the sense of limits which prevented it from running wild
in a too free speculation. In later times the subtlety, thoroughness, and clearness of the French intellectual type, when working
at its best, impressed themselves through Calvin upon our Western theology. When time has allowed for their development, may
we not expect the working of similar forces in the Churches which
are growing up on our great mission fields? In India you have a
mind naturally religious, highly speculative and metaphysical, and
moving habitually under the influence of sudden heats of religious
emotion. In China, on the contrary, you have a national temperament with little natural sympathy with the more subtle aspects of
religious thought, but strongly inclined to what is ethical and
practical, having a firm grasp of reality, and presenting a singular
combination of solidity and plasticity. Where our theology is still
one-sided and incomplete, may we not look for large contributions
to it in days to come from the independent thought and life of
Christian men in our mission fields; and may we not look forward
to the attainment, as one of the ample rewards of our mission
work, of the fuller and more rounded theology for which the
Church has waited so long? So may come at last the healing of
those divisions by which she has been torn and weakened throughout her chequered history.

"When to Jewish fervour, Greek passion, Roman restraint,
French acuteness, German depth, English breadth, Scottish intensity, and American alertness, are added Indian religious
subtlety, with Chinese ethical sagacity—all baptised into the One
Spirit—then we may reach at last the fuller theology, worthy of
the world-wide hospitalities of the kingdom of heaven, and setting
forth more nearly the very thoughts of God." [64]

Dr. Farquhar takes up this vision from the point of view of
India,

"How much will be possible when the whole world acknowl-
edges, even with meagre intelligence, the Lordship of Christ?

[64] Gibson, *Mission Problems and Mission Methods in South China*, pp.
282-286.

Aspects of His example and of His message which are latent in the West will in India find free and full expression. May not Christ's attitude to poverty find glorious illumination, His deep sense of the meaning and the sacredness of society be exhibited to the world by a people set free from Caste indeed, yet reaping its fruits as never before, and the prayer and communion with His Father to which Jesus so often gave His nights be turned to priceless account by the descendants of the rishis and yogis? Aspects of Christ which the hard practical West has failed to utilise will prove fruitful beyond our dreams in the Christian experience of the richly dowered Hindu race." [65]

It is quite possible that hopes such as these are too high and that, as many students hold, the course of human races is now a course of deterioration.[66] From the Christian point of view we should hold that only the purpose and grace of God can lift races or men,[67] that He provided the institution of race for great and beneficent ends, that the failure of those ends can result only from the disobedience and faithlessness of man, that if we will accept and follow His will for men and for races and for all racial and human relationships we shall find racial differences not an evil but an immeasurable blessing and the means of the richer and better world, pictured in St. John's vision of the City full of the glory and honour of the nations.

---

[65] Farquhar, *The Crown of Hinduism*, p. 63 f.
[66] See Adams, *The Degradation of the Democratic Dogma*, Grant, *The Passing of the Great Race.*
[67] See Warneck, *The Living Christ and Dying Heathenism*, pp. 147-156.

IV

THE EVILS AND ABUSES OF RACE

THE best of human institutions are capable of the worst perversion. It is with race as it is with sex. What God evidently intended for noble and enriching use has been often degraded to baseness and evil. Race prejudice and race strife have taken the place of race respect and race service and have poisoned the life of mankind. " I am convinced myself," says Mr. H. G. Wells, " that there is no more evil thing in this present world than race prejudice, none at all ! I write deliberately—it is the worst single thing in life now. It justifies and holds together more baseness, cruelty and abomination than any other sort of error in the world."

It is impossible to believe that men and races were created or are born with an instinctive prejudice against one another. All over the world the children of different races play together and grow up together with no more manifestation of antagonism than marks the children of any one race. Mr. Stone regards racial antipathy as congenital, a natural contrariety or repugnancy of qualities.

" To quote the Century Dictionary," says he, " antipathy ' expresses most of constitutional feeling and least of volition '; ' it is a dislike that seems constitutional toward persons, things, conduct. etc.; hence it involves a dislike for which sometimes no good reason can be given.' I would define racial antipathy, then, as a natural contrariety, repugnancy of qualities, or incompatibility, between individuals or groups which are sufficiently differentiated to constitute what, for want of a more exact term, we call races. What is more important is that it involves an instinctive feeling of dislike, distaste, or repugnance, for which sometimes no good reason can be given. Friction is defined primarily as a ' lack of harmony,' or a ' mutual irritation.' In the case of races it is accentuated by antipathy." [1]

---

[1] *The American Race Problem*, p. 212.

But we do not believe that prejudice and antipathy are inherited.
They come with education and the pressure of the social environment. Everywhere race prejudice is one of the most pervasive
elements in child training. Obedience is enforced by threats of
what the supposed ogres of disliked races will do. I heard a
young Jewish mother intimidating a three-year-old son on a railroad train a few days ago by calling out threateningly, " Come
here at once or a nigger will seize you." And such vicious training is common in many races with regard to many other races.
" I grew up with race prejudice," writes Mirza Saeed Khan of
his boyhood days as a Mohammedan Kurd in Senneh, Persia,
" but I believe it was acquired, due to bad teaching. We were
taught that the Franks and the Russians were God-hating people,
so bitterly God-hating that they made brims for their hats in order
not to see the heavens, the work of God's hand, lest they think of
Him. And I remember how I used to kill the red ants because
they were Russians and spared the black ones."

And how does race antipathy become a part of the social ideals
which control the educational process? Some think that it is because fear enters in. Professor Park, as it seems to us, over-
states the impersonal forces making for race friction, but he
points out truly one chief origin of race friction not in colour or
race characteristics but in fear. Colour and other race characteristics are merely markers. The causal factor, he holds, is fear.

" It has been assumed," says he, " that the prejudice which
blinds the people of one race to the virtues of another and leads
them to exaggerate that other's faults is in the nature of a misunderstanding which further knowledge will dispel. This is so far
from true that it would be more exact to say that our racial misunderstandings are merely the expression of our racial antipathies.
Behind these antipathies are deep-seated, vital, and instinctive
impulses. Racial antipathies represent the collision of invisible
forces, the clash of interests, dimly felt but not yet clearly perceived. They are present in every situation where the fundamental interests of races and peoples are not yet regulated by some
law, custom, or any other modus vivendi which commands the
assent and the mutual support of both parties. We hate people
because we fear them, because our interests, as we understand

them at any rate, run counter to theirs. On the other hand, good will is founded in the long run upon co-operation. The extension of our so-called altruistic sentiments is made possible only by the organisation of our otherwise conflicting interests and by the extension of the machinery of co-operation and social control.

"Race prejudice may be regarded as a spontaneous, more or less instinctive, defense-reaction, the practical effect of which is to restrict free competition between races. Its importance as a social function is due to the fact that free competition, particularly between people with different standards of living, seems to be, if not the original source, at least the stimulus to which race prejudice is the response.

"From this point of view we may regard caste, or even slavery, as one of those accommodations through which the race problem found a natural solution. Caste, by relegating the subject race to an inferior status, gives to each race at any rate a monopoly of its own tasks. When this status is accepted by the subject people, as is the case where the caste or slavery systems become fully established, racial competition ceases and racial animosity tends to disappear." [2]

The destruction of competition and the acceptance of subserviency, however, Professor Park proceeds to point out, are economically unsound and socially inefficient. And race isolation which, it might be thought, would remove the occasion of fear is likewise economically impracticable and is itself " at once a cause and an effect of race prejudice. It is a vicious circle—isolation, prejudice; prejudice, isolation."

Canon Gairdner, after a long study of the problem of race contacts in Egypt, believes that racial antipathy is the product of group self-interest.

" If the organising of goodwill as between man and man is difficult enough, that between group and group might well seem to be impossible; and for this reason:—most of these groups propose to themselves no other and no higher aim than *their own welfare:* and consequently are in immediate and absolute antagonism with any other group whose aim is or seems to be in conflict with theirs, and whose wellbeing does or seems to diminish their own. When, owing to geographical proximity, this antagonism goes on,

---

[2] Park and Burgess, *Introduction to the Study of Sociology*, p. 62 f.

generation and century after generation and century, a permanent *antipathy* is produced which distorts all vision." [3]

As between East and West, there are many who hold that there is a conflict of temper and ideals which unavoidably leads to racial antagonism. The Earl of Ronaldshay, ex-Governor of Bengal, set forth this view in a paper on the causes of India's unrest, in which he described the fear of India and the destruction of its civilisation by Western civilisation as "this potent source of racial animosity." [4] "The source of unrest," he said, "which seems to be one of fundamental importance, is the heat generated by the clash of two conflicting ideals, the offspring of two different outlooks upon the universe, those of the East and the West respectively," and he quotes Mr. Gandhi as saying, "The tendency of Indian civilisation is to elevate the moral being, that of Western civilisation is to propagate immorality. The latter is Godless, the former is based on a belief in God." This view of the fundamental conflict between the Eastern and Western races is altogether too common. No one has set it forth more intelligently and more persuasively than Meredith Townsend, editor of the *Friend of India* in Calcutta, and later of the London *Spectator*, in *Asia and Europe*. But in the first place, there is no united East nor any united West. There is no united India. The clash of ideals of which the Earl of Ronaldshay spoke is a clash in India quite as truly as between India and the West. In the second place, as Professor Reinsch argued, "there is no irrepressible conflict between Oriental and Western civilisation. On the contrary, they are complementary to each other, not necessarily competitive." [5] Nevertheless, the apparent contradiction of this complementary character of the various sections of human life, the forms of real conflict, the political controversies, the economic exploitation, the well grounded dread of men of "the flood of carnality" which Western influence has too often augmented, have produced fears in Asia which have strengthened race antipathies.

---

[3] *Orient and Occident*, Feb. 1, 1924.
[4] See whole paper in Lahore *Civil and Military Gazette*, March 23, 1923.
[5] Reinsch, *Intellectual and Political Currents in the Far East*, p. 35.

Mr. Stone also, although he believes in fundamental, immovable racial characteristics, recognises that the great source of race friction is fear, and that " the fear and effect of numbers " is one of the determining influences at the foundation of all race relations. When one race is in a distinct minority or is inoffensive in its power of competition, there will be no fear and in consequence no race friction. The friction is inevitable, Mr. Stone believes, whenever one race feels that its interest is imperiled, as it will when it is outnumbered and is unable to dictate the status of the other race.

" The practical attitude of one race or nation toward another," he says, " is determined by motives of self-interest, or instincts of self-preservation, upon the part of the one which is able to control and dictate the terms and conditions of contact between the two. It matters not whether the races concerned be white and Negro in Mississippi today, white and Negro or Indian in Massachusetts yesterday, white and Mongolian in California tomorrow. And, furthermore, it matters precious little what the so-called ' enlightened sentiment ' of the world outside may be on the subject immediately at issue. I am not just now concerned with questions of sentiment. I am endeavouring to offer you a practical consideration of practical affairs. Nor does it make much difference whether the place of such contact be the United States or Egypt, Cuba or the Philippines, Australia, or India, Japan or Santo Domingo. The rule which I state here, call it ' cold-blooded ' if you please, has not often been violated in the past; it is not likely to be in the future. . . . The only exception to this rule is in the case of nations or races between whom there exists either sufficient identity of blood and institutions or such a great disparity of numbers or strength that the controlling party has no grounds upon which to base even an apprehension of untoward consequences from unrestricted or unconditional intercourse, or from any specific or general attitude it may assume toward the weaker. Here the stronger may, if it see fit, give full play to policies wholly unselfish and altruistic, or be governed by them in so far as it may be inclined. I lay it down as a fact which cannot successfully be challenged, that the relations between the white and Negro races in every state in the Union have been, and are now, controlled by considerations ultimately governed by the factor of the relative numbers of the two." [6]

---

[6] *The American Race Problem*, pp. 54 f., 57.

A great deal that is written today on the race problem confirms this view that the pressure and fear of numbers is at the bottom of much race antagonism. The school which is seeking to arouse the white race to protect its isolation and to assert its dominance proceeds on the conviction that the coloured races are rapidly outdistancing the white races in their increase of numbers. Mr. Stoddard estimated the population of the world in 1914 at " five hundred and fifty million whites, five hundred million yellows, four hundred fifty million browns, one hundred and fifty millions blacks and fifty million ' red ' yellows and unclassified strains." Professor East, however, in *Mankind at the Crossroads*, amends these figures to over seven hundred and ten million whites, five hundred and ten million yellows, four hundred and twenty million browns and one hundred and ten million blacks, a total of seventeen hundred and fifty millions, as of 1916. Mr. Stoddard reckoned that the blacks were increasing more than twice as fast and the yellows, and the browns a third again as fast as the whites. So that the coloured races were making an annual increase of 12,655,000 compared with an annual increase of 4,780,000 on the part of the whites. Professor East has a different story to tell. He finds the European whites increasing from more than twice to nearly five times as fast as the other races. The annual increase of white Europeans is seven million, eight hundred thousand, compared to an annual increase for all the others combined of three million, six hundred thousand. The European whites at the present rate of increase would double in fifty-eight years; while it would take the browns two hundred and seventy-eight years to double and the yellows two hundred and thirty-two years. So before 1950, unless some radical and relatively permanent overturn of world affairs occurs, the white race will have a true majority in the world. In this view, on the score of numbers as well as on other grounds, it would seem that the coloured races have most to fear.

No doubt it is inter-racial fear which accounts for the intensity of race feeling in sections of the world where one race is in so great a minority that it dreads and condemns any slightest recognition of race equality. When the Rev. C. F. Andrews, an English missionary, closely associated with Gandhi and Tagore, " innocently took a little Sikh child in East Africa in his arms, a member of his own English community said to him, ' We could have killed you when we saw you there with that black child in your arms. That sort of thing is not done here!' " [7] That this is a reaction of fear and not of reason, or if of reason, then of a reason curiously but familiarly inconsistent, is shown by the fact that a white child would be entrusted without demur to black arms in Africa or India or the United States.

Race fear, race antipathy, race prejudice and race consciousness are inter-related conceptions, but fear and antipathy and prejudice are not necessary consequences of race consciousness. Mr. Stephenson thinks that they are.

" Race distinctions are not based fundamentally upon the feeling by one race of superiority to the other, but are rather the outgrowth of race consciousness. If Negroes were in every way equally advanced with white people, race distinctions would probably be even more pronounced than now ; because, in addition to physical differentiation, there would be the rivalry of equally matched races. Thus, the widespread prejudice entertained by Gentiles toward Jews, resulting in actual, if not legal, distinctions, is due, not to any notion that Jews are intellectually or morally inferior to any people, but to a race consciousness which each possesses." [8]

But neither personal nor national consciousness leads of itself to prejudice. Race consciousness per se, just like individual consciousness, would lead to social enrichment and satisfaction if not prevented or poisoned by other elements.

Professor Dewey thinks that racial prejudice springs from dislike of what is strange.

" The facts suggest that an antipathy to what is strange (originating probably in the self-protective tendencies of animal life) is

---

[7] *The Continent,* May 17, 1923, art. by Sherwood Eddy, " India Calls to Brotherhood."
[8] Stephenson, *Race Distinctions in American Law,* p. 353 f.

the original basis of what now takes the form of race prejudice. The phenomenon is seen in the anti-foreign waves which have swept over China at different times. It is equally seen in the attitude of the earlier immigrants to the United States toward later comers. The Irish were among the first to feel the effects: then as they became fairly established and the older stock became used to them and no longer regarded them as intruders, the animosity was transferred to southern Europeans, especially to the Italians; later the immigrants from eastern and southeastern Europe, became the suspected and feared party. And strikingly enough it has usually been the group which had previously been the object of hostile feelings which has been most active in opposing the newcomers, conferring upon them contemptuous nicknames if not actually abusing them." [9]

But the prejudice can be found where the strangeness is least and may be wanting where the strangeness is greatest. Elsewhere in this same article Dewey indicates deeper and more intricate causes and lifts the whole question above the plane of race:

" The question is not primarily one of race at all, but of the adjustment of different types of culture to one another. These differences of culture include not only differences of speech, manner, religion, moral codes, each one of which is pregnant with causes of misunderstanding and friction, but also differences of political organisation and habits and national rivalries. They include also economic and industrial differences involving differences in planes or standards of daily life on the part of the masses. What is called race prejudice is not then the cause of friction. It is rather a product and sign of the friction which is generated by these other deep-seated causes. Like other social effects it becomes in turn a cause of further consequences; especially it intensifies and exasperates the other sources of friction. But the cultivated person who thinks that what is termed racial friction will disappear if other persons only attain his own state of enlightenment and emancipation from prejudice misjudges the whole situation. Such a state of mind is important for it is favourable to bringing about more fundamental changes in political and economic relationships. But except as it takes effect in modifying social organisations it will always prove impotent in any crisis, to prevent racial friction.

[9] *The Chinese Social and Political Science Review,* March, 1922, art. by John Dewey, " Racial Prejudice and Friction."

"For, I repeat, this friction is not primarily racial. Race is a sign, a symbol, which bears much the same relation to the actual forces which cause friction that a national flag bears to the emotions and activities which it symbolises, condensing them into visible and tangible form. . . . The various parts of the world are now in such close contact with one another that it is very difficult for the world to endure in a condition of stable equilibrium as long as there are rival political cultures and aims operating within it. Universal disarmament would be a more powerful factor in soothing race prejudice than any amount of enlightenment of cultivated persons can be. Economic competition between countries, the race for raw materials and markets, would still, however, exist. With free immigration of the labouring classes habituated to long hours of work, to low standards of living, and to abstinence in expenditures, the economic cause of friction would continue. . . . Only by profound economic readjustments can racial friction be done away with." [10]

Much race antipathy, obviously does spring from fear and it also produces fear, because of the motive of racial self-interest in the race which is supposed to be endangered unless some other race is held down and shows itself willing to submit to a position of subjugation. The superior race dislikes the inferior unless the inferior will accept its inferior status and consent to serve. The inferior race dislikes the superior because it resents its pretensions and unequal demands. Whichever is numerically or economically weaker fears the strength of the other.

Fear is not the only evil of such racial relations. Hate is a yet more lamentable fruitage flowing from racial prejudice, and itself producing prejudice. In our contemporary world, motivated propaganda has more than once deliberately sought to foment racial hate. The war literature made us familiar with the organised campaign of education in Germany, extending over many years and designed to fill Germany with hate of Great Britain, and the calculated and government-controlled activities of falsehood and malice on the part of other nations. No other hate propaganda has ever wrought such havoc as this one, but there have been and are others. What feelings but race distrust and

---

[10] *Ibid.*, pp. 23-24.

enmity could be produced by Kipling's stab at Russia in " The Bear that Walks Like a Man "?   And where could more despicable appeals to race hatred be found than in the New York *American* of July 23, 1916, in such a set of verses as this " Anti-Japanese Hymn of Hate ":

LOOK OUT! CALIFORNIA! BEWARE!

They tell us that Uncle Sam
Would lie down like a lamb,
But he doesn't understand the situation.
He says war talk must cease
While he feeds the dove of peace
But he doesn't know the Peril to the Nation.
But something's going to happen
That will shake things up, perhaps,
If we don't start to clean out the Japs.

Chorus:

They lurk upon thy shores, California!
They watch behind thy doors, California!
They're a hundred thousand strong,
And they won't be hiding long;
There's nothing that the dastards would not dare!
They are soldiers to a man, with the schemes of old Japan
Look out! California! Beware!

There's a murmur that affirms
We're brothers to the worms,
That serve us in a meek and lowly manner;
But while we watch and wait
They're inside the Golden Gate!
Oh! God! Save the Star Spangled Banner!
With the Army and the Navy
And the White House full of gaps
And our Coast running over with Japs!

They've battleships, they say,
On Magdalena Bay!
Uncle Sam, won't you listen when we warn you?
They meet us with a smile
But they're working all the while,

And they're waiting just to steal our California!
So just keep your eyes on Togo
With his pocket full of maps
For we've found out we can't trust the *Japs!*

And the same paper featured, in an editorial page, an article by a
British writer, which purported to advocate good will and to avert
war, but which bore the title, " Millions of Americans hate and
despise England, Millions of Britishers loathe the United States,"
and which began with the paragraph, " There is no use blinking
the fact that millions of Americans either hate or despise England,
and that millions of Britishers likewise loathe the United States
and most of the things it stands for. The war with Germany
started with peace conditions just like that."

Many books of our day assume or seek to prove that such
hatred of race for race is the actual dominating feeling of the
races at the present time, and that whatever humane theory or
Christian sentiment may say, race prejudice and conflict are the
inexorable and inevitable facts. Mr. Weale construes the present
world situation as " The Conflict of Colour " and Mr. Stoddard's
view is sufficiently set forth in the titles to his books, " The
Rising Tide of Colour," " The Revolt against Civilisation," and
" The New World of Islam."

" In the modern world," says Mr. Weale, " it is in the debatable
regions—where what may be called a permanent settlement of
frontier-lines has not yet been brought about—that there will be
a constant swaying to and fro, most probably accompanied by
bloody wars, until density of population, and the consequent struggle for existence, either blots out nationality or makes its claims
undeniable. . . . The main racial contest—a contest which
must be conducted not only along frontiers, but in the heart of
densely-populated countries as well—can only be between the old
antagonists, Europe and Asia. . . . This struggle, however,
will approach slowly and methodically, and not rapidly and dra-
matically as past struggles have done. Every day will bring
nearer the inevitable settling day. . . . At the same time that
there is this large clash of conflicting ideals looming up—this clash
of two necessarily different civilisations, which is to be the mighty
problem of the future—another racial struggle of a very different

nature has already begun. This question is far more subtle and already considerably complicates the other problems. Briefly, a struggle has begun between the white man and all the other men of the world to decide whether non-white men—that is, yellow men, or brown men, or black men,—may or may not invade the white man's countries in order there to gain their livelihood. . . . It is well to understand at once that it is made peculiarly hazardous for the white man, not because he is not able to fight it in the face of all difficulties, not because it is beyond his strength to check it, but because in almost every part of the Asiatic and African worlds, he is still playing his old-world rôle of conqueror, and ruling over vast masses of the world's coloured population virtually by force. That is the real reason why this struggle must in the end prove highly dangerous. On the one hand, the white man has begun to refuse to allow coloured men of any description to enter his countries in large numbers; on the other hand, he continues to rule as conqueror immense areas of the world, the soil of which nourishes autochthonous populations having little or nothing in common with him, and therefore regarding his dominion with a natural and growing aversion." [11]

Mr. Stoddard apotheosises western civilisation and then interprets the great confused struggle of mankind, with wisdom and folly, good and evil commingled, toward a better human order and a truer brotherhood, as an indiscriminate assault of the underman, i. e., the inferior man, upon all efficiency and merit and order. It is only too easy to select one set of quotations, none too carefully appraised, and set them in inaccurate historic and economic perspective and build them as an inadequate foundation under a pre-determined thesis, which is erroneous as principle and fallacious as fact. It is quite true that there is a great racial maladjustment in the world and that the so-called " coloured " races are awakening and are unwilling longer to accept the place of inferiority and inequality assigned to them in the past by other races.

" The race questions in the United States," declares Mr. Jaime C. Gil, " are manufactured by individuals who thereby derive some pleasure or profit. Some of these individuals have been industriously and profitably endeavouring to persuade the people of

---

[11] *The Conflict of Colour*, pp. 93, 98 f.

the United States that this nation's peculiar concept of race is to be the salvation of the world. Nothing could be farther from the truth. There is no Rising Tide of Colour in this world, much as some people's groundless fears and other people's baseless ambitions have risen on a book that fools read from cover to cover and sensible people read by looking at the title. There is a rising tide of common sense that is sweeping over all the land from Calais to Vladivostock and, in its ebb, crosses the Suez Canal and flows from Cairo to the Cape. A similar tide is constantly ebbing and flowing from the Rio Grande across the Panama Canal to Patagonia. All along the path of these tides, distinctions ' in law or fact ' are becoming applied, or are already applied, to all men or to none. Sundry islands and continental areas may rise high and dry above these tides, only to find themselves bound with the bonds of their own liberty, the liberty that is there open to all of one set of people and none of another set." [12]

" There is slowly arising," says Du Bois, " not only a curiously strong brotherhood of Negro blood throughout the world, but the common cause of the darker races against the intolerable assumptions and insults of Europeans has already found expression. Most men in this world are coloured. A belief in humanity means a belief in coloured men. The future world will, in all reasonable probability, be what coloured men make it. In order for this coloured world to come into its heritage, must the earth again be drenched in the blood of fighting, snarling human beasts, or will Reason and Good Will prevail? " [13]

But the mood of the common people of the world is not a mood of hatred, of violence against prosperity, of assault upon the past. The world is not Bolshevist. The people of all races are friendly-spirited, good-willed, eager only to find a way out of the political and economic entanglements of our time into the new day of universal peace and brotherhood. It is one of the evils of race that its frictions and antipathies, whatever their cause or ground, can be used to keep men apart, to feed their suspicions and fears, to foster race pride or despair and to pervert the enriching diversity of humanity into discord and hate.

---

[12] Gil, *America, the Peacemaker*, p. 53 f.
[13] Du Bois, *The Negro*, p. 242.

We must not pass into the very error which we are deprecating, namely, of seeing the evils of the race problem in too narrow a setting or in too near a perspective. It is, after all, no modern problem of East and West or Black and White. One can see the whole problem with its good and evil in miniature in a land like India. Here are many races, conquered and conquerors, natives and invaders, Dravidians and Aryans, ignorant and intelligent, " inferior " and " superior." Here, long ago, race and colour divisions hardened into caste, and some races accepted the status of subjection and yielded to others a position of privilege close to deity. Other races like the Mahrattas refused to acquiesce in the assumption of the Brahmans. On the whole, however, race distinctions have been given in India the fullest support and sanction. India is a picture of human society where men have sought to solve the problem of race relations in almost all the ways recommended by the race inequalitarians. It is almost amusing to note in India the identical arguments made for caste which are made for the isolation and supremacy of the " Nordic " race. Dr. Farquhar sums up the Indian contention :

" To the Hindu caste is the stronghold of purity, manners, culture, and of the whole religious heritage of the race. The high-caste man thinks of himself as one of a small number of pure-blooded, cultured, religious men amidst such vast numbers of unclean, vulgar, vicious people that the light is in grave danger of extinction. Æneas-like, he bears through seething crowds of foes his ancestral heritage, bound by every duty to pass it on intact to those who follow him. Only in caste can he preserve from wrong the sacred trust of his fathers, that deposit of custom, practice, and law which regulates his religion, morals, and habits. It is this heritage which has made him what he is. In every act he does and every thought he thinks he is conscious of its influence. Each caste has its own distinct tradition. Amongst Brahmans to this day the standard of cleanliness, speech, and behaviour is far higher than in other castes. It is impossible to simulate the Brahman. A hundred trifles would betray the pretender. Feeling runs still deeper with regard to the rites of religion, the great doctrines of the faith, and the Vedanta. How can these survive if caste be tampered with? To allow these to be

shared by low-born, ignorant men would be to court not only contamination but destruction." [14]

The results of India's treatment of the race problem are there
for the world to study. The Christian solution has nowhere been
adequately tried. It is demonstrated that the other solutions are
futile and the utter breakdown of the supposed racial reconciliation of Hindus and Mohammedans has shown the inefficiency of
the forms of racial adjustment in these religions and in these races
to bridge the race gulfs and to unite men. India realises the failure of the caste system, which is simply race inequalitarianism
carried logically through, as a solution of the race question. Here
are the deliberate judgments of India's modern leaders. The first
opinion is by the Hon. Sir K. G. Gupta, a member of the India
Council: " The caste system had served useful purposes in the past,
but it had not now a single redeeming feature. If the Hindu was
again to lift his head and take part in the great work of nation-
building, he must revert to the original Aryan type and demolish
the barriers dividing the community." Mr. Shridhar Ketkar, in
his work on *Caste,* says, " The result is disunion of the people, the
worst type the world has ever seen." This testimony is from Lāla
Lājpat Rai, the Punjabi leader: " Caste . . . is a disgrace to
our humanity, our sense of justice, and our feeling of social
affinity, . . . a standing blot on our social organisation." The
editor of *The Indian Social Reformer* speaks of caste as " the
great monster we have to kill," and declares it to be utterly opposed to the modern idea of good citizenship. Such opinions
might be multiplied indefinitely. Let us add only the words of
Rabindranath Tagore, the author of " Gitanjali," who " is by
far the greatest literary force at present in Bengal, and whose
serious spirit and balanced character give his opinions very great
weight ":

" This immutable and all-pervading system of caste has no

---

[14] *The Crown of Hinduism,* p. 208. See *India Census 1911, General Re-
port,* Chap. XI, pp. 365-395, " Caste, Tribe and Race," and especially *India
Census 1901, General Report,* Chap. XI, pp. 489-557, " Caste, Tribe and
Race."

doubt imposed a mechanical uniformity upon the people, but it has, at the same time, kept their different sections inflexibly and unalterably separate, with the consequent loss of all power of adaptation and readjustment to new conditions and forces. The regeneration of the Indian people, to my mind, directly and perhaps solely depends upon the removal of this condition of caste. When I realise the hypnotic hold which this gigantic system of cold-blooded repression has taken on the minds of our people, whose social body it has so completely entwined in its endless coils that the free expression of manhood, even under the direct necessity, has become almost an impossibility, the only remedy that suggects itself to me is to educate them out of their trance. . . . Now has come the time when India must begin to build, and dead arrangement must gradually give way to living construction, organised growth. . . . If to break up the feudal system and the tyrannical conventionalism of the mediæval Church, which had outraged the healthier instincts of humanity, Europe needed the thought-impulse of the Renaissance and the fierce struggle of the Reformation, do we not need in a greater degree an overwhelming influx of higher social ideas before a place can be found for true political thinking? Must we not have that greater vision of humanity which will impel us to shake off the fetters that shackle our individual life before we begin to dream of national freedom?" [15]

And in *Nationalism,* Tagore points out the futility of setting up caste distinctions in the form of barriers which sever races.

" In her caste regulations India recognised differences, but not the mutability which is the law of life. In trying to avoid collisions she set up boundaries of immovable walls, thus giving to her numerous races the negative benefit of peace and order, but not the positive opportunity of expansion and movement. She accepted nature where it produces diversity, but ignored it where it used that diversity for its world-game of infinite permutations and combinations. She treated life in all truth where it is manifold, but insulted it where it is ever moving. Therefore Life departed from her social system and in its place she is worshipping with all ceremony the magnificent cage of countless compartments that she has manufactured." [16]

---

[15] Farquhar, *The Crown of Hinduism,* p. 175 f.
[16] Tagore, *Nationalism,* p. 137.

The evils of fixed race stratification have been adequately demonstrated in India.[17]

Race prejudice has been charged with the responsibility of hindering the development of the science of language.

" Not till that word *Barbarism* was struck out of the dictionary qf mankind and replaced by *brother*," says Max Müller, " can we look for the first beginnings of our science. This change was effected by Christianity. . . . *Humanity* is a word which you look for in vain in Plato or Aristotle; the idea of mankind as one family, as the children of one God, is an idea of Christian growth. . . . When people had been taught to look upon all men as brethren, then, and then only, did the variety of human speech present itself as a problem that called for solution in the eyes of thoughtful observers; and I therefore date the real beginning of the science of language from the day of Pentecost." [18]

Professor Müller hardly meant that the idea of humanity was not found in Greek or Latin thought. It was there, but it was not made effective, as it was, though still in such imperfect measure, under the influence of Christianity.

Race prejudice leads to partisan and embittered misreadings of history. The conflicting accounts of the Reconstruction era in the South and of the origin and results of the Fifteenth Amendment to the Constitution illustrate the effect of racial sentiments on the interpretation of historical and political movements. The partisans of particular racial views or interests constantly read into events a deliberate purpose when there was none, but where tendencies operated in which men passively acquiesced with no conscious racial motive. Du Bois furnishes an illustration of this tendency to read racial prejudice into history when the developments were not due to any intentional race discrimination: " Negroes in Africa, the West Indies, and America were to be forced to work by land monopoly, taxation, and little or no education. In this way a docile industrial class working for low wages, and not in-

---

[17] *The Missionary Review of the World*, Jan., 1923, art. " India in the Melting Pot," p. 40.

[18] Müller, *Lectures on the Science of Language*, 1st Series, p. 118.

telligent enough to unite in labour unions, was to be developed." [19]
The movement he is describing was too big and human for deliberate racial manipulation. It was a movement of social masses.

Race prejudice impeded for centuries the coming of the modern
organisation of society and it hinders today the development of
needed forms of world organisation. In its best forms, the opposition to a world association of nations and races, rests upon the
sense of racial dissimilarity and the fear of men that they are not
sufficiently kindred to be bound together in the responsibilities of
common interest and action. Mr. Lloyd George spoke of the misfortune of race disruption at the Conference of the Prime Ministers and Representatives of the United Kingdom, the Dominions
and India held in London in the summer of 1921. " No greater
calamity," he said, " could overtake the world than any further
accentuation of the world's divisions upon the lines of race. The
British Empire has done signal service to humanity in bridging
those divisions in the past; the loyalty of the King Emperor's
Asiatic peoples is the proof. To depart from that policy, to fail
in that duty, would not only greatly increase the dangers of international war; it would divide the British Empire against itself.
Our foreign policy can never range itself in any sense upon the
differences of race and civilisation between East and West. It
would be fatal to the Empire." If it would be fatal to the Empire,
can it be helpful to the world?

One of the worst effects of inter-racial relations has been the
economic exploitation and the moral abuse of the weaker races.
The races of the South Seas and of Africa have been among the
chief sufferers. The picture in Herman Melville's *Typee* of the
scene on his ship in the harbour of Nukuheva in the Marquesas
Islands in 1842 is too true an account of much of the early contact
of the white race with the primitive peoples:

" Our ship was now wholly given up to every species of riot
and debauchery. The grossest licentiousness and the most shameful inebriety prevailed, with occasional and but short-lived inter-
ruptions, through the whole period of her stay. Alas for the poor

_____

[19] *The Negro,* p. 237.

savages when exposed to the influence of these polluting examples. Unsophisticated and confiding, they are easily led into every vice, and humanity weeps over the ruin thus remorselessly inflicted upon them by their European civilisers. Thrice happy are they who, inhabiting some yet undiscovered island in the midst of the ocean, have never been brought into contact with the white man."

In *American Diplomacy in the Orient,* the Hon. John W. Foster, Secretary of State under President Harrison, tells of the struggle of the Hawaiian Islands against liquor and vice. Honolulu had been a brothel for visiting ships until, under missionary influence, the Hawaiians sought to abolish licentiousness and intemperance. " This strictness," says Mr. Foster, " interfered not only with the depraved habits of the vicious but with the profits of many traders." For a time an armed vessel of the American Navy overrode the Hawaiian authorities and insisted that the vessel should enjoy the ancient privilege of unlimited immorality.[20] Contact with the white race introduced among many of these people destructive diseases never known before.

It is not too much to say that the early contacts of the white races with the other races were generally pitched on a selfish and immoral level. As Hobson says:

" Every European nation in its early dealings with backward peoples frankly looked upon them, not as customers, but as possessors of possible treasures the worth of which they did not know, and which must be got, if possible by any peaceful means, but otherwise by force. . . . The goods we sell to the natives of these countries are largely of the most detrimental kinds and of the most inferior quality. This has always been the case. A Report to the English Council of Trade as early as 1698 upon the trade with Madagascar and the East Indies named ' liquor, arms, and gunpowder,' as the chief articles of trade. Recent reports of our trade with East and Central Africa indicate that a considerable proportion of the trade is of the same degrading character, supplemented by the cheapest and lowest grades of textile and metal wares. Such an import trade, largely appealing to the crudest wants of savage or semi-civilised natives, is fraught with manifest dangers, physical and moral. The liquor traffic, in particular, carried on by traders of several European nations in

---

[20] Foster, *American Diplomacy in the Orient,* pp. 115-118.

various parts of Africa, is a crime against civilisation, only second to the slave trade of earlier days. But equally pernicious in its effect upon the native peoples is a large portion of the export trade organised by white men in tropical countries of Africa and South America for the rapid and reckless exploitation of the natural resources of the land. The rubber trade in the Congo and in Brazil, and the cocoa trade in San Thomé, are examples of the gravest of these abuses of commerce. Such a contact of whites with backward people shows Western civilisation at its worst, for the lowest representatives of that civilisation animated by the least worthy motives, introduce among the nations the least desirable products and practices of that civilisation, while their attempt to organise industrially and commercially the tropical countries, being directed to secure the largest immediate gains without due consideration of the future, is often attended by the maximum of waste and inhumanity." [21]

Even when our commercial relations with primitive peoples are free from these unworthy elements, they are often essentially and inevitably destructive in their influence. Mr. Abel tells of the fundamental changes which contact with Western civilisation has introduced in New Guinea. The white race has introduced good government pledged to safeguard aboriginal rights, but it has monopolised the trade, and in spite of all the good which it has done, its influence has resulted in a decrease of the population and a substitution of new moral evils for the old.

" In spite of the good which these forces have brought to the Papuan in both material and spiritual things," says Mr. Abel, " his old life has been so shaken to its foundations that he is faced with racial disaster. The new order has in it destructive elements far more evident in their results upon his life than are the constructive forces. Benefits have been doled out by the handful; while the things which are bringing about his material doom have been distributed broadcast. Even peace has meant the ruin of the old Papuan life; for the peacemakers have brought in new dis-

[21] *Universal Races Congress,* 1911, paper by J. A. Hobson, "Opening of Markets and Countries," pp. 227, 230. See *The East and the West,* Jan., 1923, art. by Lord Meston, "India at the Crossways," p. 70; Page, *The Black Bishop,* p. 320; *The Country Editor,* Jan., 1923. Art. " Lubricating Revolutions with Oil ": " Bless us! What does the State Department exist for but to protect American interests in foreign countries? What is international politics but international business? "

eases hitherto unknown, and ' by compelling the Papuan to live at peace with his old enemies, many of his former industries and nearly all his arts have been destroyed.' " [22]

The white race cannot be held responsible, as though it were a racial fault, for the introduction and development of modern industrialism with its machinery organisation in Asia. It is true that this industrialism was first developed by the white race, but Asiatic capital as well as European and American capital established it in Asia, and whatever checks of humanitarianism have been laid upon it have been devised by the conscience of the white race. Nevertheless, it is not to be wondered at that the spirit of justice and humanity revolts against the evils which have appeared and is disposed to charge a heavy measure of them against the exploitation of the economically weaker race by forces awakened or controlled by the stronger races or directly drawn from them. Western students of the race problem should know what these evils of imported industrialism are in the great cities of the Far East. A careful observer writes the following from Chefoo, China:

" In Chefoo, as in other cities of China, we found a serious industrial problem. In the hair net factories seventeen thousand women and a thousand men are daily working ten hours for six cents a day. Twenty-six thousand boys and young men are here employed in forty factories making pongee silk. They work thirteen hours a day and receive an average daily wage of six cents. Skilled artisans are paid from twenty to thirty cents, but in many factories the average wage for common labour is only five cents a day. Despite these facts I found industrial conditions better in Chefoo than in any city I have yet visited in China. Owing to the early missionary work there are a number of Christian employers in Chefoo who close their factories on Sunday, though most of the other industries are running seven days a week. There is a great deal of unrest and dissatisfaction amongst the workers, but to date there has been no systematic attempt to organise. There have been three recent attempts to raise wages by strikes, but these were severely crushed by the police and a number of the leaders were imprisoned.

---

[22] *The Missionary Review of the World,* May, 1923, art. " Conflicting Forces in Papua," pp. 377-382.

" We visited Tientsin, where we found fifteen thousand boys in the weaving factories working eighteen hours a day from 5 A. M. to 11 P. M., the majority receiving no pay whatever, but only their food. In the rug factories the boys work sixteen hours a day from 5: 30 A. M. to 10 P. M., seven days a week. During the three years of apprenticeship they receive only their food and lodging. Many skilled workers are paid only four dollars a month. A large number of the boys are suffering from eye trouble and other diseases due to their working conditions and utter lack of care. In the best match factory we found boys from nine to twelve working fifteen hours a day seven days a week. Their pay runs from six to ten cents a day. Eighty of these little workers must go to the hospital each day to be treated. The fumes of the cheap phosphorus and sulphur often affect their eyes and their lungs. Much of this could be avoided by using better chemicals, but the profits of the owners would not be so large. . . .

" There are at least fifty cotton mills around Shanghai, and more are going up. Not hundreds, but thousands of children, down to the age of eight or nine years, are employed. A recent report states that small boys, ten, eleven, and twelve years of age, are working stripped to the waist. Little girls, even smaller than the boys, eight or nine or ten perhaps, were standing between double rows of whizzing unguarded machinery, steadily but wearily feeding the machines. One mite, perhaps eight years of age, was curled in an exhausted heap on the cement floor sound asleep. Over in a corner, under a pile of cotton waste, a tiny baby was spending the night while his mother worked at a machine near by. And everywhere was the unceasing roar of the machinery, the heat and humidity, and the cotton-filled air. In one small hospital there were, one day this winter, three children under ten years old. The arm of one had been caught in an unfenced machine and was all but torn off. The leg of another was mashed from hip to ankle by the teeth of a machine. The third, a little girl, had been caught by the hair in her machine and her scalp torn off. Not one of these accidents would have happened had the machines been fitted with safety devices. Most of the accidents happen on the night shifts, between two and four in the morning. The workers grow weary, heads droop with sleepiness, vigilance is relaxed, but the unguarded machines go on. Such are the terrible conditions in Chinese industry." [23]

---

[23] Federal Council of the Churches, *Research Department Information Service,* Jan. 6, 1923; see *The World Tomorrow,* November, 1923, art. on " Capitalism in China."

Two thoughts serve to ameliorate a little the shame which the white races should feel at the history of their relations with the backward peoples. One is that the moral conscience of the world has advanced and that from base beginnings the races have moved forward to a more honourable and helpful intercourse. Dr. James Stewart says that the African's " connection with the higher races hitherto has been to him a doubtful benefit," but, writing in 1902, he goes on,

" When, far on in the next century, some African comes to write the history of his continent and his race, he will probably write thus,—that up to a certain point or date—' Our contact with the higher civilised races of Europe and America invariably resulted in our further deterioration. We were shipped in multitudes across the seas to grow sugar, cotton, and tobacco. That seemed to be all we were good for, at least all that we were reckoned to be good for. When that business came to an end, other trades sprang up, the chief articles being spirits, guns and gunpowder, which we used to destroy ourselves and to destroy one another. About the end of the nineteenth century, or the beginning of the twentieth, a change for the better began to appear. It is true, the whole of the continent was partitioned among the civilised peoples of Europe, and at first we did not reap much benefit thereby. Some regions were rendered more miserable than before. But gradually, through the substitution of a humaner and wiser rule, and by the progress of education, and most of all through the introduction of Christianity, we have now reached a happier and better condition of life.' " [24]

The second comforting fact is that on the whole, evil though the past has been, it has yielded already a net result of good. Dr. Thomas Jesse Jones takes this view in the report on *Education in Africa* presented by the Commission, of which he was chairman, which visited Africa in 1920-21. In discussing " European and American Influences " he writes,

" There have been various interpretations of the contributions made by the white races to Africa. Some have thought that the

---

[24] *Dawn in the Dark Continent*, p. 365 f.

influences of Europeans and Americans have been more for evil than for good. Some have thought it would have been better to leave the African in his natural condition. Few have realised the importance of the movements that have been started and the changes that have been wrought. It must be stated that many mistakes have been made and many injustices have been perpetrated. In some sections the Africans have suffered tragically at the hands of selfish white exploiters. Evil influences originated by white people still persist in too many parts of Africa. It is, however, the emphatic conviction of the Education Commission that the gains that have come to Africa through the white man are far greater than the losses. The evidence indicates that the history of the African people resembles that of all other peoples in the world, in that their progress has been and will continue to be the result of co-operative relationships with other peoples. It seems clear that the extreme demand for the elimination of the white man from Africa represents a desire to reverse the most important lessons of history. Thoughtful Africans are increasingly realising not only the importance but the necessity of the co-operation of the white group.

" Among the most convincing evidences of this conviction are those obtained from a study of the portions of Africa now ruled by European nations. The elements of life that reflect the changes introduced by the white groups have been the improvement of physical well-being, including the decrease of sickness and death and the attendant suffering; the decrease and often the elimination of the power of witchcraft, a form of oppression exceedingly general and cruel; the overthrow of intertribal slavery; the development of friendly relations among tribes formerly hostile; the extension of the economic benefits of the country to all the tribes; and the opening of the doors of civilisation to those who were formerly limited to the narrow compass of their tribes. It is true that the extension of commercial, industrial, and even governmental influences sometimes have too often been attended with suffering on the part of the Native people. The early periods of adjustment to the new forces are especially trying. But in the long run one of the best measures of the final influence of the white group upon the Native peoples is the increase or decrease of population. So long as there are no records of the feelings of the Native masses we must rely upon the only vital measure that reflects the condition of the majority of the group, namely, the power of the group to maintain life. On this basis, the statistics of most of the colonies show a decided increase in population, and therefore an improvement of general welfare. The African areas and colonies where decreases are indicated are known from other sources to be suffering from wrong governmental, economic, or social policies. . . .

"The record of government service in Africa is a mingling of the good and the bad, the effective and the ineffective, the wise and the unwise. Despite the failures and injustices of the governments in handling the Natives, the advantages to Native life provided by the colonial governments have on the whole overshadowed the disadvantages." [25]

Even if we accept these two mollifying judgments it is indisputable that strong races have imposed on weaker races two evils whose vicious character cannot be overstated.

One of these was the traffic in liquor and opium. This traffic in liquor will be one of the terrible counts in the indictment which posterity will draw against Europe and America in their dealings with Africa. We have slowly rooted out the atrocious traffic in slaves only to plant in its place the equally abominable trade in strong drink. Some would say, more abominable. "It is my sincere belief," declared Sir Richard Burton, "that if the slave trade were revived with all its horrors, and Africa could get rid of the white man with the gunpowder and rum which he has introduced, Africa would be the gainer by the exchange." And Sir John Kirk goes so far as to declare: "The last four centuries of contact with Europeans and European trade has degraded rather than elevated or improved the people." These are strong words, but scarcely a traveller and never a missionary sends back from Africa any favourable report. Joseph Thomson was a capable and in this matter an unbiased man, and no one had better opportunity for observation, and this was his testimony:

"The notorious gin trade . . . is indeed a scandal and a shame, well worthy to be classed with the detested slave trade, in which we had ourselves ever so prominent a part. We talk of civilising the Negro and introducing the blessings of European trade, while at one and the same time we pour into this unhappy country incredible quantities of gin, rum, gunpowder and guns.

---

[25] *Education in Africa*, p. 7 f.

We are so accustomed to hearing a delightful list of the useful articles which the Negro wants in return for the products of his country that we are apt to think that the trade in spirits must be quite a minor affair. Banish all such pleasing illusions from your minds. The trade in this baleful article is enormous. The appetite for it increases out of all proportion to the desire for better things and to our shame be it said, we are ever ready to supply the victims to the utmost, driving them deeper and deeper into the slough of depravity, ruining them body and soul, while at home we talk sanctimoniously, as if the introduction of our trade and the elevation of the Negro went hand in hand. The time has surely come when in the interests of our national honour, energetic efforts should be made to suppress the diabolical traffic. There can be no excuse for its continuance, and it is a blot on Christian civilisation."

For many years a great flood of liquor poured into Africa. In 1884 the imports from Great Britain, America, Portugal and Germany were 8,751,527 gallons, of which 7,136,263 came from Germany, and 921,412 from America. The imports in 1901 into British West Africa alone were 2,319,731 gallons of gin and 1,-834,514 gallons of rum and whiskey. So firmly fixed did the cruel habit become, that in some parts of Africa gin was the only currency, and even some Roman Catholic missionaries used it for this purpose. It ruins the African physically, enslaves whole villages, men, women and children, and in the end it is as surely the death of trade as the slave traffic itself. Scarcely a true book on Africa dealing with the last half century can be found which does not expose the shame of this traffic or apologise for it. " In the poorest part," we read in the life of Mary Slessor, " she comes upon a group of men selling rum. At the sight of the ' white Ma ' they put the stuff away and beg her to stay. They are quiet until she denounces the sale of the liquor; then one interrupts: ' What for white man bring them rum suppose them rum no be good? He be god-man bring the rum—then what for god-man talk so?' What can she answer?

" It is a vile fluid, this trade spirit, yet the country is deluged with it, and it leaves behind it disaster and demoralisation and ruined homes. Mary feels bitter against the civilised countries that seek profit from the moral devastation of humanity. She cannot answer the man." [26]

Of course the real motive for the liquor traffic back of all the concocted defences made for it, is the desire for gain, or the necessity for revenue. *West Africa* frankly said: " Take the hypothesis of a total abolition of the liquor traffic—how would the colonies replace the revenue they derive from the taxation on spirit imports? As the revenue from spirits forms about sixty per cent. of the total, the part which spirits play in the administration of British West Africa has to be faced."

Little by little, beginning with the Berlin Conference in 1884, the struggle against the liquor traffic in Africa made headway in spite of political and commercial obstruction, and now there are wide zones of prohibition or heavy tariff duties which protect, though as yet inadequately, the African races from the physical and moral degradation of drink.

The opium trade in Asia is the counterpart of the liquor trade in Africa and the South Seas. Mr. Foster quotes a letter from Mr. W. N. Pethick, an American long resident in China, which had been transmitted to the State Department by Dr. Angell, then American Minister at Peking, in which Mr. Pethick stated that at that time " the single article of opium imported equals in value all other goods brought into China, and is greater than all the tea or all the silk (the two chief articles of export) sent out of the country,—which show that the black stream of pollution which has so long flowed out of India into China has been increasing in volume and spreading its baneful influence wider and wider." [27]   And Mr. Foster, one of the most careful and temperate of men, added, " There is much to be said in commendation of the British government in its relations with the Orient, but its connection with the opium traffic of China has left a dark and ineffaceable stain upon its record. In this matter the greed of the East India Company and its successor, the government of India, triumphed over the moral sentiment of the nation, which has done so much for the

---

[26] Livingstone, *Mary Slessor of Calabar*, p. 31.
[27] *American Diplomacy in the Orient*, p. 296.

amelioration of the condition of mankind." [28]   China and Japan have fought a long battle against the opium trade and have in great measure prevailed, although even now corrupt Chinese and Western or Indian allies seek to continue the destructive traffic, and Japan, still sedulously excluding the drug from its own people, co-operates with wholesale exporters of morphine in Scotland and the United States to corrupt China with this new habit in place of the old.   Does not the same principle of humanity which favours the freest interchange in wholesome trade also condemn all commerce in articles which destroy human efficiency between races of equal strength and still more between the races which have power to injure others and the races which do not have power to resist? [29]

The second great evil imposed on weaker races by the strong has been slavery.   It is true that slavery has not always been interracial.   Among the Greeks and Romans the institution had been wholly independent of race distinction.   Plato held that nature had intended some to bear rule and others to serve.   The Roman law held the slave not as an alien, but as a man, to be property like any other chattel.[30]   " The slaves at Athens were of the same blood with their masters, at least not separated from them by such apparent differences of race as separate the African or the Malaysian from the European." [31]   In Egypt races and people of any colour were enslaved.   The whole Hebrew nation bore the slave status.   In Scotland white slavery existed until the nineteenth century, as described by Hugh Miller in *My Schools and Schoolmasters* (pp. 303-305).   In the early days in America there were more white slaves than black.

" In less than a score of years after their first introduction, white servants were exported to the colonies as a species of merchandise and were dealt with as any other article of commodity.

---

[28] *Ibid.,* p. 299.
[29] Hearings before 67th Congress on " Limiting Production of Habit-Forming Drugs."   Speech by S. G. Porter, Feb. 26, 1923, House of Representatives; *Peking and Tientsin Times,* Sept. 6, 1920; New York *Times,* editorial, " The Opium Traffic," Feb. 15, 1923; *Far Eastern Fortnightly,* Jan. 17 and 31, 1921.
[30] Uhlhorn, *Conflict of Christianity with Heathenism,* pp. 131-141.
[31] Storrs, *The Divine Origin of Christianity,* pp. 154-164.

Moreover, such was the scarcity of labour and the pecuniary inducements held out, that many poor people sold themselves in order to reach these shores. A census taken in 1625 shows that there were, at that date, 464 white servants and 22 Negro slaves in the Virginia colony. Forty years later there were more than six thousand white indentured servants in the same section.

"Nor was this species of human chattelism confined to Virginia, for, notwithstanding the introduction of Negro slaves, it is reliably estimated that as late as 1680, of the great number of youthful persons sent to the colonies as indentured servants, the larger portion of them were procured by felonious means. High authorities assert that not less than ten thousand of the youth of both sexes were annually abducted from English homes. All of them did not reach the colonies, for many of them died on the passage out, owing to the scant provision made for their care and the brutality of the shipmasters." [32]

But the great development of the institution of human slavery rested on race discrimination. Among the ancients, as nations spread by military conquest, the vanquished passed under the yoke of bondage. And in the modern world outside of a few lands where there is intraracial agricultural serfdom or industrial indenture, slavery has become a matter of race relationship.

No one can be found any longer to apologise for the horrors of the African slave traffic. And it would be hard to say which races are guilty of the grosser brutality, the Arabs or the Europeans. The actual raiding of the interior villages was the work of the Moslem Arabs. Recall an eye witness's picture of one of the slave caravans with its Arab leader setting out for Zanzibar after converting " a smiling valley, called the Garden of Tanganyika, into a hungry wilderness." This was Moir's description:

" First came armed men dancing, gesticulating and throwing their guns, as only Arabs can do, to the sound of drums, panpipes and other less musical instruments. Then followed, slowly and sedately, the great man himself, accompanied by his brother and other head men, his richly caparisoned donkey walking along near by ; and surely no greater contrast could be conceived than that between this courteous, white-robed Arab, with his gold-embroidered joho, silver sword and daggers, and silken turban,

[32] Thomas, *The American Negro,* p. 5.

and the miserable swarm of naked, squalid human beings that he had wantonly dragged from their now ruined homes in order to enrich himself.

" Behind the Arab came wives and household servants, laughing and talking as they passed along, carrying the camp utensils and other impediments of their masters. After that the main rabble of the caravan, the men armed with guns, spears and axes. Ominously prominent among the loads were many slave sticks to be handy if any turned refractory, or if any likely strangers were met. Mingling with and guarded by them came the wretched, over-burdened, tied-up slaves. The men who might still have had spirit to try and escape, were driven, tied two and two, in the terrible goree or taming stick, or in gangs of about a dozen, each with an iron collar let into a long iron chain, many even, so soon after the start, staggering under their loads.

" And the women! I can hardly trust myself to think or speak of them—they were fastened to chains or thick bark ropes; very many in addition to their heavy weight of grain or ivory, carried little brown babies dear to their hearts as a white man's child to his. The double burden was almost too much, and yet they struggled bravely on, knowing too well that when they showed signs of fatigue, not the slaver's ivory but the living child would be torn from them and thrown aside to die. One poor old woman I could not help noticing. She was carrying a biggish boy who should have been walking, but those thin, weak legs had evidently given way. She was tottering already; it was the supreme effort of a mother's love—and all in vain; for the child, easily recognisable, was brought into camp a couple of hours later by one of my hunters, who had found him on the path. We had him cared for, but his poor mother would never know. Already, during the three days' journey from Liendure, death had been freeing the captives. It was well for them; still we could not help shuddering, as in the darkness we heard the howl of the hyenas along the track, and realised only too fully the reason why. Low as these poor Negroes may be in the moral scale, they have still strong maternal affection, and love of home and country.

" For ninety miles along the south coast of Tanganyika we have the entire population swept away." [33]

But the activity of the white races was no less evil and it is not improbable that it cost Africa many more lives than the Arabs

---

[33] *Church Missionary Intelligencer,* August 1, 1884, p. 505 f.

carried north or north-east. Let a spokesman of the Negro race state the case:

" The exact proportions of the slave trade can be estimated only approximately. From 1680 to 1688 we know that the English African Company alone sent 249 ships to Africa, shipped there 60,783 Negro slaves, and after losing 14,387 on the middle passage, delivered 46,396 in America.

" It seems probable that 25,000 Negroes a year arrived in America between 1698 and 1707. After the Asiento of 1713 this number rose to 30,000 annually, and before the Revolutionary War it had reached at least 40,000 and perhaps 100,000 slaves a year.

" The total number of slaves imported is not known. Dunbar estimates that nearly 900,000 came to America in the sixteenth century, 2,750,000 in the seventeenth, 7,000,000 in the eighteenth, and over 4,000,000 in the nineteenth, perhaps 15,000,000 in all. Certainly it seems that at least 10,000,000 Negroes were expatriated. Probably every slave imported represented on the average five corpses in Africa or on the high seas. The American slave trade, therefore, meant the elimination of at least 60,000,000 Negroes from their fatherland. The Mohammedan slave trade meant the expatriation or forcible migration in Africa of nearly as many more. It would be conservative, then, to say that the slave trade cost Negro Africa 100,000,000 souls. And yet people ask today the cause of the stagnation of culture in that land since 1600!

" Such a large number of slaves could be supplied only by organised slave raiding in every corner of Africa. The African continent gradually became revolutionised. Whole regions were depopulated, whole tribes disappeared; villages were built in caves and on hills or in forest fastnesses; the character of peoples like those of Benin developed their worst excesses of cruelty instead of the already flourishing arts of peace. The dark, irresistible grasp of fetish took firmer hold on men's minds.

" Further advances toward civilisation became impossible. Not only was there the immense demand for slaves which had its outlet on the west coast, but the slave caravans were streaming up through the desert to the Mediterranean coast and down the valley of the Nile to the centers of Mohammedanism. It was a rape of a continent to an extent never paralleled in ancient or modern times.

" In the American trade there was not only the horror of the slave raid, which lined the winding paths of the African jungles with bleached bones, but there was also the horror of what was called the ' middle passage,' this is, the voyage across the Atlantic.

As Sir William Dolben said, ' The Negroes were chained to each other hand and foot, and stowed so close that they were not allowed above a foot and a half for each in breadth. Thus crammed together like herrings in a barrel, they contracted putrid and fatal disorders ; so that they who came to inspect them in a morning had occasionally to pick dead slaves out of their rows, and to unchain their carcases from the bodies of their wretched fellow-sufferers to whom they had been fastened.'

" It was estimated that out of every one hundred lot shipped from Africa only about fifty lived to be effective labourers across the sea, and among the whites more seamen died in that trade in one year than in the whole remaining trade of England in two. . . .

" Such is the story of the Rape of Ethiopia—a sordid, pitiful, cruel tale.   Raphael painted, Luther preached, Corneille wrote, and Milton sung ; and through it all, for four hundred years, the dark captives wound to the sea amid the bleaching bones of the dead ; for four hundred years the sharks followed the scurrying ships ; for four hundred years America was strewn with the living and dying millions of a transplanted race ; for four hundred years Ethiopia stretched forth her hands unto God." [34]

The supreme experience of men in the matter of the enslavement of one race by another was given to us in America.   This is

---

[34] Du Bois, *The Negro*, pp. 155-159. And labour conditions still prevail in portions of Africa which differ only in name and not in reality from slavery, as is set forth in the following memorial submitted in 1923 to the Federal Council of the Churches of Christ in America:

The Fairfield County Association of Churches asks the Federal Council to undertake a study of the facts and then to initiate such activities as may be found necessary to secure the complete suppression of slavery.

The Association submits for information the following extracts from African Labor Regulations:

From a British Admiralty Report on Portuguese East Africa, 1920.

Page 184. " The disinclination of African people to work for Europeans without compensation is probably as pronounced in Portuguese East Africa as elsewhere.   In the days of slave-holding it was possible to obtain the required labour by force.   At the present time the form of compulsion is more subtle, but nevertheless as real.

" The hut tax and poll tax imposed in the different districts of the province (of Mozambique) are in reality a compulsory contribution to the labour resources of the State.   As a complement to this taxation elaborate labour regulations have been made.   Those of the Mozambique Company of July 26, 1907, may be taken as an example of these provisions."

Regulations condensed :

1. " Natives who do not properly cultivate their own small properties, (see later regulation regarding 2 acre properties), or do not offer themselves for work in the ordinary way, may be urged to enter into contracts

a true statement. It was given to us. The Southern people who lived at the time of the Civil War had not enslaved the Negro. The Negro slaves in the South at the time of the Civil War had not been raped from Africa. Both whites and blacks had come into their relationship by inheritance. While almost all the blacks were slaves, by no means all of the whites were slave owners. "The total white population of the fifteen slaveholding states in 1860 was 8,099,760, and the number of slaveholders was 383,637; of whom 277,000 owned less than ten slaves each; 10,751 owned fifty or more; 1,733 owned one hundred or more; 312 owned over

with the Company or with individuals to work for a period to be agreed upon, which is not less than three months.

2. "Failing compliance with these regulations they may be sentenced to correctional labour for not less than a fortnight nor more than a year, at one-third of the ordinary wage, to be paid in kind.

3. "With regard to the occupation of the land by natives for purposes of cultivation, the benefit of exemption from compulsory labour is only conceded to those who possess a property of a value superior to 5,000 centavos. In this connection natives are permitted to occupy vacant land to the extent of not more than one hectare (two acres) for which no rent will be charged for five years, but will be after that. After 20 years the native may become the owner.

4. "The poll tax and part of the hut tax can be paid by labour performed by the native, or may be paid in kind when the native can prove that he has laboured enough to have paid it in labour.

5. "Natives who do not perform their labour voluntarily may be invited to work for the Company or individuals, and in case of refusal and resistance may be condemned to correctional labour under the surveillance of the police, during which they will be lodged and fed and will receive a wage in kind corresponding to one-third of that paid to other labourers."

6. "The services of labourers may be requisitioned by the local authorities and holders of land, and by merchants and others, and will so far as possible be supplied, for a period not less than three months, for which the employer must pay the wages fixed by public tariff and furnish sufficient food and lodging. Such contracts to labour must not exceed five years.

7. "Employers may requisition the labour of natives condemned to correctional labour under police surveillance from the Company in the same manner. (In such cases, of course, the two-thirds wage forfeited by the native will accrue to the Company.)

8. "The regulations were revised in 1915 to entail the obligation to labour for all males over 18 and under 60 years of age, with certain specified exceptions.

9. "Natives, however, have the right to contract freely for their labour, with or without the intervention of the authorities, whilst the heads of industrial and agricultural enterprises employing over 500 natives are permitted to organise their own police to maintain order in their undertakings. Contracts cannot be for more than five years, and flogging, except by administrative permission, is not permitted.

200; fourteen owned 500; while there were practically 75,000 who owned only one each."[35]   Originally, moreover, there was a stronger anti-slavery feeling in the South than in the North. "William Pinckney, in 1789, boldly affirmed in the Maryland House of Delegates, that, 'By the eternal principles of natural justice, no master in this state has a right to hold his slave for a single hour.' Luther Martin, a delegate to the Constitutional Convention from Maryland, opposed the adoption of the Consti-

---

10. "Labourers are not required to work for more than 9 hours a day, and provision is made for at least four days' rest during the month. Moreover, labourers entering upon a new contract are entitled to have their wages raised 5 per cent. from year to year."

FROM A LAW PUBLISHED IN THE LEADING PAPER IN ANGOLA, WEST AFRICA.
From the *Nation* of Feb. 27, 1921.
1. Every able-bodied native must give not less than 90 days' labour every year to some form of industrial establishment.
2. If a native does not comply with this regulation voluntarily he "shall be compelled" to give not less than 180 days.
3. Any one "indecorously clothed" is, "without further legal form," condemned to "not less than 180 days'" labour.
4. Every official when collecting the hut tax must demand a certificate from the native tax-payer from his "patron," not having which the native is punished.
5. Natives defaulting in the service of their "patrons" "shall be condemned to correctional labour of not more than six months."
12. Every farmer is permitted a "place of detention" in which his labourers must live "outside of work hours."
13. The fixed labour conditions call upon the patron to
    1. Give two and one half lbs. of corn meal and beans—raw, daily to each workman.
    2. Pay $1.50 (15 cts. U. S. Money) up to $2.40 (24 cts. U. S.) per month to each *volunteer* labourer. Those forced to labour get 20 cts. per month less.
14. Natives in service must be given assistance and food when sick or hurt during the time of contract.
15. No patron or labourer shall be condemned without being heard.
16. A patron who shall fail to comply with any of the requirements of this regulation shall be fined, never less than $5 nor more than $150. If any patron for any reason shall attempt to evade the regulation by certifying that his natives have complied with the obligation to work when they have not, or who says that he has natives in his employ when he has not, (that is, try to protect the natives from the forced labour laws) he shall be punished with a fine of $50 for the first offense and $100 for subsequent offenses.
17. The local authorities shall ask the farmers to turn over to them any native who may be considered incorrigible from any standpoint so that he may be sent away for military service.
[35] Moore, *The South To-day*, p. 31.

tution on the ground that it contained no express provision against slavery; and General Lee, of Virginia, lamented that no provision was made in the document for the gradual abolition of slavery; while Judge Tucker, of the same state, in a letter to its General Assembly, recommending the abolition of their slaves, said, ' It is our first duty to effectuate so desirable an object, and to remove from us a stigma, with which our enemies will never fail to upbraid us, nor our consciences to reproach us.' " [36] The invention of the cotton gin, the consequent profitableness of Negro labour, the rapid growth of the slave population, numbering 700,000 in 1790 and 1,191,362 in 1810, and 2,009,043 in 1830, and 3,204,313 in 1850; the lack of education among the masses of the Southern whites, the geographical isolation of the states, the increasing struggle between diverse political principles, the commercial greed and rivalry of each section, and racial discrimination are some of the reasons given for the disappearance of the early abolition sentiment and the growth instead of the doctrine of the sanctity of slavery as a divine institution.

Some hold that slavery rests on race antipathy, others that race antipathy springs from slavery. Undoubtedly each reacts on the other, although there are those who argue that slavery accepted by the slaves is the one sure method of escaping race friction.

"The late Professor Shaler, of Harvard," says Mr. Stone, " summed up with absolute accuracy the function of slavery in making possible relations of mutual amity between the white and Negro races in this country, when he declared that, ' The one condition in which very diverse races may be brought into close social relations without much danger of hatred, destructive to the social order, is when an inferior race is enslaved by a superior.' His opinion was that ' this form of union is stronger than it has appeared to those who have allowed their justifiable dislike of the relation to prejudice them as to its consequences.' Professor Shaler struck one of the keynotes of the ante bellum situation when he said that slavery made impossible any sort of rivalry between the races. He declared his utter detestation of the institution, but said it should be recognised that ' it was effective in

---

[36] Thomas, *The American Negro,* p. 28.

the prevention of race hatreds.' To quote his words: ' Moreover, it brought the two races into a position where there was no longer any instinctive repugnance to each other, derived from the striking differences of colour or of form. If the Negroes had been cast upon this shore under any other conditions than those of slavery, they would have been unable to obtain this relation with the whites which their condition of bondage gave.' " [37]

Is not the idea of a continuous acceptance by any race of its own enslavement illusory? Has there ever been or could there ever be such an atrophy of the sense of manhood and freedom? Do not those who think that the Negro was satisfied with the status of slavery ignore the mass of evidence which disproves their idea? Is it not certainly true that if the South had won the Civil War and set up an independent Confederacy on the basis of States Rights and Slavery, it would have given them both up within fifty years?

The institution of slavery in the South bore two aspects. "One hears, on the one hand," says Du Bois, " of the staid and gentle patriarchy, the wide and sleepy plantations with lord and retainers, ease and happiness; on the other hand one hears of barbarous cruelty and unbridled power and wide oppression of men. Which is the true picture? The answer is simple: both are true." [38] Good or bad, however, the institution was a wrong institution, and the theft of the Negro from Africa was a crime of which Africa still bears the deep scar and for which both the black and the white races in America have suffered and have to suffer more. Economically and morally slavery was a curse to the South, but it has brought its blessings both to the white and black, to the black most of all. Compare the Negro population of the United States today with the Negro races in Africa. But also it has brought the blessing of a race testing and of the possibility of a greater race sympathy and service to the white race.

" We have heard much already," said the late J. L. M. Curry to a Southern audience at Montgomery, Alabama, at the Conference of the Society for the Consideration of the Race Problems

---

[37] Stone, *The American Race Problem*, p. 220.
[38] Du Bois, *The Negro*, p. 190.

and Conditions of the South, on May 9, 1900, " and will hear more before we adjourn, of slavery. It was an economic curse, a legacy of ignorance. It cursed the South with stupid, ignorant, uninventive labour. The curse in large degree remains. The policy of some would perpetuate it and give a system of serfdom, degrading to the Negro, corrupting to the employer. The Negro is a valuable labourer; let us improve him and make his labour more intelligent, more skilled, more productive. . . . Shall the Caucasian race, in timid fearfulness, in cowardly injustice, wrong an inferior race, put obstacles to its progress? Left to itself, away from the elevating influence of contact and tuition, there will be retrogression. Shall we hasten the retrogression, shall we have two races side by side, equal in political privileges, one educated, the other ignorant? Unless the white people, the superior, the cultivated race, lift up the lower, both will be inevitably dragged down." [39]

And Mr. Murphy, one of the leaders of the new mind of the South, after quoting Dr. Curry's words, adds:

" This sense of responsibility is the present residuum of the moral forces of the old South. It is a natural and legitimate development. It was under slavery that men learned the oppressive significance of the Negro's heritage from barbarism. It was under slavery that men first learned the presence of those latent capacities by which the Negro has so often transcended the limitations of that heritage. It was through the bond of slavery that the wiser South was taught, in the light of an immediate self-interest, the advantage to the white man in the Negro's integrity and skill—the disadvantage, indeed the peril, to the white man in the Negro's inefficiency and vice." [40]

Out of so great an evil as the enslavement of the black by the white race has been, there ought to be won some great good, both to the Negroes and to the whole human race. This is the deep conviction of the wisest Negro leaders.

" We are convinced," says Professor Kelly Miller, " that the whole movement must have been under the direction of a guiding hand higher than human intelligence or foresight. The incident evils that have grown out of the historic contact of these two

[39] Quoted by Murphy, *The Present South*, p. 5.
[40] *Ibid.*, p. 8; Hammond, *In Black and White*, p. 184.

races are but the logical outcome of a short-sighted and fatuous philosophy. The benefit to civilisation now flowing and destined to flow from this contact illustrates the teaching of history, that an overruling Providence makes the wrath of man to praise Him, while holding the remainder of wrath in restraint. Slavery was an institution of learning as well as of labour. There is no like instance in history where a weaker race in such large numbers has been introduced into the midst of the stronger race and has entered into the inheritance of civilisation. Inheritance is the reward of meekness. The galaxy of the Christian graces, loving kindness, humility and forgiveness of spirit are exemplified in the Negro character, and verily he has his reward." [41]

Two other instances of race injustice on the part of the white race in America were our treatment of the Indians and the method of our dealing with the problem of Chinese immigration. In the matter of the Indians, Mrs. Helen Hunt Jackson's *A Century of Dishonour* is the classic indictment of our national policy, " free from exaggeration and over-vehemence," as Col. Higginson said, and " thoroughly justified with facts and citations." And the late Bishop Whipple in repeated speeches and published statements set forth the wrongs which the Indians suffered at our hands. He charged that " in all our relations with the Indians we have persistently carried out the idea that they were a sovereign people." Yet, " they did not possess a single element of sovereignty and we never allowed them to exercise any except the matter of treaty making, and in this we habitually deceived them and habitually broke the treaties we made with them." We destroyed their tribal government and allowed no replacement of it.

" The only being in America who has no law to punish the guilty or protect the innocent is the treaty Indian. . . .   The only law administered by ourselves was to pay a premium for crime. . . .   The Government has really given the weight of influence on the side of heathen life. The sale of fire water has been almost unblushing. . . .   The system of trade was ruinous to honest traders and pernicious to the Indian. . . .   Every influence which could add to the degradation of this hapless race

---

[41] *The Missionary Review of the World,* June, 1922, art. " Negroes, both at Home and Abroad."

seems to be its inheritance. . . . The history of our dealings with the Indian has been marked by gross acts of injustice and robbery." [42]

A better day came for the Indians at last, but only after a long story of iniquitous race oppression and injustice perpetrated by a strong and intelligent race on a race that was ignorant and weak. It was not the wrong of man against man only. It was the wrong of race against race. John Quincy Adams called it in its early beginnings a "mass of putrefaction." The white race would not have thought of dealing with such faithlessness and cruelty with an equal race, able to resist it. [43]

Our dealings with the Chinese made an equally shameful though a much shorter story. It is wonderful that the Chinese should be able to cherish sucn kindly feelings as they do today toward America and in a lesser measure toward Europe when we recall what the Chinese race has had to endure. "I believe that you have the confidence of the people of China as it is possessed by no other nation," said His Excellency, Mr. Sze, the Chinese Minister to the United States, at a dinner of the China Society of America in September, 1921, "Most surely you have the good will of our Chinese millions to an almost unbounded extent. The good will of four hundred millions of people is a wonderful asset in this troubled world, and on our side we consider the good will of your hundred and ten millions as our most important haven in a stormy sea." It is good that wrongs can be so forgiven and forgotten. "It was the aggressive spirit and the violent conduct of the European nations which led the Chinese to close their ports against foreign commerce, and after two centuries of seclusion, it was a like influence of aggression and violence on the part of the same nations which was destined to compel the Chinese to reverse

---

[42] Whipple, *Lights and Shadows of a Long Episcopate*, pp. 124, 125, 140, 510-562.

[43] See our present relations to the Sioux and Pueblo Indians. New York *Times*, May 7, 1923, article, "Sioux Sue Nation for $700,000,000," and *Information Service*, Research Department, Commission on the Church and Social Service, Federal Council of the Churches of Christ in America, Feb. 3, 1923, p. 5 f., art. "The Case of the Pueblo Indians."

their policy and again to open their ports to the world." [44]   Later
the coolie trade grew up,—" the procurement from southern China
of labourers, their transportation to Peru, Cuba, and other countries nominally under a contract of service for a term of years, but
virtually constituting a system of slavery with all its attendant
hardships and horrors. The American consul at Hongkong, who
was familiar with this traffic, reported to his government that it
differed from the African slave-trade ' in little else than the employment of fraud instead of force to make its victims captive.'
Secretary Seward, who visited China on his tour of the world
about the time when it was at its height, described it as ' an abomination scarcely less execrable than the African slave-trade.' . . .
It is estimated that more than one hundred thousand Chinese
coolies were taken to Peru and about one hundred and fifty thousand to Cuba. . . . They were treated as slaves, branded,
lashed, and tortured, and their condition was so wretched that
many sought relief in death." [45]   In due time the United States
prohibited American vessels from engaging in the trade and welcomed the Chinese to come as immigrants to the country. We
shall consider later the question of the propriety of the restriction
or prohibition of immigration. We have to note here, however,
that the Burlingame treaty with China, in 1868, recognised on the
part of both governments the inherent and inalienable right of
man to change his home and allegiance, and also the mutual advantage of the free immigration and emigration of their citizens
and subjects respectively from one country to the other for purposes of curiosity, of trade, or as permanent residents, and " provided that the citizens and subjects respectively ' shall enjoy the
same privileges, immunities, or exemptions in respect to travel or
residence as may there be enjoyed by the citizens or subjects of the
most favoured nation." [46]   Thousands of Chinese labourers accordingly came over to America for railroad building and other
service. Mr. Fish, Secretary of State under President Grant,
wrote, " Every month brings thousands of Chinese immigrants to

[44] Foster, *American Diplomacy in the Orient,* p. 25.
[45] *Ibid.,* pp. 275, 277.
[46] *Ibid.,* p. 283.

the Pacific Coast. Already they have crossed the great mountains and are beginning to be found in the interior of the continent. By their assiduity, patience, and fidelity, and by their intelligence, they earn the good-will and confidence of those who employ them. We have good reason to think this thing will continue and increase;" and the Secretary said it was welcomed by the country.[47] Strong opposition soon developed and a Congressional Commission was appointed in 1876 to visit the Pacific Coast and report. The Commission held

" that an indigestible mass in the community, distinct in language, pagan in religion, inferior in mental and moral qualities, was an undesirable element in a republic, and especially so if political power should be placed in its hands; that the safety of the state demanded that such power should not be so placed, and the safety of the immigrant depended upon that power. It was painfully evident from the testimony that the Pacific coast must in time become either American or Mongolian; that while conditions were favourable to the growth and occupancy of the Pacific States by Americans, the Chinese had advantages which would put them far in advance in the race for possession; and that the presence of Chinese discouraged and retarded white immigration." [48]

As a result of this report Congress passed exclusion laws in direct violation of the Burlingame treaty, and without consulting China abrogated the articles relating to the free immigration and residence of Chinese. Several years later a new treaty was made in which it was agreed that the United States might regulate, limit or suspend immigration of labourers but not prohibit it, other classes of Chinese to enter freely and reside. In two years Congress overrode this treaty and China again assented to the policy of exclusion in more rigid terms. She assents today, and has endured also the most oppressive treatment of her scholars and merchants seeking to enter our land. If it was wrong, as it was, for Germany to treat her treaty with Belgium as a scrap of paper,

---

[47] *Ibid.*, p. 284; See Nevius, *China and the Chinese*, p. 286 f.; Denby, *China and Her People*, Vol. II, Chap. IX.
[48] Foster, *American Diplomacy in the Orient*, p. 288.

was it less wrong in principle for us to do the same with our Chinese treaties? [49]

But treaty violation is not the only feature of our wrong race relations with the Chinese. The record of terrorism and injustice visited upon the Chinese who were lawfully in the United States, was a record of racial shame. As Kok An Wee writes in his thesis on *The Status of the Chinese in the United States:*

" The Chinese were beaten in the streets, plundered by superior numbers, and burdened with excessive taxes; but they could not refuse these buffets, for they had no suffrage to protect them, and were not recognised as equals in the courts. They were sneered at as cheap labourers, but nothing was said of the Italians, the Hungarians, and the Norwegians who were paid less. They were hated as gold exporters who made the states poor; but the prosperity of the states has been partly due to them, and the benefits of their labour have accrued to the communities in which they toiled. They were scorned as pagans; but at first their teachers and ministers were prohibited entering here and their preacher was deported as a labourer. They were reviled as non-lovers of home, but nothing was intimated of the chance that their loved ones might be confronted with insult and opprobrium at the portals, because it was not stated that the wives of labourers could not enter with their husbands. They were shunned as diseased; but no hospitals were opened to them. They were denounced as criminals and paupers; but the statistics of jails, asylums, and poor-houses have shown that these places were least of all frequented by them. They were condemned as unassimilable; but the public schools were not opened for their attendance, and education and the road to citizenship was barred."

And again and again unoffending Chinese were slaughtered like rabbits and no punishment was meted out to their murderers.

There seems to have been little or no racial antipathy against the Chinese at the outset. Gradually, however, they came to be feared. Their unassimilability, their economic efficiency, their mental, moral and industrial divergence, and qualities equally good and bad on our own side brought on a racial clash. And neither

---

[49] *China and the Far East.* Paper by F. W. Williams, "A Sketch of the Relations Between the United States and China," pp. 47-82.

the spirit of justice nor the spirit of love was applied to find the right solution of the problem.

The history of race prejudice in America has not been confined to our relations with Negroes, Indians and Chinese. (1) The Italians had for years many of the same difficulties experienced by the Chinese and for some of the same reasons. The worst outbreak of race animosity against them was in the Louisiana riots in 1894-5, which led to a long negotiation with Italy over the failure of the State of Louisiana to punish the murderers and the inability of the national government to deal with crimes which could not be denied but which fell only under state jurisdiction. It was then that President McKinley raised the question as to whether the national government ought not to be equipped with all the power necessary to fulfill national obligations. Surely it could not be right, he argued, to contract national or racial obligations and then to set up the internal political policies of one party to the contract as an excuse for their violation. We would not tolerate such an excuse from the other race. How could we set it up for ourselves? Ought not races to act under codes of equal obligation in treaty fulfilment? (2) There has been anti-British feeling in the nation ever since colonial times. We have already referred to the part which the Scotch-Irish animosity to the English played in the Revolutionary War. The large number of Irish who have come to America since, their sense of grievance against England, the national sympathy of America with people under oppression, whether real or apparent, and the manipulation of racial antipathies for political or religious ends have helped to intensify the early sentiment of anti-English prejudice. The course of Great Britain in the Civil War [50] and the nature of a great deal of the intercourse of the English and the American people for three generations aggravated this prejudice. Strong forces are at work today both to perpetuate and to remove it.

The problem of race relations with the Jews will present itself later, and it is a European as much as an American question. It

---

[50] See *Education of Henry Adams*, pp. 110-179, and *A Cycle of Adams Letters*.

suffices here to remind ourselves that the race clashes which we
have known in America have been far exceeded in all the other
continents, except perhaps South America, and that there, while
intermarriage has mingled all the races, as will appear, there remains almost as sharp a racial cleavage between the old Spaniard
and the Indian as between white and black in the United States.
The history of Europe is a story of interracial struggle. It is true
that there are no pure races there and that the struggle has been
between races all of them inextricably mixed, but there has been
identity enough in the amalgams to make the conflict in reality a
conflict of race culture and ambition, languages and religions.
Africa has been the scene of a prolonged and intricate racial
wrestle. Many native races have been exterminated and some like
the Bushmen are nearly gone. Dr. Stewart said he had seen only
a few individuals: " The Bushmen have almost disappeared, having been hunted off the face of the earth by their enemies both
black and white, both colours having been their inveterate enemies." [51] Tribal wars, the slave trade and the great tidal wave of
the Bantu conquests have wiped out whole peoples and altered the
racial map of the Continent. In Asia the race struggle has been
as old as history and as new as today—between the peoples whose
story is recorded in the Old Testament, the shadowy tribes who
move about in the mists of early legend, and the composite elements now making up each Asiatic nation; between Aryan, Dravidian, Scythian, Iranian, Marathas, Brahmans, Rajputs, Mongol
in India; between Chinese, Mongol, and Tartar in China; Japanese and Korean; Malay, Chinese, Indian, Siamese and Eurasian
in the Malay Peninsula. It is all one long tale of race discord and
no race has been free from it, neither Russian nor British nor
any other.[52]

The whole story and the world's abiding problem may be summarised in two concrete illustrations, one forgotten in fact, and
the other officially forgotten though it stands in the centre of
modern history.

[51] Stewart, *Dawn in the Dark Continent*, p. 82.
[52] Vambery, *Western Culture in Eastern Lands*, pp. 60, 79; Nundy, *Indian
Unrest*, pp. 11-16; Nundy, *Political Problems*, Ch. III, VI, X.

1. The first is the story of the Cagots of France. Their origin is unknown. Some have held that they were descendants of exiled lepers; others that they were descendants of ancient Gauls enslaved by the people who drove out the Romans; others that they are a remnant of the Alans, or of the Goths. Michel traces their settlement in southern France to the disastrous return of Charlemagne from his expedition into Spain and to the battle of Roncesvalles. Whatever their origin, however, they were for centuries, as Michelet terms them, " the Pariahs of the West," and their lot typifies the possibilities of racial antipathy and injustice. Their race was regarded as infamous and its members as outcasts from the family of mankind.

" They were shunned and hated; were allotted separate quarters in towns, called ' cagoteries,' and lived in wretched huts in the country distinct from the villages. Excluded from all political and social rights, they were only allowed to enter a church by a special door, and during the service a rail separated them from the other worshippers. Either they were altogether forbidden to partake of the sacrament, or the holy wafer was handed to them on the end of a stick, while a receptacle for holy water was reserved for their exclusive use. They were compelled to wear a distinctive dress, to which, in some places, was attached the foot of a goose or duck (whence they were sometimes called ' Canards '). And so pestilential was their touch considered that it was a crime for them to walk the common road barefooted. The only trades allowed them were those of butcher and carpenter, and their ordinary occupation was wood-cutting." [53]

This hatred is past now and the Cagots have been readmitted to humanity.

2. The other illustration is the story of the Armenians and Assyrians and their expulsion from their homes in Turkey and Persia and their threatened racial destruction before the eyes of mankind. The Armenians are one of the oldest Christian races and their Gregorian Church is one of the oldest Christian Churches. They lived in their Anatolian homes centuries before

---

[53] *Encyclopedia Britannica*, art. on " Cagots." See also article in Williams's *Miscellanies*, pp. 388-391.

the Turks appeared on the pages of history. Now they have been driven from Turkey, from their own land, and save for the territory allowed them under Russian Soviet authority around their ancient seat in trans-Caucasia, the race is homeless. No doubt some of the Armenian revolutionaries committed crimes in the name of freedom. No doubt there have been dishonest Armenian people. No doubt the nation's service, both through sympathy and national interest, and the compulsion of relationship with Russia and France, was thrown with the Allies in the World War. The case against the Armenians from the point of view of the Turks may be made never so black. Nevertheless these facts are sure: the only right of the Turk to rule over the Armenian and to dispossess him of his country was the right of military force; the Western nations were bound by treaty, by official promises and by every consideration of justice to provide for the Armenian race security, freedom and a national home; Great Britain holds the Island of Cyprus under a convention with Turkey in which the first article declared, " H. I. M. the Sultan promises to England to introduce necessary reforms, to be agreed upon later between the two powers, into the Government and for the protection of the Christians and other subjects of the Porte in these territories (Armenia) and in order to enable England to make necessary provision for executing her engagements, H. I. M. the Sultan further consents to assign the Island of Cyprus to be occupied and administered by England "; France took Cilicia under mandate from the League of Nations and used Armenian troops to hold it and then instead of returning it to the League or transferring it to the Armenians for their home, betrayed its Armenian allies and delivered Cilicia to Turkey. And then on January 10, 1923, surely one of the blackest days in human history, the great Powers of Europe at Lausanne listened to the representatives of the Turks, 7,500,000 in number, scattered over a country which they had wrested from its original and surviving racial owners, larger in area than France or Germany, as these representatives announced that Turkey intended to expel all Greeks and Armenians from Turkey except, for the present, from

Constantinople.[54] Here the racial question brought in Greeks as well as Armenians, but the lesson of the tragedy of race discord is the same, and worse; and became only ampler in volume and involved more innocent people on both sides of the racial lines, when it was proposed, as part of a wholesale migration, exalting the idea of racial antipathy to the very skies, that 450,000 Turks must also be torn and exiled from their homes in Macedonia and the rest of Greece. Obviously the race problem is too great for man.[55] For the solution of expulsion is no solution. Greek and Armenian blood is running thick in Turkish veins. Can that be expelled? Turkey's own prosperity has received as heavy a blow as she has given the races she has wronged. " Of 48 Grand Viziers of note during four centuries," says Prof. Porter, of Beirut, " only twelve were of Turkish ancestry, the others were Armenian or Greek by descent. The Turks have had to depend on these races for their business and finance and in destroying them they are bringing upon themselves financial ruin." The Turks are to be pitied. Across the centuries they have suffered as well as inflicted wrong and now in the effort at self preservation and assertion they are exchanging for exploitation by the Western races what might have been made under a right solution of racial problems a happy co-operation of races in a transformed Turkish Empire. Only it could not have been transformed and remained Moslem.[56]

The Near East tragedy is also one evidence of the inevitable association of race antipathy or misunderstanding and war. There is too much warrant in history for the view which is common among students of race relationships that these relationships

[54] New York *Times*, Jan. 11, 1923.
[55] Bryce, *The Treatment of the Armenians*, Blue Book No. 31, 1916, *Reconstruction in Turkey*, edited by William H. Hall; *Report of International Commission to Inquire into the Cause and Conduct of the Balkan Wars;* Crabites, *Armenia and the Armenians;* Dowling, *The Armenian Church;* Greene, *Leavening the Levant,* pp. 33-48; Speer, *Missions and Modern History*, Vol. II, Chap. IX, and authorities cited there. For the Turkish side of the case see the New York *Times, Current History*, Feb., 1923, pp. 749-764; June, 1923, pp. 393-400; Djemal Pasha, *Memoirs of a Turkish Statesman.* pp. 241-302.
[56] Toynbee, *The Western Question in Greece and Turkey; Reconstruction in Turkey*· Koelle, *Mohammed and Mohammedanism*.

must be construed in terms of conflict, economic and social always, and if necessary, military. It is impossible to draw a clear line between race and nationality, and much may be charged to race which is really due to a false development of the spirit of nationalism. The World War was not a race war at all. Kindred races were on opposite sides and races between which the deepest antipathies are supposed to exist were on the same side. In the Civil War also, though the status of the Negro race was one of the issues, the war was between two sections of what was then and is still, the most homogeneous race in the world. Nevertheless race prejudices are the cause, or are intertwined with the causes, of war. The spirit of brotherhood and the ideal of humanity, if they were dominant over race alienation, would find a way without war to settle disagreements which can be settled by peaceable means and would prevent the development of any other kind of disagreement. If we can solve the problem of race we shall prevent war. It is conceivable that wrongs within a race might still lead to revolution, but it is not probable that in a world of inter-racial good will and justice there would be any root of war left inside any race. Consider what we have paid in the world war alone for our failure to have solved the race problem. *The Staggering Burden of Armament*, published by the World Peace Foundation, summarises the cost of the last war, under the heading " The Doom of the Taxpayer ":

" The financial aspect of armament may properly be first considered in connection with the world war. The total direct cost of the war, not counting interest charges, is officially given at $186,000,000,000 for all belligerents. The capitalised value of human life destroyed, soldiers and civilians, on a conservative basis is given as $67,102,552,560. The claims for damages against Germany, constituting part of the price she pays for the privilege of using her armament, preferred under the treaty of Versailles by the parties thereto as officially reported to the Reparation Commission, but without review, was $47,639,092,718, or about a billion a month for the duration of the war. Shipping and cargo losses are given as $6,800,000,000; loss of production at $45,-000,000,000; war relief and loss to neutrals at $2,750,000,000. These figures total $355,291,719,815.

"It may roughly be said that $350,000,000,000 is the financial handicap that the world has taken on since 1914.

"The loss of life is given in a compilation of the Danish Research Society on the Social Results of the War as follows:

	Dec. in Birth Rate.	Loss Through Inc. of Death Rate.	Among Those Killed in War.
Germany	3,600,000	2,700,000	2,000,000
Austria-Hungary	3,800,000	2,000,000	1,500,000
Gt. Britain, Ireland.	850,000	1,000,000	800,000
France	1,500,000	1,840,000	1,400,000
Belgium	175,000	400,000	115,000
Italy	1,400,000	880,000	600,000
Bulgaria	155,000	130,000	65,000
Rumania	150,000	360,000	159,000
Servia	320,000	1,330,000	690,000
Europe	8,300,000	4,700,000	2,500,000
Russia and Poland.	20,250,000	15,130,000	9,829,000

"The worst of these percentages is not their size. The worst of it is that these post-war figures would only be cut about 15 per cent. if the world returned to its former habits. The United States, which just now is setting the pace in armament competition used to spend more than 70 per cent. of its total annual budget for war purposes, not in a single year only, but on the basis of the running of the government since 1870. Here are the figures:

EXPENDITURES FOR ARMED PEACE AND WAR.

	1870-1916, Omitting Spanish-American and World Wars. 47 years.	1870-1919, Including Spanish-American and World Wars. 50 years.
Army	$3,956,346,000	$19,334,031,000
Navy	2,594,530,000	6,229,612,000
Interest	2,455,865,000	3,294,001,000
Pensions	4,906,803,000	5,469,874,000
	$13,913,544,000—71.5	$34,327,578,000—76.4
All other purposes	5,543,727,000—28.5	10,672,148,000—23.6
Total	$19,457,271,000—100.0	$44,937,065,000—100.0

" The burden of this debt brings it about that every belligerent has such staggering taxation as to hamper all the processes of national and individual life." [57]

The price which the world has paid and pays today for race misunderstanding and suspicion and conflict and maladjustment, if the race problem be soluble, proves either the incompetence or the iniquity or the insanity of mankind.

There are other forms of racial struggle which fall short of war, but which are full of political peril and fruitful of social evil. There may be good purpose in some of these and there may be real evils with which they endeavour to deal, but nevertheless they may be cast in forms of secrecy and violence which make open and righteous settlements impossible. The Ku Klux Klan in its present revival is an illustration. And the utterances of its spokesmen show the mixture of good and evil in it. An " Exalted Cyclops " spoke in a church in Newark, N. J., on March 11, 1923:

" This is a white man's organisation for exalting the Caucasian race and teaching the doctrine of white supremacy. This does not mean, as some would have you believe, that we are enemies of the coloured and mongrel races, but does mean that we are organised to maintain the solidarity of the white race.

" This is a Gentile organisation, and as such has as its mission, the interpretation of the highest ideals of the white Gentile people. However, we sing no hymns of hate against the Jew.

" It is a Protestant organisation, and its membership is restricted to those who accept the tenets of true Christianity, which is essentially Protestant. We can say to the world that our fathers founded this as a Protestant country and our purpose is to establish and maintain it as such. While we will support energetically the principles of Protestantism, we will also maintain the principle of religious liberty as essential for the future growth and development of this country." [58]

But the movement speaks with a more malicious voice. The " Imperial Wizard " is reported in the Klan paper as saying, in an address on April 30, 1923,—

---

[57] See also Col. Ayres's *The War with Germany, a Statistical Summary published by the War Department.*
[58] Reported in the New York *Times,* March 12, 1923.

" America is a garbage can, not a melting pot. . . . When the hordes of aliens walk to the ballot box and their votes outnumber yours, then that horde has got you by the throat. All of these folks of colour can take their place—they had better take it and stay in it when they get in it. . . . I am informed that every buck nigger in Atlanta who attains the age of twenty-one years has gotten the money to pay his poll tax and register, and that 6,000,000 of them are now ready to vote, and that these apes are going to line up at the polls, mixed up there with white men and white women. Lord forgive me, but that is the most sickening and disgusting sight you ever saw. You've got to change that. . . . Keep the Negro and the other fellow where he belongs. They have got no part in our political and social life. . . . To assure the supremacy of the white race we believe in the exclusion of the yellow race and the disfranchisement of the Negro. It was God's act to make the white race superior to all others. By some scheme of Providence the Negro was created a serf." [59]

With such inspiration still others commit themselves openly to doctrines of race and religious hate and exclusiveness. One writes :

" The American Idea resists and expels the Jew, the Roman Catholic and the Negro, because their character is antagonistic to the principle of Americanism.

" The Negro is the son of Ham, whose rightful heritage and natural habitat is Africa. He was torn from his native soil, brought to this country and sold into slavery, through sinister papal intrigue. The error of importing the Negro into America can be corrected only by his return to Africa. . . .

" The presence of these three foreign elements, the Jew, the Roman Catholic and the Negro, in any portion of this hemisphere, is incompatible with the peace and safety of America, with her dignity as the spiritual leader of the world, and with her prophesied destiny to be the Kingdom of God ' on earth as it is in heaven.' . . .

" The (Protestant) American people have banded themselves together in secret organisation, with the avowed and fixed purpose to drive everyone of these aliens—Roman Catholics, and their allies, the Jews and Negroes—from our midst." [60]

---

[59] Quoted in New York *Christian Advocate,* Dec. 14, 1922.
[60] Quoted in *Federal Council Bulletin,* Feb.-March, 1923. See *The Country Editor,* Feb., 1923, art. " The World Wide Vision of the Ku Klux

Such intolerance is the destruction of liberty in the name of liberty. There ought to be religious and racial freedom. If the ᴋoman Catholic Church were to attempt ecclesiastical domination, as it established it in other times and other lands, it would be necessary to resist and defeat it. If Jew or Negro were to attempt, in the case of the Jew, financial domination, or in the case of the Negro, any usurpation of rights which do not politically or socially belong to him, the rest of society would be justified in taking the measures appropriate to its protection. But race and religious injustice are not the right way to prevent the supposed threat of such injustice. They only invite and instigate it.

Still another evil expression of racial strife is our atrocious institution of lynching. It is not wholly an inter-race crime. In 1922 there were 57 lynchings in the United States, of which fifty-one were Negroes and six white. They occurred in ten states, all southern: 18 in Texas, 11 in Georgia, 9 in Mississippi, etc. The year 1923 showed great progress in the repression of lynching. In 39 states no lynchings occurred that year. Nine states bore the shame of the 28 lynchings which took place. For the first time since comprehensive records of lynchings have been kept, South Carolina and Alabama were free from the crime. The number of lynchings in 1923 was the lowest in any year recorded. The next lowest was 38 in 1917, and the highest 253 in 1892, when there were lynchings in 33 states. Of the 28 lynchings in 1923, 26 of the victims were Negroes, two being women.[61] Between 1885 and 1922, the number of persons lynched, always by mobs, was 4,154.

" Of the total number lynched during this period, 1,034 were white and 3,120 were Negro victims. Doubtless many more of whom no record was made were similarly murdered. In 1919 there were 83 persons lynched; in 1920 there were 61; in 1921, 64; and in 1922 there were at least 57 lynched.

" Some of those lynched by mobs were charged with crime; many of them were charged with misdemeanors only; some only

Klan "; March, 1923, art. " Proposed Overthrow of the United States Government."
[61] See a slightly variant report in *The Christian Work*, Jan. 5, 1924, p. 3.

with words or acts which are nowhere at any time punishable by law. All were slain without trial where they might have faced their accusers, had witnesses and had the evidence considered by a lawful judge or jury. The frenzied mob was judge, jury, and executioner.

"In many cases persons not sought by the mobs have been lynched by mistake, so wild and savage has been the procedure. Some of the victims suffered indescribable torture, such as saturation of parts of the body with kerosene or gasoline so that they could be burned piecemeal, branding with hot irons, or the gouging out of the eyes and ears with red hot rods.

"The states free from this blot are few in number. There are only four—Massachusetts, New Hampshire, Rhode Island, and Vermont—where such an atrocity has not been recorded for any community in the Commonwealth.

"Rape is usually alleged as the principal cause of lynchings. Certainly such a crime could not be attributed to the 83 women victims! As a matter of fact nearly four-fifths of all the lynchings in thirty-seven years have been for alleged crimes other than rape or for alleged acts that are not crimes or misdemeanors under any law, common or statute.

"Out of 4,097 victims only 829—60 white and 769 Negroes— were lynched on the charge of rape or attempted rape. This is only 20.2 per cent. of the total. And it should be remembered that these men had been accused, not convicted, of the crime.

"More than one-third of the victims lynched since 1889 were accused of homicide or felonious assault. About one-twelfth were accused of crime against property; some were alleged to have 'insulted' white persons; and more than 145 were not recorded as accused of any crime whatsoever.

"Mob law undermines the very foundations of government, law and order." [62]

The poison of race passions creeps back into the hating race. If white people can do wrong to Negroes, why should they not do wrong also to their own race? Mob violence against black men is a sure school for contempt of law among the whites. All race injustice has its Nemesis. "Mob law is anarchy," says an editorial in the Louisville, Ky., Times. "It brutalises the community.

---

[62] New York Times, Jan. 1, 1923; Federal Council Bulletin, Feb.-March, 1923; "Mob Murder in America," published by the Commission on the Church and Race Relations of the Federal Council of the Churches of Christ in America.

It lowers the standards of whites and blacks. It discourages the ambitions of Negroes to be good citizens. It is anarchy and has no place in civilisation." And the Christian South is resolved to suppress it utterly.[63] The Christian women of the South, moreover, refuse to allow the crime to take shelter behind the plea of chivalry. One of the strongest of their deliverances is from the representative women of South Carolina:

" Believing that the double standard of morals, in regard to races as well as sex, is a quicksand which threatens to undermine our civilisation, we appeal for the creation of a public sentiment which will no longer tolerate this condition; but which will demand protection for all womanhood.

" There is no crime more dangerous than that which strikes at the root of constituted authority, breaks all restraints of civilisation, and substitutes mob violence and masked irresponsibility for established justice. There is no greater fallacy than that which holds up the shield of Southern womanhood in defense of the crime of lynching and burning of human beings, claiming that such acts are the outcome of Southern chivalry.

" Therefore, we utterly repudiate such sentiments and condemn such practices and recommend that all people give themselves to a definite study of these vital matters relating to justice and righteousness, and that the press, pulpit, platform, and school, as well as the potent influence of the home, be used unsparingly to lead public opinion to insure justice and compel the protection and purity of both races." [64]

Stronger language with regard to lynching could hardly be used than that of a recent Georgia Baptist Convention, declaring that lynching " is a cancer on our body politic and a disgrace to our Christian civilisation. The Christian church, surely our own, must sound the knell to anarchy in all its forms; but more especially when a band of men arrogate to themselves the right to become government, court, jury, witnesses, and thus proceed to commit murder. It is diabolical. It is hellish. It puts government, so-

---

[63] See resolution of southern women, *Fisk University News*, Oct., 1923, p. 21 f.
[64] *The Southern Workman*, Feb., 1923, p. 56 f.

ciety, and the church at the mercy of the hobgoblins of the underworld. We must admit of no exceptions. There are none." [65]

The evil that lies back of all others in the abuses of race is the fundamental evil of race assumption and privilege, the idea of a race that it has a right of prescriptive precedence over other races, a false pride in the sense of superior race culture, the conception of aristocratic race-values entitling one race to dominate other races, the spirit of race suspicion and distrust, the application to race relations of the principle of gain and exploitation rather than of use and trusteeship and brotherhood. Feelings like these and the institutions which support them or which they support are bad for all races. They embitter the races which feel themselves to be wronged and they embitter the races which are accused by other races or by their own consciences of wrongdoing. Hate and evil engender themselves. As Dewey says: " The disdain and contempt of the overlord class for the inferior is moreover usually complicated by an uneasy subconscious feeling that perhaps the subject people is not really so inferior as its political status indicates." And this begets more dislike and fear. These evils are not limited to any one race or set of race relationships. Some of them characterised even the professed communism of the Russian Soviet. The Indians are prone to charge such evils against the British in India,[66] but some of these very evils are found in the most enlightened intelligence of India. Under the cry of " Bande Mataram," " Hail Motherland," the doctrine of race superiority has been preached in India as eloquently as in the West. The Ethiopian movement in South Africa has made use of the same shibboleths against the whites with which we have dealt in America in our discussions of the subject of Chinese and Japanese immigration. To get rid of the evils of race friction and conflict we

---

[65] *Ibid.,* p. 57.

[66] See C. R. Jain, *Where the Shoe Pinches,* p. 17 f., for typical illustration: "To sum up: The British rule is unpopular (1) because of the tyranny and injustice that are practiced in its name and under its shelter by the subordinate officials and their satellites, (2) because of the indifference and inefficiency of the higher officials, (3) because of the loss of faith in the administration of justice, and (4) because of the offensive behaviour of certain Europeans."

must go behind them to the fountains and establish in men's minds right thoughts about race relations and right feelings toward all their fellow men irrespective of their colour or race and secure the establishment of the economic and political ideals and relationships which will remove the cancer of race friction and injustice.

Abraham Lincoln is proof that spiritually this can be done, that the problem of race is not too great for the mind and spirit of men who seek to know and obey the laws of God. " In all my interviews with Mr. Lincoln," said Frederick Douglass, " I was impressed with his entire freedom from popular prejudice against the coloured race. He was the first great man that I talked with in the United States freely, who in no single instance reminded me of the difference between himself and myself, of the difference of colour and I thought that all the more remarkable because he came from a state where there were black laws." [67]   Lincoln never supposed that he had solved the race problem. He knew that slavery was only one aspect of it and that the abolition of slavery created more problems than it solved, and he felt the deepest anxiety over the innumerable aspects of the great questions which remained. Before the war he had not been ready for Negro franchise. In 1853 in a campaign letter he wrote: " I go for all sharing the privilege of government who assist in bearing its burdens. Consequently I go for admitting all whites to the right of suffrage who pay taxes or bear arms, by no means excluding females." In 1854 he said, " Labour is prior to and independent of capital. Capital is only the fruit of labour and could never have existed if labour had not first existed. Labour is the support of capital and deserves much the higher consideration." Utterances like these led on, however, to his statement in his last public declaration that he was in favour of extending the elective franchise to coloured men.[68] How he would have changed the conditions of its extension we do not know. He believed in equality. In 1855 he said, " Our progress in degeneracy appears to me to be pretty rapid. As a nation we began by declaring that *all men*

----

[67] *Reminiscences of Lincoln*, p. 193.
[68] *Ibid.*, p. 129 f.

are created equal. We now practically read it *all men are created equal except Negroes."* Later we enlarged the exception to exclude all but the Nordic race! At the same time he saw the coming issues and General Butler tells of a conversation in which Lincoln indicated his anxiety for some solution.[69] And yet Lincoln had found, and he himself was, the solution of the race problem, the hope and the assurance of the escape of men from the evils of race friction and injustice. By the facts of sympathy and brotherhood and truth he evaded or denied none of the facts of race difference or human inequality; he proposed no doctrinaire scheme of equalitarianism or amalgamation; nor did he, on the other hand, erect any walls of forbidden advance against any human beings nor set up the generalised abstraction of race character against capacity or virtue. With him, as with Burns, man was man. There are realities in all human intercourse—affinities, conventions, working arrangements for human happiness and well-being and progress. We must come soon to consider these. But the final thought with which this chapter leaves us is the thought of man as man, brother and friend to every other man, and transcending in this good will and helpfulness all the gulfs and chasms of race.

> " Then let us pray that come it may
>   As come it will for a' that,—
> That Sense and Worth, o'er a' the earth,
>   May bear the gree, and a' that.
> For a' that, and a' that,
>   It's coming yet for a' that,—
> That man to man, the warld o'er
>   Shall brothers be for a' that."

Mr. Mornay Williams has written a prayer which we might all profitably use:

" O God, who hast made man in Thine own likeness and who dost love all whom Thou hast made, suffer us not because of differences in race, colour, or condition, to separate ourselves one

---
[69] *Ibid.,* p. 151 ff.

from another, and thereby from Thee: but teach us the unity of
Thy family and the universality of Thy love. As Thy Son, our
Saviour, was born of a Hebrew mother and ministered first to
His brethren of the House of Israel, but rejoiced in the faith of
a Syro-Phœnician woman and of a Roman soldier, and suffered
His cross to be carried by a man of Africa, teach us also, while
loving and serving our own, to enter into the communion of the
whole human family: and forbid it that from pride of birth and
hardness of heart we should despise any for whom Christ died,
or injure any in whom He lives. Amen." [70]

And one of our American denominations, the Reformed Church
in the United States, has a special prayer for these needs: " From
the sins that divide us; from all class bitterness and race hatred;
from forgetfulness of Thee and indifference to our fellowmen;
from war and the preparation for new wars; Good Lord, deliver
us. From the corruption of the franchise and of civil government; from greed and hardness of heart against our neighbour;
from the arbitrary exercise of power; Good Lord, deliver us."

---

[70] Williams, *Prayers and Hymns*, p. 3.

V

ASPECTS AND RELATIONS OF RACE

THE race question, as has appeared, is a question not of the relation of race to race only, but also of the relation of race to colour, climate, nationality, religion, language, communications and social and moral ideals. We shall be better prepared to consider the various proposed solutions of the race problem if we first examine some of these conditioning elements.

1. Race and colour. The criterion of race now most commonly used is colour. Head measurements and indices of one kind and another have proved too confusing and erratic. Colour has seemed to be a simple and more accurate differential. And many of the modern race studies accordingly have resolved the race issue into a colour issue. Some of these, as we have seen, have gone so far as to talk of " white " and " black " blood, and less sophisticated peoples have conceived God as of their favourite racial complexion. Even Charles Carroll argued that since man was created in God's image, and as God was not a Negro, it followed that the Negro was not made after the image of God and therefore was not a man.[1] For the most part, however, colour is simply used as a synonym for race, and deep issues which are cultural or political or national are carelessly identified with colour, as by Lord Chelmsford, ex-Viceroy of India, for example, in a speech in Parliament on conditions in India in which he said that " the real root of all the unrest and agitation in India was the race or colour issue." And he proceeded in the strain now grown so familiar to us: " There was a revolt of the coloured races going on all over the world against the ascendency of the white races. But though it was not merely an Indian problem, it met them in almost every Indian question which came up—it was an all-

---

[1] *The Presbyterian Magazine,* May, 1923, p. 269.

pervading issue. Two consequences had flowed from this. In the past we governed India on the basis of the acknowledged superiority of the British race. That superiority was now challenged, and in surveying the situation, they could not ignore that the challenge had been made. The colour issue had become a unifying force in India, and through all the diversity of creeds and races, it was creating union." [2]

Two separate questions emerge. What is the relation of colour to race? What is the relation of colour to race prejudice?

a. Modern physiology is assured that colour is a matter not of race plasm or fixed heredity, but of climatic environment.[3] Von Luschan objects to racial classification on the basis of colour.

" We now know," he says, perhaps forgetting the Eskimos, " that colour of skin and hair is only the effect of environment, and that we are fair only because our ancestors lived for thousands, or probably tens of thousands, of years in sunless and foggy countries. Fairness is nothing else but lack of pigment, and our ancestors lost part of their pigment because they did not need it. Just as the Proteus sanguineus and certain beetles became blind in caves, where their eyes were useless, so we poor fair people have to wear dark glasses and gloves when walking on a glacier and get our skin burned when we expose it unduly to the light of the sun.

" It is therefore only natural that certain Indian races and the Singhalese are dark; and it would be absurd to call them ' savage ' on that account, as they have an ancient civilisation, and had a noble and refined religion at a time when our own ancestors had a very low standard of life. . . .

" It is also said of the primitive races that they are not as cleanly as we are. Those who say this, however, forget the dirt of eastern Europe, and are ignorant that most primitive men bathe every day, and that the Bantu and many other Africans clean their teeth after every meal for more than half an hour with their msuaki, while on the contrary, millions of Europeans never use a tooth brush." [4]

And another speaker at the Universal Races Congress, Pro-

[2] *The Times of India,* Nov. 17, 1921.
[3] Dixon, *The Racial History of Man,* pp. 478-480.
[4] *Universal Races Congress,* 1911, p. 14.

fessor Lyde, Professor of Economic Geography at University
College, London, declared:

"There is no doubt that difference of skin-colour is one of
the greatest 'racial' barriers, and yet there can be little doubt
that it is entirely a matter of climatic control. . . . The fundamental differences of skin-colour between the black tropical and
the white temperate types of man are, therefore, of purely climatic
origin, the climatic influence working both directly from without
and indirectly through the different relative activities of lungs and
intestines, the tropical climate throwing on the skin and the intestines work which the temperate climate throws on the lungs.
The consequent increased activity of the lungs, in the presence of
relatively little sun-light and sun-heat, favours the lighter colour
of skin, while the increased activity of the liver and other intestines, in the presence of relatively great sun-light and sun-heat,
favours the darker colour. Under these circumstances it seems
obvious that, whatever the value or the worthlessness of skin
colour as a test of 'race,' it is enormously the most important consideration in the climatic distribution of man."[5]

Colour as colour is purely a matter of the skin, not a matter of
racial character, and even as a differentiating mark it is very inaccurate and misleading. There are many Negroes with "white"
blood in their veins, who are fixed by our present idea within the
Negro race, who are nevertheless much fairer than many Caucasians. Unless it was known by some other evidence that they
were not pure white people, their colour would not mark their
race. The futility of colour as a race sign, save in the crudest
fashion, is undeniable. The *India Census Report* of 1901 deals
with this fact:

"For ethnological purposes physical characters may be said to
be of two kinds, *indefinite* characters which can only be described
in more or less appropriate language, and *definite* characters which
admit of being measured and reduced to numerical expression.
The former class, usually called descriptive or secondary characters, includes such points as the colour and texture of the skin;
the colour, form and position of the eyes; the colour and character
of the hair; and the form of the face and features. Conspicuous

---

[5] *Ibid.*, paper on "Climatic Control of Skin Colour," p. 104.

as these traits are, the difficulty of observing, defining, and recording them is extreme.   Colour, the most striking of them all, is perhaps the most evasive, and deserves further mention as a typical instance of the shortcomings of the descriptive method.   Some forty years ago the French anthropologist Broca devised a chromatic scale consisting of twenty shades, regularly graduated and numbered, for registering the colour of the eyes and thirty-four for the skin.   The idea was that the observer would consult the scale and note the numbers of the shades which he found to correspond most closely with the colouring of his subjects.   Experience, however, has shown that with a scale so elaborate as Broca's the process of matching colours is not so easy as it looks; that different people are apt to arrive at widely different conclusions; and that even when the numbers have been correctly registered no one can translate the result of the observations into intelligible language.   For these reasons Broca's successor, Topinard, reverted to the method of simple description, unaided by any scale of pattern colours.   He describes, for example, the mud-coloured hair so common among the peasants of Central Europe as having the colour of a dusty chestnut.   In the latest edition of the Anthropological Notes and Queries published under the auspices of the British Association an attempt is made to combine the two systems.   A greatly simplified colour scale is given, and each colour is also briefly described.   This method is being used in the Ethnographic Survey of India for recording the colour of the skin, but I do not expect it to yield very satisfactory results, and I doubt whether it is possible to do more than describe very generally the impression which a particular colour makes upon the observer. In point of fact the colour of the skin is rather what may be called an artistic expression, dependent partly upon the action of light, partly on the texture and transparency of the skin itself and partly again on the great variety of shades which occur in every part of its surface.   It is hopeless to expect that this complex of characters can be adequately represented by a patch of opaque paint which is necessarily uniform throughout and devoid of any suggestion of light and shade.

"The difficulty which besets all attempts to classify colour is enhanced in India by the fact that for the bulk of the population, the range of variation, especially in the case of the eyes and hair, is exceedingly small.   The skin no doubt exhibits extreme divergences of colouring which any one can detect at a glance.   At one end of the scale we have the dead black of the Andamanese, the colour of a black-leaded stove before it has been polished, and the somewhat brighter black of the Dravidians of Southern India, which has been aptly compared to the colour of strong coffee unmixed with milk. Of the Irulas of the Nilgri jungles some South India humourist is reported to have said that charcoal leaves a white mark upon them. At the other end one may place the flushed ivory skin of the traditional Kashmiri beauty and the very light transparent brown—'wheat coloured' is the common vernacular description—of the higher castes of Upper India, which Emil Schmidt compares to milk just tinged with coffee and describes as hardly darker than is met with in members of the swarthier races of Southern Europe. Between these extremes we find countless shades of brown, darker or lighter, transparent or opaque, frequently tending towards yellow, more rarely approaching a reddish tint, and occasionally degenerating into a sort of greyish black which seems to depend on the character of the surface of the skin. It would be a hopeless task to register and classify these variations. Nor, if it were done, should we be in a position to evolve order out of the chaos of tints. For even in the individual minute gradations of colour are comparatively unstable, and are liable to be affected not only by exposure to sun and wind but also by differences of temperature and humidity. Natives of Bengal have assured me that people of their race, one of the darkest in India, become appreciably fairer when domiciled in Hindustan or the Punjab, and the converse process may be observed not only in natives of Upper India living in the damp heat of the Ganges delta, but in Indians returning from a prolonged stay in Europe, who undergo a perceptible change of colour during the voyage to the East. The fair complexion of the women of the shell-cutting Sankari caste in Dacca is mainly due to their seclusion in dark rooms, and the Lingayats of Southern India who wear a box containing a tiny phallus tied in a silk cloth round the upper arm, show, when they take it off, a pale band of skin contrasting sharply with the colour of the rest of the body." [6]

"It cannot be doubted," says Finot, "that colour is the direct effect of the environment. 'A fair person (Virchow tells us) placed in a certain environment becomes brown and vice versa.'" [7] A man of the black race may be white, a white man brown, a brown man yellow, a yellow man black. Colour is a variable incident of race.

---

[6] *Census of India,* 1901, Vol. I, p. 490.
[7] Finot, *Race Prejudice,* p. 104.

b. Is colour, then, the ground of race aversion or, as is sometimes alleged, the cause of race antipathy? There does not appear
to have been any colour prejudice among the ancients. No emphasis appears to have been laid on physical differences. Today,
however, the physical differences, and especially colour, are set
forth as the chief basis of racial alienation. Professor Park says:

" The chief obstacles to the assimilation of the Negro and the
Oriental are not mental but physical traits. It is not because the
Negro and the Japanese are so differently constituted that they do
not assimilate. If they were given an opportunity, the Japanese
are quite as capable as the Italians, the Armenians, or the Slavs of
acquiring our culture and sharing our national ideals. The trouble
is not with the Japanese mind, but with the Japanese skin. The
Jap is not the right colour.
" The fact that the Japanese bears in his features a distinctive
racial hallmark, that he wears, so to speak, a racial uniform,
classifies him. He cannot become a mere individual, indistinguish-
able in the cosmopolitan mass of the population, as is true, for
example, of the Irish, and, to a lesser extent, of some of the other
immigrant races. The Japanese, like the Negro, is condemned to
remain among us as abstraction, a symbol—and a symbol not
merely of his own race but of the Orient and of that vague, ill-
defined menace we sometimes refer to as the ' yellow peril.' This
not only determines to a very large extent the attitude of the white
world toward the yellow man but it determines the attitude of the
yellow man toward the white. It puts between the races the invisible but very real gulf of self-consciousness." [8]

Mr. Weale also finds in colour the cause of race prejudice:
" There is one thing which can never be altered, and that is colour.
For here is the real root of the racial difficulty throughout the
world. There exists a widespread racial antipathy founded on
colour—an animal-like instinct, if you will, but an instinct which
must remain in existence until the world becomes Utopia. It is
this instinct which seems to forbid really frank intercourse and
equal treatment." [9]
There is a curious support given to this view by the inner social

---

[8] Park and Burgess, *Introduction to the Science of Sociology*, p. 760.
[9] *The Conflict of Colour*, p. 110.

prejudice of the race whose leaders most strenuously resent the idea of colour discrimination. A Negro writes of them:

"Social prejudices are not confined to colour or races; they pervade all segments of society, and enter into all the ramifications of human life. Nowhere are they more intense and unreasonable than among the Negroes themselves, who have established within their own ranks innumerable social distinctions which, strange to say, are based solely on colour. For example, in many sections, light-hued Negroes associate together, and hold themselves as much aloof from contact with the blacks as do the most exclusive whites. In fact, there exists among these people a graduated series of colour distinctions, with the blackest constituting the base, and the fairest the apex, of the social column. But, though there is neither logic nor sense in discriminations based on variations of racial colour, nevertheless these social antipathies of the freedmen are as pronounced in character and as relentless in effect as those which their most inveterate white enemies have shown." [10]

But this same writer proceeds to deny the validity of the view that colour is the cause of antipathy:

"Colour, we insist," he says, "is merely the incident, and not the foundation, of prejudice. Ample verification of this is afforded, by the low class of whites who inhabit our Southern states, and whose condition is infinitely inferior to that of the lowest plantation Negro, both as to opportunity for work, means of living, and social recognition on the part of a superior oversight. These people are white, and of the same race as their oppressors, nevertheless their colour neither alleviates their distresses, nor furnishes an avenue of escape from domination. . . . That race prejudices exist no sane man denies, but that colour is the prime cause of American prejudice against Negroes is not to be believed for one moment. Every shred of authentic evidence disproves conclusions so preposterous. Abstractly considered, black and white are negative colours, neither of which has any inherent superiority over the other. Whence, then, comes race prejudice? Simply through a concatenation of circumstances, by which the black represents an enslaved, and white a master class; and as a servile race is always a despised people, the logical and inevitable sequence of Negro bondage was to create an aversion for black,

---

[10] Thomas, *The American Negro*, p. 292.

not on its own account, but solely because it was the chief visible badge of personal degradation." [11]

The fact probably is that colour, as the most conspicuous of all racial characteristics, is the easiest and most natural thing to suggest, and to be made the object of, the expression of race feeling. But, also, because it is a matter entirely of the skin and not of the character of a man or of a race, it is entirely feasible for races and individuals to be free from colour consciousness. The French are largely free from it,[12] and have protested against its introduction from America. An American Committee refused permission to an American Negress to attend the Fontainebleau School of Fine Arts in France, where she would have been welcomed.[13] American patrons have required exclusion of Negroes from Paris cafés against the protest of the French. No prejudice barred Toussaint L'Ouverture when he went to France. The colour antipathy which seems to us to be so fundamental does not appear so to the French mind. As the *Temps* said editorially on August 1, 1923:

" We have nothing to do with the attitude which prevails in America among her citizens. That is not our business. But this is France, and with us the colour line is totally unknown. Our forefathers didn't write the Declaration Les Droits de L'Homme (declaration of the rights of man) for us to forget its letter and its spirit.

" Besides, our lack of all discrimination against coloured men is not inspired alone by doctrine. We are sincere about it. The blacks, with whom we come in contact, come from the French colonies. Whatever their status—citizens, subjects or protégés—they are our compatriots, and we treat them as such. How could it be otherwise when so many of them fought by our side to save France?

" That small number of our American visitors who forget that the French Republic makes no differentiation among the inhabitants of its immense Empire, whatever their race or colour of their skin, will, we hope, regard our black citizens as good as the rest of us. They will not forget that their country also accepted the services of black men in time of need.

[11] *Ibid.*, p. 294 ff.
[12] Young, *Travels in France.*
[13] The New York *Times,* April 24, 1923.

" We promise in return that when we are in the United States we will obey the dry law which American legislation has imposed on every one. And we expect our visitors to obey our rule, which proceeds not from law but from our character and customs, in virtue of which all Frenchmen form one grand family, from which none of them is disinherited." [14]

Dr. Oswald Spengler complains of this attitude on the part of France. " France," says he, " handles the Negro question in a manner virtually giving English and American institutions a blow in the face, for France is the sole power which today recognises the Negro as an equal, and which is literally breeding a Negro population in European soil, thereby injecting a spirit into the colonial Negro population which may one day prepare a frightful awakening for the European world." [15]

And even among us the manifestations of colour antipathy are peculiar. White and Negro children play together and white people call coloured nurses " Mammie " all their days. " Sam was my Negro companion, philosopher and friend," says Page of his boyhood crony. There was no colour antipathy there. Some white people in Alabama protested against the appointment by the Government of any but white officers and physicians to the new Veterans' Bureau Hospital in Tuskegee, and yet all the patients for whom these white doctors would have to care are Negroes.[16] In truth colour is only a rough external sign, of great value to distinguish races when for any reason they need to be distinguished, but external and irrelevant when the reason for distinguishment appears—and this is true whether the colour be black, yellow or white.

A southern college football team recently refused to play the team of a northern college because the latter had on it a Negro half-back,[17] but this southern team would have ridden in a Pullman car with a Negro porter. A South African of British blood

---

[14] See editorial, " American Race Prejudice in France," in The New York Times, July 3, 1923.
[15] The New York Times, March 28, 1923.
[16] The New York Times, June 22, 1923.
[17] Federal Council of the Churches, Research Department, Information Service, Nov. 3, 1923, p. 6.

has described some of the anomalies of colour prejudice in a book of observations of American life in the South:

" While the strongest resentment would be felt and expressed at a native (Negro) travelling as a passenger in a public convey- ance—a post cart or the like—especially with lady fellow- passengers, no exception is taken to his presence as a driver, and indeed ladies will manoeuvre to get the box seat at his left hand rather than take an inside place. To eat at the same table as a native would be the depth of indignity, but to eat food cooked by him, and often actually handled in the uncleanest manner by him, is taken as a matter of course. We shrink at personal contact, and would shudder to take the hand of a black man, yet to his care, or that of his sister, we entrust our most precious living treasures in their tenderest years, to be washed, clothed, tended, often ca- ressed. The presence of the cleanest native alive in the same rail- way carriage as whites is an offence which demands the immedi- ate attention of the Government; the dirtiest may make our beds. A single case of marriage between white and black by Christian rites will fill the newspapers with columns of indignant pro- test, but illicit intercourse, even permanent concubinage, will pass unnoticed." [18]

There are men to whom colour is as though it were not. " Judging from my personal acquaintance with Mr. Cleveland," said Booker Washington, " I do not believe that he is conscious of possessing any colour prejudice. He is too great for that. In my contact with people I find that, as a rule, it is only the little, narrow people who live for themselves, who never read good books, who do not travel, who never open up their souls in a way to permit them to come in contact with other souls—with the great outside world. No man whose vision is bounded by colour can come into contact with what is highest and best in the world." [19] And some institutions also have steadfastly refused to take cognizance of colour distinctions. Of Harvard University, for example, the *Harvard Alumni Bulletin* of Jan. 25, 1923, declared, " For Harvard today to deny the coloured man a privilege it ac- cords to whites, appears inevitably as a reversal of policy if not

[18] Evans, *Black and White in the Southern States*, p. 20.
[19] *Up from Slavery*, p. 229.

as positive disloyalty to a principle for which the University has hitherto taken an open and unshaken stand." And when the matter came before the Board of Overseers as to admission to the Freshman class and dormitories, it was voted that " white and coloured races shall not be compelled to live and eat together, nor shall any man be excluded by reason of his colour." [20]

And what is colour? The Rev. J. B. Cochran, of Hwai Yuen, China, reported hearing a Chinese preacher discoursing on the races of mankind. " There are five great races," said he. " There are the black coloured race, and the white coloured race and the brown coloured race and the red coloured race, and lastly there are we Chinese, the skin coloured race." Each race is skin coloured to itself. All the other races are tinted.

2. Race and climate. It seems clear that it is climate operating through long centuries of time which accounts for colour. For how much also does it account in the formation of race character? " Climate, Food and Soil," says Buckle, " have originated the most important consequences in regard to the general organisation of society, and from them have followed many of the large and conspicuous differences between nations which are often ascribed to some fundamental differences in the various races into which mankind is divided." [21] Mr. Weale goes further. In his view climate is the supreme factor, more powerful than colour. At the back of Asia's alleged hate of the white man

" there is little question of colour, no matter what there might be on the European side. The white man is not hateful because he is white, but because he is strong, confident and overbearing. The Asiatic is being therefore forced to adopt his new attitude in self-defence; and though, of course, colour has admittedly become a barrier and also a great irritant, it must be remembered that it is the white man who has largely taught the coloured man that this is so. . . . The climate of the East is responsible for the peculiar philosophy and social atmosphere of the East—both of which are totally different from the philosophy and social atmosphere of the West, and neither of which can be really changed in

---

[20] The New York *Times,* April 10, 1923.
[21] Buckle, *History of Civilisation in England,* Vol. I, p. 29; See Huntington, *Civilisation and Climate.*

their fundamentals, no matter what efforts are put forth. The changes will be in material, practical things—not in the web of life long ago woven to its final form. For though in certain portions of the Far East the climate approximates to that obtaining at the other end of the hemisphere, nevertheless subtle differences exist which in a few generations would be sufficient to change the characteristics of any white race migrating to Eastern Asia and which would assimilate that race to the autochthonous race around them. So great a rôle does this question of climate play that the attention of statesmen should be concentrated on it as a very vital question in practical politics. . . . Men, having too long been fully occupied in examining historical causation, may soon be tempted to study climatic influences. There is, in any case, a perceptible pause to be noted in the propagandist activities of the white man, probably because he instinctively realises that, though his inventions and his forms may be readily accepted, the spirit of the non-white populations of the world remains precisely the same as it has always been; in a word, that no matter how much externals may be altered, men retain certain unalterable qualities and ideas which are rooted in climate and environment." [22]

This is an extreme view, which Mr. Weale himself modifies now on one side by emphasising colour and now on another by recognising universal truths which are above climate. Finot and Bagehot balance the climatic environment with the hereditary trend, itself in part the product of long environmental influence. And they also recognise the moral elements involved. Bagehot says:

" Climate and ' physical ' surroundings, in the largest sense, have unquestionably much influence; they are one factor in the cause, but they are not the only factor; for we find most dissimilar races of men living in the same climate and affected by the same surroundings, and we have every reason to believe that those unlike races have so lived as neighbours for ages. The cause of types must be something outside the tribe acting on something within—something inherited by the tribe. . . . Old writers fancied (and it was a very natural idea) that the direct effect of climate, or rather of land, sea and air, and the sum total of physical conditions varied man from man, and changed race to race. But experience refutes this. The English immigrant lives in the

---

[22] Weale, *The Conflict of Colour,* pp. 131-133, 265.

same climate as the Australian or Tasmanian, but he has not become like those races; nor will a thousand years, in most respects, make him like them." [23]

And Finot says:

" Man, like all organic beings, is subject to the influence of the milieu, the factor which dominates all the transformations which take place in nature. Besides this force, acting slowly during an interminable number of centuries by way of modification, there is another which seems to modify its influence in working by way of preservation. This second force is heredity, owing to which acquired characteristics tend to persist in the rising generations. . . . Climate acts directly on man and animals. . . . The moral causes, such as the liberty which people enjoy, the consideration of which they are assured, the wholesome sentiment of equality before the law and the respect of human dignity, the instruction which is given them, the national system of taxation which contributes to their comfort, the facility of internal and external communications, the way in which the State exercises its privileges and monopolies, justice which respects all the legitimate aspirations of citizens, and as many other conditions of a healthy development of a country, have all likewise their counter effect on the physiological formation of human beings." [24]

The effects of climate on race character are as real as its effects on race physiology. Huntington, in *Civilisation and Climate,* sets forth the evidence for the view that the world will never be dominated from the tropics by any races. The coloured races live in the zones of low initiative and retarded progress. The conditions against which they contend would affect in some, though not the same, way and manner any other race subjected to them. If the white races move to the tropics they are sooner or later inevitably affected and may become inferior to other races already naturalised there. But the adjustment of race to climatic environment does not involve a judgment of race inferiority or superiority. It signifies simply differentiation of race function and service.

3. Race and nationality and language are three closely associated but by no means identical elements. They are found in a

---

[23] *Physics a d Politics,* pp. 183 f., 84.
[24] Finot, *Race Prejudice,* pp. 130, 137, 149.

great variety of inclusive and exclusive relationships. Nationality and race are not synonymous. Mr. Stoddard draws a very sharp but quite untenable distinction between them. " As a matter of fact," says he, " they connote utterly different things. Nationality is a psychological concept or state of mind. Race is a physiological fact, which may be accurately determined by scientific tests such as skull measurement, hair formation, and colour of eyes and skin. In other words, race is what people anthropologically really are. Nationality is what people politically think they are." [25] But as a matter of fact it might, perhaps, be as truly maintained that nationality is physiological and race psychological. Nationality is associated with physical geography, political institutions and all the material expressions of an organized corporate life. And race, as ethnologists acknowledge, cannot be accurately determined by physiological tests. It has been for this reason that all really scientific race tests have been discarded and the crude sign of colour adopted as the only acceptable mark of race distinction.[26]

The lines of nationality and race frequently overlap. Many races may be embraced in one nationality, as in India or in the United States, and there may be many nationalities in one race as in every one of the great races of the world. The more powerful of the two ideas in modern history, nationality and race, has been nationality. It has divided races which were homogeneous and it has also forced into unwilling assimilation races which were divided. It is clear that race is not the final fact so often alleged. If it is so solidly and indestructibly fixed in physiological character, how is it that an institution like nationality can overpower and obliterate it? [27] After surviving for centuries in the Balkans the ancient ethnographic composition of the people, in spite of its supposed physiological stability, was engulfed by nationalistic forces, and the perpetuation and confusion alike of the racial groups have been determined by the strength or the weakness not of race feeling or character but of nationalistic energy, sometimes

[25] *The New World of Islam*, p. 158.
[26] See Finot, *Race Prejudice*.
[27] Reinsch, *World Politics*, pp. 3-5.

measurably synonymous with race, but often blurring the racial lines.[28]

Likewise language and race are not to be too closely bound together. And yet there are those who hold language, and the mind which language expresses, to be the great racial criterion. On the other hand, Georges Rodenbach declares that a common language, and the mind behind it, transcends the bounds of nationality and race. " In truth," says he, " those who are of French nationality often feel themselves to be more different from one another than from a foreigner writing in French." [29]

It is obvious that language is not a racial mark. Language is certainly of greater consequence than type of hair or colour of skin. Two men speaking the same language have far more in common than two men speaking different languages but of the same type of hair and colour of skin. Language is no proof of racial affinity but, on the other hand, (1) a race that did not have a common language would be heavily handicapped by that lack, (2) the unity of race character is futile against the lack of a means of communication, (3) people who have the same means of communication in language are united by a bond of mental kinship which their difference in colour or race cannot annul. Once again it is clear that race is not the ultimate and sovereign fact in human relationships.[30]

Languages used to be classed among the great evidences of the ultimateness of race distinctions. That view, like most of the other views which conceive the races as doomed to perpetual segregation and conflict, has been given up. " No country more signally than our own," says Roemer in *Origin of the English People and of the English Language,* " presents examples of the fact, of which proofs abound throughout the world, that the lan-

[28] See *Report of the International Committee to Inquire into the Causes and Conduct of the Balkan Wars,* pp. 21-28; Sloane, *The Balkans, a Laboratory of History,* p. 292: " In particular the dogma that nationality, ecclesiasticism, and consanguinity [i. e., race] are the foundations of political efficiency has been discredited."

[29] Finot, *Race Prejudice,* p. 195.

[30] *Atlantic Monthly,* March, 1920, art. by John Kulamer, " Americanisation, the Other Side of the Case," p. 422.

guage spoken by a people is, by itself, no test of race at all; nor is the fallacy of the principle of 'nationalities of race' more clearly demonstrated than by the history of the people from whom our own vernacular is borrowed and whose patriotic and political nationality is founded on fusion rather than on purity of race; indeed the latter would perhaps be sought in vain throughout the world." [31]

The lesson from language with regard to the race problem is still deeper. As the writer of the article on "Ethnology and Ethnography" in the *Encyclopedia Britannica* says:

"Perhaps the greatest psychical proof of man's specific unity is his common possession of language. Theodore Waitz writes: 'Inasmuch as the possession of a language of regular grammatical structure forms a fixed barrier between man and brute, it establishes at the same time a near relationship between all people in psychical respects. . . . In the presence of this common feature of the human mind, all other differences lose their import.' [32] As Dr. J. C. Prichard urged, 'the same inward and mental nature is to be recognised in all races of men. When we compare this fact with the observations, fully established, as to the specific instincts and separate psychical endowments of all the distinct tribes of sentient beings in the Universe we are entitled to draw confidently the conclusion that all human races are of one species and one family.'" [33]

There is a fuller assertion of the same noble truth in the essay on "Language as a Link," by Professor Smith, in *Western Races and the World*. It adds all that needs to be said about race and language. He holds that

"Mankind constitutes a real unity, that there is an identity of nature running through and present in all mankind. This is not, or not merely, a natural unity. It does not lie in, or arise from, singleness of ancestry or kinship of blood; it is not merely the

---

[31] *Op. cit.*, p. 375. See also Ratzel, *The History of Mankind*, Vol. I, Book I, p. 5, "Language"; *Universal Races Congress*, 1911, paper by D. S. Margoliouth on "Language as a Consolidating and Separating Influence," pp. 57-61.
[32] *Anthropology*, p. 273.
[33] *Encyclopedia Britannica*, Vol. IX, p. 850.

result of historic accident or physical causes. I cannot think of it
as less than a spiritual unity which can neither be produced nor
destroyed from without. All men can say ' We ' with a truth and
significance incommunicable to other beings than men: they share
in a complex but single type of experience. And with this goes
a mutual or reciprocal communion in which no other beings participate; they are all literally one with one another—they form
one ' community.' They do actually and in fact communicate
with one another, actually understand, and co-operate with one
another. The whole human world is, despite all appearances to
the contrary, in act and fact, not merely in potency or promise, an
intercommunicating and interacting and co-operating whole. And,
if we take the word ' language ' widely enough, we may with truth
say that the whole human race commands and employs a single
language by means of which it maintains this world-wide intercommunication, and that of this language all forms of extant
human speech are but varieties differing in degree of perfection,
while the brutes have no corresponding language shared either
with one another or with us. Were this not so the spiritual unity
of mankind would be non-existent, or what is the same, ineffectual
and inoperative. This radical identity underlying all diversity of
human speech is difficult to grasp, but it is there at the basis—
difficult to grasp because, as I have said, it is a spiritual not a
natural or physical unity." [34]

4. Race and communications. We do not need to go further
than England and the United States for illustration of the effect
of isolation and communication upon racial and community character. The mountain people of our southern States are as pure a
branch of the old Anglo-Saxon stock as can be found in America.
But geographical isolation has wrought in them racial characteristics which may have physiological marks in colour of hair or
eyes or cranial or cephalic index, but have certainly had a distinct
effect in mental qualities. The early Colonies, and to almost as
great an extent the present States are marked by clear sectional
characteristics, due to inheritance and physical environment in part
but also to the nature of their communications. In England and
Scotland there are innumerable pockets of humanity where isolation, often within sight of a city, has left its deep results. Greek

---

[34] *Op. cit.*, p. 30.

historians have always found the explanation of much of the character and history of Greece in the physical configuration of the peninsula. The idea of a racial germ plasm, fixing unalterably the character and destiny of those who inherit it, is treated with small respect by geography, and by the influences which flow from communications. Undoubtedly the isolation of peoples, under the diverse conditions of their life, is what accounts for the racial diversity of humanity. Even the believer in racial germ plasm has to recognise this or give up the conception of the common origin of humanity which both science and revelation proclaim. Somewhere far back his germ plasms were all one. What differentiated them? How can he know that the forces and conditions which did that cannot undo it, or, if there may be a better ideal, as we believe there is, than undoing this long work of time, how does he know that new conditions and forces may not achieve that better ideal, and that adequate communications between men may not fulfill in the whole of humanity what the lack of communications will have prepared men to accept, with an understanding and capacity acquired by their education in isolation.

The late Professor Reinsch worked out these ideas in a paper on "Influence of Geographic, Economic and Political Conditions":

"Nationalism first grew in Greece and Italy, protected by mountains and by the sea, and in the modern world it was England, whose insular position enabled her first to develop a self-conscious and independent national life. In Africa the absence of such boundaries has contributed to hinder the development of civilisation. The tribes are not settled long enough, nor are their boundaries sufficiently fixed for them to develop those qualities which are based upon stability of location. . . . The growth of world unity which we have witnessed in our day has already modified, and even superseded to some extent, the effect of geographic separation, of political nationalism or particularism, and of economic exclusiveness. Economic and social forces are beginning to flow in a broad natural stream, less and less hampered by dynastic and partisan intrigue, by protectionist walls, by monopolies and all sorts of exclusive privileges. . . . We may here ask whether this development does not introduce a danger or resuscitate an old

peril under a new form?   We have seen that humanity needed
local protection against the indiscriminate onslaughts of the mass.
Now that natural boundaries have ceased to be determining factors on account of the supremacy of the human mind over physical
conditions, is it not to be feared that humanity will be reduced to
an indiscriminate mass lacking distinction—in a word, that it will
be vulgarised and barbarised?   We are still in need of cores or
nuclei about which human self-consciousness may gather.   It is
here that the usefulness of nationalism, with its ideals, lies.
When the physical conditions which gave it birth have lost in
relative importance, humanity is, nevertheless, still in need of that
distinguishing national self-consciousness under which its ideals
and achievements will be further protected and developed.   As
mere localism the national idea has lost force.   As a means by
which values fixed and gained in the struggle of history may be
preserved for the future it still has a meaning and importance.
. . .   The civilised nation today will recognise that its aim is
humanity, and that the mission of its policy transcends by far the
limits of geographical boundary, but we cannot as yet dispense
with these nuclei of human force and ideals which history has developed.   They are the great personalities which make up the system
of civilised states.   When their work is fully done, they will pass
away, but for a time still it will be their mission to organise the
efforts of humanity to higher ends and to protect mankind against
engulfment in an indiscriminate mass, with a lowering of all
ideals." [35]

These are thoughts to which we shall return.
    5. Race and social ideals.   The social relationship which is most
closely related to race and which throws most light upon it is sex.
Race, as has been said, is just expanded family, and family rests
on sex.   The conception of woman's position is one of the central
elements in race social inheritance and education.   The higher the
conception of woman, the higher the race.   The higher the race,
the higher its conception of woman.[36]
    The facts of sex suggest some significant lessons with regard to
the race problem.   (1) It is undeniable, as Goldenweiser says, that

---

[35] *Universal Races Congress,* 1911, pp. 51, 50, 53, 55.
    [36] Ratzel, *The History of Mankind,* Vol. I, Book I, par. 12; Parsons, *The
Family.   An Ethnographical and Historical Outline;* Goldenweiser, *Early
Civilisation,* Chapters XII, XIII; *Report of the Balkan Commission,* p. 271.

sex division has given rise to a set of formal and functional divisions in society. Sometimes these have implied or involved disabilities on the part of women, but often they have not done so. They have represented simply specialisation of service. In primitive societies and in modern communities also the decision has sometimes rested on the idea of woman's inferiority and sometimes of her superiority. As society has advanced the inferiority conceptions have been progressively discarded. One of the longest social struggles has been the effort of woman to achieve an equal status with man. This struggle for sex equality is analogous to the struggle for race equality. If it has involved the loss of any values, it has meant the gain of others. It has not destroyed any real facts of difference. It has simply erased artificial and unreal discriminations which hampered and impoverished society. We have thus a division, deeper and more permanent than race, and really physiological, which recognises functional differentiation without antipathy or discrimination. If this can be for sex, why not for race?

(2) Race antipathies have always melted before sex. Between all races there has been either intermarriage or intercourse without marriage. We shall consider the whole question of intermarriage presently. Here it will suffice to state that the alleged sense of race superiority or finality vanishes before the fact of sex. The moral values of life do not so vanish. They take on new solidity and inviolability. Not so with race. It is such a feeble principle that it is one of the first to crumble on the line where the sexes meet.

(3) The struggle for the emancipation and equality of women has been and is still related to the struggle against war. " It may be noted," says Goldenweiser, " that the basic politico-economic disfranchisement of woman goes back in the main, to a more primary fact, namely the monopolisation by man of the weapons and acts of war. Thus the tragedy of woman symbolises, in the last instance, the enslavement of the powers of peace by the powers of war." [37] The same thing is true of the tragedy of race

---

[37] *Early Civilisation,* p. 264.

prejudice and conflict. It rests on the philosophy of force. Mr.
Weale dismisses the Liberian experiment with the words:

" It was attempted in an age when philanthropy thought that
vague abstract principles could be applied to racial questions irrespective of the particular nature of those problems. It attempted to do by kindness (which is only a fleeting emotion) that
which can only be performed by brute movements, grounded in
human nature—that is, by the use of force called into action by an
imperative demand, such as the necessity to find elbow-room, to
find food. To bear aside those who would stay such natural
movements by mere arguments is a very natural corollary.
" Following this line of thought, it is somehow not impossible
to believe that one day the West Indies may be invaded by great
swarms of black men, unless they are stopped by force. It is also
quite conceivable that a general intercourse such as today exists
between England and Canada, and England and Australia, may
one day exist between the blacks of America and the blacks of
Africa. There will be societies and unions and churches and other
bonds—all tending to accentuate the solidarity of the Negro race—
all tending to range the race in a rival camp. Undoubtedly, in
these future days, fresh efforts will have to be made to hold the
Negro in check and to confine him in such a manner that he will
not be able to drag down the white races. Humanity has hitherto
only concerned itself with such debatable themes as the ill-
treatment of blacks by whites. The day may not be far distant
when men will pause, and openly wonder whether in the past they
have been well advised to interfere at all with solutions which,
though barbarous, are only so because men, when they are face to
face with elementary facts, can only use elementary methods." [38]

So long as this philosophy of the supremacy of the jungle-forces
in human life prevails, the race and sex problems are both impossible of solution. The races which deem themselves superior will
oppose race justice exactly as men opposed sex justice. The
achievement of justice and equality must go hand in hand with
the triumph of the powers of peace and reason over the powers of
unreason and war. As reason and peace come to prevail sex and
race come to their rational adjustment and function in humanity.

---

[38] *The Conflict of Colour*, p. 241 f.

6. Race and religion. What is the relation of religion to race and the race problem?

Is religion determined by race or is it a force which may be counted upon to mould and determine race? " Looking at things upon a large scale," says Buckle, " the religion of mankind is the effect of their improvement, not the cause of it." [39]   And Professor E. A. Ross holds that in religion the racial inheritance and the racial education are decisive, not vice versa: " Every man denies that his faith is restricted or thrust upon him by circumstances.   On the contrary, he imagines that it is a matter of intelligent free choice.   But this is all illusion.   The recognised ascendency of remote historical factors in determining the religious preferences of peoples emphasises how non-rational and unfree are the religious adhesions of men." [40]

Is religion a divisive force, provocative of war, or is it consolidating and unifying? " Differences of language and custom— and, above all, of religion—serve to intensify the hostility (of race)," says Fouillée.

" All religion is sociological in character, and expresses symbolically the conditions native to the life or progress of a given society.   The religion of a race converts it into a huge society animated by the same beliefs and the same aspirations.   Moreover, all religion is intolerant, and hostile to other religions.   It believes itself to be the truth, and thus seeks to universalise that which is only the particular spirit of one race or one nation—e. g., the Jewish spirit, the Christian spirit, the Mohammedan spirit.   When, then, the ethnic consciousness becomes at the same time a religious consciousness, the assertion of the individuality of a race implies a counter-assertion to the individuality of other races.   It is hidden warfare, passing over at the very first opportunity into open warfare." [41]

Fouillée is speaking of the decisive influence of ethnic religion, but he believes in no universal religion which would unite all men

---

[39] *History of Civilisation in England,* Vol. I, p. 185.
[40] *Social Psychology,* p. 8.
[41] *Universal Races Congress,* 1911, paper on " Race from the Sociological Standpoint," p. 25.

as an ethnic religion helps to unite the race which believes it. His faith is in scientific and philosophical ideas.

"Just as ethnic and religious ideas are dividing factors, so scientific ideas are conciliatory in tendency. . . . Over and above the consciousness of race, nationality, or religion, scientific ideas develop a *human* and *social,* not to say *human* and *cosmic* consciousness. Science, then, is the great reconciler, the fruitful germ of universal peace, realising in the world of intelligence the maxim ' All in one.' By the force that belongs to ideas union tends to pass from the intellect into the heart. Men of science, be their colour white or yellow, hail one another as brothers." [42]

Railroads, telegraph, every industrial invention " shining equally upon white and black," commerce, common philosophical ideas bind men together when " all religions, guilty of the two great capital crimes—pride and hatred, divide." Not so with the scientific man and the philosopher. " His opponents seem to him at bottom his best friends. He has no inclination whatsoever to kill or burn them." To be sure, these words were spoken in 1911. How admirably they have been authenticated! Witness Belgium and the Ruhr. " For the sociologist," adds M. Fouillée, " there is but one practical means of bringing races together, and that is to diffuse scientific, moral and social instruction as widely as possible. Instruction of this kind, spread gradually among the different nations, is the one great means of ensuring peace." [43]

The Commission which investigated the race riots in Chicago which occurred in July, 1919, asked in a questionnaire which it sent out, for opinions as to the value of religion as a solvent of racial difficulties and differences. It received such answers as these: " Utterly valueless, the average individual does not think "; " Religion has failed to solve the racial difficulties in America because its principles have never been practiced by the people. Religion has remained a beautiful theory "; " It has no utility. It had no utility in the World War "; " Unfortunately religion has little sanction over the social conduct where interest and passions are involved." [44]

---

[42] *Ibid.,* p. 25.   [43] *Ibid.,* p. 29.
[44] *The Presbyterian Magazine,* May, 1923.

Are all religions alike in this matter of their influence, or is there any special claim that may be made for any one of them as truly adapted to promoting world unity? Two answers are given apart from what we would regard as the Christian answers. One is that all religions are alike, that it is only a " pretext that one religion is more moral or more civilising than another," and " that any racial customs repugnant to the sentiment of humanity should be indirectly mollified by ethical processes and not by religion." [45] The second answer is that religion has a consolidating function, but that it will be religion not crystallised or formulated into a creed or racialised, but religion conceived as a universal human instinct. " As an instinct, deep-rooted in the heart, religion transcends the barriers of race, in offering the bond of a common aspiration between individuals. And as the day of dogmas wears on to its long twilight, and the true inwardness of religion becomes acknowledged, we may come to invert the relation between religion, as pretext, and other motives, calling themselves by its name." [46]

But these questions may all be given a different answer. In primitive society we know that religion and life covered the same sphere. The fellowship of religion and of kin are the same fellowship.[47] The Old Testament shows us a human race emerging from a tribal condition and growing into an organised theocratic state. The race was consolidated and given character by its religion. In our view it was not so much the Hebrews who produced their religion. It was rather their religion which produced the Hebrews. And throughout the East whatever may have been the origin of their religion," " the force which united people in obedience to their governments," and provided the chief influence of racial and national cohesion " has been mainly religious. This is true of races as distant and different from the Semitic people as

[45] *Universal Races Congress,* 1911, paper by Professor Giuseppe Sergi, on " Differences in Customs and Morals and their Resistance to Rapid Change," p. 72.

[46] *Ibid.,* paper by Rhys Davids on " Religion as a Consolidating and Separating Influence," p. 66.

[47] Smith, *The Religion of the Semites,* pp. 30, 47, 50.

the Chinese and the Japanese." [48]   And Sir Alfred Lyall sums up
his conclusions in his *Asiatic Studies* with a recognition of the
unifying racial influence of religion:

" It is impossible not to admit that in many instances the successful propagation of a superior or stronger creed has been favourable to political amalgamation, nor can there be any doubt of
the intense fusing power that belongs to a common religion.   In
our day the decree of divorce between religion and politics has
been made absolute by the judgment of every statesman, above all
for Christian rulers in non-Christian countries; nevertheless the
religion of the Spaniards was a part of their policy in the New
World, and this of course is still true in regard to Mohammedans
everywhere.   There have been many periods, and there are still
many countries, in which an army composed of different religious
sects could hardly hold together.   And it is certain that for ages
identity of religious belief has been, and still is in many parts of
the world, one of the strongest guarantees of combined action on
the battle-field.   It has often shown itself far more effective, as a
bond of union, than territorial patriotism; it has even surmounted
tribal or racial antipathies; and its advantages as a palliative of
foreign ascendency have been indisputable.   The attitude of religious neutrality is now manifestly and incontestably incumbent
on all civilised rulerships over an alien people; it is a principle
that is just, right and politic; but there is nothing in its influence
that makes for that kind of assimilation which broadens the base
of dominion.   Religion and intermarriage are the bonds that
amalgamate or isolate social groups all the world over, especially
in Asia, and their influence for or against political consolidation
has lost very little of its efficiency anywhere." [49]

There can be no doubt of the consolidating influence of the
great race religions each within its own race and, omitting Christianity for the moment, in the case of Buddhism at least there can
be no doubt of the influence of religion in overspreading the
bounds of race and if not unifying races, nevertheless, in a real
sense, mollifying the sharpness of race divisions.

Among the primitive people with their spirit-worship and their
spirit-fear, their fetiches and their taboos, religion is both an in-

---

[48] Curtis, *The Commonwealth of Nations,* pp. 5, 19.
[49] Lyall, *Asiatic Studies,* Second Series, p. 384.

ternal bond of the race and a bond between races as truly as it has
been the occasion of racial strife.[50]   Back of all the developed
religious conceptions and the ethical philosophy of the Chinese,
De Groot finds a " Universalistic Animism ": " The primeval form
of the religion of the Chinese and its very core to this day is
animism. . . . In China it is based on an implicit belief in the
animation of the universe and of every being or thing which exists
in it." [51]   Such a conception is comprehensive of many differences.
It is its influence, in fact, which has unified the Chinese world-
view and race-sense.   As animism works out practically, however,
it is too inchoate and motley, too full of fear, to serve as an enduring race cement or to bind together conflicting race interests.

Hinduism has never aspired, save under influences generated by
its contact with the West, to be anything but an ethnic religion.
Its principle of comprehension even of contradictory principles
and ideas, is a principle of toleration but not of organisation or
unity.   Its unifying power in India had indeed been great, but
only because it has identified itself with caste which is the religious consecration of racial and social distinction accepted as the
unalterable human order.   And it has not recognised its unsocial
and inhuman inadequacy as revealed in its exclusion, from both
society and religion, of the outcastes, comprising one-fourth of
the Hindu population of India, until it was brought into comparison with Christianity and with its democratic idea and its principle
of the unity of the human race.

Buddhism is the one non-Christian religion which most nearly
proclaims the universal principle.   The great emperor Asoka, who
united nearly the whole of India under his sceptre in the third
Century B. C., sought to consolidate all the races under his rule by
the extension and organisation of Buddhism, and it was as a
result of his activity that Buddhism spread into China.   But the
dominant passivist ideas of Buddhism have made it ineffective
even as a race cement and still more as an inter-racial bond.   Hinduism annulled it in India.   It was no more effective in preventing

---

[50] Le Roy, *The Religion of the Primitives;* Nassau, *Fetichism in West
Africa.*
[51] De Groot, *The Religion of the Chinese,* p. 3.

war between the two greatest Buddhist nations of China and
Japan than the Christianity of Germany and France was effective
in preventing the World War. " Surviving as a fossil even in
Buddhism," says Rhys Davids, " the very gospel of mutual toleration and amity, where the term ' Ariya ' has come to mean, not
race-complacency but ethical excellence, hate of the alien as alien
and not only as infidel, appears too obviously in religious wars to
need exemplifying." [52] And today one may see the King of Siam
ineffectually striving to use Buddhism once again as the inspiration of national personality. But the power of the faith in unifying either one race or two is gone.

Mohammedanism set out like Buddhism and Christianity, to
embrace all races, but in two respects it differed from them. It
did not propose to rely upon moral force alone and its strong
policy of inward consolidation was accompanied by a fiercer policy of outward exclusion. No apology can destroy the evidence
of violence in the extension of Islam.[53] But this very violence
worked as a force of racial unification among the people who accepted it. " It is one of the most striking proofs of the strength
of the creed of Islam," says Bishop Lefroy, " that it does thus
force into the background—at any rate, to a considerable degree—
the distinguishing racial characteristics of the peoples to which it
has come, and supersede them by a mind, a character, a life which
is primarily and unmistakably the outcome of the creed itself." [54]
And Mirza Saeed Khan says, " To do justice to Islam and its
founder, theoretically Islam knows no race distinction. As soon
as one is converted to it, he is in the brotherhood, no matter what
his complexion or race."

It is to be gladly recognised that there are passages in the *Koran*
which support the principle of inter-racial accord. At the Universal Races Congress Hadji Mirza Yahya, of Teheran, defended
Persian Islam, at least, against the charge of intolerance:

" The religion of the Persians makes monotheism essentially

---

[52] *Universal Races Congress,* 1911, p. 64.
[53] Haines, *Islam as a Missionary Religion,* chs. III, IV, VI; Rice, *Crusad-
ers of the Twentieth Century,* pp. 425-431.
[54] *Mankind and the Church,* p. 281.

cosmopolitan, and calls for universal peace among its disciples to whatever nationality they may belong: ' O followers of the Scriptures, come hearken to this one saying: that all may be equal between us and you. Let us agree together to worship only the one God and put naught else on a level with Him.' [55]

" It declares the equality of all men, calling to mind that they are all children of the same father and the same mother and that only virtue can give to one man preference over his fellow: ' O men, we have created you of one man and one woman; we have distributed you in tribes and families to the end that you may know one another. The worthiest before God is that man from among you who is most virtuous.' [56]

" And lastly, it stands for religious freedom: ' Let there be no constraint in religion.' [57] In such principles as these there is, then, nothing which could deter men from entering into international relationships." [58]

And he cited the Persian poets to show how truly they felt the wide sympathy of humanity:

Sadi. " The sons of Adam are members of one body; they are made of one and the same nature; when Fortune brings distress upon one member, the peace of all the others is destroyed. O thou, who art careless of thy fellow's grief, it fits not thou shouldst bear the name of man."

Sanai. " What matter whether the language be Arabic or Syriac, if so be it express the truth? What matter whether the place be east or west, if only God be worshipped there? "

Hafiz. " Thy beauty united with thy gentleness hath conquered the world. Of a truth, it is by union that the world can be conquered."

Orfi. " So behave towards thy fellow-men, O Orfi, that after thy death the Mussulman may bathe thee with the holy water of Kaaba and the Hindu burn thee in his sacred fire."

Achegh. " Thou hast read the *Koran*, Achegh, and thou knowest the verse, ' Eynema tawallou.' [59] When, then, the gates of Kaaba are closed, go worship the Eternal in the Church."

---

[55] *Koran*, Sura 3, verse 57.
[56] *Koran*, Sura 49, verse 13.
[57] *Koran*, Sura 2, verse 257.
[58] *Universal Races Congress*, 1911, p. 148.
[59] " The East and the West belong to God: whithersoever your glance be turned, you will meet His face."—*Koran*, Sura 2, verse 109.

The speaker at the Universal Races Congress from Egypt, Mohammed Sourour Bey, also had a word to say of the racial tolerance of Islam: " From the legal point of view the marriage of a Mussulman with a Christian or Jewish woman is permitted, which shows the great toleration of the Mussulman religion. The Mussulman woman marries only a Mussulman; if she unites herself to a non-Mussulman, the marriage is declared radically null and void. The children of both sexes that are born of these marriages follow the religion of their father." [60] This conception of tolerance is more characteristic of Mohammedanism than the ignored words of the *Koran* quoted by Hadji Mirza Yahya or the verses of the Persian Sufi poets. Indeed the teachings of the Persian philosophers and of religious leaders, like the Bab and Baha Ullah and their successors, have in nothing more widely departed from historic Islam than in their theory of human unity. For Mohammedanism itself is not and cannot be a solvent of the race problem.[61]

---

[60] *Universal Races Congress,* 1911, p. 170.

[61] " As you well know for Islam and Mohammed there were and are even today only two spheres, 'the abode of Islam' and 'the abode of warfare.' 'Fight against them,' *i. e.,* idolaters, Jews and Christians,' says the *Koran,* Sura 2, 'till strife be at an end and the religion be all of it God's.' This command is a real religious duty for Islam through all ages. And Bahaism which springs out of the bosom of Islam does not improve things, for the Bab ordered the Kings of the Bayan to allow no one in their country who does not embrace his religion, Christians as merchants excepted, and to take by force their wives and children and property. Do not be deceived by Baha and his son Abdul Baha's borrowed ideals and lofty phraseology." (Letter Mirza Saeed Khan, Teheran, July 9, 1923.) For evidence of the racial feelings triumphing over the religious feelings of Moslems, see Browne, *A Literary History of Persia,* pp. 232, 242, 264. Browne cites the tendency of pious Moslems of the early period, as expressed in many traditions, to disregard racial prejudices in the domain of religion, but he adds, "That the full-blooded Arabs, in whom racial feeling greatly outweighed the religious sense, were very far from sharing the views embodied in these and similar traditions is abundantly shown by Goldziher, who cites many facts and passages which indicate their contempt for the foreign *Mawali,*" (*i. e.,* "clients" or non-Arab Moslems) (*Op. cit.,* pp. 264, 229.) The contrary view, that Islam is a complete race solvent and that it furnished a true brotherhood, is, I know, the orthodox and traditional view. (*Asia,* Feb., 1922, art. by Arnold J. Toynbee, "Islam and the Western World.") Nevertheless the position taken in the text is maintained, with full knowledge of what is to be said on the other side. If others have seen Islam producing a true brotherhood, well and good. The more true brotherhood in the world the better. "There is no need for us to minimise the

It has no conception of the Fatherhood of God! How can it have of the brotherhood of man? "Outside of the mosque," Sir Narayan Chandavarkar told me once in Bombay, "there is no brotherhood in Islam." That was a sweeping statement. But in a deep sense it is true, as life in Persia or Turkey or India proves. Islam has no conception of corporate racial unity, much less of corporate human unity.[62] Bad as the failure of other peoples and other religions to deal with race problems may have been, the worst failure in the modern world has been in the case of Turkey and Islam and the Armenians. Christianity could stand to be judged against Islam by the difference between the Armenian problem in Turkey and the Negro problem in the United States.

---

greatness of Islam's brotherhood. It has had important social and political consequences in the past, and particularly in view of the message of Pan-Islamism may have even greater consequences in the future. Islam's brotherhood is great and is effective; let us confess it at the outset, and let us confess also that in some respects it may even go further as a matter of practice than our own Christian brotherhood often does. But having said so much we must not forget to recognise that there is a fundamental and far-reaching difference between Islam's conception of brotherhood and ours. . . . Islam's brotherhood, in a word, implies brotherliness only toward those within the brotherhood, and its attitude to all without the brotherhood is ever that of hostility, even if veiled hostility. . . . Within the brotherhood, we find when we come to examine the matter closely that there is again a fundamental defect. The fact is that Islam's brotherhood has not yet advanced to the position of having such ethical value that Moslems can trust one another. In Cairo, for instance, it is a notorious fact that Moslems are tremendously shy of entering into business partnerships with one another for this very reason, and the same fact has been apparent all through Moslem history. This has been the reason why Christians have been so largely employed in the bureaux of Moslem governments. As Margoliouth points out, ' public business had somehow to be transacted, and few Moslems were qualified to transact it, *while little confidence was reposed in those who were qualified.'* " (*International Review of Missions*, April, 1924, pp. 185-187. See Margoliouth, *Early Development of Mohammedanism*, p. 122.) For an able and persuasive statement of the Mohammedan position and a strong argument for the superiority of Islam in its teaching and influence with regard to race, see Ameer Ali, Syed, *The Spirit of Islam*, new edition, Part II, Chap. IV, " The Church Militant of Islam." But for a frank acknowledgment of Islam's failures see sermon by Eshuf Edih Bey, preached in St. Sophia, printed in the *Sirat-i-Mustakeem* and translated in *The Hibbert Journal*, April, 1910, pp. 647-651. And Mr. Trowbridge deals convincingly with the claim that Islam is innocent of the charge of religious war in *The Moslem World*, July, 1913, art. " Mohammed's View of Religious War." See also Freeman, *History and Conquests of the Saracens*, p. 202 f.
[62] *Mankind and the Church*, pp. 290-298.

And yet it is of the futility of Christianity as a force toward the solution of the race problem that some students of the race problem are assured. Not all. Mr. Stoddard approves of missionary effort: " In as far as he is Christianised, the Negro savage instincts will be restrained and he will be disposed to acquiesce in white tutelage." [63]   Christianity is a desirable soporific for race assertion. But Mr. Weale thinks religion a negligible factor in race development: " It is, of course, due neither to religion nor to polygamy that Europe and Asia are different—since these are rather results than first causes. Climate, soil, and environment are the great first causes of the difference—climate alone being a sufficiently powerful factor, as those who have resided in hot climates know, to produce in a few generations the most remarkable changes." [64]   And Rene Gerard likewise sees religion as only an effect and not a cause. Is this because in men's own lives religion is only a secondary and ineffectual thing?

" To believe that philosophic and religious doctrines create morals and civilisation," says Gerard, " is a seductive error, but a fatal one. To transplant the beliefs and the institutions of a people to new regions in the hope of transplanting thither their virtues and their civilisation as well is the vainest of follies. · . . . The greater or less degree of vigour in a people depends on the power of its vital instinct, of its greater or less faculty for adapting itself to and dominating the conditions of the moment. When the vital instinct of a people is healthy, it readily suggests to the people the religious and moral doctrines which assure its survival. It is not, therefore, because a people possess a definite belief that it is healthy and vigourous, but rather because the people is healthy and vigourous that it adopts or invents the belief which is useful to itself. In this way, it is not because it ceases to believe that it falls into decay, it is because it is in decay that it abandons the fertile dream of its ancestors without replacing this by a new dream, equally fortifying and creative of energy." [65]

This view is not reconcilable with history. The great religions

---

[63] *The Rising Tide of Colour,* pp. 96 f.
[64] *The Conflict of Colour,* p. 31.
[65] *The Hibbert Journal,* Jan., 1912, Art. by Rene Gerard, " Civilisation in Danger."

were not the product of great races at the apex of their vital instinct. Everyone of them had a humble beginning. The great
moral ideas were not generated by civilisations in their power.
And on the other hand a race, with no alteration whatever in its
heredity or vigour, has been again and again shaken or shattered
or remade by "philosophic and religious doctrines." Mr. Weale
does not get far with his view of the negligibility of religion before
he abandons it: "In addition to the question of colour," he says,
"it must never be forgotten that there is also the vital question
of religion." [66] So "instinct" is not the only thing that is "vital."
Two pages further on Mr. Weale becomes unconverted again:
"Religion has little to do with the standard of living; religion has
still less to do with the balance of power; and it is these things
alone which have today paramount racial importance." [67] But
presently the light breaks afresh. Colour and climate are not the
fundamental things. There is truth which is under all and over
all, independent of geography, "common to all humanity, determining history and life." [68]

We believe that Christianity is this truth and we come now to
consider the relation of the Christian religion to the race problem.

Christianity found in the Roman Empire a dream of political
world unity, a noble effort to realise that dream and the realisation that the effort had failed and that some other principle of
unity must be found. The extent to which Rome had unified the
world was one of the most notable elements in the preparation of
the world for the expansion of the Christian religion. Among
those external unifying conditions Harnack mentions (1) the
Hellenising of the East and in part also of the West, which had
gone on steadily since Alexander the Great, or the comparative
unity of language and ideas which this Hellenising had produced,
(2) the world-empire of Rome and the political unity which it
secured for the nations bordering on the Mediterranean, (3) the
exceptional facilities, growth and security of international traffic,
the admirable roads, the blending of different nationalities, the

---

[66] *The Conflict of Colour,* p. 117.
[67] *Ibid.,* p. 119.
[68] *Ibid.,* p. 189 f.

personal intercourse, (4) the practical and theoretical conviction of the essential unity of mankind and of human rights and duties, (5) the decomposition of the ancient society into a democracy, the gradual equalising of the "Cives Romani" and the provincials, of the Greeks and the barbarians, the elevation of the slave class, (6) the religious policy of Rome which furthered the interchange of religions by its toleration so long as they did not affront the ceremonial of the State religion, (7) the existence of organised associations, (8) the irruption of the Syrian and Persian religions, (9) the decline of the exact sciences and the rising vogue of a philosophy of religions, with a craving for some form of revelation.[69]

Some of those conditions were elements of strength and some were elements of weakness in the Roman world. The elements of weakness were prevailing. "Ancient life had begun to break up; its solid foundations had begun to weaken. . . . Nationalities had been effaced. The idea of universal humanity had disengaged itself from that of nationality. The stoics had passed the word that all men were equal, and had spoken of brotherhood as well as of the duties of man toward man."[70]   All these outward conditions, Harnack tells us, "brought about a great revolution in the whole of human existence under the Empire, a revolution which must have been highly conducive to the spread of the Christian religion. The narrow world had become a wide world; the rent world had become a unity; the barbarian world had become Greek and Roman."[71]

But though the ground had been made ready for the sowing the old world lacked the living seed. Notions were in men's minds which prepared the way for Christianity, but they wanted the definiteness and the energy needed to make them effective. Everything, indeed, as Uhlhorn says,

"was nothing more than preparation. The old world was not

---

[69] Harnack, *The Expansion of Christianity in the First Three Centuries*, Vol. I, pp. 19-24.
[70] *Ibid.*, p. 23 f., quoted from Uhlhorn.
[71] *Ibid.*, p. 23.

able to produce from itself a Christian universalism. The result of that great process of comminution which was wrought out in the vast Roman Empire was only uniformity, not true unity. True unity presupposes diversity. It is a comprehension of the manifold under a higher principle of organisation. Here we encounter a limitation which was insuperable to the old world. It lacked the thought of Humanity, and since it knew not the whole, it could not rightly appreciate the parts. The unity of mankind, and the organisation of the entire race in nations,—the great truths which Paul preached in Athens, the centre of ancient wisdom— were hidden from it. Therefore the meaning of nationality was not rightly understood. At first it was exaggerated. There was only national life, and nothing more. Afterwards it was undervalued. In the Roman Empire the various nationalities failed to obtain their just rights. They were completely lost in the great whole. The result was, not a living universalism but only a shadowy one, an abstract cosmopolitanism which did not know how to appreciate the meaning of nationality as a compact organism.

"The ultimate reason lies deeper. There was no religious unity. That which today holds cultivated nations in unity, notwithstanding all their diversity, is their common Christianity. Were this taken away their development in culture would gradually diverge, and the nations would again, as in ancient times, confront each other as enemies—unless, indeed, power were given to one of them to force them all into one empire. This, in many quarters today, will not be conceded. Appeal is made to the multiplied means of communication which now exist, and the consequent approximation of nations. Stress is laid on their common culture, conceived of wholly apart from religion,—as if outward union could of itself create community of life! as if the kernel of this entire common culture were not their Christianity! The thought of a humanity whose members are nations, is only possible where there is faith in one God and one Redeemer. As long as Polytheism rules, as long also as religion is purely national, humanity is split up into a multitude of nationalities rigidly secluded from each other. Even the Universalism of the Roman Empire was possible only because, in its religious development, a monotheistic tendency had already begun even within the limits of paganism,—a tendency to be sure which could not advance beyond a shadowy Monotheism. The abstract pantheistic Deity which was the result of this tendency corresponds exactly to the abstract, and pantheistically coloured, cosmopolitanism which took the place of the earlier and vigourous consciousness of distinct nationality. When, instead of a dead deity, was preached the living God, Maker of heaven and earth, the Father of our Lord Jesus Christ, then for the first time humanity was able to advance from this abstract cosmopolitanism into the true Universalism which rules the Christian era." [72]

From the very beginning Christianity came into the world with the stamp of universality.[73] The race to which Jesus belonged had developed "an intense sentiment of nationality." This displayed itself in many ways in the lifetime of Jesus. One argument advanced for suppressing Jesus was that if He were let alone "the Romans will come and take away our place and nation." [74] It was better accordingly, it was urged, to have Jesus sacrificed "that the whole nation perish not." [75] On the pleasanter side, the elders who interceded in behalf of the centurion at Capernaum, did so on the ground that He "loveth our nation." [76] Jesus was recognised as a member of their nation, sharer in its glories and high spirit.

But Jesus was not sharer in its narrowness and exclusivism. One of His earliest sermons gave great offense because He laid emphasis on the outreaching grace of God. Elijah, He pointed out, had been sent to none of the widows of Israel in the days of famine, but to a Sidonian woman, and Elisha had cleansed no lepers of Israel, but only Naaman, the Syrian. "And they were all filled with wrath as they heard these things." [77] The same spirit of nationalistic narrowness, from which Jesus was free, found expression in the sneer of the Jews at Jesus' declaration, "Ye shall seek Me and shall not find Me; and where I am, ye cannot come. The Jews therefore said among themselves, Whither will this man go that we shall not find Him? Will He go unto the Dispersion among the Greeks, and teach the Greeks?" [78] As though in contrast with this smallness of vision, John proceeds to relate the words of Jesus on the last, the great

[72] Uhlhorn, *The Conflict of Christianity with Heathenism,* p. 27 f.
[73] Luke I, 78; II, 14, 32; III, 5.   [74] John XI: 48.
[75] John XI: 50.   [76] Luke VII: 5.
[77] Luke IV: 25-29.   [78] John VII: 34, 35.

day of the Feast of Tabernacles, beginning, " If any man thirst, let him come unto Me and drink." [79]

This contrast between the attitude of Jesus and the attitude of the Jews is sharply presented in their relations to the Samaritans. The Jews had no dealings with the Samaritans,[80] and when they would be especially bitter and contemptuous in their reference to Jesus they said to Him, " Thou art a Samaritan and hast a devil." [81]   The later tradition declared, " It is forbidden to eat bread or to drink wine with the Samaritans."   But Jesus ignored and violated these restraints.   " He went and entered into a village of the Samaritans." [82]   He sent His disciples into a Samaritan village to buy food and welcomed the people of the village to faith and discipleship.[83]   And He deliberately gave to a Samaritan a place in one of His most exquisite parables above Levite and priest.[84]

It was significant that the first people to recognise the universal mission of Jesus were Samaritans.   " We know that this is indeed the Saviour of the world," they said.[85]   Yet in some sense, this sweep of the work of Jesus had been already perceived.   The song of the angels suggested it.[86]   Aged Simeon foresaw it. " Mine eyes have seen Thy salvation," he said, as the child Jesus lay in his arms,

" Which thou hast prepared before the face of all peoples,
    A light for revelation to the Gentiles." [87]

And John the Baptist hinted at it also: " The Lamb of God which taketh away the sin of the world." [88]   Thenceforward it was revealed with increasing clearness that Jesus was in the world for the world.   He said, Himself, that the field was the world.[89]   His disciples were the light of the world,[90] as He had come a light into the world,[91] and was Himself the world's light.[92]   He called Himself the bread of God which had come down for the life of the world.[93]

---

[79] John VII : 3,
[80] John IV : 9.
[81] John VIII : 48.
[82] Luke IX : 52.
[83] John IV : 39-42.

[84] Luke X : 33.
[85] John IV : 42.
[86] Luke II : 10, 14.
[87] Luke II : 31, 32.
[88] John I : 29.

[89] Matt. XIII : 38.
[90] Matt. V : 14.
[91] John XII : 36.
[92] John VIII : 12.
[93] John VI : 33, 35.

Indeed, throughout, Jesus would admit no narrower field of work and salvation for Himself than the world. There are apparently contradictory statements. "I am not sent but unto the lost sheep of the house of Israel." [94] "Go not into any way of the Gentiles and enter not into any city of the Samaritans." [95] Jesus had to make a beginning. His immediate mission was to Israel. The only way in which any larger mission could be made possible was by the discharge of this mission to the Jews. A salvation for all was to be wrought out in time and space and until the work was done the field was confined. But beyond all the immediate and preparatory work lay the universal reaches of a redemption for all mankind. Jesus was such a good Israelite in order that the mission of Israel might be fulfilled and there be henceforth neither Jew nor Greek. Accordingly the whole spirit and message of Jesus were universal. "God sent not His son into the world to condemn the world, but that the world through Him might be saved." [96] He contemplated the conviction of the world,[97] and the preaching of His gospel among all nations.[98] And even before His coming, He said, the Father had intended the temple to be a place of prayer for all nations,[99] while now all local limits were set aside and everywhere true worshippers were invited to come immediately to the Father without temple and without priest.[100]

Jesus told of a good Father over all,[101] of a light in Himself adequate for all guidance,[102] of Himself as the only way to the Father,[103] and as the truth and the life.[104] In view of all this the nation in which He was could be the starting point only, not the goal. His gospel was a message for all men everywhere.

The Book of Acts in the New Testament is a drama of the unfolding universality of Christianity.[105] The Tübingen school of

[94] Matt. XV : 24.
[95] Matt. X : 5.
[96] John III : 16, 17.
[97] John XVI : 8; XVII : 21, 23.
[98] Matt. XII. '4; XXVI : 13.
[99] Matt. XI : 17.
[100] John IV : 20-24.
[101] Matt. V : 45-48.
[102] John VIII : 12.
[103] John XIV : 6.
[104] John XIV : 6.
[105] Acts I : 8; II : 5-11, 39; III : 25; IV : 12, 24; VI : 1, 9; VIII : 5, 27; IX : 15; X : 28, 34 f., 43; XI : 12, 17, etc.

critics rewrote the history in terms of a feud between Paul and Peter, as representing the two attitudes to the race problem with which we are confronted today, the attitude of human equality and the attitude of Nordic race aristocracy. There was no such feud, but there was a real struggle in Paul's own mind and in Peter's [106] as to the right solution of the race issue and the real necessity of a living acceptance of the new and revolutionary doctrines of " the brethren who are of the races " [107] and of the organic unity of mankind. To see how vivid the teaching of Christianity was, open the New Testament and read it again, substituting the word " races " for " Gentiles." [108] And read anew its references to Greeks and barbarians.[109] And note the great utterances of Paul in Gal. III : 28; Col. III : 11, and Eph. II : 22.

" There can be neither Jew nor Greek, there can be neither bond nor free, there can be no male and female; for ye are all one man in Christ Jesus." [110]

" Where there cannot be Greek and Jew, circumcision and uncircumcision, barbarian, Scythian, bondman, freeman; but Christ is all, and in all." [111]

" Wherefore remember, that once ye, the Gentiles in the flesh, who are called uncircumcision by that which is called circumcision, in the flesh, made by hands; that ye were at that time separate from Christ, alienated from the commonwealth of Israel, and strangers from the covenants of the promise, having no hope and without God in the world. But now in Christ Jesus ye that once were far off are made nigh in the blood of Christ. For He is our peace, who made both one, and brake down the middle wall of partition, having abolished in His flesh the enmity, even the law of commandments contained in ordinances; that He might create in himself of the two one new man, so making peace; and might reconcile them both in one body unto God through the cross, having slain the enmity thereby: and He came and preached peace to you that were far off, and peace to them that were nigh: for

[106] Acts X.   [107] Acts XV : 23.
[108] Cf. Matt. XII : 21; Mark X : 42; Acts IX : 15; X : 45; XI : 18; XIV : 27; XXVIII : 28; Rom. I : 13; III : 29; XI : 25; XV : 11 f., 16; Eph. III : 6; I Thess. II : 16; I Tim. II : 7; I Peter II : 12.
[109] John XII : 20; Acts XIV : 1; XV : 4; XIX : 10; XX : 21; Rom. I : 14; X : 12; I Cor. I : 24.
[110] Gal. III : 28.   [111] Col. III : 11.

through him we both have our access in one Spirit unto the Father. So then ye are no more strangers and sojourners, but ye are fellow-citizens with the saints, and of the household of God, being built upon the foundation of the apostles and prophets, Christ Jesus himself being the chief corner stone; in whom each several building, fitly framed together, groweth into a holy temple in the Lord; in whom ye also are builded together for a habitation of God in the Spirit." [112]

Of all the foolish words spoken today none are more foolish than those spoken in depreciation of Paul. The idea that he narrowed the gospel and shadowed its freedom and joy is as wide of the truth as any idea men ever conceived. It was the truth of God which was given to him to speak which saved the Roman Empire from dissolution for a thousand years and which is yet to save and unify mankind. A fine passage of Sir William Ramsay's describes the first of these two services:

" In the mind of the ancients no union of men, small or great, good or bad, humble or honourable, was conceivable without a religious bond to hold it together. The Roman Empire, if it was to become an organic unity, must derive its vitality and its hold on men's minds from some religious bond. Patriotism, to the ancients, was adherence to a common religion, just as the family tie was, not common blood, but communion in the family religion (for the adopted son was as real a member as the son by nature). Accordingly, when Augustus essayed the great task of consolidating the loosely aggregated parts of the vast Empire, he had to find a religion to consecrate the unity by a common idea and sentiment. The existing religions were all national, while the Empire (as we saw) was striving to extirpate the national divisions and create a supra-national unity. A new religion was needed. Partly with conscious intention, partly borne unconsciously on the tide of events, the young Empire created the Imperial religion, the worship of an idea—the cult of the Majesty of Rome, as represented by the incarnate deity present on earth in the person of the reigning Emperor, and by the dead gods, his deified predecessors on the throne. Except for the slavish adulation of the living Emperor, the idea was not devoid of nobility; but it was incapable of life, for it degraded human nature, and was founded on a lie.

---

[112] Eph. II : 11-22.

But Paul gave the Empire a more serviceable idea. He made possible that unity at which the imperial policy was aiming. The true path of the Empire lay in allowing free play to the idea which Paul offered, and strengthening itself through this unifying religion. That principle of perfect religious freedom (which we regard as Seneca's) directed for a time the imperial policy, and caused the acquittal of Paul on his first trial in Rome. But freedom was soon exchanged for the policy of fire and sword. The imperial gods would not give place to a more real religion, and fought for two and a half centuries to maintain their sham worship against it. When at last, the idea of Paul was, even reluctantly and imperfectly, accepted by the Emperors, no longer claiming to be gods, it gave new life to the rapidly perishing organisation of the Empire and conquered the triumphant barbarian enemy. Had it not been for Paul—if one may guess at what might have been— no man would now remember the Roman and Greek civilisation. Barbarism proved too powerful for the Græco-Roman civilisation unaided by the new religious bond; and every channel through which that civilisation was preserved, or interest in it maintained, either is now or has been in some essential part of its course Christian after the Pauline form." [113]

And an equally fine word of Gotthard Lechler's describes the still larger meaning of Paul's influence:

" Paul has inestimable importance, both for the Church of Christ and for humanity in general. Not only was he the first to bring out the unity of the human race inherent in the person of the God-man into clear perception, but also to establish it practically and in fact. In pre-Christian times, divided and disunited humanity longed after the union and interpenetration of the different races and nationalities. But nothing good came of it. [114] Conquering Rome was just then occupied with uniting all the known world into its empire. But all its conquests and its wonderful gift of ruling produced only a formless mass of peoples, a gigantic body without a uniting spirit, naturally so, because itself had not this spirit, but was of the old man which is fleshly, being of the earth and itself earthy. When the second man came,—the Lord from heaven, who is Spirit,—it became possible to bring mankind into actual unity, beginning from within, by virtue of the one life-

---

[113] Ramsay, *Pauline and Other Studies*, p. 99.
[114] Comp. Bunsen, *Hippolytus*, i, pp. 131, 257; Schaff, *Kirchengesch*, i, 471, etc.

giving Spirit,[115] under the one head, which is Christ. The instrument of God who was called to establish this unity in thought and deed was Paul. As a true Israelite without falsehood, and, at the same time, by the grace of Christ as the apostle of the Gentiles, with deep spiritual doctrinal development, but, at the same time, with that stupendous missionary activity which he had from the grace of God, with his marvellous spiritual gift of rule and original power of organising, he united Jews and Hellenes in one Church, in one family, under one Head and Lord, in one faith and in brotherly love, and brought together the different Churches of the East and West into one body, so as to become one Church of Christ. The walls of partition thrown down by the divine-human personality and propitiatory death of Jesus, were completely destroyed by the Apostle Paul. Though he did not, it is true, complete and carry through the work of uniting the human race, yet there is still a hope at this day of reaching that goal, and we in faith expect it; but Paul put the first hand to the united structure, building on the foundation which was laid, viz., Jesus Christ; which is his world-historical, immortal work." [116]

Now it is to be recognised at once that Christianity has not as yet thus unified the races. This is something held against it as a reproach and disproof, especially its failure to prevent war. But Christianity is not automatic or self applying. It can only solve men's problems when men will accept its solution. To the extent that men have accepted it, it has worked.

It has elevated and transformed and unified races. In the case of primitive races it has preserved them from destruction and given them some support against the disintegrating influences of a different social and economic civilisation. This has been denied by teachers like Alexander Agassiz.[117] But the testimony is sufficient.[118] Two Scotch testimonies from Africa of men who knew as much of the matter as Agassiz knew of corals, will suffice. One is from James Stewart:

---

[115] I Cor. XV: 45, 47.
[116] Lechler, *Apostolic and Post Apostolic Times*, Vol. I, p. 150.
[117] *Letters and Recollections of Alexander Agassiz*, p. 369. Per contra see *The Missionary Review of the World*, May, 1923, art. "Conflicting Forces in Papua," by C. W. Abel.
[118] See Foster, *American Diplomacy in the Orient*, pp. 108, 114, 117; Dennis, *Christian Missions and Social Progress*, Vol. III, pp. 278 ff.

" Will a civilisation based on this Utilitarian or Trade and Commerce theory really do the work—the work of elevation—its supporters say it can do? That may reasonably be doubted. Trade and commerce have been on the West Coast of Africa for more than three centuries. What have they made of that region? Some of its tribes are more hopeless, more sunken morally and socially, and rapidly becoming more commercially valueless, than any tribes that may be found throughout the whole of the continent. Mere commercial influence by its example or its teaching during all that time has had little effect on the cruelty and reckless shedding of blood and the human sacrifices of the besotted paganism which still exists near that coast.

" It may be said that it is not the direct aim or duty of these commercial influences to civilise or improve morally. There is every reason for believing that they neither can nor wish to do such work, in spite of all belief to the contrary. If a wholesome and beneficial civilisation is to be introduced, that can only be done by the introduction and direct teaching of Christianity, and that is best done by Christian missions; and as the scale of the continent is large, so also would require to be the scale of missionary work.

" The fond belief of many, that the best way to Christianise is to civilise first, consequently falls to the ground. Still this is a delusion which many continue to cherish. It is a curious fact that purely philanthropic or civilising efforts, even on the West Coast of Africa, apart from the spirit of Christian missions have not succeeded. The strongest statement has yet to be made, and it rests on a conclusion gathered from observation and experiment. It cannot be said that civilisation sprang out of Christianity; nor yet that civilisations have not existed apart from Christianity; both statements would be untrue. But, speaking of races that have fallen to a certain low level, all modern experience seems to show that they are never truly civilised by the direct processes, hasty methods, or incidental influences of a civilisation which settles down among them chiefly for its own ends or private gain.

" This denial of the power of a purely Utilitarian Civilisation to civilise effectively, beneficially, and permanently, may be rejected by some as resting only on African missionary evidence; and missionary opinion, as some think, is often lacking in breadth and calmness. It requires to be used, however, as it is sometimes all we can get. Similar evidence comes from other parts of the world from missionaries who have spent their lives in close contact with these backward races, and it should have some value. From New Guinea there comes the same conclusion as from any part of the

African continent. James Chalmers, one of those simple great
souls who do their duty and scorn the consequence, even if that
should be the loss of life itself, says: 'I have had twenty-one
years' experience among natives. I have lived with the Christian
native, and I have lived, and dined, and slept with cannibals. But
I have never yet met with a single man or woman, or with a single
people, that civilisation without Christianity has civilised.' " [119]

The other is from Robert Laws, testifying of Nyasaland:

" It was a vast region where cruelty, suffering, and bloodshed
prevailed unchecked. The people were riven into thousands of
independent units warring continuously against each other. Every
circle of huts was the scene of endless disputes, witchcraft-trials,
beer-drinks and moonlight revelries. It was a country where the
thoughts and desires of the heart were evil continually. No
woman would venture on the bush-paths alone. She would have
been a victim of the first man who met her and would probably
have been left stabbed to death. Terror made it a sleepless land.
' We want sleep,' was the cry of the people to Dr. Livingstone."
" Everywhere now there is sleep profound. Peace lies upon
the Lake and the wide-spreading bushland and the villages. Men
still carry spears, but it is to ward off the wild beasts. The faces
of the women are free from the old sullenness and suspicion. In
the deep heart of the forest far from the symbols of ordered law
they travel alone in absolute security. Industry is unrestricted
and workers have more property than their chiefs in former
days." [120]

It is a fact which history amply illustrates in India among the
low caste people and in Africa among the primitive and savage
peoples, that Christianity lifts races. The witnesses are unim-
peachable both for competence and for veracity. Of Christianity
and the low castes in India the Government Census reports witness to " the brilliant achievements of the Christian missions in
this noble work of civilising and elevating the aborigines in Chota
Nagpur," " the moral regeneration of the race (the Mundas),"
the uplifting by Christianity of the outcaste.[121]   As to the

---

[119] *Dawn in the Dark Continent*, pp. 24-26.
[120] *Life of Robert Laws*, quoted in *Sunday School Times*, Dec. 10, 1922,
p. 784.
[121] *Census of India*, 1911, Vol. I, pp. 136-139.

African, the testimony of the Inspector of Schools in Natal will suffice:

"The history of native education in South Africa is the history of South African missions, for it is due entirely to the efforts of the missionaries that the Natives of South Africa have received any education at all, and to this day all but three of the several thousand Native schools are conducted by missionary agencies." [122] "It is said that a certain wise old Native chief divided Europeans into two classes, viz., white men and missionaries. The distinction is significant. To the thoughtful Native the white man is the disintegrating force which has broken down his tribal customs and sanctions, and has replaced them with nothing but innumerable and vexatious governmental restrictions introduced for the benefit of the white man. On the other hand, he knows the missionary to be his friend. It is the missionary who educates his children, who writes his letters, who cares for him in sickness and sorrow, who acts as a buffer between him and the local storekeeper or Government official, and whose motives are always altruistic." [123]

Mr. Loram does not exempt missionaries from error in breaking down good or innocent moral and social customs, but he lays that to human misjudgment and not to Christianity, and he quotes Lord Selborne's statement that the missionaries in South Africa "should be regarded as the people who have saved the situation, because they are the people who have taken far the most trouble, and who alone have sacrificed themselves in order to ensure that the education of the Native, inevitable from the moment that he came into contact with the white man, should contain something good." [124]

Not only is it a fact that Christianity elevates and unifies low races. It is also a fact that it does it by moral ideas and spiritual force. The climate does not change. The physiology of the race continues the same. It is obvious that climate and physiology are not the determining factors, but that race elevation and unifica-

---

[122] Loram, *The Education of the South African Native*, p. 46.
[123] *Ibid.*, p. 73.
[124] *Ibid.*, p. 78. See Ratzel, *The History of Mankind*, Vol. I, p. 65; Watts, *Dawn in Swaziland*.

tion are moral processes. The competent students of African life recognise this.[125] It is the "moral forces which are chief powers in the progress or recuperation of any race." [126] And this view may be generalised. The development of races and of race relationships is a moral development. It is only secondarily a physical problem. Kidd asserts that we must discard colour and heredity as the basis of race judgment: " Neither in respect alone of colour, nor of descent, nor even of the possession of high intellectual capacity, can science give us any warrant for speaking of one race as superior to another. The evolution which man is undergoing is, over and above everything else, a social evolution. There is, therefore, but one absolute test of superiority. It is only the race possessing in the highest degree the qualities contributing to social efficiency that can be recognised as having any claim to superiority." [127] And he proceeds to press this view as furnishing the true judgment of our own race. It is not a matter of white skin or long heads or Nordic heredity. It is a matter of humanity, of strength and uprightness of character and of devotion to the call of duty, and he quotes Lecky on *The Political Value of History:*

" Its foundation is laid in pure domestic life, in commercial integrity, in a high standard of moral worth and of public spirit, in simple habits, in courage, uprightness, and a certain soundness and moderation of judgment which springs quite as much from character as from intellect. If you would form a wise judgment of the future of a nation, observe carefully whether these qualities are increasing or decaying. Observe especially what qualities count for most in public life. Is character becoming of greater or less importance? Are the men who obtain the highest posts in the nation, men of whom in private life, and irrespective of party, competent judges speak with genuine respect? Are they of sincere convictions, consistent lives, indisputable integrity? . . . It is by observing this moral current that you can best cast the horoscope of a nation." [128]

---

[125] *The South African Native*, pp. 3, 229.
[126] Stewart, *Dawn in the Dark Continent*, pp. 14, 33.
[127] *The Control of the Tropics*, p. 98.
[128] *Ibid.*, p. 100 f.

And what is thus spoken of nations is equally true of races. The Christian ideals and forces are the only salvation of races and the only solution of the race problem.[129]

The Christian view has a right to assert itself. If it is the duty of patriotic men to know and spread the biological facts about society,[130] it is still more clearly their duty to know and spread the Christian facts. For Christianity is the judge and standard of all our race judgments and contacts. It is its business, as Lord Meston says, to bring home to us whatever fundamental errors there are in our treatment of national relationships, to point out where in our contact with other races " we have deflected our own standards and our own best traditions, founded on Christian precepts." [131]

But can Christianity bind together alien races? It may unite a race. Can it unite the races? We must proceed to inquire. But meanwhile let it be quite clear to us that this is what It came to do,[132] and that, if failure comes, the responsibility for it belongs not to Christianity but to men, and that man must not fail, and with God's help need not fail. As a wise race teacher has said: " Out of all the many confusing interpretations of Christ's teachings, this is clear to me: That He meant to bring together the alienated, to harmonise the discordant, to heal the ancient wounds caused by the mere struggle for self, and that into the world's disorder He intended to bring a new order, which He called: The Kingdom of Heaven.

" The most valuable possession which Christianity holds for me is this conviction: That the task is unfinished, that the conflict

---

[129] *Mankind and the Church,* pp. 240, 245 f. With regard to Christian missions as a conciliating and uniting force see Hunter, *The India of the Queen,* p. 219; Seeley, *The Expansion of England,* p. 323.

[130] *Yale Review,* April, 1917, art. by Conklin, " Biology and National Welfare, p. 486: " The time has come when one cannot be a good citizen without some knowledge of biology."

[131] *The East and the West,* Jan., 1923, art. by Lord Meston, " India at the Crossways," p. 73.

[132] " For me the mention of Christ's name, 'poured out as ointment,' touches such a chord of love and response, that, no matter what the race or colour, I am drawn to that Soul more firmly than to any dearest and nearest relation in the flesh who is a stranger to Him." Letter from Mirza Saeed Khan, M.D., Teheran, Persia, July 9, 1923.

is still on and that it is my business to invest my life in such a way as to make true the dream of the Son of Man." [133]

[133] Steiner, *Against the Current,* p. 204.

VI

AN INDIAN STATESMAN'S VIEW OF RACE

IN preparation for this book I wrote to several friends in Asia, members of different races, asking them for their help. The letter from one of these, Sir Narayan Chandavarkar, of Bombay, deserves to be printed in full. It must have been one of the last documents he prepared. It is dated April 18, 1923, and he died on May 14, 1923. Sir Narayan was one of the most remarkable and most honoured men in India. His full title and official record ran: The Honourable Sir Narayan Chandavarkar, Kt., B.A., LL.B., LL.D., Late Judge of the High Court, Bombay, Ex-Vice Chancellor of the University of Bombay, President of the Bombay Legislative Council.

He was a member of the Prarthana Samaj, the most progressive of the Indian reform societies within Hinduism, and a great devotee of the poet Tukaram. But he had strong intellectual and spiritual sympathies with Christianity. In one confession he declared:

" I am a Hindu, but I believe in Christ as the highest fulfilment of Hinduism. I have a picture of Christ crucified in my bedroom where I can look daily upon it. . . . I believe Jesus Christ to be unique in His character, His teaching, His power to save and help men and especially in His dynamic and world-wide social programme. No one else ever did for suffering oppressed humanity what He did. I am a Christian already, yet I cannot dogmatically say that Christ was God. Though a follower of Christ in my daily life I do not take the outward step of baptism because, as at present interpreted in the popular mind, it means not only to accept Christianity but to reject and denounce Hinduism. This I cannot do, for I believe that God has been in our past history and revelation."

And some years ago, in an address entitled, " The Kingdom of Christ and the Spirit of the Age," he said:

"Let me tell you what I consider the greatest miracle of the present day. It is this: that to this great country, with its 300 millions of people, there should come from a little island, unknown by name even to our forefathers, many thousand miles distant from our shores, and with a population of but fifty or sixty millions, a message so full of spirit and life as the Gospel of Christ. This, surely, is a miracle if ever there was one. And this message has not only come, but it is finding a response in our hearts. The process of the conversion of India to Christ may not be going on as rapidly as you hope, or in exactly the same manner as you hope but, nevertheless, India is being converted; the ideas that lie at the heart of the Gospel are slowly but surely permeating every part of Hindu society, and modifying every phase of Hindu thoughts."

His statement on the race question, which comprises the rest of this chapter, will show how these questions appeared to such a mind in India.

I. What is the Origin and what do you conceive to be the divine purpose of race and racial differences?

The object of these questions being, as stated in the Questionnaire, "to set before our own people the Christian view of race and racial feeling, and the solution of the race problem," I should content myself with starting in these answers with the Biblical view as to the origin of race and racial differences. In Chapter XI of Genesis, in the Old Testament, we are told that at the beginning of its creation the whole earth was of one language and of one speech. I understand that to mean that but one race of people existed at the beginning of the creation. The science of Comparative Philology supports that statement of fact. The account in Genesis goes on to say that it came to pass, as the single race that then existed journeyed from the east, they dwelt in the land of Shinar; that they started building a city and a tower; and that the Lord "confounded their language and scattered them abroad from thence upon the face of all the earth," to prevent their being "one people," and having "all one language." In Chapter XII of Genesis we have it that God asked Abram to get out of his country and from his kindred, and from his father's house unto a land which God would show him with the object of making him the

father of "a great nation." These historical facts, put very
pithily in the Bible, show that the family first and the tribe afterwards gave origin to race; and that racial differences have been
due to differences of climate, language, religion, traditions, and
other circumstances that compose a people's environment. While
these main facts of the story in the Bible find support from the
discoveries of science and the researches of history, the view
propounded in Chapter XI of Genesis that God, having become
jealous of the men who started building the city and the tower,
confounded their language and scattered them abroad, to restrain
their ambition and prevent them from becoming all-powerful
against the Almighty, represents the crude primitive view as to
the origin of race. The later conception of God is Love promoting Unity, not Jealousy and Fear. The Bible must be studied as
a book dealing with the evolution of Man and the human race—
their growth from crude ideas to the highest conceptions of humanity as revealed by the life and teachings of Christ. To the
primitive view expressed in Genesis God appeared to deal with
men on the principle subsequently enunciated by the Romans for
the government of their Empire—the principle, viz., of "divide
and rule." That principle has been corrupted to mean that the
safety of a ruler lies in breeding differences among the ruled that
they may not prove powerful against the ruling authority by reason of union among themselves. But the true meaning of "divide
and rule" as the divine law of life is given to us in Genesis itself
and also in some other books of the Old Testament when the
writers of those books merely state *facts* as distinguished from
their understanding of the implications of those facts. For instance, the first true glimpse of the divine law of "divide and
rule" is afforded in Chapter IV, Genesis, in the second verse of
which we are told that the two sons of Adam and Eve were not
alike, because "Abel was a keeper of sheep but Cain was a tiller
of the ground." "Orders and degrees," says Milton in the *Para-
dise Lost,* "jar not with liberty but well consist." A wise ruler
promotes the cause of good government and contributes to Unity
among his people by dividing the government into gradations and
ranks such as we know now by the name of departments, division

of labour, delegated authority, or decentralisation. Nature is our
best teacher on this point as to the divine purpose of race and
racial differences. It is out of variety and diversity that Nature
exhibits her harmony and beauty. The poet Browning brings that
out in these lines:

> " Rather learn and love
> Each facet-flash of the revolving year :—
> Red, green, and blue, that whirl into white,
> The variance, the eventual unity,
> Which makes the miracle."

Or take these lines from Wordsworth's *Prelude:*

> " The immeasurable height
> Of woods decaying, never to be decayed,
> The stationary blasts of waterfalls,
> And in the narrow rent at every turn
> Winds thwarting winds, bewildered and forlorn,
> The torrents shooting from the clear blue sky,
> And rocks that muttered close upon our ears,
> Black drizzling crags that spake by the wayside
> As if a voice were in them, the sick sight
> And giddy prospect of the raving stream,
> The unfettered cloud and region of the Heavens,
> Tumult and peace, the darkness and the light
> Were all like workings of one mind, the features
> Of the same face, blossoms upon one tree,
> Characters of the great Apocalypse,—
> The types and symbols of Eternity,
> Of first, and last, and midst, and without end."

In short, unity must come and can only come out of diversity.
What doubt is to faith, as an incentive, diversity is to unity. All
the different races have each its peculiarity of contribution to the
happiness and progress of all the world. All depend upon one
another. In St. Paul's phrase, all are intended to be members of
one another. No race is nor can be self-sufficient without stunt-
ing itself. Even as between and among the people of one race,
sameness of all without diversity in points of view, capacity, and

personality, is apt to lead to imbecility and retard the cause of truth. "Assemblies that are met," wrote Burke, "and with a resolution to be all of a mind, are assemblies that can have no opinion at all of their own. The first proposal of any measure must be their master." The same law applies to races. Each has its own mission allotted to it by Providence to promote the unity of the world—the brotherhood of the whole human race under the fatherhood of God.

It has been remarked by some writers that two essential problems enter into the problem of Life, viz., (1) the food problem, and (2) the race problem. The former is indispensable for the self-preservation of a race and the latter for its self-realisation.

Let me briefly consider the true aspect of each of these problems, on which depends primarily the very existence and continuance of a race.

In its primitive conditions a people belonging to a country have, comparatively speaking, but a few wants, whether in point of food or other necessities of life. But as they advance in civilisation, the wants increase with their standard of life, so that every country comes to be more or less dependent on others. Hence the growing value of commerce. Commerce, which in its accepted sense means the exchange of goods between one country and another, represents the spiritual value of what St. Paul has termed *Charity*, meaning the brotherliness of love. This interdependence of races or nations for food gives rise to the terms familiar to Political Economy—such as production, distribution, exchange, value, currency, etc. These terms mean that St. Paul's pithy saying that "none of us liveth to himself and no man dieth to himself" applies to races and nations as well. Mr. Harry F. Ward, in his book on "The New Social Order," has well pointed out that during the last war "it became glaringly apparent that no nation was sufficient unto itself for its economic life." In 1915, Mr. Lloyd George, who was then the British Prime Minister, said in a public speech that the commandment "'Love thy neighbour as thyself' is not only good religion, but also good business." The idea of Free-Trade first came into the thoughts of the late Mr. Gladstone when he was at the Board of Trade. He saw there

a letter from a Chinese Official at Canton to the head official at
Pekin, suggesting that " no ships should be allowed at Chinese
ports without heavy dues, but that ships bringing food for the
people—that was quite another affair." [1]   That puts the Divine
purpose of different races in a nutshell, so far as their interdependence in respect of the food problem is concerned.

Writing as a Hindu, I may here supplement what I have said
by an appeal to the voice of the Hindu religion in its highest aspects.   The Hindu Scriptures declare that " food is the form of
Brahma," *i. e.,* the Universal Soul.   That is to say, it is a symbol of the Divine—because it is " the life of the whole world."
It is a current proverb in India: " Meat and Matrimony are
Unifiers."

Turning now to the question of the self-realisation of a race as
an indispensable condition of Life, we must first settle what self-
realisation means in the case of a race.   In the case of an individual, we know that there are two selves—the animal self and
the spiritual self.   Self-realisation in the case of an individual
means growing from the lower animal to the higher spiritual
plane of life, man rising (to use the familiar lines of Tennyson)
" on the stepping stones of his dead self."   This he can do only
by trying to realise in his own person the *Ideal of the Absolute,*
the life of the Universal Soul.   What is true of Self-realisation in
the case of an individual man is also true in the case of his race.
Every race has its own peculiar genius, by means of which it is
ordained to express and realise itself to fulfill its allotted mission,
to make its contribution to the good of humanity as a whole, and
thereby to help the cause of the unity of the world and civilisation.   What St. Paul has explained in Chapter XII of I Corin-
thians holds good of races as well as individual persons.   " There
are diversities of gifts but the same spirit; and there are differences of administrations but the same Lord.   And there are diversities of operations but it is the same God which worketh all
in all.   . . .   All these worketh that one and the self-same spirit,
dividing to every man severally as he will."   " There is no differ-

---

[1] Page 193, Sir Algernon West's Diaries.

ence between the Jew and the Greek, for the same Lord over all
is rich unto all that call upon Him." That this law applies to races
also has been so tersely expressed in an article which appeared in
the *International Journal of Ethics* [2] that I shall take the liberty
of citing it here :—After stating that national genius is expressed
only " by aiming at the absolute ideal," that self-consciousness
both in a nation and an individual is a hindrance to self-expression
and " self-realisation," the writer observes, " when a nation has
produced great original work, it has not been by trying to be char-
acteristically *national*, but by seeking to find the absolute truth.
It is by keeping steadily in view the ideal and in obedience to the
universal claims of truth and love that nationality will reach its
highest expression."

To each race, then, its peculiar genius is given in order that all
races may serve one another and out of diversities of gifts constituting the brighter side of racial differences help and promote
mutual good. As beautifully sung by the Scotch divine, Dr.
George Matheson, in his hymn, " One in Christ ":

> " Thine is the mystic light that India craves;
> Thine is the Parsi's sin-destroying beam;
> Thine is the Buddha's rest from tossing waves;
> Thine is the Empire of vast China's dream;
> > Gather us in.
> Thine is the Roman's strength without his pride;
> Thine is the Greek's glad world without its graves;
> Thine is Judea's law, with Love beside—
> The Truth that centres and the Grace that saves.
>
> .   .   .   .   .   .
>
> Within Thy Mansion we have all and more.
> > Gather us in."

II. What is your definition of race? Are the different races fundamentally unlike or are their variations superficial and re-
   movable? If so, to what extent, and through what processes
   or forces?

---

[2] May, 1921.

I do not feel equal to the task of defining the term *race*. That is a task for experts.

I should venture to think that the different races are fundamentally alike if by *fundamentally* we mean *at the core*. The proverbial sayings that "human nature is the same everywhere," and that "one touch of nature makes the whole world kin," record centuries of world-wide experience. Years ago an English Divine—Rev. Mr. Fielding—wrote and published a book on *The Soul of a People*, which then attracted much attention. The author there described the character of the people of Burmah and displayed an insight into it which was the result of his personal contact with and life for a number of years amongst them in their own country. The purport of the book was that it is one Soul, one human heart with the Divine as its indwelling Spirit, which animates all the different races of mankind; that such racial differences as divide peoples and lead to mutual hatred are, however strongly marked, more or less superficial and can be removed by mutual sympathy between race and race. Since then, I believe, "the soul of a people" has become not only a classic phrase, but a familiar expression in literature representing the truth embodied in the English proverbs above cited. Similar proverbs have been from ancient times current in India. It should be easy to prove by facts from history that racial differences are superficial and that *fundamentally*—meaning, at the bottom,—deep down in the recesses of the human heart—all races are alike. The celebrated Darwin, to whom we owe the doctrine of Evolution, has told us that certain Fuegians, who were brought to England in his time, were found by him on close examination to be at the bottom not unlike Englishmen or any other civilised race. The Africans who loved the great Livingstone, and served him faithfully, ready to die for him; the Samoans whom Louis Stevenson gathered about him and who became his ardent followers on account of his loving service to them, so much so that they built a road in his honour and called it "The Road of the Loving Heart," because they called him "the loving heart,"—these are not stray illustrations from actual life. The Old Testament has made us familiar with

the expression that " the Ethiopian cannot change his skin." The
skin no doubt is tough and it may not be easy to eradicate the
habits and qualities, mental and moral, due to the environment of
climate, religion, and traditions which it connotes and breeds. But
after all the skin is an external covering of the human body and
if you creep inside it, you can discover God in the germ in every
man, woman and child of every human race. The Biblical saying
that an Ethiopian cannot change his skin has been taken to mean
that racial nature is ineradicable. If that is so, why has the Bible
used the word " skin " instead of employing the word " nature "
to convey that idea? The studious use of the word " skin " is
significant. And, as General Gordon used to say, we must creep
inside the skin of a man to find his human point of view. The
same God dwells in all—our differences are, after all, but
skin-deep.

While that is so, to each race is given its own genius. The
ancient Greek was different from the ancient Romans ; the Jews
had their own racial characteristics. Just as every individual has
his own personality differentiating him from other individuals, so
every race has its own peculiarities, enabling it to develop itself
on their lines and thereby contribute to the civilisation of mankind as a whole. Those peculiarities may prove a blessing if the
development on their basis is directed by the knowledge and consciousness that all the races are the children of one God bound
together by the chain of the brotherhood of Love. They prove a
curse where the race becomes hidebound and is led by conceit of
itself and treats other races as inferior doomed by nature to
serfdom.

I think that such of the racial variations as are skin-deep, due
to the environment, traditions, and religion of a race and as retard its progress can be removed without detriment to or loss of
those racial variations which constitute the peculiar genius of the
race fitting it to contribute its quota to the civilisation of mankind
as a whole. The racial variations which have proved a hindrance
to that civilisation have persisted either because some races have
lived a self-contained life of isolation, hidebound and separated

from the rest of the civilised world, or because when they have been brought into contact with it, the more civilised and powerful race has treated the backward race as a race of helots, doomed by nature to inferiority, and exploited it for its own aggrandisement. The idea has prevailed that some races have been created by God as superior beings, destined to lord it over other races doomed to inferiority and remain in the lower scale of civilisation. This idea dates from the ancient times and has done much mischief in our own days owing to a misunderstanding of the laws of biology and the doctrine of Evolution made familiar to us in the nineteenth century by Darwin and Spencer. At the Annual Meeting of the Universities Mission to Central Africa, held in London, in May, 1921, Bishop Gore presiding, Archdeacon H. W. Woodward, who had served the Mission since 1878, recounted his experiences which illustrate the way in which this race problem is treated by some European races in the name of Christianity. Archdeacon Woodward said:

" We are told that the best way to civilise the African is to make him work. That depends upon what is meant by civilisation. Work does not necessarily Christianise and does not necessarily lead a man to Christianity. Once a man told me that the best way to help the Africans was to teach them to love strong drink and then they would work well in order to get money to buy it. He was a man with a title. I have often talked with settlers on the subject of work and they speak as though it were the remedy for all evils of body and soul." [3]

The Venerable Archdeacon further stated:

" I was in that country ten years before any other European (except the members of the Mission) came to it. I know that the general moral character of the tribe was higher than it is at the present time. Conduct, which would have been then condemned by the whole tribe, is now treated as a matter of no consequence. I will not say that this is entirely due to the presence of Europeans. It is due also very much to the presence of foreign labourers like the Chinese and the Japanese. It has made our

[3] See *The Guardian;* a London Weekly; 20th May, 1921; page 372.

work harder than it would have been. It has been made harder still by the aloofness from religion on the part of many of our European brothers. In pre-war days the people looked upon most Europeans as non-Christians, if not absolute heathen. It was thought a most remarkable thing last year when an Assistant Political Officer went into a Church to say his prayers. The news went through all the country."

As another illustration of the mischievous and false view which a superior race takes of the races it considers inferior, I would cite what Lord Stanmore told the British Parliament in 1907. He said that a very large proportion of white settlers in Fiji held the view that the natives there ought to be deprived of the ownership of lands, because the natives would then be obliged to sell their labour. The late Hon. James Mason, a large planter and a member of the Legislative Council in Fiji, met His Lordship one day and grumbled at the state of things generally and the state of planting. Lord Stanmore said to him: he had just been moving about the Colony and witnessed more prosperity than had been two years ago,—in every native village new and better houses and extended civilisation, the people looking well-fed, and happy, more pigs and more poultry. Mr. Mason's reply was: " Yes, Sir, of course they are better off; and they are much better off; but we do not want them to be better off; we want them to be ill-off; when they are ill-off, they will come and work for us, but when they are well off, they will not." Lord Stanmore, having recounted that experience, told Parliament:

" I took these words down at the time, and I have often thought of them since. They are an index of the antipathy which is displayed on the part of many settlers to native occupation of land." [4]

This exploitation of the backward races by those higher in civilisation is really at the root of the mischiefs due to the race problems. Providence has intended that the different races should be inter-dependent and history shows that races have risen in the scale of civilisation by coming into contact with one another; but that contact should be one of sympathy, of love as the

[4] See the Official Reports of Parliamentary Debates: House of Commons: IVth series: Vol. 178; Cols. 476 and 478.

golden rule of life for all races, and not one of exploitation for
greed and selfish interests. History also proves—and the Bible
is the most terse and trenchant history on the subject—that a
superior race which exploits an inferior race for its own interests
and aggrandisement digs its own grave by contracting the vices
of the latter—giving to the world (as the Italian statesman Cavour
said) a great lesson and teaching the most powerful nations that
their crimes and their errors recoil sooner or later on those who
commit them.

It follows then:

1. Providence has intended that the different races should be
interdependent. It is a law of nature that a race which lives
isolated from the rest of the world lives a life of stagnation
and decay.

2. Conquest and commerce are the two main agencies employed
by Providence to bring the different races into contact with one
another and learn from and help one another.

3. Races superior in point of civilisation should help the inferior races, when they come in contact with the latter by means
whether of conquest or commerce, by diffusing the blessings of
education, sound religion, sanitation and the like. It should not
be the help of exploitation. The inferior race should be encouraged to stand on its own legs instead of being treated as inferior,
doomed to servitude and unfit to rise in the scale of civilisation.
Christ's teaching: " Be ye perfect as your Father in heaven is
perfect," " Be ye merciful as your Father in heaven is merciful," is the soundest principle for wholesome practice in the regulation of intercourse between superior and inferior races. It is
by following Christ's golden rule of Life that racial differences
can be gradually removed and the two Divine agencies of world-
unity—conquest and commerce—be used, not abused, in fulfilment of the Divine purpose of racial differences. There is no
other sovereign remedy for the eradication of those differences.
It is a long and perhaps painful process, but as St. Paul truly said
in Romans VIII:

" We know that the whole creation groaneth and travaileth in
pain together until now. We are saved by hope. . . . Likewise

the Spirit also helpeth our infirmities. . . . And we know all things work together for good to them that love God, to them who are the called according to his purpose. . . . Nay, in all these things we are more than conquerors through him that loved us."

To what extent racial differences can be removed is a question which it is difficult to answer. Ours is to work, directed by the golden rule of Christ—the results are in His hands, whose instruments we are. So far as the world has moved forward, it has moved by the light of that rule.

" Nothing," wrote Kant, " can possibly be conceived in the world or out of it, which can be considered good without qualifications except a good-will. Intelligence, wit, judgment, and other talents of the mind, however they may be named, or courage, resolution, perseverance, as qualities of temperament, are undoubtedly good and desirable in many respects ; but these gifts may become extremely bad and mischievous, if the Will which is to make use of them and which, therefore, constitutes what is called Character is not good."

On that Mr. Pringle Pattison in his Gifford Lectures on *The Idea of God* remarks : " The most perfect realisation of unity in variety is as naught, if there is nowhere anything to which we can attach this predicate of Value."

This principle of good will is in theory praised. There is no conquering nation which has denied in profession at least that its duty is to govern the conquered for the good of the latter. But the practice has more or less departed from the profession and measures designed in reality to serve the selfish interests of the conqueror have been supported on the ground that they are for the good of the conquered. That has been more or less the character of modern diplomacy. The ancient conquerors, not having the benefit of expanded ideas of religion and the brotherhood of the human race which we moderns have, made their professions consistent with their practice. Modern conquerors have no excuse for the *camouflage* which marks the dealings of most, if not all of them, with the backward races, whether conquered or not.

4. The scholars and learned men of the different races should form a brotherhood and become the bond of union among them.

Emerson has well defined a scholar as a man of all climes and ages. The Universities as seats of learning should take up this question and become among the centres for propagating the ideas of human brotherlihood and propagate correct ideas on racial differences.

5. The Press has come to be a most powerful agency for spreading ideas and forming opinions in these times. It is to this age what the Prophets were to the old ages. While the Press has done much good to the world, it has done much harm also. As has been said, wars and racial animosities have often been made by the Press. The worst of it is that with the growth of industrialism and commerce, the Press has also been becoming more and more a commercial venture, fostering racial prejudices and pandering to racial vanity. The prophet of the age is becoming its pedlar. In these times of democracy, men and women hang on the newspapers and have no time to think or reason for themselves. It is a great deal in the hands of the Press to diffuse sound ideas on the question of race and racial differences.

6. *Above all,* the churches should fulfil their proper function by insisting that races shall deal with one another on the cardinal principle of religion embodied in Christ's teaching: " Love thy neighbour as thyself "; " All things whatsoever ye would that men should do to you, do ye even so to them." It has been recorded of Alfred the Great that he gathered the laws of England together and ordered many to be written which the forefathers of Englishmen had held; he promulgated such of those laws as he approved, rejected those he disapproved and had other ordinances enacted with the counsel of his Witan; and he introduced the laws so enacted by quoting these rare and everlasting words of Jesus: " Whatsoever ye would that men should do to you, do ye even so to them." And quoting that he added: " By this one commandment a man shall know whether he does right, and then he will require no other law book."

III. What is the teaching of Hinduism and Mohammedanism with regard to race? Please compare these religions and Christianity in their relation to the race problem.

Hinduism: To understand the teaching of Hinduism with regard to race, it is necessary to bear in mind that Hinduism is not one creed, but a conglomeration of creeds, ranging from the highest form of Monotheism to the lowest form of Animism. Just as Christ preached both to Jew and Gentile, " Be ye perfect as your Father in Heaven is perfect," thereby declaring to men of all races whatsoever, in spite of their racial differences, it is given to be perfect, and grow in point of character and personality, so also the Hindu Scriptures known as the *Upanishads* maintain that growth in perfection is open to all and within the reach of all because the Universe and every element, animate or inanimate in it, has the seed of perfection. Just as Christ sought to help that growth by leading His followers step by step, so also Hinduism maintains that men must be led gradually to the attainment of perfection. But there the comparison ends and the contrast begins. Christ chose His followers from amongst the most ignorant and sinful of people. He worked from the bottom to the top. He held before them the ideal of the Absolute and by its help raised them to " perfection." There He proved the true psychologist of human nature. Elevate the lower, the higher are necessarily elevated, being provoked to emulation (to use St. Paul's words). But elevate the higher, it does not follow that the lower are also elevated. Hence Christ devoted His service to the finding and saving of " the lost sheep." Christ has also proved that the masses and the most backward classes can be gradually raised more effectively by a straight and simple appeal to what is called " the tremendous dialectics " and " the audacious logic " of the human heart than by an appeal to the logic of reasoning or the subtleties of Metaphysics or Theology. That was Christ's way of winning men to the path of perfection. He made that path open to all without distinction of race. Hinduism, on the other hand, by its doctrine of caste, has practically inculcated the principle that a man's destiny in life is determined by his birth; he cannot rise into a higher caste. An appeal to the Absolute, it holds, is for the highly cultured classes only—the lower classes, the average man must be left to conform to lower forms of worship and life. In its operation, this way of Hinduism has had the effect of separating caste from caste and retarding the brotherhood of races. Hinduism for centuries, has banned travel to foreign lands for fear that its followers may get corrupted thereby. At the same time it has allowed foreigners to come and settle in India and live as a separate race. It has never put a ban on immigration from foreign lands and of foreign races into India.

This paradoxical attitude of Hinduism—its fear of the mixture of castes and races, its toleration of other races and faiths, represents both its weak and strong points. Toleration is good, but when allied to unreasonable fear of corruption from caste and race mixture it leads to stagnation. We see the result—Hinduism has become a mixture of multitudinous creeds and castes and disunion. This evil side of Hinduism has not been without a protest and a revolt against it from within its own fold. That protest and revolt came from Buddha first and after him from the saints of the school called *Bhakti* (Devotion), whose Bible is the *Bhagavad-Gita* and who flourished in the fourteenth and fifteenth centuries after Christ. According to popular and orthodox Hinduism, the world has passed through certain Ages such as the Golden and the Iron Age; the present Age is called the Age of *Kali* (the Destroyer). The popular belief about that Age is that it is destined to end in the mixture of castes and races, when anarchy will prevail and each man and each woman will break away from the bonds of authority and religion; and the world will become a chaos first and ruin afterwards.

This Hindu belief formed the subject of a prophecy foretold in a Hindu Purana (mythological book) dating from 1000 B. C. There it is written of the present age: " The man who owns most gold and lavishly distributes it will gain dominion over all. Religion will consist in wasting alms at large and self-willed women will seek for power. They who rule the State will rule the people and abstract the wealth of merchants on the plea of raising taxes. And in the world's last age the rights of man will be confused, no property be safe." [5] The present Age, then, stands in the eye of

---

[5] See this quoted by Sir F. Banbury in the House of Commons on the 17th May, 1909, in opposing the Budget Resolutions of Mr. Lloyd George: Parl. Deb. Vth Ser: Vol. V: Col. 10.

popular Hinduism as the Age of Sin and Unrighteousness, bringing in its train all the evils of what is called *Sankara,* an Indian word meaning the corruption and ruin of mankind through mixture of the different races.

Against this belief the saints I have above mentioned have fought hard and striven to dislodge it. They have praised the present Age as the Age of Hope and Salvation for human kind, especially the weakest and lowest of the human race. They have, therefore, represented it as the Golden Age of the World and described its virtues in glowing terms. According to them, in the past ages the masses were kept down by the higher classes and the true knowledge of God was made inaccessible to them. Rights of humanity were thereby withheld from the masses. But in the present age God has manifested Himself to all, irrespective of caste and race; even the meanest menial can now win God by simple devotion and a righteous life without the aid of' formal rites and ceremonial religion which made religion and life a matter of outward observances in the past and the privilege of the higher castes only. That in essence is the teaching of the *Bhagavad-Gita*—that God is no respecter of persons or races; that distinctions of *colour* (meaning race) have been ordained by Him not by the test of *birth,* but by the test of each man's qualities and actions. Following that teaching, another Scripture of the Hindus —the *Bhagavad Purana*—declares that the Golden Age of the World was not in the Past, but that the present *Kali* Age is the Golden Age because it brings together all the different races and castes, high and low, into the bonds of brotherhood. This idea is the theme of numerous hymns composed by nearly all the Indian saints. As a sample may be quoted here a hymn of the well known Maratha Saint Tukaram, who is the most popular saint among the masses in Western India and who lived in the sixteenth century A. D. In that hymn he sang:

" God's Liberty has come into the market places of the world. Let all freely partake of it. Come unto it, ye people of all castes; accept the free gift and share it to your heart's content and be blessed." There is no distinction here of caste between man and man, high or low.

In short, I may adopt the language of St. Paul and say that according to the saints in India, in the present Age we are no longer under the dominion of the Law (called the *Shastras* by Hinduism), but we are under grace, called upon to "serve in newness of spirit and not in the oldness of the letter." This is the common meeting ground for Hinduism and Christianity with reference to the race problem.

Coming now to the question of the race problem as viewed by Mohammedanism, the Prophet Mohammed made no distinction between race and race—he opened his creed to all.

Now, to compare Hinduism, Mohammedanism and Christianity in their relation to the race problem, the defect of Hinduism (in its popular sense) is that it regards racial differences as *natural* and countenances the idea of fatalism. Hinduism is a religion of toleration—its doctrine is " Live and let live." These words sum up its popular creed. When I was a boy and was sent to a school kept by a Christian Missionary, the Missionary who taught us the Bible, every day for an hour, used to denounce Hinduism in violent terms. My maternal grandfather, who brought me up and sent me to the school for education, was an orthodox Brahmin. I naturally resented the Missionary's abuse of Hinduism. One day, unable to stand the abuse any longer, I complained to my grandfather. Instead of resenting the conduct of the Missionary, my grandfather counselled me to pay no heed to the Missionary's view of Hinduism. " But, Grandpapa," I said, " is the Missionary right in saying that Hinduism is a false religion, and that Christianity is the only true religion? " My grandfather replied as follows:

" God is One but men are many. To each man God has given his own peculiar religion to follow. Man's religion is determined for him according to the race he is born in. It happened in this way. Once upon a time a Christian, a Mohammedan and a Hindu approached God. The Christian asked: ' How am I to worship Thee, O Lord? ' God made a cross of two fingers of His hand and so Christians worship the Cross. The Mohammedan next asked the same question. God held up the palm of His hand and showed him the five fingers of His hand. Therefore Mohammedans worship God in the form of those five fingers. Last of all the Hindu enquired likewise. To him God showed Himself as an idol and bade him worship God in that form." "If that is so," I asked my grandfather, "all the three religions are true. Why, then, does the Christian Missionary abuse our Hindu religion as false?" My grandfather quieted me with the following answer:

"Each man ought to be proud of his own religion. So the Christian is proud of his. My boy, be proud of your own religion and be tolerant of the rest! Listen quietly to the Missionary, but go on your own way, not minding what he says, but following the religion prescribed by God to us, Hindus."

I cite this for the purpose of illustrating my point that Hinduism is a religion of toleration sometimes carried to excess. It has no aggressiveness about it. It has enrolled even the Apostle of Atheism—Kapila—as one of its objects of worship. Thus Hinduism survives by yielding even where it ought not to yield and perpetuates among other evils the evil of caste and race differences.

The defect of Mohammedanism is that it errs on the other side —it is intolerant. It treats all races not brought within its fold as "infidels." That proves a hindrance to the right solution of the race problem and racial differences.

Christianity as taught by Christ is wisely tolerant. He lived and taught by

"Working miracles
Not on the waves and winds but in the wills
Of men, upon the hearts of multitudes,
Healing, restoring, blessing."

But the question is whether Christianity, meaning by it the Christianity of the Churches, has been "healing, restoring, blessing," by walking in the footsteps of the Master as it should. The doctrine of "the White Man's Burden," "the Open Door," and other phrases of modern polity in Europe have intensified the problem of racial differences with the result that, as remarked by the Archbishop of York in his address at the Church Congress

held at Sheffield (England), in October, 1922, " Religion attracts
but the Church repels." The Church repels because it has not
kept faith with the Master as it should and has left the field of
the race problem to politicians, statesmen and economists who have
no vision beyond " my country and race, right or wrong."

IV. What do you conceive to be the right solution of race problems? In what senses are races equal or to be considered
equal? What is your view of racial inter-marriage?

In my answer to Question No. II I have stated what, in my
opinion, are the processes or forces to be employed for the removal of the superficial variations of the different races. To that
I would here add that the right solution of race problems primarily depends on Education.

Dr. Lester F. Ward, a great American authority upon the New
Science of Sociology, has said in his book, *Applied Sociology,*
that the only solution of racial problems lies in Education.
" Wars," so stated the *London Times Literary Supplement,* in its
issue of the 16th of July, 1921, " are made in class rooms before
they ever come up for discussion in the Council room of the
States." The last war, which has made havoc of the world and
laid bare the evils of modern civilisation, was due (it is generally
admitted) to the fact that the wells of youth had been poisoned
by false notions of *patriotism* and *nationality* taught and encouraged in the home and the school. If we are to solve the race
problem, we must first solve the educational problem. The future
citizens of a country must be caught young for that purpose.
The education of a people does not mean education in schools and
colleges only. It means the home also. Both in the home and the
class room an atmosphere of wholesome patriotism and sound
nationality should be created. Youth should be taught and
brought up on and in the idea that *patriotism* and *nationality* are
and ought to be paths leading to love of the human race—the
brotherhood of the races. It is a wise saying of Bacon's: " If I
might control the literature of the household I would guarantee
the well-being of the Church and the State." How can peace and
amity be secured among the different races when in the class

rooms and homes youth are fed, so to say, on knowledge fostering false notions of love of one's own country and race hatred or jealousy or contempt of other races?

It is just three years since I had a painful experience in this matter. An Indian friend of mine, who occupies a high position as a member of the Indian Civil Service—a gentleman who has been to England and moved in English society and is widely cultured—was staying in a hotel with his accomplished wife— also an Indian—and their son, a boy ten years of age. In the same hotel resided a European lady with her son, about six years old. I used to go every morning to the hotel to see my Indian friend and his wife. For some days I found their son and the European boy playing together on friendly terms. The Indian boy spoke English as well as any English boy and both took kindly to each other. One morning, however, when I went up to the hotel, I heard the European boy say to the Indian boy: " I am not going to play with you. Don't come near me. Mamma has asked me not to play with you, not to speak to you because you are a black man." This is how race conceit and hatred are fostered in the home.

Home life, they say, is gradually declining in Europe and America and is being replaced by club life. I do not know how far that is true. But a good home or family life is the fountain of sound national life. The right solution of the race problem must begin with sound education in the atmosphere of the home and the class room. The infinite worth of man, whatever his race, of even the downmost man, should animate that atmosphere.

The present is an industrial and economic age; and its industrial and economic arrangements have proceeded on lines which intensify the evil of class and racial differences. The right solution of the race problem will come if the Age realises the value of the conclusions arrived at in 1920 by the Conference, held at Lambeth, and composed of 253 Bishops of the Anglican Church. In the Report issued by the Conference they say that experience has shown that the doctrine that the best possible condition of society as a whole is that in which different individuals, sections, interests, or classes pursue their own self interest is absolutely false; and that nothing less than a fundamental change in the spirit and working of our economic life is necessary. And they remark: " This change can only be effected by accepting as the basis of industrial relations the principle of co-operation in service for the common good in place of unrestricted competition for private profit. . . . As God is our Father and as the Eternal Son of God took our whole human nature upon Him, every son and daughter of God is of infinite and equal value. There are wide differences in capacity, but such differences do not warrant any loss of liberty or failure to give to the children of God the opportunity of a full human life."

In this alone lies the right solution of the race problem.

Now, as to the question " in what sense are races equal or are considered to be equal."

Races, like individuals who compose a race, may not be equal— in fact are not—in point of intellectual, moral or physical endowments, but they are all *equal* in the sense that every race, like every man, is equally entitled to (1) life, (2) liberty, (3) the pursuit of happiness. These are the natural rights of every race as of every human being. That every human being is of worth goes without saying. No one in his senses, I believe, disputes that. As to *liberty*, every race has a right to live its own life and mould its own destiny, and to resist enslavement by another race. If we understand liberty in the only sense in which it makes man worthy—that is to say, the liberty to be a free man of God, living a life of service—a life of self-renouncing love—all races are equally fitted for it.

I think St. Paul has helped us to discern in what sense all races are equal or are considered to be equal. " Are all apostles? Are all prophets? Are all teachers? Are all workers of miracles? Have all the gifts of healing? Do all speak with tongues? Do all interpret? But covet earnestly the best gifts." All races are equal in that power to covet which alone can solve the race problem.

As to racial intermarriage, I do not agree with those who disapprove of racial intermarriages and condemn them wholesale as leading to racial degeneracy. Why should an intermarriage prove a failure if it is really a love marriage? Intermarriages have proved unhappy (within my knowledge) because they have not been love marriages. Have not marriages between persons of the same race proved failures? I would not actively encourage a racial intermarriage. At the same time neither would I actively discourage and condemn it. The prejudice against intermarriage is rooted in racial prejudices and hatred. Remove the causes of the latter—the problem of racial intermarriage will solve itself.

V. (a) What is the relation of Colour to the race problem?
(b) What is the relation of Race to Nationality?
As to (a):
Though colour has not been the sole determining factor of racial differences, and even the different races of the same colour have prejudices against one another, leading to grave misunderstandings, sometimes ending in wars, yet colour is a more potent cause of those differences than anything else. It is in fact day by day proving the greatest hindrance to the solution of the race problem. Judging from the present, the world-struggle of the future threatens to be between the white races and the so-called coloured races.
As to (b):
Race at one time played a very important part in the formation of nationalities. As pointed out by Mr. A. F. Pollard in his book on *The Evolution of Parliament,* "there are various means by which unity has been stamped upon the peoples of the world. In primitive times and backward communities it has been simply a matter of race." But conquest, commerce, and other agencies of modern civilisation, which have brought the different races of the world into more or less contact and communion with one another, have tended to minimise the place of race upon nationality. Nationality—a term difficult to define precisely—has grown out of several elusive elements; but in the main it has come to be the product of a common political consciousness. In the words of Renan, " nationality grows among a people composed of different races not out of identity of speech or race, but from the fact of having accomplished in the past great things in common with the

desire to achieve like things in the future." Nationality, in short, represents the idea of community of *State* or political sovereignty; a race represents community of blood and descent.

VI. What is the cause of racial prejudice?

The proverb runs: "Blood is thicker than water." That is the root of all prejudice, racial included. To keep one's blood pure is an instinct implanted by Nature in man to conserve all that is good in him. In that respect and so far racial prejudice is a virtue because it conserves society. But we do not often see rightly what is good and what is bad and our habit becomes a second nature, so that in the case of race, differences of colour, customs, manners, and religion intensify racial prejudice. Some years ago an American lady, a Professor in one of the Women's colleges there, visited India. I met her and we had a long interview. In the course of our conversation she narrated to me an incident, which I shall describe here as a pointed illustration of how racial prejudices possess us, as it were, instinctively. The American lady met a fellow passenger on board the steamer carrying her to India. The English lady was coming out to India to join her brother, a military officer, stationed at Poona in the Bombay Presidency, and to keep home for him. The English lady told the American Professor that she felt so keenly interested in the people of India that on arrival at Poona and during her residence there and elsewhere in India, she was going to move among Indians and try to be friendly, useful, and serviceable to them. " But," remarked the American lady, " to be useful and serviceable you will have to overcome your racial prejudice. You will find Indians different from you in point of colour, habits, customs, and manners; and that may change your mind. Are you prepared to overcome your racial prejudice?" The English lady replied: " Certainly I am prepared and I have no prejudice. I mean to rise above all prejudice." A few days after this conversation, the steamer arrived at the port of Aden. There both ladies with other passengers were watching the sight of black Negroes yelling, diving into the sea and coming up to amuse and get money out of the passengers, as their reward for all their quaint feats in

the sea. The English lady, shocked at the sight of the half-naked
and black Negro boys and men, said to the American lady: " How
queer! " The latter asked: " Why do you say *queer?* It is queer
because it is a new sight to you. You may more properly call it
a strange sight, but to say it is queer means it is absurd, unnatural
or foolish, but is it so really? Is not your racial prejudice accountable for your view of the sight? Is not your view queer, not the
sight? " The English lady said to that: " It did not strike me
that way." The American lady advised: " It ought to strike you
that way or else your racial prejudice will thwart your resolution
to be useful, friendly and sympathetic to the people of India."
Racial prejudice is thus the result of differences of colour, customs
and habits. The only way to get over it is to educate ourselves, so
to say, in what Wordsworth finely calls " the sanctity of nature
given to Man " in

> " That kind
> Of prepossession without which the soul
> Receives no knowledge that can bring forth good,
> No genuine insight ever comes to her."

VII. To what extent do the Indians admit or deny feelings either
of racial superiority or racial inferiority between themselves
and other races?

The bulk of India's people consists of Hindus and Mohammedans. Hindus have from ancient times regarded all other races
as *Mlenchas* (a term carrying the same meaning as the word
barbarian which the ancient Greeks used of foreigners with a
view to exclude them from Greek morality). But the Hindus,
notwithstanding that racial prejudice, have been distinguished for
their spirit of toleration, so that their feelings of racial superiority
have not been of a hostile or even contemptuous character. The
Mohammedans of India share the Mohammedan feeling of racial
superiority—all those who are not Mohammedans are " infidels."
While that is so, it is to the credit of Indians that their feelings
of race superiority have never been intense and aggressive as those
of the European races. But modern politics, I am afraid, are

tending to breed in Indians that intensity and aggressiveness of racial superiority.

VIII. Are you yourself aware of having any feelings of race consciousness or racial prejudices?

I am aware of having feelings of *race consciousness*, but I am not, I believe, aware of having any feelings of racial prejudice.

I ought to make myself as clear as possible as to this answer.

By *race consciousness* I understand the feeling of legitimate pride one has in one's race by reason of its achievements and contribution to the *service* of mankind without being blind to its blemishes. *Racial prejudice* I take to mean the conceit one has of one's own race accompanied by contempt or hatred of or indifference to the interests of other races. Race consciousness is love of other races as love of one's own, because all are parts of one whole. *Racial prejudice* is loving one's own race at the expense of other races. When Pasteur, on seeing his country, France, conquered and humiliated by Germany in 1870, felt for his race, and, resolving to raise its *prestige* in the eyes of the whole world and so to remove that stigma of humiliation, devoted himself, heart and soul, to the cause of medical science and relief for the benefit of the whole human race, and when at last he proved one of the world's benefactors, thereby increasing the honour of his race, it was race consciousness which prompted him to his glorious task. Bismarck was an instance of racial prejudice—the man of blood and iron who, proud of his Fatherland, worked to make Germany great at the expense of other races.

The prophets of Israel had race consciousness, no race prejudice.

Above all, the finest illustration of race consciousness was given when Jesus uttered: " O Jerusalem, Jerusalem, which killeth the prophets and stonest them that are sent unto thee! How often would I have gathered thy children together, as a hen *doth gather* her brood under her wings, and ye would not! "

IX. In what respects is the caste problem in India like and unlike the inter-racial problem?

Caste in India would seem to have originated in the idea of distinction by colour. That appears from the fact that in those of the ancient Hindu Scriptures in which it is mentioned it is designated by the Sanskrit word *Varna,* meaning " colour." But the idea of colour has in process of time disappeared altogether from the *signification of caste,* which has come to be determined solely by the Hindu community in which a person is born. So in respect of that signification, the caste problem and the inter-racial problem are alike. Birth is the determining factor of both. In point of prejudice against inter-dining and intermarriage, both problems are alike, but with this difference that, in the case of the inter-racial problem, the prejudice is not necessarily sanctioned by law, but only by the social opinion of the race concerned, whereas the prejudice sanctioned by caste had legal sanction from the state. A man who marries outside his caste—and for that purpose race is included in the term caste—lost some of his civil rights and his *status,* and the children by such marriage were deemed by law illegitimate. That was the original Hindu law, but British enactments have softened its rigours to some extent, so that a Hindu can now marry outside his caste or race without any forfeiture of civil rights. Thus both the caste problem and the inter-racial problem have become alike in that the prejudice against inter-dining and intermarriage can be enforced only by social but not legal penalties.

While the two problems so far present common features, the caste problem is day by day becoming more easy of solution than the inter-racial problem. In the first place, caste has survived, so many centuries after its birth, because it has gone on adapting itself quietly and without revolution or the bloodshed of civil wars to the changing conditions of time and circumstance. It has gone on conquering by yielding. The Hindu is nothing if not an adept in compromise—that is his strength in some respects; his weakness in many. Inter-dining and intermarriages are not treated with the same attitude of hostility and excommunication and social persecution that they aroused, say, even twenty years ago. The conditions of modern civilisation, the play of world forces, and the acuteness of the racial problem both in India and outside where Indians have emigrated and settled, have awakened Hindus to the weakness of their position created by caste distinctions. So caste is losing gradually its old force, whereas the inter-racial problem seems to be gathering strength. In the second place, although caste was an institution devised in its inception for the economic arrangements of society on the principle of division of labour, it has since several centuries ceased to have that economic character. It is now merely a matter of religious and social arrangement, whereas the inter-racial problem is day by day becoming more and more a political and economic problem—a struggle between the different races for political power for economic ends—for food and wealth and over-lordship of the earth.

VII

THE SOLUTION OF THE RACE PROBLEM

"YE need na pray for peace," remarked a character in *Wee Macgregor*, "gin the Lord gie ye laddies." A world of races is no static world. The dream of a settled, undisturbed order in such a world is an illusion. Perhaps that is one reason why God made races. Every race and all race relationships are undergoing change. There is no stability of human types, and the heredity of racial superiority is as insecure as racial character.[1]

> "The Lord's at the loom
> Room for Him, room!"

The races are here with a divine purpose, namely the diversification and enrichment of the whole life of humanity, and there is a right solution of the problem of their relationships. It is a confused spectacle which we witness if we look back over history or survey the world today, but a very little faith can see in it the struggle of the truth and love of God toward a world of unity and unselfishness, toward the subjugation of what is partial and transient and evil to the higher and perfect law.[2] But there are many who disbelieve this and there are many different conceptions both of the process and of the goal.

1. There are those who see no future different from the past. The story of race in their view will be a story of continued struggle and conflict. These are the terms in which one school of stu-

---

[1] *Universal Races Congress,* 1911, p. 103. Compare Meredith Townsend's ideas of race stability and fixedness in *Asia and Europe* with the facts set forth in Gulick, *Evolution of the Japanese; China Today through Chinese Eyes;* Temple, *Native Races and Their Rulers.*
[2] Kidd, *Western Civilisation,* p. 409.

287

dents of the race problem conceive it. The titles of their books, so
frequently cited in these pages, express their view. They see the
evidence of it all over the world.

"Let the brown world once make up its mind that the white
man must go, and he will go," says Stoddard, " for his position
will have become simply impossible. It is not solely a question of
a 'Holy War'; mere passive resistance, if genuine and general,
would shake white rule to its foundations. And it is precisely the
determination to get rid of white rule which seems to be spreading
like wild fire over the brown world today. . . . The crux of
the African problem therefore resolves itself into the question
whether the white man, through consolidated racial holds north
and south, will be able to perpetuate his present political control
over the intermediate continental mass." [3] And speaking of the
Great War, " As coloured men realised the significance of it all,
they looked into each other's eyes and there saw the light of
undreamed-of hopes. The white world was tearing itself to pieces.
White solidarity was riven and shattered. And—fear of white
power and respect for white civilisation together dropped away
like garments outworn. Through the bazaars of Asia ran the
sibilant whisper : ' The East will see the West to bed ! ' "

The chorus of mingled exultation, hate, and scorn sounded from
every portion of the coloured world ! [4] I have gone through the
coloured world of Asia twice since the great War began and heard
this chorus nowhere,—not one word of exultation, hate or scorn,
but only the common sentiment of grief and shame at the old order
and of hope and longing for a better day. No doubt writers of
books and manipulators of parties in Asia talk the talk of strife,
but the people are weary of the jungle with its raven and its
fangs.[5]

We must recognise that there are some who regard the continuance of racial struggle as a good thing. Professor von
Luschan, of the University of Berlin, ended his paper with this
note at the Universal Races Congress in 1911 :

---

[3] Stoddard, *The Rising Tide of Colour*, pp. 83, 89.
[4] *Ibid.*, p. 13 .
[5] Townsend, *Asia and Europe*, p. 214 f.

" Racial barriers will never cease to exist, and if ever they should show a tendency to disappear, it will certainly be better to preserve than to obliterate them.

" The brotherhood of man is a good thing, but the struggle for life is a far better one. Athens would never have become what it was, without Sparta, and national jealousies and differences, and even the most cruel wars, have ever been the real causes of progress and mental freedom.

" As long as man is not born with wings, like the angels, he will remain subject to the eternal laws of Nature, and therefore he will always have to struggle for life and existence. No Hague Conferences, no International Tribunals, no international papers and peace societies, and no Esperanto or other international language, will ever be able to abolish war.

" The respect due by the white races to other races and by the white races to each other can never be too great, but natural law will never allow racial barriers to fall, and even national boundaries will never cease to exist.

" Nations will come and go, but racial and national antagonism will remain; and this is well, for mankind would become like a herd of sheep, if we were to lose our national ambition and cease to look with pride and delight, not only on our industries and science, but also on our splendid soldiers and our glorious ironclads. Let small-minded people whine about the horrid cost of Dreadnoughts; as long as every nation in Europe spends, year after year, much more money on wine, beer, and brandy than on her army and navy, there is no reason to dread our impoverishment by militarism." [6]

And Americans and Englishmen have yielded to or even advocated this same theory of the jungle solution of race as the only possible solution. Mr. Mann, of Illinois, said in Congress in a discussion of the Philippine Islands: " I have no doubt that a conflict will come between the Far East and the Far West across the Pacific Ocean. All that is taking place in the world, the logic of the history of the human race up to now, teaches us that the avoidance of this conflict is impossible. I hope it will be only a commercial conflict. I hope war may not come, but I have little faith in this world of ours that people and races are able to meet in competition for a long period of time without armed conflict.

---

[6] *Universal Races Congress,* 1911, p. 23.

A fight for commercial supremacy leads in the end to a fight with arms, because that is the final arbiter between nations." And Professor Dicey, of Cambridge University, declared: " In every part of the world where British interests are at stake, I am in favour of advancing and upholding these interests, even at the cost of annexation and at the risk of war. The only qualification I admit, is that the country we desire to annex or take under our protection, the claims we choose to assert, and the cause we decide to espouse, should be calculated to confer a tangible advantage upon the British Empire." [7]

The classic enunciation of this view of the inevitable continuance of the present order of rival races, with the tables ever turning more and more against the white peoples is the picture of C. H. Pearson in *National Life and Character*:

" The day will come, and perhaps is not far distant, when the European observer will look round to see the globe girdled with a continuous zone of the black and yellow races, no longer too weak for aggression, or under tutelage, but independent, or practically so, in government, monopolising the trade of their own regions, and circumscribing the industry of the European; when Chinamen and the nations of Hindustan, the States of South America, by that time predominantly Indian, and it may be African nations of the Congo and the Zambesi, under a dominant caste of foreign rulers, are represented by fleets in the European seas, invited to international conferences, and welcomed as allies in the quarrels of the civilised world. The citizens of these countries will then be taken up into the social relations of the white races, will throng the English turf, or the salons of Paris, and will be admitted to intermarriage. It is idle to say that, if all this should come to pass, our pride of place will not be humiliated. We were struggling amongst ourselves in a world which we thought of as destined to belong to the Aryan and to the Christian faith, to the letters and arts and charm of social manners which we have inherited from the best times in the past. We shall wake to find ourselves elbowed and hustled, and perhaps even thrust aside, by peoples whom we looked down upon as servile and thought of as bound always to minister to our needs."

---

[7] *Nineteenth Century,* Sept., 1899, art. on " Peace and War in South Africa."

We cannot feel very greatly indebted to those who offer us this as the only solution of the problem of race relationships.[8]

2. A second solution is offered by those who believe in the isolation and segregation of the races. Some argue that the West should leave the East alone, or at least interfere as little as it can. Some years ago a book appeared under the title, " What Social Classes Owe to One Another," and the answer given was, " Above all to keep apart." [9] With some this is a counsel of sheer desperation. So Mr. Rowell argues in his defense of Japanese exclusion from California.

" Our people have learned their racial lessons in a dangerous school. We have dealt with two inferior darker races, but never with an equal one, and we have dealt always unjustly. We have dealt unjustly with the Negro and he submits. We have dealt unjustly with the Indian and he is dead. If we have many Japanese, we shall not know how to deal otherwise than unjustly with them, and very properly they will not submit. The only real safety is in *separation*. Nature erected a barrier which man will overpass only at his peril. . . . On the great problem let this nation resolve as firmly as California is resolved that one side of the Pacific shall be the white man's and the other side the brown man's frontier. Only so is our race, our civilisation, or the peace of the world secure." [10]

Generally, however, in the field of race relationships one seldom hears this view urged in behalf of the lower races except as against Christian missions. It is usually advanced in behalf of the white races, either by those who want to protect the supremacy of those races or by those who regard the invasion of other racial territory by white men as right, but all invasion of white men's territory by other races as wrong.[11] Mr. Madison Grant repre-

---

[8] Dean Inge does not offer a much more hopeful view in his essay on " The White Man and His Rivals " in *Outspoken Essays,* Second Series, pp. 209-230.

[9] *Western Races and the World,* p. 18.

[10] *The New Republic,* Sept. 15, 1920. Art. by Chester H. Rowell, " California and the Japanese Problem."

[11] " The mass of the European population in South Africa knows very little about the situation. Its imagination has been captured by the loose use of that blessed word ' segregation,' so that it now declares that *segre-*

sents the first group. He would not even share the white race's ideals with other people: "Democratic ideals among a homogeneous population of Nordic blood, as in England or America, is one thing, but it is quite another for the white man to share his blood with, or entrust his ideals to, brown, yellow, black or red men. This is suicide pure and simple, and the first victim of this amazing folly will be the white man himself." [12] Of the other group Wu Ting Fang once spoke plainly:

"It is said that some countries should be reserved exclusively for white people, and that no race of another colour should be permitted there. When such a doctrine is openly approved by statesmen in the West, the yellow or coloured race should in fairness be allowed to act upon it themselves. Patriotism is an excellent quality; but to preach the dogma of colour, race, or nationalism is a matter of grave international importance, and should not be handled without serious consideration. If such a doctrine should spread and be generally followed, men would become more narrow-minded than ever, and would not hesitate to take undue advantage of peoples of other colour or race whenever an opportunity occurred. Altruism would certainly disappear. Instead of friendly feelings and hearty co-operation existing between Occidental and Oriental peoples, there would be feelings of distrust, ill-will, and animosity towards each other; constant friction and disputes would take place and might ultimately lead to war. I have noticed that this cry of 'White policy' has been raised, not by the aborigines, who might have some excuse, but by the descendants or settlers who had conquered and, in many cases, killed the aborigines of the country, which they now want to keep for themselves, and by politicians who recently migrated to that country. Is this fair or just? To those who advocate such a policy, and who no doubt call themselves highly civilised people, I would remark that I prefer Chinese civilisation. According to the Chinese civilisation, as interpreted in the Confucian classics, we are taught that 'we should treat all who are within the four seas as our brothers and sisters; and that what you do not want done to yourself you should not do to others.'

---

gation is the policy of South Africa, by which it understands that a place will be found somewhere for the native far enough away to prevent his mixing or competing with the Europeans, but not so far away that he cannot return periodically to do their rough manual labour."—London *Times*, April 24, 1923.

[12] Introduction to *The Rising Tide of Colour*, p. 32.

" Until racial and national feeling is eliminated from the minds of Occidental peoples, it is to be feared genuine friendship and coöperation between them and Oriental peoples cannot really exist." [13]

As a matter of fact the principle of segregation rightly interpreted and applied is a sound and just principle and essential to the educational processes through which God is putting each race and all humanity.[14] Each people needs room to develop its own character and contribution to the common wealth of mankind. And there is valid ground in this principle for righteous and reasonable immigration laws on the part of the white people and there is equally valid ground for the claim of other races for protection against white invasions which hinder and do not help their own racial development.[15]

Marcus Garvey zealously argues for the segregation of the Negro people in a republic of their own in Africa :

" We believe that the black people should have a country of their own where they should be given the fullest opportunity to develop politically, socially and industrially. The black people should not be encouraged to remain in white people's countries and expect to be Presidents, Governors, Mayors, Senators, Congressmen, Judges and social and industrial leaders. We believe that with the rising ambition of the Negro, if a country is not provided for him in another 50 or 100 years, there will be a terrible clash that will end disastrously to him and disgrace our civilisation. We desire to prevent such a clash by pointing the Negro to a home of his own. We feel that all well-disposed and broadminded white men will aid in this direction. . . . Looking forward a century or two, we can see an economic and political death struggle for the survival of the different race groups. Many of our present-day national centres will have become overcrowded with vast surplus populations. The fight for bread and position will be keen and severe. The weaker and unprepared group is bound to go under. That is why, visionaries as we are in the

[13] *Universal Races Congress*, 1911, p. 131 f.
[14] For a statement of the argument against the " Separation of Black and White in the Church," see *The East and the West*, July, 1914, pp. 330-334.
[15] See *World Dominion*, March 15, 1924.   Art. by C. T. Loram, " Race Relationship in South Africa," p. 43 f.

Universal Negro Improvement Association, we are fighting for the founding of a Negro nation in Africa, so that there will be no clash between black and white and that each race will have a separate existence and civilisation all its own without courting suspicion and hatred or eyeing each other with jealousy and rivalry within the borders of the same country." [16]

The same issue of *Current History* which publishes Garvey's article prints also a paper by Judge Robert Watson Winston, of North Carolina, advocating the same solution of the race problem in the southern states. Judge Winston writes as a friend of the Negro, *i. e.,* of " the white man's Negro," " unambitious, likable," " with his hat in his hand." " I sucked the breast of a Negro woman," he writes, " listened to the wonderful tales of my father's slaves, rode ' horse ' on their backs, swam and fished with them, and ate their ash cake in the cabin. The Negro, I think, is my friend; I know I am his." Judge Winston's view is that the Negro and the white are homogeneous races and that " no two homogeneous races will long continue to exist side by side in the same country on terms of perfect equality without race blending," that there ought not to be race blending, that accordingly the colour line must be maintained and the Negro be held under unyielding social and political inequality, that the Negro will not submit to this and ought not to submit, that " self determination is of God, not of man." " The Negro desires to be free, and he is right. The white man claims that the South is his to rule and control, and he, too, is right." The solution is the removal of the Negro from the South, either to sections of the United States which will accord him equality, or preferably to Africa.[17] While Judge Winston advocates the Negro's departure, southern legislatures are proposing to make it a felony for any one to lure him away.[18]

No principle of segregation, however, whether viewed practically or in the form of some chimerical isolation of all races from

---

[16] *Current History,* Sept., 1923.   Art. by Marcus Garvey, " The Negro's Greatest Enemy," p. 957.
[17] *Ibid.,* " Should the Colour Line Go? " pp. 945-951.
[18] The New York *Times,* July 20, 1923.

contact with other races, can solve the race problem. The removal of the Negro race from the South would not solve the race problem in the southern states. It would be simply a temporary evasion of it. Wherever the Negroes should go, white men from the South would still have dealings with them unless such white men were to separate themselves from the indissoluble common life of the world. Complete isolation is an absolute impossibility. For good or for ill, and our faith is that it is for good, the intercourse of the races is ever to increase and the race problem is inherent in that intercourse. All that proper segregation can do is to protect each race in its just rights and liberties, supply it the opportunity of true self-development, and strip the problem of relationships of as many unnecessary friction contacts as possible.

The problems of race separation emerge in their most difficult forms in the question of Oriental immigration to the United States and Canada and Australia, in the exploitation of tropical lands and of undeveloped resources in other lands by the entrance of white men, and in the relation of the white and coloured races in our own country. The third of these, of which Judge Winston and Mr. Garvey have just been speaking, is the one that presses most upon our thought. We shall return to it and to the difficult social problems which it presents. Meanwhile it will suffice to quote the careful statement of E. G. Murphy, one of the best leaders of the New South, and one of the most sympathetic friends of the Negro race, regarding the principle of segregation in the southern states. He assumes the impossibility of any removal of the Negro race from the South. He has recognised the unity of interest in the two races, living on the same soil under one flag a common life, and he proceeds:

" Ours is a double population, a population divided by the felt and instinctive diversities of race. The land is occupied by two families of men between whom the difference in colour is, perhaps, the least of the distinctions which divide them. The differences in racial character are accentuated by the differences of social heritage—one is the population of the free-born, one has been the population of the slave-born.

" The doctrine of race integrity, the rejection of the policy of racial fusion, is, perhaps, the fundamental dogma of southern life. It is true that the animalism of both races has at times attacked it. The formative dogmas of a civilisation are reflected, however, not in the vices of the few, but in the instincts, the laws, the institutions, the habits of the many. This dogma of the social segregation of the races, challenged sometimes by fault of the black man, challenged sometimes by fault of the white man, is accepted and approved and sustained by the great masses of our people, white and black, as the elementary working hypothesis of civilisation in our southern states.

" The great masses of our coloured people have themselves desired it. It has made our public school system, however, a double system; and it is inevitable that it should have often made the Negro schools inferior to the white schools. But the social and educational separation of these races has created the opportunity and the vocation of the Negro teacher, the negro physician, the Negro lawyer, the Negro leader of whatever sort. It has not only preserved the coloured leader to the Negro masses by preventing the absorption of the best Negro life into the life of the stronger race; it has actually created, within thirty years, a representation of Negro leadership in commerce, in the professions, in Church, and School, and State, which is worthy of signal honour and of sincere and generous applause. The segregation of the race has thrown its members upon their own powers and has developed the qualities of resourcefulness. The discriminations which they have borne in a measure by reason of their slavery, and which have established the apartness of their group-life, are the discriminations which are curing the curse of slavery—an undeveloped initiative—and are creating the noblest of the gifts of freedom, the power of personal and social self-dependence. The very process which may have seemed to some like a policy of oppression has in fact resulted in a process of development." [19]

A social principle of segregation which will protect race rights and personalities on both sides, when two races occupy common ground and live in the same communities, is vastly more difficult than when they live in different continents, and wise men, both white and black, recognise the need of the most sympathetic common study and readjustments of many relationships. One of the finest things in the world today is the way in which the people of the South, white and black, are facing the situation.

---

[19] Murphy, *The Present South,* pp. 34 f.

Just as the attempt to find a basis of relationship which would be mutually protecting and mutually respecting and self-respecting has been beset with many difficulties and failures among us, so has it been in the contact of races in other continents. The impossibility of race separation, the inevitableness of the contact of commerce, culture, government and religion in these continents has brought much wrong and injustice. If these contacts of race with race had been wrong in principle or avoidable in practice, the evil of them would doubtless have outweighed the good. But racial associations are both right and desirable and necessary and, much as we lament the evils of them, there is ground for believing that these evils have been less than the policy of isolation would have entailed. Even with all the horrors of the slave and liquor traffic in Africa, this view may be maintained, and still more in the case of North and South America, where the Indians are more numerous and more happy than they ever were in the days before the European conquest. And of Asia, too, we have Vambery's deliberate judgment:

" If we start with the assumption that every man has a right to his own opinion and to the views which best correspond with his ideas of morality and material comfort, our pretended crusade in the name of civilisation must look like an unwarrantable interference. But the correctness of this assumption has so far been contradicted by historical events, for no community can remain in absolute isolation. Even China, the prototype of a seclusion extending over thousands of years, has before now migrated far into neighbouring lands. If Rome and Greece had remained within the narrow precincts of their native lands humanity would not have reached the present height of culture, and if Western nations had checked their passion for migration the aspect of things in Asia would now be even worse than it actually is. . . .

" During the much-extolled golden era of the history of Asia, tyranny and despotism were the ruling elements, justice a vain chimera, everything depended on the arbitrary will of the Sovereign, and a prolonged period of rest and peace was quite the exception. . . .

" When fanatics and enthusiasts profess that our culture in Asia has only engendered poverty and misery, and that the coming of the Westerners has been a curse to mankind in the East, these

expressions are merely the outcome of a morbid fancy, or of total
ignorance of the real situation. Wherever, and in whatever garb,
the influence of the modern world of culture has asserted itself,
the transformation period may have caused a temporary disturb-
ance in social and economical life; but, as soon as the time of trial
was past, peace, prosperity, and contentment have taken up their
abode there, and even poverty, which still shows itself here and
there in spite of the prevailing well-regulated conditions, is less
oppressive than in the time when these countries were dependent
upon themselves. Only arrant malevolence or wilful blindness can
persist in seeing a disadvantage in the activity displayed by Western lands in favour of the Asiatic world." [20]

No isolation of the races is possible. They are mingled now
beyond all possibility of separation. The race problem cannot be
solved by any futile proposals of segregation.[21] In two cases, the

---

[20] *Western Culture in Eastern Lands.* pp. 4 f., 394.
[21] "Exclusion is no solution of the problem. Its most ardent supporters
will sometimes admit that it can never be more than a temporary expedient.
Since the Jews, the most exclusive of peoples, became scattered among the
nations of the world, it has become more and more evident that men,
nations and races were made to mingle. No man can live to himself; nor
can any nation, permanently; nor any race. The western nations showed
their appreciation of this law of creation when they forced open the barred
doors of the Far East and rudely disturbed the contented Asiatics from the
sleep of ages. In their turn the Asiatics, having had the principle of free
intercourse thus forced upon them, feel that they have a right to demand
that the principle be mutually observed. Forbidden to exclude, they resent
being excluded. . . . Deeply offended, the Asiatic is nevertheless too
wise to kick against steel spikes. The West closes her lands to him.
'Very well,' he says to himself, 'she cannot close the sea. I shall go to
sea.' To sea he has gone. Asiatic crews man nearly all the big mercantile
vessels that trade now in the Pacific, and many besides in the Atlantic.
"If it is unfair to allow Asiatics to compete with whites side by side in
the colonies, it is doubly unfair to allow goods to be made by Asiatics in
Asia to compete with colonial products. Asiatic workers, admitted to the
colonies, would have to conform in some degree to white men's standards;
in Asia they can be sweated without restraint. To sum up:—Exclusion of
Asiatic immigrants, without exclusion of Asiatic imports, becomes economically foolish. . . .
"The policy of exclusion seemed to be the means of averting strife in the
past; it now appears that it was a mere dam against the natural current,
and that the waters are rising behind the dam to break over with doubled
and redoubled power of destruction. Exclusion fails. The inevitable meeting of East and West is near. Both sides recognise the fact. And both
sides are preparing, in time-honoured manner, to celebrate their meeting
with a trial of strength on the field of death."—(Report of Commission
II of the Committee of the Peace Conference of All Friends. John A.
Brailsford, "National Life and International Relations.")

Negro and the Jew, the problem of the relationships of the race is
greatest when the race is furthest from that original home where
alone it might have preserved its integrity and distinctions. Scattered about in other lands, over all continents, these two peoples
are losing ever more and more their segregation and are undergoing, whether for good or for evil, an ever extending infiltration
of other blood.[22]

Fundamentally, moreover, a rigid and mechanical racial segregation, even if it were possible, would have the same deadening
effect on humanity that it has had for centuries in China and India.
The Indian system of caste carried segregation to its completion, ·
as we have already seen, and with fatal results, as Tagore has
unflinchingly pointed out.[23]

3. A third solution of the race problem is the proposal that the
civilised races should rule all the rest of the world. This proposal
is now, however, only a reminiscence of another day. There was
a time when the notion was seriously held. It is still seriously
held, if Professor Josey is really serious in his view in *Race and
National Solidarity,* in which he argues that the white race is
justified in its policy of world domination in order that other races
may do the heavy tasks and give the white race leisure for æsthetic
and artistic self-expression.

" It may be taken as certain," he writes, " that we wish for a
rich and complex culture, one that is highly organised, one that
provides many opportunities for making life worth while, one that
encourages artistic fruitfulness. It is no less certain, (he continues) that such a society is only possible where there is a considerable surplus of wealth. An account of the sources of our

---

This is the dark view. There is another and brighter one, namely, that
the races are not preparing for a struggle on the field of death but are
seeking for the solution of the problem of their destiny and relationships
in the establishment of a rational world life. The League of Nations, the
Court of International Justice, disarmament, economic co-operation under
true economic principles and with adequate common instrumentalities, and
service and unity under the Headship of Christ are elements in the Christian program which to many men are quite chimerical, some more and some
less so, but to other men are as reasonable as light and as sure as time.
[22] Cf. Belloc, *The Jews,* p. 185.
[23] Tagore, *Nationalism,* p. 137.

wealth reveals how largely it is used in a world specialisation of
function of which we are the beneficiaries. *Unless we are able
to maintain our position of advantage we shall be deprived of the
wealth that is the necessary basis of our rich and colourful
culture."* [24]

But why have " colour " in our culture if coloured races are to be
excluded from our civilisation? Would it not be more consistent
to bleach our culture pure white? Professor Josey's view, however, is nothing but the Prussian doctrine of the German State
transferred to the white race. It is fatuous to think that the other
races will take this doctrine lying down, or that the attempt to
apply it, whether by military force, which is impossible, if for no
other reason, simply because the young men of the white race will
not fight for such a lie, or by economic processes, would have any
other consequences than those which followed the Prussian delusion. Its echoes can still be heard in Kipling's " Recessional,"
and even in " The White Man's Burden." The white man was to
govern the coloured man. The governors would supply the character and brains, for compensation and retiring allowance, but
there must be no prohibition law, a reasonable laxity in the matter
of concubinage and the coloured man must do the chores. Eliminating the immorality and conceiving the task in terms of service,
good men preached this doctrine two decades ago. Some thought
that the subordinated races really enjoyed their place. Kidd cited
Milner's words that British influence in Egypt " is not exercised
to impose an uncongenial foreign system upon a reluctant people.
It is a force making for the triumph of the simplest ideas of honesty, humanity and justice, to the value of which Egyptians are
just as much alive as any one else." [25] Others thought that Anglo-
Saxon domination of the world was the predestination of Providence. In the year 1895, when relations between Great Britain
and America were shadowed by the difficulty over the Venezuelan
boundary question, at the English service on Christmas morning
at the American Mission Church in Teheran, Persia, the custom-

---

[24] *Op. cit.*, see pp. 61, 87, 213, 219.
[25] Kidd, *The Control of the Tropics*, p. 94.

ary prayer for the Queen and the President " that they may vanquish and overcome all their enemies " was omitted and a prayer for peace substituted. An English officer present was much impressed and wrote an ingenuous prayer in the form of a sonnet, referring to the incident, and closing with the lines:

> " Two mightiest nations, may we sheathe the sword
> That our great destiny be not refused,
> The common faith we hold from common birth,
> To spread Thy glory and to rule Thine earth."

Careful students like Sir Alfred Lyall thought that it was inconceivable that China would remain " under the oppressive burden of an antiquated and discredited official hierarchy." He saw the whole of Asia subject to the white people: " Every part of it, whether decaying or reviving, lies under the shadow of Europe, and the whole region has exchanged the old state of chronic warfare, dynastic insecurity, and perpetual shifting of frontiers, for submissive acquiescence in the ascendency of the white races. And such, it has been confidently asserted, will before long be the condition of the whole continent, whenever the western shadow shall have lengthened until it falls over China." [26] But he could not believe that this would be Asia's ultimate destiny:

> " It seems to me, in short, that those who believe the tide of European predominance in Asia to be still rising must take into account the growth of various forces and circumstances which hold it in check and throw it backward. The paramount fact that all the temperate zone is virtually occupied by firmly planted nationalities or strong governments, has altered and is transforming the course and character of the vicissitudes of dominion. The old conquests, wherever they were permanent, rested upon multitudinous invasion, upon intermixture of races, and upon acclimatisation. The armies or hordes subdued a country, settled down among the people, intermarried with them, imposed new customs and creeds or adopted those of the subject races. All this blending of blood, of manners, and of religions produced material and moral acclimatisation, whereby the ruling or foreign element usually consolidated its dominion." [27]

[26] *Asiatic Studies,* Second Series, pp. 371, 375.
[27] *Ibid.,* p. 380.

This is not the character of white dominion over other races. And nowadays it is pretty generally recognised that that dominion is doomed. The race problem is not to be solved by white sovereignty over coloured peoples. Even in South Africa, where the white race has dominion and is likely to retain it for some time, men see that the repressionist policy as applied to race education and advancement is impossible.[28] And in general the idea of the subjection of race to race is surrendered. " I do not believe," says the late Lieutenant-Governor of the Northern Province of Nigeria, " that one race can remain subject to another for an indefinite length of time. I hold strongly that fusion, extermination, or the reclamation of liberty of action must sooner or later be the destiny of the subject race." [29] And Mr. Weale quotes John Stuart Mill's words, " Such a thing as government of one people by another does not and cannot exist," and adds,

" Did he mean that it is a foolish dream to conceive it possible for one people permanently to rule over another people? He did mean it, and he was quite right in meaning it. . . . Men now fully understand that it is not mere suzerainty, but actual ownership, which is claimed by the white man wherever he has raised his flag; and since it has been clearly proved by past history that this virtual slavery of the coloured man is unnatural and can never lead to the fusion of the races, it is only just and logical to admit that the attitude of the man of colour in demanding back rights long usurped by intruders, is one which is bound in the end to be crowned with signal success." [30]

And fundamentally, as William James asks in one of his letters, " what right of eminent domain has the white man over darker races? " [31]

Once again, it may be said that the race problem is not to be solved by the subjection of race to race. Economic subjection may be attempted when it is seen that political subjection is im-

[28] Loram, *The Education of the South African Native*, pp. 17-20.
[29] Temple, *Native Races and Their Rulers*, p. 78.
[30] *The Conflict of Colour*, pp. 189 f., 291.
[31] *The Missionary Review of the World*, June, 1922, art., " The Negro View of the White Man."

possible, but this, too, will fail as a solvent of race friction and prejudice.[32] Sooner or later it will aggravate it. The true solution must still be sought.

4. A fourth solution which is offered to us is eugenics. As between race and race, eugenics leads us on to the wider question of inter-racial marriages, but eugenics may deal either with inter-marriage between races or with the attempt so to breed any one race as to check tendencies of deterioration or to lift it to higher levels of character and efficiency. The forerunner of our modern race eugenics was Francis Galton. He was thinking chiefly of eugenics within a race, but his view was also inter-racial. " Eugenics," he wrote, " is the science which deals with all influences which improve the inborn characters of a race, also with those which develop these to the utmost advantage." In *Inquiries into Human Faculty,* a germinal book, in 1883, he wrote:

" Whenever a low race is preserved under conditions of life that exact a high level of efficiency, it must be subjected to rigourous selection. The best specimens of that race can alone be allowed to become parents, and not many of their descendants can be allowed to live. On the other hand, if a higher race be substituted for the low one, all this terrible misery disappears. The most merciful form of what I ventured to call ' eugenics ' would consist in watching for the indications of superior strains or races, and in so favouring them that their progeny shall outnumber and gradually replace that of the old one. Such strains are of no infrequent occurrence. It is easy to specify families who are characterised by strong resemblances, and whose features and character are usually prepotent over those of their wives or husbands in their joint offspring, and who are at the same time as prolific as the average of their class. These strains can be conveniently studied in the families of exiles, which, for obvious reasons, are easy to trace in their various branches.

" The debt that most countries owe to the race of men whom they received from one another as immigrants, whether leaving their native country of their own free will, or as exiles on political or religious grounds, has been often pointed out, and may, I think, be accounted for as follows:—The fact of a man leaving his compatriots, or so irritating them that they compel him to go, is fair

---

[32] See Olivier, *White Capital and Coloured Labour.*

evidence that either he or they, or both, feel that his character is alien to theirs. Exiles are also on the whole men of considerable force of character; a quiet man would endure and succumb, he would not have energy to transplant himself or to become so conspicuous as to be an object of general attack. We may justly infer from this, that exiles are on the whole men of exceptional and energetic natures, and it is especially from such men as these that new strains of race are likely to proceed.

" The influence of man upon the nature of his own race has already been very large, but it has not been intelligently directed, and has in many instances done great harm. Its action has beer by invasions and migration of races, by war and massacre, by wholesale deportation of population, by emigration, and by many social customs which have a silent but widespread effect.

" There exists a sentiment, for the most part quite unreasonable, against the gradual extinction of an inferior race. It rests on some confusion between the race and the individual, as if the destruction of a race was equivalent to the destruction of a large number of men. It is nothing of the kind when the process of extinction works silently and slowly through the earlier marriage of members of the superior race, through their greater vitality under equal stress, through their better chances of getting a livelihood, or through their prepotency in mixed marriages. That the members of an inferior class should dislike being elbowed out of the way is another matter; but it may be somewhat brutally argued that whenever two individuals struggle for a single place, one must yield, and that there will be no more unhappiness on the whole, if the inferior yield to the superior than conversely, whereas the world will be permanently enriched by the success of the superior." [33]

But the eugenics solution does not appear easy to biologists. Mr. Spiller speaks of it as " the eminently plausible but almost certainly unscientific doctrine." [34] And Professor Conklin writes:

" The eugenical dream of a single human breed in which every individual would be a superman would make a highly organised society impossible; it is an anti-social and wholly individualistic ideal. It would be possible theoretically, though perhaps not prac-

---

[33] Galton, *Inquiries into Human Faculty*, Everyman's Library Edition, Sections on " Influence of Man upon Race " and " Selection and Race," pp. 199-201, cf. pp. 206, 218.
[34] *Universal Races Congress*, 1911, p. 58.

tically, to breed a race of men of greater intellectual ability than any the world has known, but if all people were of this highly intellectual type, who would dig coal and build railroads and work in factories or on farms? It is as undesirable that persons of marked intellectual capacity should be forced into mere routine tasks as that persons of small ability should be placed in great positions.

"But a great variety of human types is beneficial only if every individual is able to find the work and place in society for which he is best suited, and if those are eliminated from reproduction who are incapable of filling any useful place. Furthermore, the best biological and social results would be obtained if intermarriage occurred only between individuals of similar hereditary types. Such a segregation is no impossible ideal, for it is what takes place naturally and normally where instinct and inclination are not interfered with by purely artificial restrictions and conventions. Even our oldest families are of such mixed lineage that their children vary greatly in intellectual capacity, and it is contrary to instinct and to good breeding for a woman of talent to marry the stupid son of a distinguished family or for a man of genius to marry a shallow-minded heiress. It would be good for society in general and for its individual members in particular, if every person were free to find his or her proper level both in occupation and marriage, irrespective of family obscurity or pride." [35]

The eugenic principle is like the principle of segregation, true enough with its right limits and governed by the right spirit. As a process of deliberate breeding of race excellence it is impossible.[36] But as a principle of action to be wrought into the

---

[35] *Yale Review,* April, 1917, Art. "Biology and National Welfare," pp. 481 f.

[36] "The biological fear proposes no remedy, except that the blondes must outbreed the brunettes or hold them under if they cannot outbreed them. If these are the remedies, then, of course, the great race is doomed. Unfortunately, the families of 'Great Race' parentage are not being increased; a bad example, which, by the way, 'the lesser breeds' are following as soon as they achieve a certain status. The masses—long heads and broad heads —are 'out of hand,' and 'all the king's horses and all the king's men cannot put "the old order" together again.'

"Against this unrelievable pessimism we must recover a challenging faith. Nature has not laid all her best eggs into Nordic baskets; civilisation is not measured by the cephalic index alone; democracy is not degradation, and mongrelisation within limits is not doom. I believe in race because I believe in heredity, though the two are not necessarily identical. I believe in the fine strain of folks who came with their sublime faith to the rockbound coast of New England; but I do not believe that the cour-

sense of race pride and effort it is a sound principle. Society has a right to demand a great deal more than it has been accustomed to demand, and public opinion ought to make marriage as difficult as possible for those who are not fit for it, and especially for those who have been unfitted by sin. But here again the problem is moral. So far as eugenics can make any contribution to race improvement it will be due to higher moral ideals controlling the character and relationships of men.[37]

5. We come next to the difficult question of miscegenation or amalgamation in its relation to the problem of race. On two points the anthropologists appear to be agreed, namely, the facts as to the universal operation of race assimilation in the past and the probable development of the future. The really difficult question is as to the present. And as to the present, the fact of steadily progressing racial intermixture is unquestionable. The real issue is as to what is wise and right and how can what is wise and right be secured.

a. As to the past, Galton says that the past has left us with nothing but mongrel races. In his *History of Rome,* Prof. Frank writes of the amalgams which made up the Greek and Roman races, neither of which in its maximum power was a pure race. " About 2,000 years B. C., various Indo-European tribes began to push their way across the Alpine ranges into the Mediterranean countries. They were apparently a tall, well-built, fair-haired race, closely related to the ancestors of the modern Celts, Germans and Anglo-Saxons. In Greece, these migrants were called Hellenes, and became the basic element of the remarkable Greek people." These Hellenes " mingled along the Aryan coast with the most cultured people then in existence." Of Italy, he writes,

---

age with which they faced the odds of the New England winters, the strength with which they drove the stakes of homestead, church and school into the new and reluctant soil, will pass from America when the last drop of New England blood blends with that of Celt, Latin, Slav or Semite."— *The Christian Century,* Sept. 20, 1923, art. by Edward A. Steiner, " The Myth of a New Race."

[37] " Moreover, the ultimate fruits of any eugenic movement will, by the nature of the case, require many generations."—*Eugenical News,* Aug., 1923, p. 80.

" This tall light race, though far from precocious and seldom the originator of a new culture, has nevertheless shown a marked capacity for analytical thought and for orderly government, as well as a distinct ability to assimilate and appreciate high artistic ideals. Their capacities have to be sure been variously dulled or quickened by intermixture with other races. In Greece, for instance, they doubtless gained in artistic power and lost in political genius by freely mixing with the native Ægean peoples. In Italy however, one may study them in their more normal development, since there the more thorough elimination of the native element seems to have kept the immigrant stock for a long time fairly pure." [38]

In later Rome, there was an almost universal intermixture of blood. Prof. Frank concludes that perhaps ninety per cent. of the free plebeians in the streets of Rome in the time of Juvenal and Tacitus had Oriental blood in their veins, and he has compiled equally remarkable statistics for various towns in Italy, Gaul and Spain. " It is evident," he concludes, " that the whole Empire was a melting pot and that the Oriental was always and everywhere a large part of the ore." [39] Some lay the fall of Rome to this amalgamation. Others believe, as we have seen, that Rome got more than she gave and that the foreign elements saved her. What happened in Rome has been going on continuously through history. The specialisation of race has been undergoing a vast regeneralisation. As Professor Conklin says:

" Existing races have arisen by mutation and hybridisation, but they have been established by the isolation of certain of these mutants or biotypes. The present tendency to the breaking down of isolation and the commingling of races is a reversal of the processes by which those races were established. If in the past ' God made of one blood all nations of men,' it is certain that at present there is being made from all nations one blood. By the interbreeding of various races and breeds there has come to be a complicated intermixture of racial characters in almost every human stock, and this process is going on today more rapidly and extensively than ever before. Strictly speaking, there are no ' pure '

[38] Frank, *A History of Rome*, p. 6 f.
[39] *American Historical Review*, Vol. XXI, (1916), p. 689 ff., quoted in *Western Races and the World*, p. 102.

lines in any human group. If so-called ' pure ' English, Irish, Scotch, Dutch, German, Russian, French, Spanish, or Italian lines are traced back only a few generations they are found to include many foreign strains, and this is especially true of American families, even those of ' purest ' blood." [40]

"If we assume," says Ratzel, looking both forward and backward, " with the majority of anthropologists at the present day, a single origin for man, the reunion into one real whole of the parts which have diverged after the fashion of ' sports,' must be regarded as the unconscious ultimate aim of these movements of mankind. This in the limited space of the habitable world, must lead to permeation, and as a consequence, to mingling, crossing, levelling. But again as a similar organisation has spread among men, the possibility has increased of migration to places the most remote from the original abode ; and in the whole world, there is hardly a frontier left which has not been crossed." "A thousand examples show," Ratzel adds, " that in all this change and movement, the races cannot remain unaltered, and that even the most numerous, counting their hundreds of millions, cannot keep their footing in the tumult that surges around them. Inter-breeding is making rapid strides in all parts of the earth." [41]

b. As to the future. Here again the anthropologists agree. Professor Conklin, of Princeton, says:

"Even if we are horrified by the thought, we cannot hide the fact that all present signs point to an intimate commingling of all existing human types within the next five or ten thousand years at most. Unless we can re-establish geographical isolation of races, we cannot prevent their interbreeding. By rigid laws excluding immigrants of other races, such as they have at present in New Zealand and Australia, it may be possible for a time to maintain the purity of the white race in certain countries, but with the

---

[40] *The Direction of Human Evolution*, p. 47.
[41] *The History of Mankind*, Vol. I, pp. 10, 12. See Galton, *Inquiries into Human Faculty, Influence of Man upon Race;* Roemer, *Origin of the English People and of the English Language*, pp. 85, 197 f., 212; Taine, *History of English Literature*, p. 71; Dixon, *The Racial History of Man*, p. 516; *Atlantic Monthly*, June, 1920, art. " The Future of Central Europe," p. 834 f., as to the disappearance of racial marks.

constantly increasing intercommunications between all lands and peoples such artificial barriers will probably prove as ineffectual in the long run as the Great Wall of China. The races of the world are not drawing apart but together, and it needs only the vision that will look ahead a few thousand years to see the blending of all racial currents into a common stream." [42]

And Professor Dixon, of Harvard, thinks that the Negroid peoples will hold the tropical heart of Africa, " but for the rest of the world, if the theory here proposed be true, that the racial history of man is in final analysis that of the struggles for dominance among the descendants of differently dowered types, together with their gradual blending into an ever more homogeneous form, the answer to the riddle of the future would seem to be written in the past. The more primitive types and races, those least endowed, must tend to pass from the stage and merge into the complex of their victors, and among these amalgamation and absorption must continue to reduce more and more the remnants of the original types, until in the end, out of many types, through a multitude of races, may come one race, which will be the consummation of them all." [43]

This is the biological prophesy. We believe that there is a better solution of the race problem than this, that there is a richer destiny possible for man than, to use Professor Reinsch's phrase, " engulfment in an indiscriminate mass," a common amalgam of all human blood.

c. As to the present the statements already made indicate how deeply the forces of inter-racial amalgamation are operating. In Siam and the Malay Peninsula, Chinese blood is pouring in a steady flood into the already composite population. The whole of Latin America, as we shall see, is a gigantic experiment in racial intermingling. In India the population is made up of " races as fundamentally differing from each other as any in Europe," [44] but ever more and more melting together. The number of Anglo-Indians or mixed English and Indian blood, reported in the Census

---

[42] *The Direction of Human Evolution*, p. 52.
[43] *The Racial History of Man*, p. 523.
[44] *General Report, Census of India*, 1881, p. 8.

of 1911 was 15% more than in 1901, while the total population increased 7%. In the census of 1921 the Anglo-Indian increase during the decade was 12.6%, while the total population increased 1.2%. The most startling evidence of racial intermixture is in the United States. " There are now one-quarter as many mulattoes as full-blooded Negroes in the United States, and the former are increasing at twice the rate of the latter." [45] The census of 1920, however, raises some perplexing questions. The following table shows the growth of the mixed population and the comparative growth before and since the abolition of slavery.

Census Year	Negro Population			Per cent of Total Negroes	
	Total	Black	Mulatto	Black	Mulatto
1920	10,463,131	8,802,577	1,660,554	84.1	15.9
1910	9,827,763	7,777,077	2,050,686	79.1	20.9
1890	7,488,676	6,337,980	1,132,060	84.8	15.2
1870	4,880,009	4,295,960	584,049	88.0	12.0
1860	4,441,830	3,853,467	588,363	86.8	13.2
1850	3,638,808	3,233,057	405,751	88.8	11.2

Between 1890 and 1910 the pure black population increased 31% and the population of mixed " white blood " and " black blood " increased 81%. Between 1910 and 1920 the pure black population increased 13% and the population of mulattoes, of mixed " white blood " and " black blood " decreased 24%. It is obvious that these figures are impossible. There cannot have been such a decrease in the number of mulattoes. Either the number of mulattoes reported in 1910 was too great or the number in 1920 was too small. As a matter of fact the Census Returns show that the number of mulattoes nearly doubled between 1870 and 1890. The same rate of increase between 1890 and 1910 would justify the figures of the 1910 Census. A corresponding increase between 1910 and 1920 would suggest a present mulatto population of

[45] *The Yale Review,* April, 1917, p. 479.

nearly 3,000,000, which would be almost double the actual returns and which would require the conclusion that the pure black population had not increased at all. What explanation can there be of such confusion? The explanation of the Census authorities is as follows:

" According to the census returns, *the proportion of mulattoes in the Negro population increased from 12 per cent. to 15.2 per cent. during the 20 year period from 1870 and continued to increase to 20.9 per cent. during the following 20 year period, but decreased to 15.9 per cent. during the 10 year period from 1910 to 1920.* Thus on the face of the returns the proportion of mulattoes in 1920, although nearly one-fourth smaller than in 1910, was nevertheless slightly larger than that in 1890. (See Table 9.)   ·

" It is likely that the explanation of *the relatively large proportion of mulattoes shown for 1910 may be found in part in the fact that a larger proportion of the Negro population was canvassed by Negro enumerators in that year than in any other census year.* It is probable that the practice of returning as black those mulattoes who had but a small admixture of white blood was greater among the white than among the Negro enumerators. Moreover, the Negro enumerators may have taken somewhat greater care than did the white enumerators to ascertain whether Negroes whom they were not able to interview personally were blacks or mulattoes. The difference between the proportions of mulatto in 1920 and in 1910, as shown by the returns, cannot, however, be accounted for as resulting wholly or mainly from these causes.

" In order to ascertain the probable effect of the employment of Negro enumerators in 1910 upon the proportion of the Negro population returned as mulattoes in that year as compared with 1920, a special tabulation was made for the 16 Southern states and the District of Columbia and for 10 Northern states—Massachusetts, New York, New Jersey, Pennsylvania, Ohio, Michigan, Indiana, Illinois, Missouri and Kansas—in all of which a part of the Negro population was canvassed by Negro enumerators in 1910. The total Negro population of the area covered was 10,-303,399 in 1920 and 9,714,770 in 1910, or between 98 and 99 per cent. of the total Negro population of the United States in each year. The number of enumeration districts in this area in which Negro enumerators were employed in 1910 was 2,055. This special tabulation brought out the following facts:

"Considering as one group those counties in each of which three or more Negro enumerators were employed in 1910, the percentage mulatto in the Negro population decreased from 21.8 in that year to 16.1 in 1920; considering as another group those counties in each of which one or two Negro enumerators were employed, the percentage mulatto decreased from 21. to 14.2; and considering as a third group those counties in which white enumerators only were employed, the percentage decreased from 19.6 to 15.9. Thus the decrease in the counties in which white enumerators only were employed in 1910 was nearly two-thirds as great as the decrease in those counties in each of which three or more Negro enumerators were employed in that year.

"Moreover, in every one of the 26 states covered by the comparison a decrease in the percentage mulatto between 1910 and 1920 is shown for the group of counties in which white enumerators only were employed in 1910, and in a number of cases this decrease was equal to or greater than that for the groups of counties in which Negro enumerators were employed in 1910.

"It appears, therefore, that the employment of Negro enumerators in certain counties in 1910 and of white enumerators only in 1920 had some effect in reducing the proportion of mulattoes in the Negro population, as shown by the returns for 1920 in comparison with those for 1910, but that this was not the sole nor principal cause of the indicated decrease." [46]

What was the cause? Or was there really a decrease? It would be very desirable to know the facts. Judge Winston holds that prior to 1876 racial amalgamation was common; " there was no public sentiment on the subject, neither was there race consciousness nor conflict." [47] And yet the number of mulattoes according to the census increased 45% between 1850 and 1860 and decreased slightly between 1860 and 1870, but leaped upward 93.8% between 1870 and 1890 and 81% between 1890 and 1910. There is something unexplained in these figures.

Is this mixture of all races good or evil? Some say good. Some, good within limits. And some have a different answer.

(1) Some say good. Man is one species and race intermarriage is not an attempt at hybridisation of different species. The fertil-

[46] *Fourteenth Census Reports,* Vol. II, Chap. I, p. 17, " Colour or Race, Nativity, and Parentage."
[47] *Current History,* Sept., 1923, p. 948.

ity of human cross breeding, it is argued, is its biological justification. Professor Finch argues that " race blending, especially in the rare instances when it occurs under favourable circumstances, produces a type superior in fertility, vitality, and cultural worth to one or both of the parent stocks. . . . While race blending is not everywhere desirable, yet the crossing of distinct races, especially when it occurs with social sanction, often produces a superior type; certainly such crossing as has occurred tends to prove absurd the conclusion that the dilution of the blood of the so-called higher races by that of the so-called lower races will either set the species on the highway to extinction or cause a relapse into barbarism." [48]   And he quotes G. Stanley Hall:

" The Ainos of Japan, who are vanishing by amalgamation, are a very different and more primitive type than the Japanese, and both appear to be benefited by the process of absorption. The Portuguese and the Dutch have been intermarrying for several centuries in farther India to the advantage of both races, as is true of the Russians with the older natives of Siberia. The mixture of Arabs with the North Africans has produced the Moors; many crossings of the Turks, the mixture of the Spaniards and Indians in South America and Mexico, especially in Chile, which have resulted in Neo-Indian and Neo-Aryan types, show how favourably the crossing of races may act if differences are not great and if both sexes of both races marry with each other instead of only the men of one with the women of the other." [49]

Wu Ting Fang also spoke a word in behalf of intermarriage, with a characteristic touch:

" With regard to the question of inter-racial marriage, in my opinion the principle is excellent, though I fear it is not easy to carry out. Broadly speaking, it is proper that Occidentals and Orientals should intermarry, as this would be the best means of diffusing knowledge and creating ties of relationship and friendship. But some of our customs, habits, and modes of living, though excellent in themselves, are different from those of Western countries, and may not be agreeable to Occidental people.

[48] *Universal Races Congress*, 1911, paper on " The Effects of Racial Miscegenation," pp. 108, 112.
[49] *Ibid.*, p. 111, from Hall, *Adolescence*, Vol. II, p. 722 f.

Within the last few years the people of China, especially those on the Coast, have been adopting some of the Western habits and ways of living. It is not impossible that these persons will make good partners for life with Westerners; in fact, there are cases of mixed marriages which have turned out to be happy. I am inclined to the opinion that when a nation has a large number of its people who marry with foreigners, it is a sign of progress. It has been proved that children inherit the traits of their parents, and, as the Chinese are noted for their patience, perseverance, honesty, and industry, these characters will naturally be imparted to the Eurasian children, who will have the good points from both sides." [50]

Permanent racial dominion of any race would seem to be dependent upon its amalgamation with the races it is to rule. It purchases power at the price of its blood.[51] But this is not always a loss. Indeed this was the way many societies or races were formed. "The mixture of races," says Bagehot, "was often an advantage, too. Much as the old world believed in pure blood, it had very little of it. Most historic nations conquered prehistoric nations, and though they massacred many, they did not massacre all. They enslaved the subject men, and then married the subject women. . . . What sorts of unions improve the breed, and which are worse than both the father-race and the mother, it is not very easy to say." [52] And he quotes M. Quatrefages as holding "that the mixture of race sometimes brings out a form of character better suited than either parent form to the place and time; that in such cases, by a kind of natural selection, it dominates over both parents, and perhaps supplants both, whereas in other cases the mixed race is not as good then and there as other parent forms, and then it passes away soon and of itself." [53] And Bagehot concludes, " In the early world many mixtures must have wrought many ruins; they must have destroyed what they could not replace—an inbred principle of discipline and of order. But if these unions of races did not work thus; if, for example, the

[50] *Ibid.*, p. 128 f.
[51] Lyall, *Asiatic Studies,* Second Series, pp. 364 f., 368 f.
[52] *Physics and Politics,* p. 68 f.
[53] *Ibid.*, p. 69.

two races were so near akin that their morals united as well as
their breeds, if one race by its great numbers and prepotent organisation so presided over the other as to take it up and assimilate it, and leave no separate remains of it, then the admixture was
invaluable." [54]

And Professor Conklin, while disapproving indiscriminate
amalgamation, indulges the thought of an imagined composite race
combining all the good of all the races:

" No race has a monopoly of good or bad qualities; all that can
be said is that certain traits are more frequently found in one race
than in another.

" In love of adventure, of discovery, and of freedom within the
limits of social order the white race is probably supreme, and these
qualities under favourable environment have led to its great
scientific, industrial, and political development. In virility, conservatism, and reverence for social obligations the yellow race, as
a whole, is probably superior to the white. If the white race wor-
ships liberty, the yellow race deifies duty; if the former is socially
centrifugal, the latter is centripetal. The brown, red, and black
races each have their characteristic virtues and defects which have
become proverbial. Every race has contributed something of
value to civilisation, though there can be no doubt that the white,
yellow, and brown races lead, and probably in the order named.

" No doubt if all the good qualities of different races could be
combined and all of the bad qualities eliminated the result would
be a type greatly superior to any existing race." [55]

(2) Some say amalgamation is good within limits, *i. e.,* between
kindred races or between the best of two races even though not
kindred. Dr. Jordan is prepared to make these limits pretty wide.
" When European blood," he writes, " mingles with Asiatic strains
as good, there is no evidence that the progeny is inferior to either
parent stock. . . . In general, other things being equal, the advantage seems to be on the side of the blended races which belong
to the same general stock. Moreover, in civilised lands, there are
only blended races." [56] An American physician living in India is
disposed on the whole to favour amalgamation. He writes:

---

[54] *Ibid.,* p. 71.
[55] *The Direction of Human Evolution,* p. 51.
[56] Jordan, *War and the Breed,* p. 29 f.

"Caste is a term which connotes social distinctions and differences, differences in 'purity' of blood and breed, heredity, etc. It indicates social organisation based on birth, *i. e.*, blood. Lower castes may marry upward, and thus bring about improvement of breed, but not vice versa. Marriage downward seems in some respects to cause a deterioration, the resultant being 'inferior.' It seems certain that caste is based on differences in race. For example, among Hindus, the Brahmins are of pure Aryan race and fair complexion. The Kshatriyas are somewhat mixed, the Vaishnavas more so, and the Sudras are of aboriginal origin and black in complexion. (I think Sudra means black.) In America, the 'coloured' people form a different caste. So do the Jews. Biologically speaking, I think there is no inherent objection to interracial and inter-caste marriages. In many cases the results seem happy and suitable. For example, in India my observation is that inter-marriages between Europeans and Indians in many cases give good results, and would be advantageous to India if they took place between equal classes and religions, and in large numbers so as to exert a decided influence. The Eurasians (or Anglo-Indians) may be 'inferior' in some qualities, but in some fine qualities they may be 'superior' to the European. In present conditions (rather abnormal) the children of Anglo-Indian mixed marriages are doubtless in an unfortunate position, but I speak above of ideal or theoretical conditions."

Within the broad colour distinctions, those who hold this view, would approve of wisely ordered assimilation. They recognise the fact of inextricable mixture already existing and, while some of them deprecate the disappearance of specialised types, like the long-headed, fair-haired, blue-eyed north European, they assent to the inevitability of white amalgamation and would assent to similar amalgamation of the other colours. As to marriage between the best individuals of two diverse races, there would be greater difference of view.[57] We shall come to a judgment of our own in a moment.

---

[57] "Probably, and I should say more than probably, where nature herself obliterates the distinction of race, and allows a mighty and permanent affection between man and woman to cross the limits of race, then, I should be inclined to say nature herself gives sanction which may set the lesser utilities at defiance and consecrates the union of distinct breeds; but without so mighty a permit it is perhaps well that we who are but children in this matter, and cannot see farther than our hands can reach, should pause

(3) But others deem the intermarriage solution of the race problem the wrong solution. The Capper Marriage-Divorce bill which was before Congress in the spring of 1923, entirely prohibited marriages between feeble-minded persons, between Whites and Mongolians, and between Whites and Negroes. It was reported that Senator Capper had agreed to remove these last clauses in response to protests.[58] This solution cannot, however, be condemned off hand on the ground that the result of intermarriage between the races will be a product inferior to each race. For two reasons, (a) Amalgamation often takes place under the worst conditions instead of under the best, on the fringes where too often the weakest and most lawless elements of both races bring together the inferior and uncontrolled qualities of each. Usually it is the men of the supposedly stronger and superior race who take the women of the other race, sometimes in lawful marriage, more often in concubinage or in even more indiscriminate relations. And often the laws force upon even legalised marriage and its offspring a degrading status. In South Africa such persons " are outside the pale of tribal influences; they are not brought within the white community. Yet, as a rule, they are monogamists, and conform their lives to civilised usages, and their aspirations, notwithstanding many drawbacks, are impressively towards the legal position of their ' white father,' objecting to being thrust down to the level of their ' black mother '; they do not receive the status which, having regard to their culture, they might fairly claim." [59] If the best of two races were joined on the highest and worthiest basis the test would be fair, as the illegitimate mixture along a low boundary line can never be. (b) But even such amalgamations as we have are not to be lightly set down as failures. The Chinese blood is improving the stock of all south-eastern Asia. It is a popular misapprehension that hybrids are always inferior to pure breeds or that they resemble

---

and move with caution. For the future of the race on earth is bound up in this matter."—Olive Schreiner, *Some Thoughts on South Africa*, pp. 385-386.

[58] *The World Tomorrow*, March, 1923, p. 88 f.; New York *Times*, Jan. 24, 1923.

[59] *The South African Natives*, p. 127.

the inferior parent. "As a matter of fact it is well known that while some hybrids are inferior to either parent, others are superior. . . . Combinations of the best qualities yield only the best types, combinations of the worst characters yield the worst types; and between these two extremes all combinations of good and bad characters occur." [60] A man like Booker Washington was a far better and greater man than the white man who was his father.

(4) But when all has been said that can be said for amalgamation, some things remain to be noted as weighing against it as a solution of the race question.

(a) It cannot be operated on a scale sufficiently great or speedy to solve the race issue. It would be generations, probably centuries, perhaps millenniums, before amalgamation could erase the lines of race. Meanwhile the friction and prejudice and malrelationship which constitute the problem would remain. They might be mollified by the acceptance of the principle of race-equalitarianism which the policy of universal miscegenation would imply, but on the other hand any such alleviations would be offset by the certainty of increased friction between the growing hybrid groups and the pure blood groups from which they were composed. Experience shows that this is the case and that the only method of avoiding it in any measure is by the incorporation of the hybrid group in one of the other two, and inevitably in the supposedly lower race. In South Africa the illegitimate son of a native woman by a European father is in law a native.[61] This has been the course pursued in the United States. The race of mixed white and black parentage has been absorbed in the black race. In India the Anglo-Indian or Eurasian community has had a separate status but has steadfastly striven for recognition in the white race. This has led to increased race friction. The new political situation in India is compelling the Anglo-Indian to reconsider this position and their wisest leaders are advocating their throwing in their lot politically as they must and socially as

---

[60] *The Yale Review*, April, 1917, p. 480.
[61] *The South African Natives*, p. 128.

they ought, with the Hindu people.[62] Racial amalgamation within
limits will no doubt proceed and of course it must proceed, as the
white blood already in the Negro race will spread more and more
and as the Chinese blood will spread in all eastern continental
Asia. But the dimensions and acuteness of the race problem will
not be diminished and may even be aggravated.

(b) Amalgamation, as has been suggested, imperils race personality and autonomy and self-development.[63] If a race has fulfilled its mission and needs no further opportunity to work out
its destiny and its distinctive contribution to humankind, perhaps
it might as well melt into some other race or some new amalgam,
but this would be racial euthanasia, not the protection and use of
racial freedom and activity. There is no evidence that any of the
great races has accomplished its mission. Until it has done so,
even though amalgamation may filter in along its margins, it is
better that its essential race integrity be preserved. Marcus
Garvey's power, as President of the Universal Negro Improvement Association, with its project of an independent African republic, lay in his appeal to the sense of Negro race personality.
" We believe," said he, " in a pure black race just as all self-
respecting Whites believe in a pure White race as far as that can
be." [64] In an article on the Negroes who were opposed to Garvey
as " The Negro's Greatest Enemy," Garvey complained of the
antagonism to him on the part of Negroes who had white blood:

" I was a black man and therefore had absolutely no right to
lead ; in the opinion of the ' coloured ' element, leadership should
have been in the hands of a yellow or a very light man. On such
flimsy prejudices our race has been retarded. There is more bitterness among us Negroes because of the caste of colour than there
is between any other peoples, not excluding the people of India.
. . . Being black, I have committed an unpardonable offense
against the very light coloured Negroes in America and the West

[62] Allahabad, *Pioneer*, May 14, 1923, art. " Future of Anglo-Indians."
There are some writers who charge the mulattoes in the United States with
responsibility as the " prime cause of social friction." See *Current History*,
March, 1924, pp. 1065-1070, art. " The Mulatto—Crux of the Negro
Problem."
[63] Oldham, *The World and the Gospel*, p. 189; Murphy, *The Basis of
Ascendancy*, pp. 51-69.
[64] *Century Magazine*, Feb., 1923.

Indies by making myself famous as a Negro leader of millions. In their view, no black man must rise above them, but I still forge ahead determined to give to the world the truth about the new Negro who is determined to make and hold for himself a place in the affairs of men. The Universal Negro Improvement Association has been misrepresented by my enemies. They have tried to make it appear that we are hostile to other races. This is absolutely false. We love all humanity. We are working for the peace of the world which we believe can only come about when all races are given their due.

"We feel that there is absolutely no reason why there should be any differences between the black and white races, if each stops to adjust and steady itself. We believe in the purity of both races. We do not believe the black man should be encouraged in the idea that his highest purpose in life is to marry a white woman, but we do believe that the white man should be taught to respect the black woman in the same way that he wants the black man to respect the white woman. It is a vicious and dangerous doctrine of social equality to urge, as certain coloured leaders do, that black and white should get together, for that would destroy the racial purity of both." [65]

"Race assimilation," says a recent sensible writer on India, "is desired neither by the Indian nor by the British." [66]

(c) Amalgamation, which is sometimes urged on the principle of race equality, is in reality the subversion of race equality. Men of a stronger race treat women of a weaker race as they could not treat women of their own. Some Indian writers are inclined to look back regretfully to the early days when Englishmen under the East India Company kept their establishments as a matter of course and left behind them troops of half-breed children. There was once a furious dispute in Calcutta as to whether these children and their mothers were not a legitimate charge against the Civil Fund of the Company.[67] And some modern writers imagine that

---

[65] *Current History*, Sept., 1923, art. by Marcus Garvey, "The Negro's Greatest Enemy," pp. 954, 956.

[66] *The Yale Review*, April, 1924, art. by Philo M. Buck, Jr., "What India Wants," p. 515.

[67] Marshman, *Life and Times of Carey, Marshman and Ward*, Vol. I, pp. 202 ff.

THE SOLUTION OF THE RACE PROBLEM

these old conditions represented a recognition by the British of race equality and understanding.[68] Precisely the contrary. They were an expression of intolerable race inequality. And even when the amalgamation is legitimate it would certainly imperil race equality if it were on a sufficient scale. It would deprive each race of the conditions requisite to its full freedom and self-expression. No argument is offered here against amalgamation on the ground of race inequality. And the disapproval of inter-racial marriage does not imply our surrender of the ideals which this little book has maintained. We view the matter just as we view marriage within any one race.[69] All the considerations which counsel good sense, the conservation of moral and physical values, the union of harmonious strains, consideration for offspring, and the rational application of eugenic principles in marriages within a race operate as presumptive objections to inter-race amalgamation.

(d) To amalgamate races is to reverse the process of differentiation. There come times when new syntheses are desirable and certainly a new spiritual synthesis of the races is essential, but the progress of nature and of mankind has been a process of enlarging heterogeneity. Amalgamation turns this process backward. All the great gains of humanity have been painfully won by the specialised experience and sacrifice and achievement of the races. We cannot see that this work is yet finished. The races appear still to be necessary to accomplish the tasks for which they came into being.

---

[68] Nundy, *Political Problems*, p. 102. See Mrs. Burton, *Life of Sir Richard Burton*, Vol. I, pp. 109, 135 f., setting forth the advantages and disadvantages of the system of Indian mistresses for British officials: "At last the Búbú (*i. e.*, the native mistress) made her exit and left a void. The greatest danger in British India is the ever growing gulf that yawns between the governors and the governed; they lose touch of one another, and such racial estrangement leads directly to racial hostility." Any account like Burton's of life in India before the Indian Mutiny is enough to explain the existence of race antipathy on the part of the Indian people.

[69] A newspaper despatch from Nobleville, Indiana, in March, 1923, reported that a coloured woman had filed suit for divorce against her husband on the ground that he had represented himself as a coloured man in marrying her but had subsequently filed in court a petition for recognition as white and of white parentage.—New York *Times,* March 19, 1923.

Three of the instances of racial amalgamation with which we are familiar have some special lessons for us.

(1) The Eurasian peoples in Asia. We know them best in the Anglo-Indian community, as it is now called rather than Eurasian, in India. Mr. Andrews calls them "a warm-hearted and emotional people, with high qualities of character when properly developed but apt very quickly to degenerate when left without proper care and training." [70] A friend has sent us from India the following report of an interview with the President of the Anglo-Indian Society:

"(1) While in America the mulatto was repudiated by white society and became a leader in Negro society, in India the Eurasian was repudiated by Indian society (due, no doubt, to the caste system) and became the bottom of European society, adopting the European civilisation, manners, customs, religion and language, but not accepted among Europeans. This is an interesting contrast, and the lot of the mulatto has in the past been much to be preferred.

"(2) In my early years in India I came in contact with, and was shocked by, the intense dislike of the English by the Eurasian. I thought within myself, 'These people owe all they have to the English. They and their children would have no chance in India in the midst of the teeming Hindu and Mohammedan population but for the position the British Raj gives them. How ungrateful and foolish of them to hate the British.' I had not learned that help and favours given as by a superior to an inferior, even though accepted because needed, create not gratitude, but usually bitter resentment. This was the fact. The experience of Jean Valjean with the poor family in Paris he befriended and gave money to, is an illustration.

"(3) The Anglo-Indian community has always feared the competition of Hindu as the Californian labourer fears that of the Chinaman—only the one has had to accept it, the other could check it.

"(4) Now the Anglo-Indian sees the fact clearing before his vision that the British are foreigners and cannot be always in power in India, that the permanent factor is the Indian. To try to be like the bat in the fable that wished to be bird at one time and animal at another, must bring disaster. Hence we must decide

---

[70] Andrews, *The Renaissance in India*, p. 285.

what we are. And our only hope lies in taking our place squarely as Indians.

" Taking this line the Anglo-Indians of India will get full recognition in India and I believe will be treated fairly."

And the American who sent this spoke of his own love of India, where he had been born and spent his life, and yet of the sense of race difference which new movements made only the sharper, not on his side, but on the side of the Indians:

" I have had many Indian friends, Hindus, Mohammedans and Christians and I confess to having often felt a pang when I saw how different, however friendly, their attitude towards me was from their attitude towards each other. I work along with and see and talk with Indians only, from week's end to week's end. I think I draw as close as any to the Indian in sympathy and thought and mutual regard, and yet I feel at every turn that I am a foreigner. It makes one hungry for his own people. You will remember Lafcadio Hearn's experience, even marrying a Japanese lady in order to really be one with the Japanese, and how bitterly disappointed he was—he found it could not be, they did not accept him.

" The early English in India got closer to the Indians than we do now—they seldom went ' home,' they got little home news, they smoked the huqqa, even their English wives did; many married Indian and Eurasian women. They did not become one with the people even then, but the nearer they came to getting rid of race distinctions the lower they sank in the scale of life—and the lower they sank the less were they of help or service to the Indian."

The mention of Lafcadio Hearn is relevant. He married a Japanese wife and sought to bridge the gulf between the races and to interpret Japan to the world. The result was perhaps as happy as it could be, but it was not a vindication of the proposal to solve the race problem by amalgamation. And Hearn seems to have felt keenly the problem of such race union in the life of the child. Writing of his little son he said, " The spirit of him is altogether too gentle, a being entirely innocent of evil—what chance for him in such a world as Japan! Do you know that terribly pathetic poem of Robert Bridges, ' Pater Filio '?

" ' Sense with keenest edge unused
    Yet unsteel'd by scathing fire
Lovely feet as yet unbruised
    On the ways of dark desire
Sweetest hope that lookest smiling
    O'er the wilderness defiling!

" ' Why such beauty to be blighted
    By the swarms of foul destruction?
Why such innocence delighted
    When sin stalks to thy seduction?
All the litanies e'er chanted
    Shall not keep thy faith undaunted.' "

It may be truthfully said that this refers to any pure child life launched anywhere into the world, and that it is not a distinctive picture of Eurasian childhood, but far otherwise. Nevertheless the plight of the children of interracial marriage is one of the greatest difficulties in the way of accepting amalgamation as the solution of race. All over the world we see these children and only a heart of stone would be insensible to their plight. Often the white fathers have gone back to the home land and the little ones are left to work out their colossal problem themselves. Nothing more clearly proves that race honour and colour antipathy are secondary forces than the readiness with which the white race has strewn the world with half breeds. And where white men have gone and lived in honour and purity, it has been moral forces rather than race pride or colour prejudice which have governed them.[71] Possibly the sacrifice of some generations of children and of adult life might be the necessary price of the solution of amalgamation, and possibly there might not need to be any such price if the world were agreed that amalgamation is the wise and right solution. In that case a special respect might attach to those who were courageously carrying it through. But as the world is, amalgamation imposes a terrible burden on its offspring in many lands. There are " 450,000 coloured or Euro-Africans in South

---

[71] *The East and the West,* Oct., 1922, art. "Coloured Races in South Africa," pp. 330-337.

Africa, 100,000 of them in Johannesburg. Five of these hybrid people to every five whites. Their position is hard. They resent being called ' natives ' and are not received on equality with whites. The native women have suffered harshly at the hands of white men—mostly Dutch, who keep native women openly on their farms as concubines." [72]

(2) South America. South America is an illustration of amalgamation on a continental scale.[73] This was the deliberate policy and ideal of some of the great liberators and leaders. " We shall not see nor the generation following us," wrote Bolivar in 1822, " the triumph of the America we are founding : I regard America as in the chrysalis. There will be a metamorphosis in the physical life of its inhabitants ; there will finally be a new caste, of all the races, which will result in the homogeneity of the people." [74] There are still distinct racial divisions in South America, but the mixture of Portuguese and Indian and Negro in Brazil, of Spanish and Indian and Negro in the Caribbean lands, of Spanish and Italian and Indian in Argentina and of Spanish and Indian in the rest of the Continent has gone further than any mixture of such dissimilar races has gone elsewhere. One-third of the population of the continent is estimated to be of pure white or dominant white blood, one-tenth of Indian blood and all the rest of mixed blood.

Has the result justified the policy of amalgamation? In his later years, Bolivar gave up hope. In a letter to General Flores, of Ecuador, shortly before his death, he wrote : " I have been in power for nearly twenty years ; from this experience I have gathered only a few definite results :

(1) America for us is ungovernable.
(2) He who dedicates his services to a revolution plows the sea.
(3) The only thing that can be done in America is to emigrate.

---

[72] *The Missionary Herald*, Feb., 1923, art. " Johannesburg, South Africa's Melting Pot."

[73] One of the richest bodies of material on the race question in Latin America is the *Report of the Panama Congress on Christian Work in Latin America*, 1916. See references to race and racial problems in index, Vol. III, p. 545.

[74] Calderon, *Latin America, Its Rise and Progress*, p. 74.

(4) This country will inevitably fall into the hands of the unbridled rabble, and little by little become a prey to petty
tyrants of all colours and races.

(5) Devoured as we shall be by all possible crimes and ruined
by our own ferociousness, Europeans will not deem it
worth while to conquer us.

(6) If it were possible for any part of the world to return to
the state of primitive chaos, that would be the last stage
of Spanish America."

Sr. Calderon sums up the facts and expresses his judgment:

" In the Argentine, where Spanish, Russian, and Italian immigrants intermingle, the social formation is extremely complicated.
The aboriginal Indians have been united with African Negroes,
and with Spanish and Portuguese Jews; then came Italians and
Basques, French and Anglo-Saxons; a multiple invasion, with the
Latin element prevailing.   In Brazil, Germans and Africans
marry Indians and Portuguese.   Among the Pacific peoples, above
all in Peru, a considerable Asiatic influx, Chinese and Japanese,
still further complicates the human mixture.   In Mexico and Bolivia the native element, the Indian, prevails.   The Negroes form
a very important portion of the population of Cuba and San Domingo. Costa Rica is a democracy of whites; and in the Argentine,
as in Chili, all vestiges of the African type have disappeared.   In
short, there are no pure races in America.   The aboriginal Indian
himself was the product of the admixture of ancient tribes and
castes.

" In the course of time historic races may form themselves; in
the meantime, an indefinable admixture prevails.

" This complication of castes, this admixture of divers bloods,
has created many problems.   For example, is the formation of a
national consciousness possible with such disparate elements?
Would such heterogeneous democracies be able to resist the invasion of superior races?   Finally, is the South American half-
caste absolutely incapable of organisation and culture?

" Facile generalisations will not suffice to solve these questions.

" The three races—Iberian, Indian and African—united by
blood, form the population of South America.   In the United
States union with the aborigines is regarded by the colonist with
repugnance; in the South miscegenation is a great national fact;
it is universal.   The Chilian oligarchy has kept aloof from the
Araucanians, but even in that country unions between whites and
Indians abound.   Mestizos are the descendants of whites and

Indians; mulattoes the children of Spaniards and Negroes; zambos the sons of Negroes and Indians. Besides these there are a multitude of social sub-divisions. On the Pacific coast Chinese and Negroes have interbred. From the Caucasian white, bronzed by the tropics, to the pure negro, we find an infinite variety in the cephalic index, in the colour of the skin, and in the stature.

" It is always the Indian that prevails, and the Latin democracies are mestizo or indigenous. The ruling class has adopted the costume, the usages, and the laws of Europe, but the population which forms the national mass is Quechua, Aymara, or Aztec. . . .

" One may say that the admixture of the prevailing strains with black blood has been disastrous for these democracies. . . .

" The zambos have created nothing in America. On the other hand, the robust mestizo populations, the Mamelucos of Brazil, the Cholos of Peru and Bolivia, the Rotos of Chili, descendants of Spaniards and the Guarani Indians, are distinguished by their pride and virility. Instability, apathy, degeneration—all the signs of exhausted race—are encountered far more frequently in the mulatto than in the mestizo.

" The European established in America becomes a creole; his is a new race, the final product of secular unions. He is neither Indian, nor black, nor Spaniard. The castes are confounded and have formed an American stock, in which we may distinguish the psychological traits of the Indian and the Negro, while the shades of skin and forms of skull reveal a remote intermixture. If all the races of the New World were finally to unite, the creole would be the real American.

" He is idle and brilliant. There is nothing excessive either in his ideals or his passions; all is mediocre, measured, harmonious. His fine and caustic irony chills his more exuberant enthusiasms; he triumphs by means of laughter. He loves grace, verbal elegance, quibbles even, and artistic form; great passions or desires do not move him. In religion he is sceptical, indifferent, and in politics he disputes in the Byzantine manner. No one could discover in him a trace of his Spanish forefather, stoical and adventurous.

" But is unity possible with such numerous castes? Must we not wait for the work of many centuries before a clearly American population be formed? " [75]

Calderon's own present conclusion is that the Latin American

[75] Calderon, *Latin America, Its Rise and Progress, pp.* 311 f., 356 f., 359 f.

democracies " are degenerate. The lower castes struggle successfully against the traditional rules: the order which formerly
existed is followed by moral anarchy; solid conviction by a superficial scepticism, and the Castilian tenacity by indecision. The
black race is doing its work and the continent is returning to its
primitive barbarism.

" This retrogression constitutes a very serious menace. In
South America civilisation is dependent upon the numerical predominance of the victorious Spaniard, on the triumph of the white
man over the mulatto, the Negro, and the Indian. Only a plenti-
ful European immigration can re-establish the shattered equilibrium of the American races." [76]

Lord Bryce's view of South American amalgamation was not
so unfavourable, and he saw clearly the fallacy of the idea that
race hostility is a primary instinct:

" It might seem natural to assume *a priori* that men of pure
European Race would continue to hold the foremost place in these
countries, and would show both greater talents and a more humane
temper than those in whose veins Indian blood flows. But I doubt
if the facts support such a view. Some of the most forceful leaders who have figured in the politics of these republics have been
mestizos. I remember one, as capable and energetic and upright
a man as I met anywhere in the continent, who looked at least half
an Indian, and very little of a Spaniard. Nor have there been any
more sinister figures in the history of South America, since the
days of Pedro de Arias the infamous governor of Darien who
put to death Vasco Nunez de Balboa, than some who were pure
Spaniards. . . . The Brazilian lower class intermarries with
mulattoes and quadroons. Brazil is the one country in the world,
besides the Portuguese colonies on the east and west coasts of
Africa, in which a fusion of the European and African races is
proceeding unchecked by law or custom. The doctrines of human
equality and human solidarity have here their perfect work. The
result is so far satisfactory that there is little or no class friction. The white man does not lynch or maltreat the Negro; indeed, I have never heard of a lynching anywhere in South America except occasionally as part of a political convulsion. The
Negro is not accused of insolence and does not seem to develop

[76] *Ibid.*, p. 262. See also Ross, *South of Panama*, pp. 213, 216, 248.

any more criminality than naturally belongs to any ignorant population with loose notions of morality and property.

" What ultimate effect the intermixture of blood will have on the European element in Brazil I will not venture to predict. If one may judge from a few remarkable cases, it will not necessarily reduce the intellectual standard. . . ." [77]

And Bryce concludes:

" The fusion of two parent stocks, one more advanced, the other more backward, does not necessarily result in producing a race inferior to the stronger parent or superior to the weaker. . . .

" The second conclusion is this: Conquest and control by a race of greater strength have upon some races a depressing and almost ruinous effect. . . .

" Thirdly, the ease with which the Spaniards have intermingled by marriage with the Indian tribes—and the Portuguese have done the like, not only with the Indians, but with the more physically dissimilar Negroes—shows that race repugnance is no such constant and permanent factor in human affairs as members of the Teutonic peoples are apt to assume.   Instead of being, as we Teutons suppose, the rule in this matter, we are rather the exception, for in the ancient world there seems to have been little race repulsion; there is very little today among Mohammedans; there is none among Chinese.   This seems to suggest that since the phenomenon is not of the essence of human nature, it may not be always as strong among the Teutonic peoples as it is today.   Religion has been in the past almost as powerful a dissevering force as has racial antagonism.   In the case of Spaniards and Portuguese, religion, so soon as the Indians had been baptised, made race differences seem insignificant." [78]

It would seem, accordingly, that we must allow longer time to the South American experiment before passing judgment.   And there can be no doubt that if the experiment fails it will be not solely on ethnological grounds, but because the forces of true education and religion which ought to govern and direct so great a human development were not supplied by other races who under a just and generous principle of race relationships would have done their utmost to assure the success of a racial venture of such significance to all mankind.

---

[77] Bryce, *South America, Observations and Impressions*, pp. 477, 480.
[78] *Ibid.*, p. 481 f.

(3) The problem of white and black amalgamation. What makes this problem the more difficult is the apparent impossibility of its prevention. The white race has thus far been unwilling to accept any law of race integrity. It proclaims a principle of segregation which it persistently violates. Booker Washington once asked pertinently, " If your segregation wall be high enough to keep the black man in, will it be high enough to keep the white man out?" Twenty-six states, more than half of them outside the South, have laws forbidding the marriage of white and black.[79] Such a law as established in the State of Illinois entered again and again into the debates between Lincoln and Douglas.[80] In South Africa such marriages are prohibited in the Transvaal. " In the Free State the licenses issued to marriage officers do not permit of the celebration of mixed marriages. In the Cape Province and Natal such marriages can be contracted legally, though the tendency of recent legislation has been to place obstacles in the way of these unions." [81]

This book has already stated the broad grounds on which it seems wise to deprecate amalgamation. The special view of the South on the question is stated with characteristic care and sympathy by Mr. E. G. Murphy. " The South," he says, " does not base disapproval of intermarriage on an assertion of universal ' inferiority '—for in that case every gifted or truly educated Negro might shake the structure of social usage. It bases its distinctions partly upon the far-reaching consideration that the racial stock of the two families of men is so unlike that nothing is to be gained and much is to be lost from the interblending of such divergent types; partly upon the broad consideration of practical expediency, in that the attempt to unite them actually brings unhappiness; partly upon the inevitable persistence of the odium of slavery; partly upon a complex, indefinable, but assertive social instinct." The South in recognising the principle of race integrity, Mr. Murphy says,

---

[79] Stephenson, *Race Distinctions in American Law,* pp. 348-350; Mecklin, *Democracy and Race Friction,* p. 147 f.
[80] *Reminiscences of Abraham Lincoln,* pp. 113, 446.
[81] Temple, *Native Races and Their Rulers,* note to preface, p. iv.

" has done so, not in order to enforce a policy of degradation, but simply to express her own faith in a policy of separation. Her desire is not to condemn the Negro forever to a lower place, but to accord to him another place. She believes that where two great racial masses, so widely divergent in history and character, are involved in so much of local and industrial contact, a clear demarcation of racial life is in the interest of intelligent co-operation, and—in spite of occasional hardships—is upon the whole conservative of the happiness of both. During the opening of the great Southwest to private settlers there was an extended period of a quasi-collective ownership upon the unrestricted prairies. Men grazed their herds at will. There soon arose, how-ever, the confusion of boundaries and a consequent multiplicity of feuds. Then a number of the settlers, in order to define their lim-its, began to put up fences. Those who first did so were regarded as the intolerant enemies of peace. Soon, however, men began to see that peace is sometimes the result of intelligent divisions, that the attempt to maintain a collective policy through the confusion of individual rights had broken down; that clear lines, recognised and well defined, made mightily for good will; that the best friends were the men who had the best fences. And so there arose the saying, ' Good fences make good neighbours.' " [82]

The objection to amalgamation does not rest on colour antip-athy or on race inequality, but upon the principle of race person-ality, integrity and mission. On this ground Du Bois rests the Negro's best view. " I believe in Pride of race and lineage and self; in pride of self so deep as to scorn injustice to other selves; in pride of lineage so great as to despise no man's father; in pride of race so chivalrous as neither to offer bastardy to the weak nor beg wedlock of the strong, knowing that men may be brothers in Christ, even though they be not brothers-in-law." [83] Illegitimate amalgamation is the repudiation of colour antipathy, but also of race equality and integrity. Legalised amalgamation would recog-nise race equality. Either legitimate amalgamation should be allowed or illegitimate should cease. And the burden of re-sponsibility in the matter is not on the Negro. It is on the white. It is not the Negro who has sought an intermixture with the white

---

[82] Murphy, *The Present South*, pp. 275-277.
[83] Du Bois, *Darkwater*, p. 3 f.

race. It is the white race which has forced its blood upon the Negro. The violation of race integrity all over the world is the offense of the white race. It is a curious fact that the race which has most highly exalted the theory of race integrity should have done most to destroy it. How familiar are words like these of Senator Vardaman, of Mississippi:

" This is a white man's government and therefore must remain a white man's country. And everything that interferes in any way with the industrial and political supremacy of the white race, betokens evil and ought to be avoided.

" Race purity is indispensable to Caucasian supremacy. And the only way to maintain the supremacy is to prohibit by law the commingling of the races. It has been well said: It is idle to talk of education and civilisation and the like as corrective or comprehensive agencies. All are weak and beggarly as over against the almightiness of heredity, the omnipotence of the transmitted germ plasma. Let this be shorn in some measure of its exceeding weight of ancestral glory, let it be soiled in its millennial purity and integrity and nothing shall ever restore it; neither wealth nor culture, nor science, nor art, nor morality, nor religion—and even Christianity itself." [84]

How familiar are such words, and how futile, over against the plain fact of increasing racial intermixture between black and white. Some of the states, as has been already said, forbid by law the marriage of black and white people and some of them, like Virginia, are striving earnestly through competent and conscientious officials to protect the purity of the two races. But in these respects, the effort is beset by difficulties: (1) The births in white families are diminishing. (2) Unlegalised mingling of the races seems to be unpreventable. (3) All who bear any trace of Negro blood, however slight, are classified as Negroes, so that the " white blood " already in the Negro race is ever more and more widely distributed.[85]

But, it may be asked, if the human race is one and its ultimate goal is a unified humanity, why are not those men and women of

---

[84] New York *Sun,* April 23, 1913.
[85] See *Bulletins of Virginia Bureau of Vital Statistics; The Nation,* Jan. 10, 1923, art. " Alabama, A Study in Ultra Violet."

various races to be praised who pioneer the road by intermarriage?
For two reasons: Because the ideal of organic unity in humanity
is not identical with racial uniformity. And, because, as St. Paul
argued in his day, while races have the right to intermarry and it
is better for them to intermarry than to burn, and far better than
to breed an amalgam of illegitimacy, the course of rational race
respect and race relationship and race discharge of duty is to be
preferred to the course of those who yield these values for the
sake of lesser goods.

6. From the proposed solutions of the race problem which offer
us no hope we turn to the only reasonable and right answer. We
are our brothers' keepers. Those who are strong ought to bear the
burdens of the weak. We live in the bonds of a universal trusteeship. Colour and climate and language and physiological traits
are all secondary matters. Heredity and education alike entail
obligations but entitle to no privilege except the privilege of
service. All the races are in the world to help one another, to
work together for their common good, to build unitedly on the
earth a human commonwealth. Even in his gloomy prediction of
the day when the white men are to be jostled from their place of
supremacy, Mr. Pearson takes comfort in the thought that the
white races will themselves have brought the new day in: " The
solitary consolation," he adds to the words already quoted, " will
be that the changes have been inevitable. It has been our work to
organise and create, to carry peace and law and order over the
world, that others may enter in and enjoy." [86] The entering in of
others will not be our exclusion. In their joy our joy will be fulfilled. And they also will have their contribution to make to us
and to all. The right solution of the race problem is the simple
solution of justice and righteousness, of brotherhood and good
will. It is quite true that innumerable difficult problems of politics and economics are to be solved and that right thought as well
as right feeling is essential but, except on the philosophy that
economic and physical determinism is more powerful than moral
liberty and social purpose, man is equal, under God and with the

---

[86] Pearson, *National Life and Character*, p. 84.

guidance and help of God, to the work that is to be done. It involves elements which are already clear to us and, as we go on with courage and a right spirit, other elements will appear.

(1) Races must recognise their economic inter-dependence and common interests. No race, as we have seen, can permanently profit by the loss of other races. Trade must be mutually beneficial or it cannot endure. Capital must be employed where it can serve all men best or it will not serve best either its owners or the race to which they belong. It cannot be said that tariffs designed to promote racial or national independence have not their place, but they reach their limit when they advantage one race to the detriment of the mass of human well being. Generalisations like these can be multiplied indefinitely. But the principle underlying them is simple and fundamental. Lowell expresses it in a single line in " The Crisis," " In the gain or loss of one race all the rest have equal share."

This economic unity of the world is a fact from which there can be no escape. It is as sure and inevitable as common sunlight or the common laws of nature. No political isolation or tariff barriers can deliver us from it. They are themselves a recognition of it and an attempt to reach an adjustment with it. And this economic unity will become still clearer and more inexorable. The whole human race must use together the whole world. Every solution of the race problem which proceeds on any other assumption will break down.

(2) This community of racial interest is moral and social as well as economic, and the races must recognise this as an essential element in their solution of the race problem. All races must be lifted or the lower will drag the upper down. Races can fall as well as rise.[87] What Dr. J. L. M. Curry said long ago is clear to all today with regard to the Negro and the white in the South. Unless the white race lifts the black race " both will be inevitably dragged down." The South African Native Races Committee, of which Sir John Macdonell was Chairman, put this view plainly in their second report:

---

[87] Kidd, *The Control of the Tropics,* p. 50 f.

" Nothing could be more unworthy, or in the long run more disastrous, than that the whites in South Africa should regard the natives as a mere ' labour asset.' If this view prevailed—and it is to be feared that it still has some advocates—it would inevitably result in the demoralisation of the white communities. ' We have to bear in mind,' writes Sir Marshal Clarke, ' that where two races on different planes of civilisation come into such close contact as do the whites and blacks in South Africa, they act and react on each other, and where the higher race neglects its duty to the lower it will itself suffer.' Neglect of this duty has many serious consequences, but perhaps none more disastrous than its effects on the white children. Mr. P. A. Barnett, the late Director of Education in Natal, in his report for 1904, draws special attention to this vital matter. ' Of the baser and more cruel contamination,' he says, ' liable to result from the intimate domestic contact of little European children with people whose life, thoughts, and speech are habitually at a low level, it is hard to speak in the measured terms that decorum requires. One may have the most real respect for the Zulu folk in their places, and in regard to the stage of their development; but, apart from the hard pressure of social difficulty, here, where so many influences fight against the refinement and elevation of life, little Zulu drudges are the worst trainers of youth that we can employ.' As Mr. Barnett justly says, ' the mental and moral development of the white children is inextricably involved in that of the black.' " [88]

Even where races are not living together their community of moral and social interest is not less real. The thoughts of every race, like its diseases, are not segregable. There is no quarantine that can wholly bar disease, and the barriers against ideas are still less effective. The only safety of any one race is not in isolation, but in a pure and clean world.

(3) It is quite true that these are ideas of which we are speaking, and it is often said that the relations of life are governed not by these sentimental considerations, but by the hard economic facts. But these ideas are facts. They are the hardest economic and physical facts with which we have to deal. " The sympathies of peoples with peoples," said J. R. Green, " the sense of a common humanity between nations, the aspirations of nationalities

[88] *The South African Natives*, p. 187.

after freedom and independence, are real political forces." And no one can escape from them. And a third fact, equally hard and equally fruitful of effect with these, is the fact of racial thought and feeling toward other races. The right solution of the race problem requires that each race shall cultivate a feeling of respect and tolerance toward other races, and of sympathy with them in struggles which our race has often made more difficult for them. Lord Meston speaks of this in the case of the British race and India: " We must study the new conditions with a sympathetic endeavour to understand them; and we must look back on our own relations with these Eastern lands, on a good deal for which we have to make amends, but on much else which we have given as a pledge that we mean to give more and of our best." [89] Each race is bearing a great burden. Napoleon's adage as he met a labourer beneath a heavy load and stepped deliberately out of the way, is a good racial counsel, " Respect the burden "—and respect the human bearers of it. [90]

(4) Whatever the advanced races have of knowledge or power they ought to conceive in terms of trusteeship. There are some today who discredit the idea that the white races are in possession of any great trust for the world. Mr. Pepper thinks that our American literacy is not education and is little to be preferred to the illiteracy of Asia. [91] And Mr. Russell thinks Chinese civilisation superior for the Chinese to our own. Nevertheless these men personally adhere to and make use of the civilisation and education which they criticise and go abroad to teach the nations. We may not have all that we think we have. Every race, no doubt, exaggerates itself and its acquisitions and powers. But whatever any race really does have it holds not for itself alone, but for all the races. And we have come at last, after long delay, to what ought from the first to have been in our sense of trusteeship. Not only do we hold what is ours for all men, but we hold what we have taken over from other races for all men. At last we

---

[89] *The East and the West,* Jan., 1923, p. 77.

[90] See art. in *The East and the West,* Jan., 1923, on " The Japanese Treatment of Korea," p. 61.

[91] *Century Magazine,* June, 1923, art., " The Real Revolt Against Civilisation."

realise that what we hold of any other race we hold for that race as well as for civilisation. Articles XXII and XXIII of the Covenant of the League of Nations embody this acknowledgment and indicate the long distance we have come from the old days of imperialistic expansion. These articles read as follows:

" ARTICLE XXII.

" To those Colonies and Territories which, as a consequence of the late War, have ceased to be under the sovereignty of the States which formerly governed them, and which are inhabited by peoples not yet able to stand by themselves under the strenuous conditions of the modern world, there should be applied the principle that *the well-being and development of such peoples form a sacred trust of civilisation,* and that securities for the performance of this trust should be embodied in this covenant.

" The best method of giving practical effect to this principle is that the tutelage of such peoples should be entrusted to advanced nations who, by reason of their resources, their experience, or their geographical position, can best undertake this responsibility, and who are willing to accept it, and that this tutelage should be exercised by them as Mandatories on behalf of the League.

" The character of the mandate must differ according to the stage of the development of the people, the geographical situation of the territory, its economic conditions, and other similar circumstances.

" Certain communities formerly belonging to the Turkish Empire have reached a stage of development where their existence as independent nations can be provisionally recognised subject to the rendering of administrative advice and assistance by a Mandatory until such time as they are able to stand alone. The wishes of these communities must be a principal consideration in the selection of the Mandatory.

" Other peoples, especially those of Central Africa, are at such a stage that the Mandatory must be responsible for the administration of the territory under conditions which will guarantee freedom of conscience or religion, subject only to the maintenance of public order and morals, the prohibition of abuses such as the slave trade, the arms traffic, and the liquor traffic, and the prevention of the establishment of fortifications or military and naval bases and of military training of the natives for other than police purposes and the defence of territory; and will also secure equal opportunities for the trade and commerce of other Members of the League.

" There are territories, such as South-West Africa and certain of the South Pacific Islands, which, owing to the sparseness of their population, or their small size, or their remoteness from the centres of civilisation, or their geographical contiguity to the territory of the Mandatory, and other circumstances, can be best administered under the laws of the Mandatory as integral portions of its territory subject to the safeguards above mentioned in the interests of the indigenous population.

" In every case of mandate, the Mandatory shall render to the Council an annual report in reference to the territory committed to its charge.

" The degree of authority, control, or administration to be exercised by the Mandatory shall, if not previously agreed upon by the Members of the League, be explicitly defined in each case by the Council.

" A permanent Commission shall be constituted to receive and examine the annual reports of the Mandatories and to advise the Council on all matters relating to the observance of the Mandates."

" ARTICLE XXIII.

" Subject to and in accordance with the provisions of international conventions existing or hereafter to be agreed upon, the Members of the League

"(a) will endeavour to secure and maintain fair and humane conditions of labour for men, women, and children, both in their own countries and in all countries to which their commercial and industrial relations extend, and for that purpose will establish and maintain the necessary international organisation ;

"(b) undertake to secure just treatment of the native inhabitants of territories under their control ;

"(c) will entrust the League with the general supervision over the execution of agreements with regard to the traffic in women and children, and the traffic in opium and other dangerous drugs ;

"(d) will entrust the League with the general supervision of the trade in arms and ammunition with the countries in which the control of this traffic is necessary in the common interest ;

"(e) will make provision to secure and maintain freedom of communications and of transit and equitable treatment for the commerce of all Members of the League. In this connection the special necessities of the regions devastated during the war of 1914-18 shall be borne in mind ;

"(f) will endeavour to take steps in matters of international concern for the prevention and control of disease."

The League is also charged with duties in behalf of the protection of racial, religious and linguistic minorities.[92]

Under these provisions the League has assigned mandates to the Allied nations and established a Permanent Commission to which the Mandatory powers must report.

" To secure impartiality, a majority of the members of the commission are citizens of non-mandatory countries. Their task will be scrupulously to examine all reports and present their advice to the Council of the League.

" The supreme object is to prevent the mandatory system from developing into something akin to annexation and to insure the establishment of a world colonial policy under international supervision. Each administrating country, it is hoped, will be stimulated through publicity and the resultant force of public opinion to exercise the best possible government for the many millions of people under its control. The chief interest of the League is to ascertain whether the territories are being governed in the highest interest of the native populations formerly under Turkish or German rule.

" England has the greater part of German East Africa, Mesopotamia and Palestine under mandate. Australia has New Guinea, and New Zealand has Samoa. The Pacific islands north of the Equator were turned over to Japan. France received Syria and the major part of Togoland and Kamerun, and Belgium the district of German East Africa bordering on the German Congo.

" Separate reports are submitted on the question of slavery and labour in the affected territories, as well as education and the liquor traffic." [93]

At the meeting of the Mandates Commission in Geneva, in July, 1923, the newspaper dispatches reported:

" In answer to the Commission's questions, the Japanese reported that there was no liquor problem in the South Sea Islands, as the use of alcohol was forbidden to the natives. There was freedom of trade and religion, especially Christianity, to which almost all the natives have been converted. Thirty-four missionaries, among them three Americans and twenty-six Spaniards,

---

[92] *Handbook on the League of Nations,* published by " World Peace Foundation," p. 308 f.
[93] New York *Times,* July 20, 1923.

received every facility in spreading Christianity, which Japan considers is powerful in elevating the moral standard of the people.

"The Mandates Commission of the League supervises the welfare of 16,000,000 people governed under the mandates of various Powers. It will insist on its prerogative of criticising the management of these territories. This was made clear at today's session of the commission when Marquis Thedoli, its President, protested against the assembly's criticism of the Commission's policy of publicity. He insisted that the Commission's views should always be freely voiced, as otherwise abuses might develop.

"The President appealed to all the mandatory countries to take more interest in the work of the Commission and in the great experiment of the League to advance the welfare of the backward peoples under the new form of colonial policy, based upon the public opinion of the world.

"A letter was read from Premier Smuts of the Union of South Africa, saying that he believed the mandatory system was a great step forward. He also said that 7,000 Germans of former German Southwest Africa may elect to become citizens of the Union of South Africa, choosing a popular council and sending representatives to the Parliament of the Union.

"The Commission invited representatives of all the mandatory States to come to Geneva for an examination of the conditions in their territories, after which the Commission will draft its report." [94]

Thus far, the chief complaint of racial injustice in the execution of the Mandates has been the protest of the Arabs and of the Pope against the establishment of "absolute Jewish preponderance over all other peoples of Palestine, constituting a grave breach of existing rights of other nationalities." [95]

There are strong races and there are weak races, advanced races and backward races. The problems of their relations will not be solved for many years. But the solution will be hastened by recognition of the principle of trusteeship. Economically that principle is the only sensible principle. The expedition into Mexico after Villa cost the United States $112,000,000. The Mexican unrest of which the Villa incident was a part has cost our nation and the world vastly more. A small portion of these

---

[94] New York *Times*, July 21, 1923.
[95] New York *Times*, June 16, 1922.

amounts spent in a spirit of brotherly helpfulness in Mexico in education would have averted all this loss and advanced Mexico on her way by at least two generations.

Trusteeship, however, as a solution of the race problem includes and involves that very problem itself. Many of the wards of such trusteeship deem themselves ready for independence before the trustee is assured and the trustee invariably finds the task of dissolving the trust and emancipating his charge more difficult than the original establishment of the trustee relationship, or even than the process by which he came to accept theoretically the idea of trusteeship in lieu of the imperialism by which the original authority was established. As Sir Valentine Chirol has said: " So long as we can treat such peoples as children, all the best qualities of our race, our instincts of justice and fair play, our natural kindliness, our sense of responsibility as trustees of the material welfare of all those committed to our care, find full and congenial scope. Our difficulties begin when those children grow up and, claiming the benefits of everything that we have ourselves taught them, ask to be released from our leading strings and to be treated as equals.

" That is where the trouble begins, for the claim to equality, though we may be willing to admit in principle, conflicts with the racial pride which is undoubtedly one of the defects of our qualities." [96] It would be a happy thing if racial pride were the only difficulty. A true racial pride on both sides would assist and smooth the transition.

(5) The right of racial integrity, to be developed wherever possible into national autonomy, should be recognised. The success of civilisation would involve the realisation of both these ends. They are both consistent with and involved in the ideal of democracy whether national or universal. " Democracy does not mean the erasure of individuality in the man, the family, or the race. Its unity is truer and richer because not run in one colour or expressed in monotony of form. Like all vital unities, it is composite. It is consistent with the individuality of the man, it is

---

[96] *Outward Bound,* August, 1923, p. 804, art., " Social Relations and Race Feeling."

consistent with the full individuality and the separate integrity of the races. No one has ever asserted that the racial individuality of the Jew, preserved for sixty centuries and through more than sixty civilisations, by conviction from within and by pressure from without, was a contradiction of democratic life. Democracy does not involve the fusion of races any more than it involves the fusion of creeds or the fusion of arts. It does not imply that the finality of civilisation is in the man who is white or in the man who is black, but in the man—white or black—who is a man. Manhood, in a democracy, is the essential basis of participation." [97] It is the business of the strong races to help on the weak races in the hope that they may be able to stand alone in the exercise of self-government and in the accomplishment of the world's work. The advance of such a democratisation would inevitably mean the recession of Islam, and the approach of any race toward full self realisation means its approach to Christianity.[98]

7. Is this true? Does the solution of the race problem belong to Christianity? May we believe, as the " International Creed " of the Commission on International Justice and Good Will of the Federal Council of the Churches of Christ declares, "that the Spirit of Christian brotherhood can conquer every barrier of trade, colour, creed and race "? We may believe this. This is what we must believe. All the conceptions which have emerged as involved in the true view of race and the true solution of the race problem, are Christian conceptions. Historically they came into the thought of man through Christianity. They derive what vitality and power they possess from the Christian spirit. In closing this chapter three of the great ideals of Christianity may be suggested as fundamental.

(1) Its ideal of equality. Christianity affirms human equality in the sense in which it is true. The races are not equal in their capacities or achievements or progress. Professor Conklin is quite right: " Every human race has its good qualities and its bad ones, but human history as well as biology refutes those idealists

---

[97] Murphy, *The Present South*, p. 19.
[98] *Atlantic Monthly*, Nov., 1920, art. " Islam," p. 680.

who claim that there are no lower races or types, that all men are born equal." [99]   In many respects men are not born equal, and even if they were they would not remain so.   And races are only kindred and measurably assimilated groups of men.   They differ both by and in inheritance and education and character.   But in the true sense Christianity affirms that all men and all races are equal.   They have equal rights to justice and to life, to happiness and to work, to self development and to liberty.   They have the capacity each to do his own duty and to fulfill his own functions. Christianity asserts the equal right of man as man to be his best and to do the most, and it asserts this equal right for every man of every race.   This assertion is essential to the production of the human values which the whole race needs.   Any theory of race inequality which prevents this will rob humanity of potential human capacity; for, as Prof. Thorndike has shown, " selection by race of original natures to be educated is nowhere nearly as effective as selection of the superior individuals regardless of race.   There is much overlapping and the differences in original nature within the same race are, except in extreme cases, many times as great as the differences between races as wholes." [100] These individuals have their right to the freest and largest life, unforbidden because of race connection.   And each race has its right to self fulfilment according to its highest possibilities.[101]

(2) Its ideal of service and love.   The military and economic education through which we have passed has derided the sentimental considerations.   But love and sympathy and service, nevertheless, are the primary forces.   Even the military and economic appeals make use of love of country and of service to race and of duty to symbols like the flag, thus confessing the supremacy of the moral sentiments.   The race problem will not be solved by men who are driven to the philosophic conclusion that only brotherhood will solve it.   Brotherhood is not a force which will come to such a summons.   It is to be found only where men look upon other men with a brother's love.   The idea and power of such a

[99] *The Yale Review,* April, 1917, p. 480.
[100] Thorndike, *Educational Psychology,* Vol. III, p. 224.
[101] See paper by H. D. Griswald, *Jesus Christ and Human Personality.*

love is historically and peculiarly Christian. And the great inter-racial services of the world are all traceable to a Christian source.

At Indianapolis, Indiana, during the Christmas holidays in December, 1923, between six and seven thousand students were gathered under the auspices of the Student Volunteer Movement for Foreign Students. Only a fraction of those present expected to go as missionaries, but all were there because of their interest in the present-day problems of world relationships. The two subjects which commanded most attention and interest were race and war. The students broke up for several sessions into discussion groups of about a hundred each, where the whole discussion was in the hands of the students themselves. Naturally not all that was said was judicious or well informed, but one thing was unmistakably clear, namely, that these students wanted to view the problems of race and war in the light of the principles of Christ. Whatever criticism might be made of some of their suggestions it is certain that none but Christian students could ever have brought in such proposals as those which the discussion group leaders, all students, brought from their groups to the whole Convention:

"Eliminate the white superiority complex ingrained in primary schools;

"Get together various races in groups on the campus for prayer and thought and fellowship together;

"Bring in leaders of other races to speak and meet students;

"Utilise every opportunity to become friends with members of other races whenever we meet them (this in some sections would involve visits to segregated areas);

"Oppose organisations working toward the attitude of racial superiority;

"Work through journalism in every possible way to change the press feeling of the country. (The suggestion was made to begin tackling the problem by converting our own families.);

"Work for breaking down discriminations because of race in dormitories, societies, athletics, fraternities, churches, in college life generally;

"Give money to support organisations which are working for these ends;

"Promote education; do all we can for the inclusion in the curriculum of courses in history which present a fairer and more Christian attitude than the ones now given;

"Be living examples of Christ's spirit whenever a race issue appears;

"Indulge in real thinking and study on the reasons for the present prejudiced attitude;

"Right concrete racial wrongs and work together with those from other nations for the same great cause." [102]

(3) Its ideal of unity. The conception of human unity which Christianity has propagated and which resides in its universality of character and claim, has happily spread widely over human thought and effort. Dr. Reinsch has summarised the facts of the new world mind:

"The cardinal fact of contemporary civilisation is the unification of the world, the emergence of organic relations, world-wide in scope, uniting the branches of the human family in all parts of the earth. . . . Great types of character are no longer merely national household names, but their lineaments are known the world over and everywhere interest is taken in their views and actions. There is a world-wide sympathy, so that if evil befall in California, or Chile, or Italy, or China, the entire world is affected and all nations are anxious to offer their aid and bear their share of the burden.

"The growth of world unity which we have witnessed in our day has already modified, and even superseded to some extent, the effect of geographic separation, of political nationalism or particularism, and of economic exclusiveness. Economic and social forces are beginning to flow in a broad natural stream, less and less hampered by dynastic and partisan intrigue, by protectionist walls, by monopolies and all sorts of exclusive privileges. . . .

"Through participation in the scientific spirit, those deep-lying differences in point of view, which had been developed through centuries of historic experience, are giving way to a unified mode of seeing and solving the problems of life. . . .

"While national policy still strives to reserve some special benefits to citizens, the dominant note in industrial life is no longer national but international. This is also indicated by the manner in which practically every economic interest has organised itself

---

[102] For an illustration of the right spirit of inter-racial friendship and good will, see Fraser, *Among Indian Rajahs and Ryots*, pp. 60-74.

on an international scale. Such great unions as those in which the activities of insurance, of railway management, of shipping, of agriculture, of building, of law, of education, and of science are discussed and acted upon, are the final proof that economic organisation has for ever abandoned the narrower field and recognises no confining local limits." [103]

But these unities are frail and need some deeper spiritual basis. And also they need some principle which will protect us against the risk of world uniformity. A universal social mind filled with the whole world content is our goal, but how is personal and racial individuality to be preserved in it? [104] Christianity has the only adequate assurance. Read again Paul's great passages in I Cor. XII, 12-27 and Eph. II and III and IV and Col. I. In the New Testament conception, humanity is a body of which Christ is the Saviour and Head. The races are members of an organism living one common life, sharing alike the honour and health of the whole body of which each is a part. There is unity of body, variety of function, identity of interest, equality of life and joy.[105]

" After all," as Mr. Mornay Williams writes, " it is the personal and living Christ, not the body of ideas, or philosophy of life, which most persons have in mind when they speak of Christianity, which is the reconstructive principle. Our Lord's own words are both the explanation and the demonstration of His place and power: ' I am the way, the truth and the life.' Apart from His person there is no access to the Father or to the unity of mankind. A striking illustration of the inevitableness of this personality of the truth is the scene in Pilate's judgment hall where Jesus, the Word of God manifest in the flesh—the embodied Truth—stood before His Roman judge, who, vacillating and harassed, cried out, ' What is truth?' and the next moment, looking to the Jews, said: ' I find in Him no fault at all.' In much the same fashion the wisdom and science of our modern world faces the problems which confront it, and not least, the racial problems, and as men

---

[103] *Universal Races Congress,* 1911, paper on "Influence of Geographic, Economic and Political Conditions," pp. 49 f., 52, 54.

[104] Ross, *Social Psychology,* p. 363 ff.

[105] See *The Christian Union Quarterly,* April, 1924, art. by Dean Inge, " Reunion: An Englishman's View," p. 355.

eagerly question: 'What is truth? How shall we conserve the best? How shall we save life, individual life and racial life? How shall we escape war and bloodshed?'—over against them stands the calm figure of Jesus Christ, the King of Righteousness and Prince of Peace, saying, 'I am come that ye might have life and have it more abundantly. Whosoever shall seek to save his life, shall lose it, and whosoever shall lose his life shall preserve it.' In the Te Deum of history the noble army of martyrs and the glorious company of the apostles as they praise God, continually affirm and prove the truth of these words for the individual, and gradually, here a little and there a little, the races and families of the earth are spelling out the truth in an anthem of praise that is a deepening echo of the song of peace on earth, good will to men; for the method of Jesus is to make men friends to one another through Himself and the purpose of Jesus is to create a new heaven and a new earth wherein dwelleth righteousness."

Here is the solution of the race problem. If, looking out over humanity, torn with race feuds and embittered with race hatreds, we ask with Paul, "Who can deliver us from the body of this death?" the answer is simple and clear, "Christ is the Saviour of this body." And this is not a mere pious vagary. It is the hardest and most fundamental social and political fact.

In many races we begin at last to see light. We shall meet in the next chapter the new mind which is taking shape in America. And Gabriella Mistral, the Chilean poetess, speaks the highest thought of Latin America: "Every day I see more clearly the necessity, yea, the tragical necessity, that all of those who by one road or another are looking for Christ and who desire to hasten His reign on the earth, must unite, facing such an inferior and dense materialism as we find at this hour, which probably will bring to death our modern civilisation if it is not totally cleaned of this gangrene. We people of faith have the most urgent duty of forgetting our various petty divisions and remembering only that we belong to Christ."

SOME SPECIFIC RACE PROBLEMS OF TODAY

1. Our greatest American race problem is the problem of relations between the white and black races. In some respects the situation is more hopeful, in others more alarming than it has even been. It is more hopeful because among both the black and the white people there is a growing body of the best men and women who realise the gravity of the situation, who are ready to co-operate in dealing with it, who believe that the application of Christianity to the problem is its only solution and who are convinced that Christianity must be applied to its solution. Indeed the Christian forces are the only forces which are really grappling with the issue. Nothing has ever shown the inadequacy and the helplessness of all other forces in facing a real and perilous race situation more sharply than it has been shown in this matter. And no one can read the literature on this subject of twenty years ago and then the literature which the South is producing today without realising the immense progress that has been made in the courage and justice and hopefulness with which the Christian people of both races in the South are meeting this real crisis.

Among the evidences of this spirit and as illustrating the right method of approach to race problems nothing has been more notable than the growth of inter-racial co-operation, especially since the inauguration of the Southern Sociological Congress in 1912, in Nashville, Tenn. Its program covered the whole field of social and moral need in the South and it specifically included among the things for which the Congress stood " the solving of the race question in a spirit of helpfulness to the Negro and of equal justice to both races." It issued " a challenge to Southern chivalry to see that justice is guaranteed to all citizens regardless of race, colour or religion and especially to befriend and defend the friendless and helpless," and " a challenge to the present generation to show its gratitude for the heritage bequeathed to it through the toil and blood of centuries by devoting itself more earnestly to the task of making the nation a universal brotherhood." [1] Out of the first meeting of the section on Race Relations came the appointment of a Southern University Commission on the Negro, with a representative from nearly every Southern State University. This commission met for organisation in December, 1912. It reported to the Atlanta Congress a broad outline of investigation to be undertaken in regard to conditions—religious, educational, hygienic, economic and civic; the duty of whites in improving these conditions; and the ideal of race-relations towards which the South should move. [2] The spirit in which this Commission has been working is revealed in its letter of Jan. 14, 1922, to the college men of the South, signed by representatives of ten southern State Universities, calling on the students of the South

" to assist in moulding public opinion and to co-operate in all sane efforts to bring about a more tolerant spirit, more generous sympathy, and larger measure of good-will and understanding between the best elements of both races.

" In this letter the Commission wishes to call attention to the progress made in the last few years in interracial co-operation. Already there are agencies at work developing such co-operation in local communities throughout the southern States. Noteworthy in this connection is the establishment of more than eight hundred county interracial committees in the southern States, as a result of the efforts of the Commission on Interracial Co-operation, organised in 1919 by representative southern men and women, with its headquarters in Atlanta. This is a practical method of putting into service the leadership of both races. Sane, thoughtful men, who love truth and justice, can meet together and discuss problems involving points of even strong disagreement and arrive at a common understanding, if only they remember to look for the next best thing to do rather than attempt to determine for all time any set of fixed policies or lay down an inclusive program for the future. The most fruitful forms of co-operation have been found in connection with such vital community problems as better schools, good roads, more healthful living, and more satisfactory

[1] *The South Mobilising for Social Service*, p. 11 f.
[2] Hammond, *In Black and White*, p. 212.

business relations. In all these community efforts the good of
both races is inseparably involved.

" No fact is more clearly established by history than that hatred
and force only complicate race relations. The alternative to this
is counsel and co-operation among men of character and good will,
and above all, of intelligent and comprehensive knowledge of the
racial problem."

Not only have these inter-racial committees been established in
800 counties, but the inter-racial State Committees also, likewise
organised under the Commission on Inter-racial Co-operation, with
larger power and influence have faced courageously the immense
task before them.[3] The report of one Committee, made by a
Negro, will be sufficiently representative of all, namely, the Inter-
racial Committee of Kentucky for 1922. A few quotations will
be adequate:

" Although the coloured people of Kentucky are at this moment
suffering from many grave injustices and handicaps, it is nevertheless my conviction that never before in the history of the state
were the relations between the races so pleasant and helpful as at
the present time, and that the spirit of good will and co-operation
was never so evident as it is today. The ground of this conviction
is found in the ready and frank admission on the part of our white
friends of these injustices and handicaps, their desire to know the
facts and their willingness to discuss these grave inequalities with
their coloured neighbours, with the purpose of devising ways and
means by which these injustices may be corrected and these handicaps removed, together with the progress actually made to
that end.

" In practically every county, through the influence of inter-
racial committees or other agencies, school authorities have come
to admit the right of Negro schools to their pro rata of the cor-
poration tax. In some counties the officials are still slack in the

---

[3] For striking evidence of what these Inter-racial Commissions are ac-
complishing, see the reports of their work, *e. g., Progress in Race Relations
in Georgia,* issued by the Georgia Committee on Race Relations, 416 Pal-
mer Building, Atlanta, Ga.; Annual Meeting of the Commission on Inter-
Racial Coöperation in the South, *Fisk University News,* Oct., 1923, pp.
18-22; "An Adventure in Good Will," in *Fisk University News,* March,
1924, pp. 17-20; Conference of the Commission of the Federal Council of
the Churches on the Church and Race Relations, Feb. 23, 1923, *Federal
Council Bulletin,* Feb.-March, 1923, p. 31 f.; accounts of the observance of
Race Relations Sunday, *Ibid.,* p. 30.

observance of this law, but nowhere in the state is the right of the coloured people to such pro rata seriously questioned. It is the task, therefore, of the coloured people in each county, assisted by their white friends, to see to it that there is an equitable and legal division of these funds."

The Report cites the insufficient protection which the laws give coloured girls and coloured women against assault and refers to an unpunished assault on a little four year old coloured girl and to a Florida judge who had dismissed a similar case with the declaration that no white man could be convicted in his court on the testimony of Negroes only. But the report quotes also the resolution of the Commission's Conference in 1921:

" Resolved: that appreciative attention be called to the fact that in Louisville, coloured tax-payers serve on both petit and grand juries apparently in just ratio to their respective numbers. What is safe in Louisville is certainly safe elsewhere in the state, and we express our earnest hope and expectation that the Negro will be given his full share in this field of service."

The resolutions adopted by this Commission at its meeting in Louisville, Dec. 15-16, 1922, are also representative and significant:

" That race differences are based on prejudice, the basis of which is misunderstanding.
" That race friction and false judgment between the races are hindrances to economics and to ethical and moral problems which can only be solved by knowledge on the part of both races. This knowledge will best be attained by a fair and mutual study of race relations.
" There can be no question that righteousness, racial or other-wise, calls for equal justice and impartial enforcement of law in our courts regardless of race or colour. This each race should call for and support.
" We also urge that Negroes who, under the law, are qualified for jury service be given their full opportunity thus to serve.
" Further: we recommend that the press be urged to exercise care to publish impartially violations of law on the part of either race and also that it set before the public an impartial account of the meritorious achievements of both races.

" We recommend that a constant and determined effort be made to judge the Negro not by any traditions of the past, but by the advance guard who are looking to the highest possibilities of the future. The Negro should be judged, not by the disorderly and light minded of the race, but by those who are trained to meet the issues and bear the responsibilities of life today.

" The committee is in thorough accord with the view that good will, founded upon intellectual, moral and spiritual knowledge, will produce a compelling power which, linked with the proper commanding physical forces, will combat the destructive work of prejudice and build constructive and well founded community life.

" That a scale of adjustment of salaries in city high and normal schools be adopted which shall remove all racial inequality.

" Realising that many white women have no adequate idea of the tragedy of the Negro woman's upreach to the virtue of purity, we recommend a most sympathetic study of the question."

A new day has come among the students of the South in the matter of inter-race relations among the students, white and black. The first Southern Conference of the Student Fellowship for Christian Life Service, held in Atlanta, April 6-8, set a new standard for the conduct of such meetings. The Committee on Local Arrangements, made up of students from some of the white institutions in Atlanta, voted unanimously and without debate to invite the Negro students to be present and participate fully in the Conference. They agreed that it would be un-Christian to hold such a Conference otherwise. Among the speakers on the program were Peter Shih, a Chinese, and Professor Isaac Fisher, of Fisk University, a Negro. The meetings were held at one of the white Baptist churches and at the Y. M. C. A., and throughout the sessions there was no suggestion of racial discrimination. Students of both races served on the Committee on Findings, and the Conference adopted a resolution declaring " that the Student Fellowship Movement make a careful study of racial relationships, foster a spirit of kindliness and goodwill among all men, and endeavour to bring about peace and harmony among the races.

The Emory Wheel, the student newspaper of Emory University (Georgia), in reporting the Conference said: " A unique feature of the Conference was the presence of delegates from the coloured institutions of Atlanta. There could have been no better manifestation of Christian spirit than the friendship and fellowship that existed between the representatives of these colleges and the other colleges." One of the leading Negro students, writing after the Conference, said: " I was much impressed with the attitude of the white students; the type of association which was ours was something unique in the realm of Christian experience in the Southland." Those who know the condition of the past can appreciate the significance of such a development as this.

The women of the South, both white and coloured, have taken their place in this forward movement.[4] They are members of the

---

[4] At the Fourteenth Annual Meeting of the National Association for the Advancement of Coloured People, in Kansas City, August 29th to September 5, 1923, one of the notable incidents was the address of Mrs. B. W. Bickett, of North Carolina, wife of the late ex-Governor of that state. She gave an account of the work of the Inter-racial Commission and added:
"We are a long, long way from solving the race problem in the South, but we have made a hopeful beginning. As interested, thoughtful, white men and women we are seeking through our civic and religious organisations to meet in a spirit of coöperation the leading men and women of the Negro race in the community in which we live. We are coöperating in a study of Negro community life, in housing and sanitation, better neighbourhood conditions, educational opportunities and the needs of Negro women and children, especially. We are becoming increasingly conscious of the fact that as those in authority, our responsibility towards the Negro cannot be evaded and many of our people are going forward with a determination that no unfair advantage shall be taken of the Negro, but that he shall receive justice and fair treatment which is his due, and which we cannot withhold if we wish to retain our self respect."
In a message to the people of the United States the annual convention at which Mrs. Bickett spoke, called attention to the fact that: " the destinies of the Negro and white races of the American continent are inseparable; that the races must, therefore, in the fullest sense work together for the realisation of the principles on which the American nation was founded. That unless the humblest citizen is guaranteed his citizenship rights there can be no true security for any one in the land."—(Federal Council of the Churches, Research Department, *Information Service*, Nov. 3, 1923, p. 4.)
And no one has spoken more fearlessly against violence and the organisations of violence than Mrs. W. C. Winsborough, one of the leading women of the South, Superintendent of the Women's Auxiliary of the Southern Presbyterian Church, at a public meeting of the Executive Committee of the Federal Council of the Churches in Columbus, Ohio, in December, 1923:
"The Ku Klux Klan, that organisation known as the 'Invisible Empire,' under the guise of patriotism is sowing seeds of race hatred, lawlessness and anarchy which, if not checked, will strike at the very life of our national life itself. I come from a denomination which does not sanction a union of Church and State, which does not intermingle politics and religion. Were the Ku Klux Klan a political organisation only, Christians might remain silent. Important as is the political side of its activity, how-

inter-racial commissions, and, acting both in separate racial groups and together, they are looking the race issues squarely in the face. On October 12, 1922, eighteen North Carolina white women met in Raleigh and, having accepted membership on the State Committee on Race Relations, drafted and gave to the public the following declaration:

"We believe that unrest existing between two different races, dwelling side by side under the same economic system and the same government can be lessened and eventually dispelled by a course of justice and fair play. When one race exceeds another in numbers, in possessions, and in opportunity, there is but one solution. As a Christian people we hold the elements of that solution. It lies in the cultivation of an attitude of fairness, of good will, and of conscious determination to establish an understanding sympathy.

"We believe that every human being should be treated not as a means to another's end, but as a person whose aspiration toward self-realisation must be recognised; that we must cherish racial integrity and racial self-respect, as well as such mutual respect as will lead to higher moral levels, to mutual trust and mutual helpfulness. We believe that in this process certain values must be developed and maintained.

"No family and no race rises higher than its womanhood. Hence, the intelligence of women must be cultivated and the purity and dignity of womanhood protected by maintenance of a single standard of morals for both races.

"The right of childhood to health and safety, to the training of

---

ever, there is a moral and religious side which should not be overlooked by the Christian people of America. This organisation combines many of the evils which the Church has been decrying for years. Mob violence in its unlovely reality repels honest men, but the Ku Klux Klan disguises mob law under the guise of benefaction.

"While persecuting the race from which our Master came, they have adopted the Cross as their symbol, and saddest of all, have enlisted among their followers thousands of those who profess to be followers of the lowly Nazarene who came to bring peace to the world and who called all men His brethren.

"This organisation is confined to no one section of the country but is reaching its terrible tentacles into every state in the Union. The time for inaction has passed. If this monster is to be crushed, it must be done by the Christian people of America. If we who believe that 'He has made of one blood all nations of the earth' remain silent in the face of so great an evil, the very stones themselves will cry out against us."—*Federal Council Bulletin,* Jan.-Feb., 1924, p. 12 f.)

body and mind in right habits and the soul in right purposes, is unchallenged.

"The childhood of every race must be safeguarded, for races move forward on the feet of little children.

"As a foundation for social security for all races, the family ideal must be made possible by economic justice, by religious sanction, by legal safeguards, and a single standard of morals.

"We believe that violence has no place where people lend their support in every possible way to the agencies constituted by the people for the apprehension, trial, and punishment of offenders against society. We resent the assertion that criminality can be controlled by lawless outbreaks, and woman's honour protected by savage acts of revenge.

"We believe it our highest duty to pursue these methods toward harmonious racial adjustment.

"We believe that bitterness, resentment, and strife will yield to mutual trust only as we steadfastly cultivate in both races these attitudes and this faith in our common humanity.

"To these ends we pledge ourselves." [5]

Thousands of concrete instances of good feeling and good action between white and black could be gathered, and the daily papers could publish ten of these to every contrary instance of bad feeling and bad actions, but only the evil finds publicity or an occasional unique occurrence like the following from The New York *Times* of March 8, 1923:

"WILL PENSION OLD SLAVES.
"*South Carolina Rewards Negroes Faithful to Masters in Civil War.*

"COLUMBIA, S. C., March 7.—Faithful Negroes who stood by their masters during the Civil War were voted pensions by the South Carolina Legislature today. The House passed the Johnstone bill providing such pensions, which already had passed the Senate by a vote of 67 to 34.

"The bill provides that slaves who served the State and their masters in the Confederate Army during the war shall be granted pensions under virtually the same conditions as those now paid to Confederate veterans."

But the significant thing is not such an isolated incident. It is

---

[5] *Home Mission Monthly,* April, 1923, p. 129.

the steady patience and the growing intelligence of the Negro race and the ever developing purpose of the white race to see that absolute justice is done both to the Negro race and to its individual members.

But this is only the hopeful side of the picture. There is a darker one. As Dr. Haynes says:

" A generation of Negroes who know not slavery has grown up with an increasing race consciousness and aspiration for American opportunities. The descendants of the non-slave-holding white people now make up the majority of the population of the southern states and have come into power of two kinds: they have acquired a large share in the increasing industrial occupations and a large voice in civic and political matters.

" With the race consciousness of the Negro gradually rising like the tides of the sea, has come a restlessness under the existing restructions, limitations, and racial discriminations.

" The races have been drawing apart; a cleavage from the cradle to the grave. Separate neighbourhoods in cities and impersonal relations on large plantations and in large industrial operations where both races are employed are only the larger outlines of a more detailed segregation that ramifies in many directions. In city and in country communities, Negroes and white people attend different churches. In the last fifty years, Negroes have built up national and international church organisations managed and controlled by Negroes. Separation in schools, public and private, except in most northern states, is well-nigh universal. There have grown up the mission colleges and secondary schools for the Negro youth, fostered by the Church Educational and Home Mission Boards. In the southern states, on all railroad trains there are separate cars or compartments in cars for white and coloured passengers. State laws or local ordinances require separation regulations on street cars. The old feeling of dependence of man upon master is rapidly disappearing on the Negro side, and the old feeling of paternal protectiveness is disappearing on the white side of the line. Many white people and Negro people, especially women and children, spend weeks, months and even years without any personal contact with those of the opposite race. In many places Negroes are buried in separate cemeteries." [6]

But this is no new discrimination. Thaddeus Stevens, half a cen-

---

[6] Haynes, *The Trend of the Races*, p. 9 f.

tury ago, in the State of Pennsylvania, chose his last resting place deliberately in a cemetery where black and white might sleep side by side. "In the chief cemeteries of Lancaster it was stipulated by charter that no person of colour should be interred therein," says one of Stevens' biographers.

"Stevens had lots in both cemeteries, but he sent back the deeds, preferring to be laid to rest in Shreiner's cemetery, a private and humble burying-ground not far from the center of Lancaster and near one of its public schools. There on a worthy monument erected to his memory the visitor may read these characteristic words composed for his epitaph by the Great Democratic Commoner himself:

"'I repose in this quiet and secluded spot,
Not from any natural preference for solitude,
But finding other cemeteries limited by charter rules
    as to race,
I have chosen this that I might illustrate in my death
The principles which I advocated through a long life,
Equality of man before his Creator.'

"He died as he lived, the relentless foe of Privilege, the uncompromising advocate of Democracy—of equal rights for all and special privileges for none beneath the law. 'I know not what record of sin awaits me in the other world, but this I know—that I have never been guilty of despising a man because he was poor, because he was ignorant, or because he was black.' These words fitly apply to the life and character of Thaddeus Stevens. Before all else he stood for liberty and the equal rights of men. To this faith he bore his consistent testimony from early life to the open grave and beyond." [7]

With growing co-operation between black and white, there is also growing divergence. There are white elements which behave with anti-social hatred and in a spirit of race arrogance toward the Negro. There are other white elements too high-minded for such an attitude which nevertheless are satisfied with an inadequate ideal of justice for the Negro. There are black men whose patience is worn thin or who despair of a peaceful solution of the

---

[7] Woodburn, *Life of Thaddeus Stevens*, p. 609.

problem. And there are black men who are intemperate and who have accepted the war philosophy that the right way to right wrong is by force and violence.

And who will say that the Negro has not been given already too great provocation for an increasing spirit of resistance to injustice and mistreatment?

" The following are some concrete illustrations from statements of Negroes: In 1919, at the time of the Washington (D. C.) riot. a most reliable Negro, a man of the rank and file of workers, said: ' During the riot I went home when through with my work and stayed there, but I prepared to protect my home. If a Negro had nothing but a fire poker when set upon, he should use it to protect his home. I believe all the men in my block felt the same way. I know they stayed 'round home more than usual.' Another Negro, a porter, said: ' We are tired of bein' picked on and bein' beat up. We have been through the war and given everything, even our lives, and now we are going to stop bein' beat up.' A third, commenting on the Chicago riot, said: ' These things (meaning riots) will keep on until we peaceable, law-abiding fellows will have nothing to do but to prepare to defend our lives and families.' A Negro teacher said, ' The accumulated sentiment against injustice to coloured people is such that they will not be abused any longer.' " [8]

The situation is made more acute by the fact that so much of the contact between the races is in the marginal land of idleness, shiftlessness and crime into which the lees of both races settle down.

As we face this existing race situation in the United States what are the most living and significant aspects of the problem?

(1) The most important thing is the temper of mind which will allow time for a solution and which will assure all parties to the issue that there is an adequate will to reach a just solution. Fortunately these two essentials are just the qualities with which the two races involved are most strongly endowed. The most notable gift of the Negro race is its patience and long suffering. In spite of all that the race has endured it has kept its good spirit and

---

[8] Haynes, *The Trend of the Races*, p. 17.

kindness. Its songs are free from all hate and vengeance. They breathe only friendship and steadfastness and hope. It is true that a more menacing note is beginning to appear, but still the true Negro heart hesitates to go further than young Joseph Cotter in his verse, " And What Shall You Say? "

> " Brother, come!
> And let us go unto our God.
> And when we stand before Him
> I shall say—
> ' Lord, I do not hate,
> I am hated.
> I scourge no one,
> I am scourged.
> I covet no lands,
> My lands are coveted.
> I mock no peoples,
> My people are mocked.'
> —And, brother, what shall you say? "

Influential Negro leaders, both moderate and radical, still advocate this policy of patience even in the face of growing unrest among their people. " The way of hatred and bitterness and the sword," says Isaac Fisher, " has failed to bring human justice and human rights, and if men cannot be moved to deeds of righteousness through the power of good will and kindness, there is no hope." [9] " I believe in Patience," says W. E. Du Bois, " patience with the weakness of the Weak and the strength of the Strong, the prejudice of the Ignorant and the ignorance of the Blind; patience with the tardy triumph of Joy and the mad chastening of Sorrow;—patience with God! " [10]

When the Negro is asked to be patient a little longer he is asked only to be his own best self. And, on the other hand, the one thing that the American race can be counted on to come to at last is justice. Many interests may befog the road. Many weak and evil elements in each race may seek to argue that what is wrong is really right in order that they may do injustice with peace of

---

[9] *Fisk University News,* May, 1923, p. 11.
[10] Du Bois, *Darkwater,* p. 4.

conscience. *The Advertiser,* of Montgomery, Alabama, declared the right policy twenty years ago when it was not as easy to say these things as it is today:

> " That principle of eternal justice which bids the strong protect the weak, makes it our duty to protect the Negro in all his legal, industrial and social rights. We should see that he has equal and exact justice in the courts, that the laws bear alike on the black and the white, that he be paid for his labour just as the white man is paid, and that no advantage be taken of his ignorance and credulity. . . .
> " And the task is a simple and easy one. The courts and juries should know no difference between whites and blacks when a question of right and justice is up for settlement. The man who employs a Negro to work for him should deal as fairly with him as he would deal by a white man. The life of a Negro who has done no wrong should be as sacred as the life of a white man. He is in our power politically and otherwise, and justice, humanity, and good policy unite in demanding for him equal and exact justice. Keep the Negroes among us, give them the full protection of the laws, and let them have justice in all things. That is the solution of the race question." [11]

Sooner or later this nation will see right and will do right. But what is just and right in the matter of the status of the Negro in America?

(2) One thing that is obviously right is full economic freedom and opportunity. That was one of the issues settled when slavery died. Slavery had been the economic bondage of both the slave and his owner. Emancipation set them both free and left them both penniless. The economic recovery and advancement of the whole South is a romance. But we are concerned now with the Negro. His has been the labour which has largely made the New South. And what has been his share in the new industry and the wealth which he has produced? The Negro race constitutes between one-seventh and one-eighth of the total working population of the country. In the South he has been a far larger fraction. Nearly nine-tenths of the Negroes in the South over ten

---

[11] *The Advertiser,* Sept. 16 and Oct. 6, 1903, quoted by Murphy, *The Present South,* p. 182 f.

years of age are wage earners and nearly all of these are employed by white people. The number of those employed in manufacturing and mechanical pursuits more than doubled in the years between 1890 and 1910. A summary in round numbers will suffice to show the progress of the Negro since the Civil War.

	1866	1922
Negro population	4,000,000	10,500,000
Homes owned	12,000	650,000
Wealth	$20,000,000	$1,500,000,000
Farms operated	20,000	1,000,000
Business conducted	2,100	50,000
Per cent. literate	10	80
Colleges and normal schools	15	500
Students in public schools	100,000	2,000,000
Spent for Negro education	$700,000	$20,000,000
Negroes spent on education	$80,000	$2,000,000
Number Negro churches	700	45,000
Communicants	600,000	4,800,000
Sunday school pupils	50,000	2,250,000
Value of church property	$1,500,000	$90,000,000 [12]

The most significant item in this advance is the creation of the Negro home and all that it represents as a social and moral force, in the life of the race and the nation.[13] The Negro has vindicated his right to full economic freedom, and all the rights of associations in labour and capital within that freedom, and has proved himself to be a priceless asset to the nation. The South would have been economically handicapped without him.

This progress of the Negro has come so steadily and gradually that we have been scarcely aware of it. But competent visitors

[12] See *The South Mobilising for Social Service*, pp. 368-397; and Moton, *The Negro of Today*, pp. 7-15; especially his comparison with Russia: "The serfs were emancipated in 1861. Fifty years after it was found that 14,000,000 of them had accumulated about $500,000,000 worth of property, or about $35 per capita—about $200 per fami'.. After this same lapse of time only about 30 per cent. of the Russian peasants were able to read and write. After fifty years of freedom the 10,000,000 Negroes in the United States have accumulated over $700,000,000 worth of property, or about $70 per capita and $350 per family, while 70 per cent. of them have some education in books."
[13] Hammond, *In Black and White*, pp. 90-128; Haynes, *The Trend of the Races*, pp. 41-47, 169-172.

from abroad discern it and are amazed at it. Dr. James Henderson, of Lovedale, one of the leading Scotch missionaries in Africa, visited America in the spring of 1923, and this was his competent judgment:

" I was impressed, first of all, with the fine physique of the Negro boys and girls in the United States. In Charleston I saw a parade in which the coloured boys were as fine in physique as the white. And the coloured boys and girls at schools like Tuskegee are remarkable. What I experienced in the South far transcended anything I had expected. The progress is marvellous. As to language, I pictured to myself the Scotch carried to Greece in early centuries, and mastering Greek. But that would be nothing in comparison with what the African slaves have done, in mastering English. One is amazed to see this ex-slave race thinking and speaking in the full moral power, wealth and freedom of the English language. In the classes at Hampton one sees in glorious reality the liberty of the sons of God. In Africa we are trying to get Christianity into the people. Here it is in them. Christianity is not a thing superimposed, it is there in nature and reality."

(3) The Negro's rights include full political equality. Any limitations of franchise which debar him from voting ought to do so on other grounds than race. They ought to apply equally to all races. The question whether he should or should not have been enfranchised after the Civil War is an interesting but academic question. General S. C. Armstrong's judgment on it is probably as fair and good as any man's. In a public address in 1887 he said:

" After all, being a citizen and a voter has more than anything else made the Negro a man. The recognition of his manhood has done much to create it. Political power is a two-edged sword which may cut both ways and do as much harm as good. In the main, it has, I believe, been the chief developing force in the progress of the race. It is, howeveʳ, probable that this would not have been so had it not been for the support of a surrounding white civilisation which, though not always kind, has prevented the evils which would have resulted from an unrestricted black vote.

" The political experience of the Negro has been a great education to him. In spite of his many blunders and unintentional crimes against civilisation, he is today more of a man than he would have been had he not been a voter. . . . Manhood is best brought out by recognition of it. Citizenship, together with the common school, is the great developing force in this country. It compels attention to the danger which it creates. There is nothing like faith in man to bring out the manly qualities.

" Suffrage furnished him (the Negro) with a stimulus which was terribly misused, but it has reacted and given him a training which it was out of the power of churches and schools to impart. The source of American intelligence is not so much the pedagogue as the system which gives each man a share in the conduct of affairs, leading him to think, discuss and act, and thus educating him as much by his failures as by his successes. Responsibility is the best educator." [14]

Whatever may have been wise in the past, the fact is that under the Constitution of the United States the Negro is explicitly protected against any denial or abridgement of his right to vote " on account of race, colour or previous condition of servitude." This law has been annulled,[15] and its annulment is now made a pretext for the annulment of the Eighteenth or Prohibition Amendment, as well. Contempt for one law is offered in justification for contempt of the other. There ought to be loyal compliance with both laws. It may well be that there should be qualifications for the suffrage which would disenfranchise Negroes, but the same qualifications should apply to whites as well. And ultimately they will do so. As Mr. Murphy wrote to the Alabama Constitutional Commission in 1901 :

" Southern sentiment will not approve the disfranchisement of the illiterate Confederate soldier. In any civilisation, there is a deep and rightful regard for the man who has fought in the armies of the State. But, with that exception, the State must eventually protect itself, and protect the interests of both races, by the just application of the suffrage test to the white and black alike. The South must, of course, secure the supremacy of intelligence and property. This we shall not secure, however, if we begin with the

[14] Talbot, *Samuel Chapman Armstrong*, p. 260 f.
[15] Stephenson, *Race Distinctions in American Law,* p. 320 f.

bald declaration that the Negro is to be refused the suffrage although he have both intelligence and property, and that the illiterate white man is to be accorded the suffrage although he have neither. Such a policy would, upon its face, sustain the charge that we are not really interested in the supremacy of intelligence and property, but solely in the selfish and oppressive supremacy of a particular race. . . .

" It is not merely a question of justice to the negro. It is a question of enlightened self-interest. No State can live and thrive under the incubus of an unambitious, uneducated, unindustrious, and non-property-holding population. Put the privilege of suffrage among the prizes of legitimate ambition, and you have blessed both the Negro and the State.

" If, on the other hand, we accept the administration of an educational and property test which is to enfranchise the Negro on his acceptance of its provisions, and is to enfranchise the white man whether he accepts them or not, we shall have adopted a measure which will be an injustice to the white citizenship of the South. It will be an injustice to the white man for the reason that it places for the Negro a premium upon knowledge and property—makes for him a broader incentive to the acquisition of an education and a home, leaves the white boy without such incentive, makes the ballot as cheap in his hands as ignorance and idleness, and through indifference to the God-given relation between fitness and reward, tempts the race which is supreme to base its supremacy more and more upon force rather than upon merit. . . .

" The absolute supremacy of intelligence and property, secured through a suffrage test that shall be evenly and equally applicable in theory and in fact to white and black—this will be the ultimate solution of the South for the whole vexed question of political privilege." [16]

Adhering literally to Mr. Murphy's argument, the illiterate Negro soldier who fought in the World War might protest against disfranchisement, but he will not do so if the same law lays its requirement upon white and black alike. And Lord Bryce was on the whole convinced that it should do this, that the Negro should have full political as well as full economic equality. He raises the question as the South has faced it and he replies:

---

[16] Murphy, *The Present South*, pp. 194-197.

" The answer seems to be that as regards political rights, race and blood should not be made the ground of discrimination. Where the bulk of the coloured race are obviously unfit for political power, a qualification based on property and education might be established which should permit the upper section of that race to enjoy the suffrage. Such a qualification would doubtless exclude some of the poorest and most ignorant whites, and might on that ground be resisted. But it is better to face this difficulty than to wound and alienate the whole of the coloured race by placing them without the pale of civic functions and duties." [17]

On the part of the Negro also there is need of restraint and modesty. Some of his vain and boisterous leaders do his cause no good.

(4) The Negro race should have also full educational opportunity. Not only should there be no educational discrimination against it, but on the contrary, for the sake of the State and of Society as a whole, there should be special and preferential care to bring the race onward. The idea of racial intellectual inferiority or incapacity for education is disputable, and even if it were not it would not be relevant.

It is disputable. Psychological and educational tests among children and in the army have revealed an average intellectual superiority of the white over the black, but the difference has not been great enough to warrant any special racial pride on the part of the white when the heredity and educational advantages of the two races are taken into account. And in the case of individuals many blacks have demonstrated a marked superiority over white comparisons. And a worthy list of Negro authors, poets, inventors, painters, musicians, soldiers, doctors, teachers, orators, scientists, preachers and others proves the capacities and latent resources of the race.[18]

But even if the Negro race should be inferior to the white, the real question is, will it not be a better race and of more value to

[17] Bryce, The Romanes Lecture, 1902: *The Relations of the Advanced and the Backward Races of Mankind,* quoted by Murphy, *Ibid.,* p. 334 f.

[18] See the New York *Times, Current History,* June, 1923, art. " The Negro Problem as Viewed by Negro Leaders."

the nation and the world, if it is given opportunity to be its best?
"We may even expect," argues Professor Thorndike, "that education will be doubly effective, once society recognises the advantages given to some and denied to others by heredity. That men
have different amounts of capacity does not imply any the less
advantage from or need of wise investment. If it be true, for
example, that the Negro is by nature unintellectual and joyous,
this does not imply that he may not be made more intelligent by
wiser training or misanthropic and ugly-tempered by the treatment
he now receives." [19] The experience of fifty years shows what
new social values there are to accrue to all races in the United
States from the fullest development of each.

It is life or death to the white race to lift or fail to lift the
black race with it. As Dr. Weatherford said at the second meeting of the Southern Sociological Conference,

"The South is a solid South in more than a political sense. We
are a solid South in a social sense. I mean whatever affects the
social welfare of one man affects the social welfare of every other
man in the section. We are bound together by the fact of proximity, we are bound together by economic relations, we are bound
together by the traditions of the past, we are bound together by all
the forces of present life which demand the guarding of our
health, our ideals, and our civilisation. We are not eight million
Negroes and twenty million whites; we are twenty-nine million
human beings, and whatever affects one of our company must of
necessity affect all the other 28,999,999. The sin of the immoral
will destroy the safety of the moral, the disease of the weakest
will destroy the health of the strongest, the prejudice of the most
ignorant will warp the judgment of the most learned, the lawlessness of the most criminal will blacken the fair name and drag into
criminal action the law-abiding instincts of the highest citizens.
We must stand or fall together. Thank God this is true! This
insures that the learned shall not despise the ignorant, that the
physically sound shall not despise the physically weak, the rich
man cannot scorn the poverty-stricken, the righteous cannot become self-righteous in their contempt for the morally weak.
Every welfare movement for whites must become a welfare movement for Negroes as well. This interest in the whole will keep us

---

[19] *Educational Psychology,* Vol. III, p. 311.

from dying with the dry rot of complacency. God has put upon the religious, educational, and social workers of both races of the South a tremendous load of responsibility; but by His help we will carry it like men, and be all the stronger because of our manly exertion." [20]

The problem of adequate racial education in the South is in part a financial problem. The school funds have been inadequate and the Negro children have suffered in the distribution. " In 1909 the Southern Educational Association made open acknowledgment of the existence of this evil in the following demand: ' We insist upon such an equitable distribution of the school funds that all the youth of the Negro race shall have at least an opportunity to receive the elementary education provided by the State.' In appealing for a ' larger share ' of the school funds for the Negro, the University Race Commission, a body of Southern white men, recognised the existence of the evil by saying that ' The inadequate provision for the education of the Negro is more than an injustice to him; it is an injury to the white man.'

" Here are certain figures based on the report of the United States Bureau of Education for 1916 on Negro education (No. 39, Volumes 1 and 2); and the Negro Yearbook of 1918-1919, which show how grave has been the handicap under which Negro children in the South labour, and concerning and against which the Southern white men quoted above have protested.

" ANNUAL PER CAPITA EXPENDITURES PER CHILD OF SCHOOL AGE IN CERTAIN STATES.

	For Whites	For Negroes	Of Population Whites were	Of Appropriations Whites receive	Of Population Negroes were	Of Appropriations Negroes receive
Alabama	$11.21	$2.00	57.5%	89%	42.5%	11%
Arkansas	9.07	4.14	71.8	84	28.1	16
District of Columbia	33.00	32.00	71.3	73	28.5	27.
Delaware	11.53	5.23	84.6	91	15.4	9

[20] *The South Mobilising for Social Service*, p. 359 f.

	For Whites	For Negroes	Of Population Whites were	Of Appropriations Whites receive	Of Population Negroes were	Of Appropriations Negroes receive
Florida	$19.23	$2.44	58.9%	92.6%	41%	7.4%
Georgia	13.16	2.59	54.9	87	45.1	13
Kentucky	11.43	9.70	88.6	91	11.4	9
Louisiana	16.46	1.81	56.8	92.6	43.1	7.4
Maryland	14.63	7.04	82.0	90.5	17.9	9.5
Mississippi	8.20	1.53	43.7	80	56.2	20
Missouri	22.00	16.66	95.2	96.2	4.8	3.8
North Carolina.	9.64	3.70	68	85	31.6	15
Oklahoma	22.60	11.52	87.2	96.8	8.3	3.2
South Carolina.	11.97	1.23	44.8	89	55.2	11
Tennessee	11.44	5.76	78.3	88	21.7	12
Texas	9.06	6.90	82.2	88	17.7	12
Virginia	14.08	4.13	67.4	87	32.6	13
West Virginia..	17.80	17.00	94.7	95	5.3	5

" Since these figures were compiled there has been some notable progress made in curing some of these inequalities; but the general relative proportions have not yet been seriously changed." [21]

It is argued that the Negroes receive a larger proportion of school funds than they pay of the taxes. Probably, but it was their labour in large part which created the wealth which paid the rest of the taxes. In any case it is true that the resources have been inadequate and it is a fair question whether the rest of the nation has not left too heavy a burden in this matter to be borne by the South alone. For the advancement of the Negro race is the concern of the whole nation.

The newspapers of the South are taking an enlightened leadership in the movement for good will and fair dealing, especially in education. The example of fifty editors of leading papers in Virginia has been followed by editors of daily papers in six other

[21] *Fisk University News*, Oct., 1922, p. 2. For a courageous and honest discussion of the situation in our southern states see the Arkansas Survey Report made by the Federal Bureau of Education at the request of the Honourary Educational Commission appointed by Governor McRae, of Arkansas, in 1921. Chapter X of the report, dealing with the Negro public schools, is printed in *Fisk University News*, Dec., 1922, pp. 8-15.

southern states. In a signed statement they ask for mutual helpfulness and co-operation between the white and coloured people in the South, for adequate educational advantages for coloured people, for equality before the law, and for abolition of mob violence. They stress particularly the influence of published news, saying,

" The Negroes of the South are largely dependent upon the white press for current news of the day. It would be well if even greater effort was made to publish news of a character which is creditable to the Negro, showing his development as a people along desirable lines. This would stimulate him to try to attain to a higher standard of living.

" It is a generally accepted fact that in both races if the entire mass were educated industrial problems would adjust themselves automatically and the less fit of either race would find the work and place for which he was best equipped. It has been authoritatively stated that the Negro demand would absorb all teachers, preachers, physicians and lawyers the schools may turn out. . . . In the harmonious co-operation of the thoughtful and exemplary men and women of both races lies the prospect of larger understanding and better inter-racial relations." [22]

(5) The Negro situation in the United States, both in the South and in the North, has been radically altered by the startling redistribution of the race, and by the steady decrease of the Negro population in proportion to the white. The Negro now represents one-tenth of the total population. A hundred years ago he was one-fifth. Even the steadily improving hygienic conditions are not sufficing to offset the death rate in the Negro population. A generation or two ago the South had a Negro population in some states equalling and in South Carolina and Mississippi exceeding the white population. In the sixteen states and the District of Columbia, which are included by the Government Census in the South Atlantic, East South Central and West South Central divisions, the total white population in 1860 was 7,033,973, and the total Negro population was 4,097,111. In 1920 the white popu-

---

[22] Federal Council of the Churches, Research Department, *Information Service,* Jan. 12, 1924, p. 4.

lation in the same states was 24,132,214 and the Negro population 8,912,231. In other words, the white population multiplied three and one-half times, while the Negro population a little more than doubled. In separate states the change has been even more startling. In 1860 in Florida the Negro population nearly equalled the white; in 1920 the whites were nearly double the Negroes. In 1860 in South Carolina the Negroes were one-third more than the white; in 1920 they were about equal, and on April 17, 1923, for the first time in a century, the whites outnumbered the Negroes. The movement of Negroes from the South had been especially rapid in the last decade. Until 1910 each decade showed an increase of Negro population in every southern state, but between 1910 and 1920 the Negro population diminished in Alabama, Delaware, Kentucky, Louisiana, Mississippi and Tennessee. In the nation as a whole the Negro element, which was 16% in 1860, sank to 11% in 1920. In other words, one of the most conspicuous elements in the Negro problem fifty years ago has disappeared. Then it was predicted that the rate of the Negro increase was so great that in a few years the South certainly and in a little longer time the nation would be engulfed in an overwhelming Negro numerical ascendency. Out of this idea grew the fear which tainted the whole atmosphere in which the race question had to be dealt with. Already one can see the new aspect which the arithmetic of the Census has given to the entire discussion.

And the situation in the North has changed also. The decade from 1910 to 1920 has seen an acceleration of the movement of Negroes into almost all the northern states. In Illinois the number advanced in this decade from 109,049 to 182,274; in Indiana from 60,320 to 80,810; in Ohio from 111,452 to 186,187; in Michigan from 17,115 to 60,082; in New York from 134,191 to 198,-483; and in Pennsylvania from 193,919 to 284,568. There are now more Negroes in Pennsylvania than in Kentucky, Maryland or Missouri. The growth of Negro population far exceeded the growth during the preceding decade and surpassed in ratio the white growth. Great Negro communities grew up in cities like Detroit and Indianapolis, which had never before had a Negro problem. The presence of Negro masses which had constituted the gravamen of the problem in the South and which the North had never known now brings the whole problem home to it.[23]

Two questions arise from this movement. What is its cause? What will be the effect? The cause is twofold, social and economic. A committee of representative Negroes of Jackson, Miss., stated the social reasons to their white fellow citizens as follows:

"Having been informed that the object of your meeting is to take steps to try to stay the present exodus of Negroes from the State of Mississippi and being ourselves property holders, citizens of the State and most deeply interested in the future welfare of the commonwealth, realising that anything that is detrimental to the common good of the State is equally detrimental to us, and being Negro citizens ourselves, we beg to submit the following as a few of the many reasons which cause the Negro to be so easily induced to leave his native State:

"(1) The Negro feels that his life is not safe in Mississippi, and that it may be taken with impunity at any time upon the slightest pretext or provocation, by a white man.

"(2) The record filibuster, vote and defeat by the Southern representation in the last Congress of the Dyer anti-lynching bill has caused the Negro to believe that the South is irrevocably determined to perpetuate therein lynch-law and mob violence.

"(3) The Negro has generally despaired of obtaining his rights as a citizen in this section. He has lost faith, and a few of the following facts all tend to force him to this conclusion." [24]

The statement proceeds to specify these: inequality before the law, unequal participation in the use of taxation for education for Negro children and training of Negro teachers, for reformation of Negro derelict youth, for care of the tuberculous and feeble-minded and the blind, unfair treatment of tenant farmers which holds them in serfdom for debt, discrimination against Negroes and Negro sections of towns, political disfranchisement of Negro boys who had gone to the war but " on their return home found

[23] *Public Affairs,* Sept., 1923, art. by Phil H. Brown, " Southern Negroes Move North "; *Current History,* Sept., 1923, art. by Eric D. Walrond, " The Negro Exodus from the South."
[24] New York *Evening Post,* Jan. 14, 1923.

themselves with no more voice in the State and Government which they fought to defend than the German enemy whom they helped to stay from American soil," and exclusion from jury service. " In our humble judgment," the statement said in conclusion, " there is no hope whatever of bringing back the Negroes who have already left the State, but the only hope now lies in taking the proper steps to retain as many as possible of those who are here. The Negroes feel that most of the foregoing facts are, in a measure, true throughout the South." [25]

Economic reasons were included in the statement of the Jackson Negroes. These have been interlaced with the others. Seeking freedom from restraints which were galling and which he hoped to find less in the North, the Negro was drawn also by the demand for labour and by the higher wages. For some years this type of workman has moved North in small numbers, but now the farm labour class also has begun to move. It is estimated that thirteen per cent. of the farm labour of Georgia and three per cent. from Alabama and South Carolina moved North in the twelve months ending in the spring of 1923.[26]

Even if this movement could be checked, and some of the southern states are attempting to check it by legislative measures which cannot be effective, its effects have already made themselves felt. The South, feeling the mass of unskilled labour on which it has rested slipping from under, has been led to deal further with the cause of racial discontent. As the New York *Times* remarked in an editorial on " Laws Against Negro Migration ":

" The real solution lies in removing the incentive to migrate. Already various southern newspapers have pointed out this fact, and there are indications that the more enlightened opinion in the South appreciates it. It is generally recognised that, while higher wages have been the principal bait with which the Negroes have been induced to go North, there have been other reasons of a deeper sort which have had a great influence. These include the

[25] See also Federal Council of the Churches, Research Department, *Information Service*, March 15, 1924, art. " Inter-racial Sentiment in Mississippi."
[26] The New York *Times*, April 23, 1923; New Haven *Courier Journal*, April 9, 1923.

hope of better social conditions, of better educational facilities for children, of better health and sanitary arrangements both in work and at home, and of better prospects for the ambitious. In an article printed in the New York *Times* in May, Mr. Robert R. Moton, President of Tuskegee Institute, mentioned among other factors in the South which encouraged migration the ever-present haunting fear of mob violence. There has also been a widely spread conviction among the coloured people that they are not accorded fair play. The editor of the Columbus (Ga.) *Enquirer-Sun* frankly admits that the white men know this and states that as a matter of fact the Negro does not receive justice in the same measure as the white man, and that he is given inadequate protection.

" To keep the Negro at home can be effected by improving his condition rather than by legislating against his going. In other words, by removing those factors which at present incite him to leave, much more can be done than by punishing those who help him on his journey. In various important southern centres the truth of this is being realised, and even such organisations as local Chambers of Commerce and some of the civic associations have recommended acting accordingly, and urge giving the Negro better protection, improving his schools, and helping him rather than seeking to keep him down. The South wants the Negro, and, given equal treatment, the Negro prefers the South. Unless he receives this, however, no legislation nor fines nor attempts to prevent his learning where there is a labour market will stop his migrating." [27]

The President of the Cotton Growers' Association said recently in Charleston, " The Negro can be kept on the cotton plantation by kindness and personal attention. The landowner needs to get on the job. . . . There has been a lack of brotherly feeling between the landlord and tenant largely because they rarely saw each other. Leaving the management of plantations to overseers is seldom satisfactory. We may soon have to come to a profit-sharing basis of dealing with plantation labour." [28] In other words, the old, old lesson, justice and brotherhood. And the South, the true South, perceives this and the communities which

---

[27] The New York *Times*, July 21, 1923.
[28] Federal Council Commission on the Church and Social Service, Research Department, *Information Service*, May 5, 1923, Nov. 3, 1923.

act in justice and brotherhood are not afraid. In *The Morning Herald,* of Durham, N. C., Jan. 13, 1923, Mr. C. C. Spaulding, President, Mutual Life Insurance Company, a coloured business organisation of that city, speaking as a Negro for his group, describes the favourable conditions in Durham where nearly 8,000 Negroes live on " peaceful and friendly terms with their white neighbours." They find employment in tobacco factories and hosiery mills; the vote is not denied them because of colour; adequate educational opportunities are provided; they receive an honest hearing in the courts, and the white people of Durham show a desire " to make the Negro population a permanent and valuable part of its citizenry." In such southern communities the Negro desires to remain.

(6) We come now to the last and most difficult matter, social equality. What does this mean? Dr. Du Bois answered:

" I mean no half-way measure; I mean full and fair equality. That is, the chance to obtain work regardless of colour, to aspire to position and preferment on the basis of desert alone, to have the right to use public conveniences, to enter public places of amusement on the same terms as other people, and to be received socially by such persons as might wish to receive them. These are not extravagant demands, and yet their granting means the abolition of the colour line. The question is: Can American Negroes hope to attain to this result?"

And to this Mr. Stone replied:

" With equal clearness and precision, and with full comprehension of its larger meaning and significance and ultimate possibilities, the American white man answers the question in the language of another eminent American sociologist, Professor Edward A. Ross, in contrasting the attitudes of Anglo-Saxons and Latins toward other races on this continent: ' The superiority of a race cannot be preserved without pride of blood and an uncompromising attitude toward the lower races. . . . Whatever may be thought of the latter policy, the net result is that North America from the Behring Sea to the Rio Grande is dedicated to the highest type of civilisation; while for centuries the rest of our hemisphere will drag the ball and chain of hybridism.' And thus the issue is joined. And thus also perhaps we find an answer to our own question, whether racial friction in this country is increasing and inevitable." [29]

Such an apparent deadlock would seem to promise nothing but war, a growing demand and a determined denial. But these words were written twenty years ago, and while the race problem is here as really as then and while the new conditions have aggravated the situation, we are nevertheless more hopeful of the solution of the problem than we have ever been. The matter of social equality does not so greatly trouble us. We are coming to see the race problems in far larger terms than the old issue of " social equality " implied. " Social equality," says Dr. Moton, " is a myth that makes trouble. It is a smoke screen and barrage that is often used by politicians. Social equality, as white people understand that term, is not wanted by coloured people, who would rather be with one another than with anybody else. All that coloured people ask for is the fair execution of the law." [30] The issue of social equality is of diminishing significance as the conception of true race personality and integrity and true inter-racial brotherhood and service comes into view.[31] In the first place social equality cannot be defined. It cannot be defined as between individuals,

---

[29] Stone, *The American Race Problem*, p. 240 f.
[30] *Racial Relations and the Christian Ideal*, p. 17.
[31] The resolutions adopted by the Inter-racial Conference held in Birmingham, Alabama, Jan. 22, 1924, indicate this:

I.

" That the race problem is not one of social equality, but a human problem which can best be solved by thoughtful consideration of definite needs for the advantages of both races, and since neither race, the black any more than the white, wishes racial amalgamation, the misleading phrase 'social equality' should no longer be permitted to hold back the co-operation of the white people from giving fair life opportunity to the Negro.

II.

" Race relations in Alabama are improving, respect for law and order is growing and no lynchings are charged to this State during the last year.

III.

" Since the South will perhaps always remain the residence of the majority of the Negro race the mutual inter-dependence of the two races must be continually kept in mind.

still less as between races. It is a phrase readily used because it looks clear and plain, but the moment it is examined it crumbles away. Men are not socially equal because they go to the same theatre or eat in the same hotel. In the second place what substance the phrase really signifies cannot be demanded. If it is felt and accorded it is real. If it is not felt and accorded, the demand cannot secure it and any one demanding it would not be capable of receiving it. He might be given its form, but its reality can never be possessed by any one who is capable of conceiving it as a demandable thing. All this is absolutely true of social equality without regard to race, and it is true of it with regard to race.

What we need to be rid of is all race servility and race arrogance, all discrimination for or against men on arbitrary and unreal grounds, all racial demand and racial assertion, all impatience and injustice. There are multitudes of men and women who are true friends across the line of race. They understand and respect one another. They are working together with a unity

---

IV.

"We recommend that new school buildings for coloured people be located with a view to healthy, sanitary surroundings, that school funds be equitably divided, and that opportunity be given for the adequate training of teachers for coloured schools.

V.

"That in every community effort be made to apportion to each race a just share of the comforts and benefits derived from facilities for recreation, good housing, sanitation, sewerage and street lighting and other necessities which contribute to better living conditions.

VI.

"We affirm our belief that a righteous settlement of race relations everywhere may be found through the application of the principle of Christianity and we therefore recommend that church groups make careful and sympathetic study of conditions surrounding the Negro home, church and school, using the knowledge thus gained to quicken the public conscience concerning responsibility for the conditions.

VII.

"Realising the large part played by racial suspicion and hatred in multiplying stubborn world problems, this Inter-Racial Conference desires to make every possible contribution to the right adjustment of our own racial difficulties in order that our Christian civilisation may not be discredited throughout the world."—(*Birmingham Reporter*, Jan. 26, 1924.)

of purpose and spirit in which there is no colour line nor any wraith of a colour line. They have transcended the old issues and know in their hearts that for them the new day has come. Our hope is in the increase of this company and their triumph over the agitators, the men of both races who use race to confirm or to refute race and who then use both the confirmation and the refutation as a means of intensifying race assertion or authority. Once again, the old and only solution, justice and brotherhood, justice to each race and to all the trusts and values of each race and brotherhood within and across all the races, the maintenance by each race of its self-respect and racial dignity, and the unity of all races in the fulfillment of their distinct and their common tasks. President Harding put it all in a few words spoken to the third annual meeting of the National American Council, commenting upon one phrase in the preamble of the Constitution of the United States:

" Consider one phrase in the preamble: ' To establish justice.' In our mechanism of government, we have set up an elaborate organisation to insure this: the Federal and State Judicial systems. But the courts cannot insure equal justice to all the community if some individuals shall strive for special privileges for themselves, or seek to establish subtle forms of injustice not specifically prohibited by the letter of law. The task of the courts will be difficult, slow, sometimes impossible, unless citizens subject to their jurisdiction are sincerely desirous to do justice and to see it done in the affairs of day-by-day life.

" Thus the immediate and continuing opportunity for every citizen to contribute toward the accomplishment of this particular objective by the nation as a whole, lies in so guiding one's personal affairs that they shall fall into coincidence with this injunction ' to establish justice.' If we sincerely wish to leave a better and a greater nation to the next generation, to bequeath institutions better adapted to accomplish the great aim of social organisation, we shall accomplish these things by adhering in our daily conduct to the rule of seeking and doing justice."

No better counsel has been given to both races as they face their common problem than the Recommendations of the Chicago Commission on Race Relations appointed after the Chicago race riots of 1919. A few of the more significant of the fifty-nine recommendations may be cited:

Inter-racial Tolerance.

27. We are convinced (a) that measures involving or approaching deportation or segregation are illegal, impracticable and cannot solve, but would accentuate, the race problem and postpone its just and orderly solution by the process of adjustment; (b) that the moral responsibility for race rioting does not rest upon hoodlums alone, but also upon all citizens, white or black, who sanction force or violence in inter-racial relations or who do not condemn and combat the spirit of racial hatred thus expressed; (c) that race friction and antagonism are largely due to the fact that each race too readily misunderstands and misinterprets the other's conduct and aspirations.

We therefore urge upon all citizens, white and Negro, active opposition to the employment of force or violence in inter-racial relations and to the spirit of antagonism and hatred. · We recommend dispassionate, intelligent, and sympathetic consideration by each race of the other's needs and aims; we also recommend the dissemination of proved or trustworthy information about all phases of race relations as a useful means toward effecting peaceful racial adjustment.

28. Since rumour, usually groundless, is a prolific source of racial bitterness and strife, we warn both whites and Negroes against the acceptance or circulation by either of reports about the other whose truth has not been fully established. We urge all citizens, white and Negro, vigourously to oppose all propaganda of malicious or selfish origin which would tend to excite race prejudice.

29. We recommend race contacts in cultural and co-operative efforts as tending strongly to mutual understanding and the promotion of good race relations.

Fostering Race Antagonism.

30. We condemn the provocation or fostering of race antagonism by associations or organisations ostensibly founded or conducted for purposes of patriotism or local improvements or the like.

Information About Negroes.

36. We recommend that white persons seek information from responsible and representative Negroes as the basis of their judg-

ments about Negro traits, characteristics, and tendencies, and thereby counteract the common disposition, arising from erroneous tradition and literature, to regard all Negroes as belonging to one homogeneous group and as being inferior in mentality and morality, given to emotionalism, and having an innate tendency toward crime, especially sex crime.

RACIAL DOCTRINES.

37. We recommend to Negroes the promulgation of sound racial doctrines among the uneducated members of their group, and the discouragement of propaganda and agitators seeking to influence racial animosity and incite Negroes to violence.

RACE PRIDE.

42. While we recognise the propriety and social values of race pride among Negroes, we warn them that thinking and talking too much in terms of race alone is calculated to promote separation of race interests and thereby to interfere with racial adjustment.

ATTITUDE TOWARD NEGRO WORKERS.

43. We have found that in struggles between capital and labour Negro workers are in a position dangerous to themselves and to peaceful relations between the races, whether the issues involve their use by employers to undermine wage standards or break strikes, or efforts by organised labour to keep them out of certain trades while refusing to admit them to membership in the union in such trades. We feel that unnecessary racial bitterness is provoked by such treatment of Negro workers, that racial prejudice is played upon by both parties, and that through such practices injury comes, not alone to Negroes, but to employers and labour organisations as well.

We therefore recommend to employers that they deal with Negroes as workmen on the same plane as white workers; and to labour unions that they admit Negroes as workmen on the same plane as white workers; and to labour unions that they admit Negroes to full membership whenever they apply for it and possess the qualifications required of white workers.

46. We have found that Negroes are denied equal opportunity with whites for advancement and promotion where they are employed. As a measure of justice we urge that Negroes be employed, advanced, and promoted according to their capacities and

proved merit. We call to the attention of those concerned the high qualifications of many Negro workers in sleeping-car and dining-car service and recommend that when they deserve it and the opportunity offers, they be made eligible for promotion to positions as conductors and stewards.

SEPARATE LABOUR UNIONS.

50. We strongly condemn the efforts of self-seeking agitators, Negro or white, who use race sentiment to establish separate unions in trades where existing unions admit Negroes to equal membership with whites.

RELATIONS WITH UNIONS.

51. We recommend that qualified Negro workers desiring membership in labour organisations join unions which admit both races equally, instead of organising separate Negro labour unions.

EQUAL RIGHTS IN PUBLIC PLACES.

57. We point out that Negroes are entitled by law to the same treatment as other persons in restaurants, theaters, stores, and other places of public accommodation, and we urge that owners and managers of such places govern their policies and actions and their employees accordingly.[32]

This is the fullest and most courageous discussion of the Negro problem which has appeared.

If we fail in America to solve this problem of relation between the white and black races it will be only one more proof of the incapacity and weakness wrought in man by sin. The guilt of failure will be wholly and clearly our own.

2. Immigration and the race problem. The population of the 48 States and the District of Columbia in 1920 was 105,710,620. Of these more than one-half, 58,421,957, were native white of white parentage; more than one-fifth, 22,686,204, were native white of foreign or mixed parentage; one-eighth, 13,712,754, were foreign-born white; one-tenth, 10,463,131, were Negroes.

---

[32] Report of Commission, *The Negro in Chicago,* pp. 640-651.

The foreign born population and the total population at each decennial census were as follows:

	Foreign Born	Total Population	Per cent.
1860...........	4,138,697	31,443,321	13
1870...........	5,567,229	38,538,371	14.4
1880...........	6,679,943	50,155,783	13
1890...........	9,249,560	62,947,714	14.6
1900...........	10,341,276	75,994,575	13.6
1910...........	13,515,886	91,972,266	14.7
1920...........	13,712,754	105,710,620	13.2

It is apparent at once that the ratio of foreign born has changed only slightly. The foreign born population in 1900 was 13.6 per cent. of the whole and in 1910 it was 14.7 per cent. and in 1920 it was 13.2.

On the other hand the character of the races to be assimilated has changed from 1890 to 1910 and again from 1910 to 1920, as the following table of the foreign born shows:

	1890	1910	Per cent. in 1910	1920	Per cent. in 1920
Austria	241,377	1,174,973	8.8	575,625	4.2
England	909,092	876,455	6.6	812,828	5.9
Germany	2,784,894	2,501,181	18.7	1,686,102	12.3
Greece	1,887	101,264	0.8	175,972	1.3
Hungary	62,435	495,600	3.7	397,282	2.9
Ireland	1,871,509	1,352,155	10.1	1,037,233	7.6
Italy	182,580	1,343,070	10.1	1,610,109	11.7
Mexico	77,853	219,802	1.6	478,383	3.5
Norway	322,665	403,858	3.	363,862	2.7
Russia and Finland ...	182,644	1,732,421	13.	1,685,313	11.3
Scotland	242,231	261,034	2.	254,567	1.9
Sweden	478,041	665,183	5.	625,580	4.6
Wales	100,079	82,479	.8	67,066	.5

The number of English, Scotch, Irish and Welsh-born people in the United States has decreased in each period. The number of Greeks, Italians and Mexicans has increased. The south-eastern and eastern Europeans who leaped ahead from 1890 to 1910 have fallen off slightly. The effects of the war are evident, especially on the Germans, Austrians and the Hungarians. The figures show that the races from north Europe which are more easily assimilable and more available to aid in the process of assimilation have fallen off steadily, while the dissimilar and less assimilable races of southern and eastern Europe which sprang forward so rapidly between 1890 and 1910 have dropped between 1910 and 1920. What has been gained in the probability of successful assimilation, in the latter case by the reduction of the problem, seems to have been about offset in the percentages by the loss in the former case. Most of those who return to Europe, however, are from southern Europe. In 1923, 6,054 English immigrants came and 7,979 left, but 39,226 southern Italians came and 21,029 went back. It is interesting to note the continued Italian gain and the steady Irish decline. In the fiscal year ending in 1923, the largest number of aliens admitted to the United States were Germans, 65,543. Others in large numbers were Mexicans, 62,709; English, 60,524; Hebrews, 49,719; south Italians, 39,226; Scotch, 38,627; Scandinavians, 37,630; French, 34,731; Irish, 30,386. The largest number of those who left to return to their own countries were south Italians, 21,029.[33] Professor Conklin is " certain that our general level of intelligence has been going down ever since the great influx of immigration from southern and eastern Europe began thirty or forty years ago," and he quotes Dr. C. C. Brigham as estimating after " a most careful study " that " since 1901 we have added to our population more than two million white immigrants below the average Negro in intelligence." Professor Conklin holds that the chief menace is not the foreign-born, but their children. Only 725 out of 15,656 inmates of State and Federal institutions for feeble-minded were foreign-born, but 5,574 of those inmates were the children of foreign-born parents.[34] In 1910 there were 13,345,545 foreign-born whites in the United States and 12,916,311 of foreign white parentage and 5,981,526 of mixed native and foreign white parentage, a total of 32,243,382.

[33] The New York Times, Aug. 21, 1923.
[34] The American Legion Weekly, Aug. 3, 1923, art. " The Price We Pay."

In 1920 about 34% of our population consisted of foreign-born and their children. Yet this 34% furnished 55% of the insane, 46% of the paupers and 40% of the feeble-minded. On the other hand a report in the *American Journal of Sociology* finds "that the children of mixed foreign and native parentage have greater vitality than the children of native stock." [35] It is clear that we have not all the facts yet for a judgment. For it cannot be said that we have yet done our full duty in educating and helping these children. What they are is in part our fault. And after all, most of us are the children of foreign-born or their children's children.

The problem has been modified also by the redistribution of immigration among the states. It is interesting to note the facts in a few races. The states which contain most English born in order are as follows: New York, Pennsylvania, Massachusetts, California, Illinois and New Jersey. The states which contain most Irish born in order are, New York, Massachusetts, Pennsylvania, Illinois, New Jersey, Connecticut. The states which contain most German born are in order, New York, Illinois, Wisconsin, Pennsylvania, Ohio, New Jersey. The Poles are chiefly, in order, in New York, Pennsylvania, Illinois, Michigan, New Jersey and Ohio; the Russians, in New York (529,240), Pennsylvania, Illinois and Massachusetts; the Italians, in New York (545,173), Pennsylvania, New Jersey, Massachusetts, Illinois and California.

Valuable studies have been made of various races in the New Americans Series published through the Home Missions Council, covering thus far the Czecho-Slovaks in America, the Poles, the Russians and Ruthenians, the Italians and the Greeks.[36] No adequate study has yet been made, however, of the intermixture of racial strains in the United States. We know that since 1841 the proportion of southern and eastern European immigrants has risen steadily, while the proportion from northern and western Europe declined. Croxton and Lauck presented the following table at the Universal Races Congress in 1911:

[35] New York *Evening Post*, Jan. 3, 1923.
[36] See also Shriver, *Immigrant Forces*, p. 43.

Year ending June 30th.	Total Number of Immigrants	Per Cent. From		
		Northern and Western Europe	Southern and Eastern Europe	Other Specified Countries
1820-1830	124,640	86.5	3.4	10.1
1831-1840	528,721	92.3	1.2	6.5
1841-1850	1,604,805	95.9	0.4	3.7
1851-1860	2,648,912	94.6	0.9	4.4
1861-1870	2,309,878	89.2	1.6	9.2
1871-1880	2,812,191	73.7	7.1	19.2
1881-1890	5,246,613	72.0	18.3	9.7
1891-1900	3,687,564	44.8	52.8	2.5
1901-1910	8,795,386	21.8	71.9	6.3

This table does not indicate how many immigrants returned to Europe (it was one-third for the five years ending June 30, 1912), and we know that the number going back to the South and East was a larger percentage than the number going back to the West and North of Europe. But even so, a grave economic and social problem was left. Croxton and Lauck summed up their conclusions as follows:

" 1. The extensive employment of southern and eastern Europeans has seriously affected the native American and older immigrant employees from Great Britain and northern Europe by causing displacements and by retarding advancement in rates of pay and improvement in conditions of employment.

" 2. Industrial efficiency among the recent immigrant wage-earners has been very slowly developed owing to their illiteracy and inability to speak English.

" 3. For these same reasons the general progress toward assimilation and the attainment of American standards of work and living has also been very slow.

" 4. The conclusion of greatest significance developed by the general industrial investigation of the United States Immigration Commission is that the point of complete saturation has already been reached in the employment of recent immigrants in mining and manufacturing establishments. Owing to the rapid expansion in industry which has taken place during the past thirty years and the constantly increasing employment of southern and eastern Europeans, it has been impossible to assimilate the newcomers, politically or socially, or to educate them to American standards of compensation, efficiency, or conditions of employment." [37]

This was in 1911. The War and the new restrictions upon immigration have checked the flow of immigrants from all lands, and in 1921 the total incoming stream of alien immigrants numbered 309,556 and of non-immigrants 150,487, as compared with 1,218,480 in 1914; 298,826 in 1916; 110,618 in 1918; 430,001 in 1920; and 1,285,349 in 1907. In 1923 the alien immigrant newcomers numbered 522,919, while 81,450 left the country to return to Europe.

Current periodical literature supplies illustration of almost all conceivable views on the question of immigration and its restriction. Some would have it as nearly unrestricted as possible. Some would close the doors as tight as possible. Some would work with a quota principle, making immigration proportionate to the number of members of any race or nationality in this country at the time of some specified census. And some specify the census of 1890, some the census of 1900 and some the census of 1910 and some the census of 1920. The tables already given show how different results these different census returns would yield. Some would add other elements to the sifting process than mere numerical quota, such as racial kinship, moral and economic worthfulness, demonstrated assimilability, literacy, eugenic principles, etc. Some would frankly face the issue between the north European Protestant culture and the south European Roman Catholic or east European Greek Catholic, and seek to perpetuate the early American tradition, although there is difference of opinion also as to what this tradition was.[38]

Mr. E. V. Wilcox, in *The Country Gentleman*, Nov. 24, 1923,

---

[37] *Universal Races Congress,* 1911, p. 222.
[38] *E. g.,* New York *Times,* May 25, 1923, "Welcome Immigration"; Dec. 3, 1923, "Pictures Pilgrims Facing Quota Law"; Jan. 26, 1924, "Curb Aliens to Save Nation, Curran asks"; Feb. 10, 1924, "Like-Minded or Well Born", Feb. 16, 1924, "Eugenics and Immigration"; Feb. 28, 1924, "Assails Alien Quota Basis"; March 1, 1924, "Eliminating the 1890 Census," "Quotas for Immigration," etc., etc. See also the suggestive series of articles in *World's Work* beginning Nov., 1923, "The Immigration Peril," by Gino Speranza.

objects to the arguments for more immigration which rest on the
ground that cheaper labour means lower costs and more mouths
to feed and therefore better markets for the farmer.   He holds
that more immigration means more financial drain.

"Quoting from a study made jointly by the Department of
Commerce and Harvard University he states that the foreign
born in this country sent $400,000,000 abroad during the last fiscal
year.   This sum, the expenses of our tourists in Europe, our gifts
for relief purposes and other items not only wipe out the trade
balance in our favour, but it even appears that Europe 'in 1922
got the better of us by about $500,000,000.'   Mr. Wilcox says,
'We are supporting millions of Europe's paupers.'   He even
claims that if more immigrants came they would live 'as far as
possible on foreign products.'   Therefore, he urges that 'restriction laws, even if faulty, are a boon to farmers.'" [39]

Dr. Sidney L. Gulick has worked out as thoughtfully as any
one a reasonable, and, as he believes, a Christian basis of regulated
immigration, as follows:

"There are certain fundamental principles that should characterise any immigration law which seeks to limit the numbers of
aliens entering the United States.   Among them are:
1. "Only so many aliens coming for permanent residence in
the United States should be admitted as we have good reason to
believe can be wholesomely assimilated and incorporated into our
body politic.
2. "This number differs with different peoples and races and
may be broadly estimated by noting the reactions of those already
among us to our national, social and economic conditions.
3. "The determination of this number should be made in the
light of sound sociological, psychological and economic principles
as they reveal themselves in objective verifiable facts.
4. "Even from peoples that are highly assimilable, no more
should be admitted year by year than can be wholesomely incorporated into our industrial system.   It is vital that American
standards of wages and living for our industrial workers be
maintained.

[39] Quoted in Federal Council of the Churches, Research Department, *Information Service*, Feb. 9, 1924, p. 4.   See also *Information Service*, March
1, 1924, art. "American Immigration Policy."

5. " The determination of the number of immigrants to be admitted annually should be free from personal bias or race prejudice.

" If these principles are correct, then it is a mistake to base the quota of permissible immigration from any given people on the number of that people that happened to be in the United States at the time of a given census. Such a method completely ignores vital questions regarding assimilability and economic and industrial conditions.

" There are two objective criteria of wholesome assimilation:

1. " Naturalisation: This shows whether or not the alien is wholeheartedly severing his connection with his native land and throwing in his lot with us. It shows the degree of his political assimilation. Long-continued allegiance to a foreign government by a large proportion of any given people residing among us shows certain mental traits undesirable from the American standpoint.

2. " American-born children of foreign parentage: These are American citizens and if educated in our public schools are pretty thoroughly assimilated. This principle may be still more closely defined. The intermarriage of the foreign-born of a given race or people with native Americans proves a high degree of social assimilability and tends to the elimination of hyphenated citizenship and of race-group consciousness. Intermarriage across lines of nationality tends to produce a homogeneous people. The number of children, therefore, of ' foreign stock ' one of whose parents is native-born is a valuable objective criterion of the assimilability of the race of that foreign-born parent.

" The sociologically correct, objective basis, therefore, for the calculation of the quota of immigrants for each people should be:

1. " The number of that people in the United States who have become American citizens by naturalisation, plus

2. " The number of American-born children of that people only one of whose parents is foreign-born.

" In order, moreover, to be thoroughly scientific and impartial, the basic figures to be used should be those of the latest available census.

" No attempt has been made to work out a full table of quotas on these principles, but by way of illustration, a few examples, making use of the census of 1920, have been calculated.

" On account of a certain lack of parallelism of the tables the figures here given are not exact. They do, however, give a fairly correct view of the statistical results of the principles advocated.

Mother Tongue Groups	Naturalized Plus American- Born Children, One Parent Only Foreign-Born	Permissible Immigration (2%)	Quotas of the Present Law
English-Celtic	4,522,707	90,454	77,342
Germanic	3,618,963	72,379	72,777
Scandinavian	1,660,069	31,201	37,863
Latin-Greek	1,288,961	25,779	61,645
Slavic-Lettic	462,495	9,249	81,814
		229,062	331,441
Italy	622,014	12,440	42,057
Germany	3,323,347	66,466	67,607
Denmark	536,742	10,734	5,619

" I have provisionally used 2 per cent. for estimating the quotas. Whether or not this is the best percentage I do not undertake to say. I believe personally that it would be wiser for Congress to adopt the general principles to govern immigration and to determine certain maximum permissible quotas and then to leave to an Immigration Board the final determination of the actual numbers —which may change from year to year according to economic conditions—together with many other matters of detail of administration.

" The United States needs a flexible law administered in the light of changing conditions without fresh Congressional legislation; frequent emergency legislation to meet successive crises should be avoided just so far as is possible."

The nation has slowly come to the purpose of trying at least so to control immigration and so to care for what is admitted that the process of assimilation can operate efficiently and all races be welded together harmoniously into one national life.   Both this purpose and the effect of measures then in force were described by Mr. Husband as Commissioner General of Immigration, in an address in New York on April 3, 1923.   He recognised that the quota law is an experiment in race assimilation, an attempt to admit each year a certain percentage of the people of any given nationality already in the country on the theory that such a percentage could be wrought into the common life of the nation, and added:

"Immigrants from the south and east of Europe have not demonstrated that they can be readily assimilated into the population of the United States in the sense that the old type of immigrants could. With their coming there were fears and speculation on the part of the American people.

"The quota law has produced hardship, but it has realised in a way the principle upon which an immigration law may be made checking the new immigration. There were probably a quarter of a million people in the countries of southern and eastern Europe in the last year who would have come to America but for the quota law.

"We are now getting from the old sources, England, Ireland, Scandinavia, Switzerland, Holland and Belgium, the same class of immigration as before. The British quota will be exhausted in May and the Swedish quota in June. The demand here has been so great that the old-time immigration is coming to us again, and we are receiving a class of immigrants who are just as good, if not superior to those who came after 1852.

"We are getting into this country some of the finest people in the world. If that is so, the quota law is an unqualified success. It is not perfect and it ought to be amended, but it is a cornerstone upon which a future immigration policy can be framed."

Mr. Husband said an investigation had shown that of the people coming from the south and east of Europe less than 50 per cent., and in some cases as low as 30 per cent. had become naturalised in that period, whereas of the old type of immigrants of the north and west of Europe more than 50 per cent., and in some instances 85 per cent. had become naturalised.[40]

During the Congress of 1923-24 public opinion in America moved very rapidly and legislation was adopted stringently reducing the volume of immigration, retaining the quota principle but basing it on the census of 1890, with the result of curtailing the south European immigration and favouring the immigration from the northern Europen races. The general purpose of this legislation to safeguard the integrity and unity of the nation is

---

[40] New York *Times*, April 4, 1923. For one of the best summaries of the issues involved in our present immigration problem, see *The Congressional Digest*, Vol. II, Nos. 10-11, July-August, 1923, "America and Her Immigrants." See also *Public Affairs*, Dec., 1923, art. by W. H. Husband, "Immigration Up to Date," and art. by E. J. Hemming, "The Problems of the Alien."

certainly sound. Some of its methods and even some of its principles, however, are sure to undergo revision.

America has not solved the race problem yet in the case either of the Negro or of the immigrant, but real progress has been made toward its solution. The " melting pot " metaphor is at present a little discredited and it does not represent the mode of dealing with race relationships set forth in these studies. But the unity which it suggests, though still unattained, is nearer to us in the United States, in spite of the heterogeneity of our racial elements, than in any other country in the world, and it is interesting to see the increasingly clear and steady recognition of the fact that our problem in America must be worked out under a rational and Christian conception of racial values and relationships. An editorial in The New York *Times* will suffice for illustration:

" In formulating a permanent policy two considerations are of prime importance. The first is that the country has the right to say who shall and who shall not come in. It is not for any foreign country to determine our immigration policy. The second is that the basis of restriction must be chosen with a view not to the interest of any group or groups in this country, whether racial or religious, but rather with a view to the country's best interests as a whole. The great test is assimilability. Will the newcomers fit into American life readily? Is their culture sufficiently akin to our own to make it possible for them easily to take their place among us? There is no question of ' superior ' or ' inferior ' races or of ' Nordics ' or of prejudice, or of racial egotism. Certain groups not only do not fuse easily, but consistently endeavour to keep alive their racial distinctions when they settle among us. They perpetuate the ' hyphen ' which is but another way of saying that they seek to create a foreign block in our midst.

" The more the population of the United States is recruited from divers racial groups, the more essential is it that all racial distinctions be eliminated. So long as racial consciousness is fostered, whether it be in the form of the dual loyalty preached by the representatives of certain nations, or in the banding together of the foreign born or their descendants to further the political or other interests of their group as a group, the fusing of the American nation will be delayed. Particularly true is this as bearing on immigration restrictions. A policy must be formed without discriminating unfairly against any given groups, but at the same time with regard to the interests only of the whole and not of any special part." [41]

The good which we seek to attain will be brought steadily nearer if we will do our national, and as Christian churches our Christian, duty toward all who come to us, (1) by a rational and humane policy of assimilation untainted by the mania of war psychology, (2) by adequate education which will do for all our children what the army tests showed our education in the past has not done for the young men of the present generation, (3) by absolute and equal justice to all and by good will which will make race rioting and intimidation of aliens and their children impossible, (4) by proper selective processes which will bring to us the right elements to be wrought into the body of American life, (5) by preserving the real Christian character of our nation and its life and allowing those classes to go elsewhere which do not wish to become a part of a Christian nation or which are not willing to accept the authoritative declaration of the Supreme Court as to what is the true nature of our institutions and government,[42] (6) and by doing our duty to all who come in this regard, not by political measures but by the persuasive and convincing service of the Christian Church.

3. There are two particular racial issues involved in our general immigration problem, the Mexican and the Japanese. The figures already cited show that our Mexican population trebled between 1890 and 1910 and more than doubled between 1910 and 1920, due to the unsettlement of Mexico and the security and industrial opportunity here. Of the 478,382 Mexicans reported in 1920, 249,652 were in Texas, 86,610 in California, and 60,325 in Arizona. In Texas they constituted one-tenth of the population and in Arizona not quite one-fifth. The total foreign born population of New York City is nearly two-fifths of the whole, and the children of foreign or mixed parentage are two-fifths more. In proportion, the Mexican element in the south-west is a far

---

[41] The New York *Times,* March 1, 1924. Editorial, " Eliminating the 1890 Census."
[42] See Justice Brewer's little book, *The United States a Christian Nation.*

simpler problem with the same simple solution, justice and brotherhood, involving the adequate provision of facilities for education and race advancement.

The Japanese problem has been the most perplexing of all, and the facts of the case and the right solution have been matter of dispute. The Chinese problem would be joined to the Japanese but for the acceptance, for the present at least, by China of the principle of race discrimination and the earnest rejection of that principle by Japan.

As to the number and increase of the Japanese in the United States, there can be no reasonable disagreement. The Census returns give 63,070 Japanese males and 9,087 Japanese females in 1910, and 72,707 males and 38,303 females in 1920. Some alarmists have calculated that even under the Dillingham Immigration Law " the Japanese population of the United States in forty years would be two million, in eighty years ten million and in one hundred and fifty years, one hundred million." [43] Opponents of the admission of the Japanese to the United States have argued that they were not assimilable, and that they were an economic and ethical and political menace. On the other hand evidence has been offered that they will and do assimilate, and are ready for naturalisation and Americanisation. Attorney-General Webb, arguing for the California Alien Land Laws which forbade aliens ineligible to citizenship to hold land in the state, was asked by the Chief Justice, " What we want to know is what the Japanese are doing to which you take objection." Mr. Webb did not answer that the Japanese would not assimilate. He replied, " The white people refuse to assimilate with the Japanese and as the Japanese line advances we retreat and we do not like to retreat." [44] No doubt many of the Japanese in the United States propose to retain their Japanese nationality just as the Americans in Japan and China do, but many of the Japanese desire to be full Americans. Dr. Waterhouse recently conducted an investigation among 1,600 American born Japanese young people with the following conclusion:

[43] McClatchey, *Our New Racial Problem*, p. 6.
[44] New York *Times*, April 24, 1923.

" The Japanese in this country will not be assimilated by inter-marriage, but the second generation is apparently being assimilated in a cultural and social way, adopting American ideals, standards of thought, living and character.

Sixteen hundred replies from Japanese children under 15 years of age who were born in this country, to a questionnaire show:

> That practically all are attending American public schools.
> Nearly two-thirds are attending Protestant Sunday Schools.
> Thirty-five per cent. gave their religion as Christian.
> Nineteen per cent. were Buddhists.
> The rest gave no answer.

Three hundred forty-two replies from American-born Japanese between 15 and 22 years of age, representing 40 per cent. of the Japanese of that age born in California, show:

> Fifty-one per cent. were attending or planning to go to high school.
> Fifty per cent. were expecting to go to College.
> One-half were Christians.
> One-fifth were Buddhists.

Without hesitation we join the ranks of those who argue that the Japanese can be assimilated, and the more thoroughly we study the situation, the more powerful is the conviction that the debate about the Japanese would cease to be a debate at all, if only all who argue against them could come into personal contact with the second generation of young men and women.

It is not the purpose of this article to advocate, in any sense of the term, an open door for Oriental immigration. The sole reason for making this investigation was to get some first-hand, verified information as to the trend of thought and life in the second generation of Japanese in California upon which to base a judgment as to the right policy for treating those who are already here in this country." [45]

The sentiment of the Christian element of the Japanese in America was expressed in the action taken by the group in southern California on May 31, 1920, entitled " Americanisation Ideals of Japanese Children in Southern California."

---

[45] Paul B. Waterhouse, *Can the Japanese Be Assimilated?*

" We, the pastors and laymen of 26 Japanese evangelical churches and missions of southern California, believing that Americanisation can only be realised through Christianisation of these people, believing further that no one can fully appreciate, without acquiring the fundamental teachings of Christ, the mighty spirit of the foundation of the nation of liberty, equality and humanity which emanates throughout her history, do hereby adopt the following principles and policies for the Americanisation of 100,000 Japanese who are enjoying peace and prosperity in this country.

(1) We who are in the United States are to be first of all loyal to the land of our adoption.

(2) We are to endeavour to embody consistently in our daily life the fundamental principles and spirit of the American Government and Christianity respecting her customs and institutions and abiding by the law of the land.

(3) Having chosen our life work here we deem it our first duty to promote the welfare of our adopted country and contribute our share to its civilisation. Furthermore will we gladly be regarded as a forsaken band by the country that gave us our births.

(4) As to the education of our children we think it best and sufficient to give them wholly American education, thus enabling them to become loyal and useful American citizens. By further affording them the spiritual education based on the teachings of Christ, we are not to place any obstacles and burdens in their Americanisation.

In order to carry out the purpose of this resolution, irrespective of our religious affiliation, we do hereby unite and co-operate in our utmost endeavour to Americanise the Japanese in this country with hope, patience and justice, the fundamental teachings of Christ whose followers we are."

The Japanese are not allowed to be Americanised, however. The Supreme Court has ruled that the privilege of naturalisation is confined to white persons and those of African nationality and descent. Justice Sutherland, in the Court's decision, maintained that there was no intent to assert any offensive racial distinction and then disposed of the idea that colour is a practicable criterion of race, but held that the term " white person " meant a member of the Caucasian race. He was not ready to say who were and who were not Caucasians, but clearly Japanese were not, and therefore they could not be naturalised:

" Manifestly," said he, " the test afforded by the mere colour of the skin of each individual is impracticable, as that differs greatly among persons of the same race, even among Anglo-Saxons, ranging by imperceptible gradations from the fair blonde to the swarthy brunette, the latter being darker than many of the lighter-hued persons of the brown or yellow races. Hence to adopt the colour test alone would result in a confused overlapping of races and a gradual merging of one into the other without any practical line of separation. . . . The appellant, in the case now under consideration, however, is clearly of a race which is not Caucasian." [46]

This does not mean, however, that there are no Japanese American citizens. The Constitution gives American citizenship to all American-born children of whatever race. Until 1906 alien Japanese could become American citizens. A few were naturalised. Then, without act of Congress, by a rule of the Bureau of Naturalisation clerks of court were forbidden to give application forms to any but " free white men " and " persons of African birth or descent." Since that date no Japanese have been permitted to become naturalised citizens, except some 400 who had waived their right of exemption and joined our army in the war. By that act they earned the right to become citizens, and did so in 1919.

The total increase of the Japanese population by immigration during the past twelve years is 12,174. This number consists chiefly of wives and children, who were lawfully admitted. Practically no new labourers were given passports by Japan or admitted to this country.

What is the rational and Christian racial policy for us to pursue toward the problem of the Japanese in America? The Japanese Exclusion League proposed:

1. To enact Japanese exclusion laws like those dealing with Chinese.

2. To prevent Japanese from owning or leasing any farm land whatever, and to reduce all Japanese agriculturalists to the status of day labourers.

[46] The New York *Times*, Nov. 14, 1922.

3. To forever prevent Japanese from becoming American citizens.

4. To deny American citizenship to all American-born Japanese children.

5. To have Congress pass the discriminatory drastic laws required to secure the above objects.

How much land do the Japanese own in California? The State Board of Control reports (1920) that the Japanese cultivate 458,056 acres, most of it under short term leases. Of this they own 74,769 acres. California has an area of about twenty-eight million acres of farm land. Of this, only one and six-tenths per cent. is cultivated by Japanese. They produce, however, 13% of California's total food output. Their produce is valued at $67,000,000, or which 35% is paid to land owners as rentals and 45% to labour as wages. The balance of 20% is the reward for Japanese tenants or contractors.

The National Committee for Constructive Immigration Legislation proposed a different course of action from the Exclusion League:

1. Congress should provide for the complete stoppage of Japanese immigration, until it is clear that those in congested areas can and have become truly Americanised, establishing wholesome relations with the rest of the population.

2. The needed legislation should be free from features humiliating to Japanese, therefore free from offensive race discrimination. The new immigration law should be general in scope and apply equally to all peoples.

3. The standards for naturalisation should be raised and the privileges of citizenship should be extended to all who qualify.

Which is the rational and humane course? Which course is in accord with the actual facts of race and race relationship which we have faced in these studies? The last Congress answered in a way which the public opinion of the nation, uttered in the press and through the churches, disapproved. *Life* expressed the prevalent view when it sent to Congress an award of a prize for " Bigger and Better Wars," in recognition of its action in formulating "a plan so simple and inevitable in its potentialities for the promotion of ill-will." [47]

The race problem between American and Japanese in the Hawaiian Islands is more difficult than on the Pacific Coast. The Japanese constitute 43% of the population of the Islands. The Immigration Committee of the U. S. Senate presented a report on March 1, 1923, in which it said: "On account of their close adhesiveness and characteristic collective manner of action, the Japanese have it in their power to control the industries of the territory by being able, either to furnish or fail to furnish the labour without which those industries cannot live. Immigration to supply the immediate needs of the agricultural industries and relieve an existing acute shortage must take into consideration the overwhelming preponderance of Japanese in the islands, their control of the labour situation and the possibility amounting to practical certainty, under existing conditions, that the American control of the island industries may pass into the hands of this alien race."

And the Labour Department's "Hawaiian Labour Commission" in its report made public in Jan., 1923, expressed great concern over both the labour and political conditions.[48] The report says that

"attention should be specially called to the menace of alien domination, and the present policy of 'parental adoption' and importation of 'picture brides' by the Japanese should be stopped, because these practices have defeated the purpose of the 'gentlemen's agreement' to curtail common 'labour importations' by augmenting the supply to such an extent that it 'will soon overwhelm the territory numerically, politically and commercially.'

"The menace from a military standpoint," says the report, "can be fully verified by referring to the records of related Federal departments.

"The question of national defense," the report continues, "submerges all others into insignificance. If these islands are to remain American the assured control of the political, industrial,

---

[47] Millis, *The Japanese Problem in the United States; The Congressional Digest,* Vol. II, Nos. 10-11, July-August, 1923, pp. 317-319.
[48] See, however, Romanzo Adams, *The Japanese in Hawaii.*

social and educational life of the islands must also be American, and the sooner we wake up to a fuller appreciation of this imperative and immediate need the sooner we will make the people of the Hawaiian Islands feel generally a greater sense of security and control of all that contributes to make continued living in the Territory of Hawaii worth while.   In the interests of national defense and the welfare of American citizenship in the territory, the commission respectfully and earnestly recommends that the question of alien domination be immediately referred to the Congress of the United States for the necessary remedial legislation."

Why not solve the problem by right and friendly relations, rather than by suspicion and war ideals?   It ought to be solved also on grounds of racial justice and consideration, and not of discrimination against race as race.   The Japanese are ready for its solution on such grounds, Baron Shibusawa declares:

"In order that there shall be no possible apprehension in America in regard to the nature of our ideas and desires, let me assure all Americans that we have no thought of asking for our labour people any privileges of free immigration to the United States.   We distinguish quite clearly between the questions of immigration and those of discriminatory legislation against Japanese already lawfully residing in your country.   Your discriminatory legislation seems to us to be contrary to the principles of humanity and of the great Christian faith which so many of you profess.   We ask for nothing from the people and Government of the United States, in their dealings with members of our race in your land, except that which is fair and honourable.   We seek no special privileges or favours.   We ask only, and we ask earnestly, that nothing be done in respect to our people that is essentially humiliating to them, nothing that discriminates between them and other races in the United States merely on the ground of colour or difference of facial contour and expression.

"It may not be amiss to state in this connection that since the adoption by Japan, in the last half of the last century, of the main principles of Occidental government, we have no discriminatory laws based on differences of race or nationality or religion.   This principle we learned from the West, chiefly from your own country.   Americans in Japan enjoy the same privileges and rights of land ownership, naturalisation, and everything else that we grant to individuals of any other nation or race.

"It may be also well for me to state in the clearest terms that we do not have the least objection to the deportation of individual Japanese who are found to be unlawfully in the United States; nor do we object to the rejection of Japanese travellers who may be lawless or who do not conform to general standards of moral character, literacy, and the like, such as are applied generally to all travellers from every race and people. But I think you will easily understand why we as Japanese cannot but resent proposals and laws that discriminate against Japanese merely as Japanese, regardless of their individual and personal qualifications." [49]

It will be little to the credit of our good sense, our political capacity or our spirit of justice if we cannot find a peaceable and adequate solution of this question.[50]

4. Two other internal race problems enter into our American thinking, the Indian and the Jew.

It is very difficult to arrive at a just racial picture of the Indian. Was he a savage? Was he a noble savage? Was he no savage at all? John Heckewelder, one of the early Moravian missionaries to the Indians, who came to America in 1754 and became Zeisberger's assistant, in his account of the Indians, whom he had known intimately for fifty years, wrote, in 1817, that nothing was so false as this savage picture of Indian character.

" Every person," he says, " who is well acquainted with the true character of the Indians will admit that they are peaceable, sociable, obliging, charitable, and hospitable among themselves, and that those virtues are, as it were, a part of their nature. In their ordinary intercourse, they are studious to oblige each other. They neither wrangle nor fight; they live, I believe, as peaceably together as any people on earth, and treat one another with the greatest respect. That they are not devoid of tender feelings has been sufficiently shown in the course of this work. I do not mean to speak of those whose manners have been corrupted by a long intercourse with the worst class of white men; they are a degener-

---

[49] Letter from Baron E. Shibusawa, June 5, 1923.
[50] See Gulick, *Should Congress Enact Special Laws Affecting Japanese?* and *New Factors in American Japanese Relations and a Constructive Prospect;* Axling, *On the Trail of the Truth about Japan;* The American Committee of Justice, *California and the Japanese;* per contra, McClatchey, *Our New Racial Problem; The Literary Digest,* March 1, 1924, p. 14. As to the assimilability of the yellow races, especially the Chinese, as illustrated in Hawaii see *China and the Far East,* Clark University Papers, pp. 295, 315.

ate race, very different from the true genuine Indians whom I have attempted to describe." [51]

If we are in doubt as to whether to accept Heckewelder's estimate, which he supports with facts and testimonies as to the Indian races before contact with the whites, and are disposed to set against it the account which history gives of the Indians and of the wars waged against them, it is well to remember that the histories were written by the race which invaded the land and waged the wars, although we have also tried to do justice to the record, and *A Century of Dishonour* will endure as an honest attempt to tell the truth and to right wrong.

The story of race relationship between Indian and white is a long story of the wrong and deadly way to deal with such issues. It is clear that the Indians had no exclusive title to North America, that the white race was warranted in coming here and opening the continent to its intended uses. And no doubt, man being what he is, such a process will be filled with blunder and waste as every decade of human life has been for centuries.

Our consolation is that we have come at last to a better mind regarding the Indian, and that reason and justice and Christian duty have at last been applied, in a measure at least, to this race problem. The evidence is found in the increase of the Indian population, its advancing prosperity and intelligence, its health and character. Any estimate of the number of Indians who were here on the discovery of America is mere guess work. Dr. Eastman thinks the total number of natives of North America could not have been far from half a million.[52] " Since that period," he says, " they have fallen off in numbers but not to the extent popularly supposed, and are now slowly increasing." The census returns show that the Indians in the United States decreased from 256,127 in 1880 to 243,504 in 1890, and then increased to 270,544 in 1900 and to 340,838 in 1921. The Hon. Cato Sells, when Commissioner of Indian Affairs, declared, " I repudiate the suggestion

---

[51] Heckewelder's *Indian Nations, Memoirs of the Historical Society of Pennsylvania*, Vol. XII, p. 330.
[52] *Universal Races Congress*, 1911, p. 367.

that the Indian is a 'vanishing race.' He should march side by
side with white men during all the years to come. It is our chief
duty to protect the Indian's health, and to save him from premature death. Before we educate him, before we conserve his property, we should save his life." [53] The Indian's life seems to have
been saved. At the same time the line of demarcation between
the two races becomes increasingly indistinct. The break up of
the reservations, the allotment of land in severalty, the education
of the Indians, the increase of wealth among them, the steady
progress of Christianity, their economic community with the rest
of the life of the land, the progress of intermarriage with other
races are all helping to heal their old sore and to merge the Indian
both into the nation and into the race.[54]

There is still need of the working of the right interracial spirit
in this wide and scattered field. The Indians are divided into
more than 150 tribal bands and clans with as many different languages and dialects. They are scattered on 147 reservations and
many hundred communities in many states of the Union. Okla-
homa has nearly one-third of the entire number, with Arizona
second. The Dakotas or Sioux, the Chippewas and the Navajos
are the largest tribal groups.

As to means of support and advancement in education and
citizenship the following tabulations are indicative:

> 133,193 speak English
> 91,331 read and write
> 84,462 are citizens.

Of 62,138 adult men enumerated

> 40,962 were engaged in farming
> 44,847 raised stock
> 26,949 were engaged in other industries.

Practically one-fourth of the children eligible for school attendance are not in school.

Conditions of health and sanitation have improved with stricter

---

[53] Moore, *The South Today*, p. 137.
[54] Talbot, *Samuel Chapman Armstrong*, Chap. X; Lindquist, *The Red Man in the United States*.

402   RACE AND RACE RELATIONS

federal supervision, but tuberculosis and trachoma are the two diseases which are very prevalent, a study of 207,000 Indians revealing 24,773 cases of the former and 30,795 of the latter.

To this great task the white race has at last begun conscientiously to apply itself. It will have a great deal to contend against in its own base elements and in the effect of its past mistreatment of the Indian race, but it means to do right. The Secretary of the Interior, Mr. Work, expresses its mind in his letter constituting a Committee of one hundred citizens to advise on a right Indian policy:

" The Indians, many having suddenly acquired wealth, with their citizenship rights, allotted lands, agricultural development, schools, religions and diseases, present an appeal more acute than ever before. For many years the Government has been charged intermittently with having no policy, or with exploiting the Indian, or with acquiescing in his extinction, or with permitting the dissipation of his wealth.

" Although the Indian Bureau has recently received encouraging approval from advised sources of its altruistic attitude, the present Secretary of the Interior desires, of course, to plan the best possible policy in its relation to these people and execute it in a manner that will work the greatest good.

" A determination of the Government's commitments to the Indian must either lead to an educated, self-sustaining Indian citizenry or the ultimate dependency of a majority of them." [55]

A still more perplexing problem is that of Semitic race and anti-race feeling. Both these words raise at once the question about which both Jews and Gentiles are disagreed—Are the Jews a race and is the question of their relations to others a race question? Prof. Boas answers no. There is no Italian or French or German race, he says. Each of these groups is a mixture. Racially the South Germans are of the same type as the Central French.

" Even in antiquity while the Jews still formed an independent state they represented a thorough mixture of divergent racial types. . . . Even in antiquity, therefore, we cannot speak of a

---

[55] The New York *Times*, May 12, 1923.

SOME SPECIFIC RACE PROBLEMS OF TODAY   403

Jewish race as distinct from other races in Asia Minor. . . .
The dispersion of the Jews all over the world has tended to increase considerably the intermixture. . . . The Jews of North
Africa are, in their essential traits, North Africans. The Jews of
Europe are in their essential traits Europeans, and the black Jews
of the East are in their essential traits members of a dark-
pigmented race. . . . It is often claimed that the Jews have
certain mental characteristics which are due to hereditary causes.
There may be a certain truth in this statement, but not in the sense
in which it is generally taken. Among all the Jews there are certain rather small groups which are thus characterised—the merchants of Europe and America, the journalists, musicians, etc. It
must be recognised that the groups to which these individuals
belong represent on the whole a very small, closely inbred portion
of the Jewish population of the world. The amount of inbreeding
which occurs in human life is generally very much underestimated.
Statistical inquiries in regard to the increase of population show
that the European nobility and the European peasantry are both
closely inbred, while the lack of inbreeding is rather characteristic
of our unstable industrial population, particularly of our modern
city populations. The inbreeding which occurs among the Jews
may, therefore, have produced a number of small groups representing certain hereditary strains who are characterised by certain
physical and mental characteristics, probably in the same way as
in ancient Athenian society the smallness of the group and the
consequent inbreeding developed a number of strains characterised by very definite mental traits. Taken as a whole, however,
the Jews do not show any such traits that cannot be adequately
accounted for by the influence of the social environment in which
they live. The mental characteristics of certain strains must not,
of course, be taken to mean that the actual mental life of the individual is determined solely by these hereditary traits, but rather
that under certain social conditions these will become operative in
one way or another.

" There is certainly nothing that would indicate the existence of
any definite mental characteristics which are the common property
of the Jews the world over, or even of a large part of the Jews of
any one community. The mental reactions of the Jews in each
community are determined by the social conditions under which
they live.

" Summing up the whole evidence we may conclude that we
have just as little right to say there is a Jewish race as that there
is a French race or a German race or a Spanish race. All of them
are descendants of various strains which have developed anatom-

ically and mentally according to the historical fates which each nation has undergone." [56]

While he includes the Jews among the racial groups, Professor Dixon seems to incline to the view of Dr. Boas.

"The questions of the racial origin and unity of the Jews," says he, "have long been fertile themes for discussion. The traditional view has always been that they were a true Semitic people, and, indeed, the term Semite has popularly come to be practically synonymous with Jew. They were regarded as a people whose purity of blood had, in spite of wide dispersion, been jealously preserved throughout the centuries. As soon, however, as detailed investigations in regard to Jewish physical types began to be available, it appeared that it was extremely doubtful whether either of these assumptions was true, for the Jews proved to be by no means uniform in their physical characteristics, and the great majority appeared to be of a different type from that found among other Semitic-speaking peoples. . . . One of the main causes which has been suggested as responsible for the variation in the physical type of the Jews is that of intermarriage with the Gentile population among which they live, and it has frequently been pointed out that the Jew thus generally approximates the character of the surrounding peoples, whatever this may be. That such intermarriage does indeed occur, and has occurred throughout the past, can be demonstrated, although the extent of the practice is very hard to determine. The belief that the Jew merely reflects the physical type of the Gentile population among which he lives we shall find to be borne out in general by the facts." [57]

This view, that the Jews are not a race but an artificial nationality cemented by religion, is set forth by a writer in *The Living Age:*

"The so-called purity of the Jewish race is a fable. The word 'Jew' has no ethnological significance. 'The whole controversy, so far as it rests upon race, is based on a groundless myth. It is essentially an empty and irrational dispute, because, from the physical standpoint, there are no such races as alluded to. There

---

[56] Art. in *The World Tomorrow*, Jan., 1923, p. 5 f.
[57] Dixon, *The Racial History of Man*, pp. 162, 164.

is no such thing as a Semitic nation. A Semitic nation is solely a philological conception. The Semitic-speaking peoples differ radically from each other, and have no anatomical features in common with the Jews, or, in many cases, with each other. There is no pure Semitic type. The Jews are a mixed race. They have few traits in common with the Arabs, who come nearest to being pure Semites of any people. They resemble the Europeans among whom they live much more than they do the Bedouins.'

" But the honest reader will ask: ' Do you mean to say there is no difference between a Jew and a Christian?' Certainly there is, but a difference due to historical rather than anatomical causes. The key to the puzzle is found in segregation, which was partly voluntary and partly involuntary. At first the Jews lived apart from other peoples of their own volition; later they were forced to do this whether they so willed or not.

" The saying is as old as it is true that the Jews are what the people among whom they live make them. What are the Jews really? The Jews are an artificial nation, sprung from an intermingling of countless nationalities, and forming a religious community. The existence of this religious community is maintained by voluntary accessions, the forced exclusion of its members from other social groups, and the prohibition of mixed marriages. This brings us to Count Coudenhove's definition: ' The Jews are an artificial nationality created by a religious discipline out of innumerable racial elements." [58]

This view of the Jews as neither a real nation nor a pure race, nor a religious denomination, but a " religious people," was recently set forth by one of the American Jewish leaders, Rabbi Nathan Krass, in Temple Emanu-El in New York:

" Dr. Krass denied emphatically that the Jews constitute a nation or an ' imperium in imperio,' since for almost 2,000 years they have not possessed the essentials that constitute a nation, namely, a common sovereign, soil and a common political government. The Jews, he said, ceased to be a nation when Jerusalem was destroyed by the Romans in the first century of the present era.

" The Jews, he maintained, are not a pure race. Through their

[58] *The Living Age*, June 23, 1923, art. by Bertrand Alexander, " Anti-Semitism," pp. 699, 701. Disraeli, in *Coningsby*, exulted in the idea of the absolute and unequalled racial purity of the Jews. *Coningsby*, Book IV, chs. X, XV.

pilgrimage during the ages they drew into their ethnic circle individuals and groups of other origins, but managed to absorb and assimilate them, so that by and large the Jews maintained their ethnic integrity up to the present day. But this ethnic subdivision of the human family was not merely a race. It was much more than that, he declared. It was a ' holy people,'—that is, a people of common origin, dedicated to a common task, the guardianship of ethical monotheism, the religion of righteousness based on the fatherhood of God and the brotherhood of man.

" ' The Jews are not a religious denomination, for denominations have only surface value in the language of mathematics,' said Dr. Krass. ' The Jews are more than a religious community; they are a religious people, though many among them today may be non-religious or irreligious. The Jews are a divine amalgam of race and religion, and this amalgam has never been broken or separated. All attempts to do so must be futile, for the Jew has no reason to exist as a separate race unless he dedicates himself to the noble task of religious service. Though the Jews have achieved fame in all fields of human endeavour, they are unique and unexcelled in the realm of religion. Moses, the Hebrew prophets, Jesus and Paul were all Jews. The Bible is the greatest religious literature in the annals of history. This sublime and unique literature is the product of the Jews.

" ' Not by forsaking his faith, but by living up to its principles will the American Jew contribute to the development of a country still in the making.' " [59]

But there are Jews and Gentiles who dispute this view. Mr. Leo Newmark, in a letter to *The Nation*, May 16, 1923, quotes against it the judgment of Dr. Arthur Kirth in a lecture at Oxford on " Nationality and Race from an Anthropologist's Point of View ":

" If we except the Lapps and other Mongolian elements in Russia, there is only one people in Europe with a legitimate claim to be regarded as racially different from the general population. That exception is the Jewish people. . . . The Jews maintain a racial frontier, such as dominant races surround themselves with; they carry themselves as if racially distinct. Their original stock was clearly Eastern in its derivation; the peoples of Europe sprang from another racial source. . . . However much the Jewish racial frontier may be strengthened by the faith which is the standard of the race, raids have been made, are now made, across the frontier and a certain degree of hybridisation has occurred. Even thus exposed in the eddying seas of modern civilisation, the race spirit of the Jews has preserved the greater part of the original characters carried into Europe by the pioneer Semitic bands. In 90 per cent. of the Jews the physical or Semitic characters are apparent to the eye even of the uninitiated Gentile. In the Jewish people we see nature steering one of her cargoes of differentiated humanity between the Scylla and Charybidis of the modern sea of industrial civilisation."

Whether or not the Jews are a race, they are a human group distinguished from other groups, for all practical purposes, as races are distinguished, and the question of the relations between them and other groups is identical with the general question of race relations, with three peculiar differentiations, namely, a special prejudice, just or unjust, against some of the characteristics of the Jews; an inheritance of evil incidents of wrong done on both sides, perhaps predominantly on the side of the non-Jews; and an unequalled resistance to religious assimilation on the side of the Jews. To the extent that the view of Judaism not as a race but as a religious culture is sound, the problem of relations will be dealt with efficiently only as a religious and cultural problem. And while there will be many who will reject the idea, nevertheless, the facts of American life will support it, namely, that the problem of Jewish race and anti-race feeling would be more quickly resolved if any considerable number of Jews were to become Christians. But if Judaism is not a race but a religious nationality, such a solution would mean the disappearance of the religion into Christianity, which already includes the Hebrew Scriptures, and of the nationality into Americanism. On the other hand it is clear that Judaism is not a homogeneous religion. There is a wider religious gulf between old and new Judaism than between the latter and some non-Jewish religious groups. Professor Ellwood, who pleads " for the unity of Jews and Christians upon the basis of a humanitarian religion and ethics," [60] holds that " there is really no difference today between liberal Christianity

---

[60] Ellwood, *The Reconstruction of Religion,* p. 283 f.

and liberal Judaism." [61]   What, then, is it that holds all these Jewish groups together against all outside groups?   Is there, after all, a racial bond, if not physiological, then social and moral, which is as real as any other racial bond?

It is no simple problem.   And it is clear that there are faults in both races, Jews and non-Jews in America.[62]   How can we make some progress in America with its 3,900,000 Hebrews, with "the world's largest and most influential Jewries?" [63]   By dealing, personally and socially, with the causes of ill will and prejudice and seeking to remove them.   What are they?   A small conference between Jewish and Christian leaders recently named these:

1. Sheer misunderstandings.
2. Differences in habits and customs.
3. Economic competition.
4. Jealousy of success.
5. Fear of losing leadership.
6. Personal aggressiveness.
7. Bad manners.
8. Pride of intellect.
9. Gregariousness and its accompanying provincialism.
10. Dogmatic moods and utterances.
11. The air of superiority.
12. Selfishness.

The problems which the Jews themselves face and which they present to the rest of society are indicated by a few utterances of Jewish leaders at the time of the Golden Jubilee Convention of the Union of American Hebrew Congregations in New York, in January, 1923.   The gravity of the problem justifies a full presentation of material for the reader's judgment:

Dr. Marius Ranson: " It is essential that a selection be made of the important historical, ethical and religious productions of

[61] Letter Dr. Charles A. Ellwood to Dr. Isidor Singer, Jan. 25, 1923, published by Dr. Singer.
[62] See *The American Hebrew*, July 28, 1922, art. by Dr. Joseph Jastrow, "What is Prejudice and Why?" and Sept. 22, 1922, art. by Col. Harris Weinstock, "The Case Stated."
[63] *The Missionary Review of the World*, March, 1923, p. 166 f.

our Bible and that the great mass of inconsequential, trivial and tautological material be eliminated. The union prayerbook represents a bold revis'on of this character. The Bible cannot attain the respect it deserves until it, too, is modernised in this manner.

"A twentieth century Bible must recognise the universality of revelation. The ethics of Buddha as well as of Confucius and all the other god-intoxicated seers of the human race must be included in a Bible that is intended for the brotherhood of man.

"The Jewish Bible must begin to establish a rapprochment between Christianity and Judaism. For many centuries the ethics of Jesus, the great Jewish prophet, have been a closed book to the Jew. The Christless antagonism of Christianity and Judaism of sixteen centuries can be wiped out in our day by the adoption of a revised life of Jesus in which, on the one hand the Christians will abandon the New Testament slander against the Jews and on the other hand, the Jew will accept the Jewish ethics of Jesus. . . .

"For a century the Jews of western lands have believed and have loudly proclaimed to the rest of the world that Judaism is a religion and Jewry a religious community and not a nationality. In this position they have abandoned the ancient and medieval belief that the Jews are in exile from Palestine as a punishment for the sins of their ancestors; and they have also abandoned the hope or ambition of returning en masse to Palestine, there to re-establish the ancient Jewish State.

"Most emphatic of the Jews of any country have been the Jews of the United States in declaring that we are Americans in nationality, Jews only in religious belief."

President Charles Shohl: "The best product of the half century is the new Jewish point of view. Fifty years ago the Jewish people of America were torn by factionalism. This was not improved by the increasing tide of immigration. Each year brought from widely separated parts of Europe, Jewish groups whose ideas were at variance, whose habits clashed and whose religious observances seemed to be mutually incompatible. Misplaced loyalties, sentimental attachment to regional antecedents, produced the appearance of endless sects and sectaries. Religion being the ruling passion of the Jew became under these circumstances the cause of bitter disputation. The outlook for many years was chaotic and discouraging.

"The last fifty years have witnessed an important change

in this direction. The Jews have achieved a certain degree of homogeneity. I doubt if there is yet a well developed and distinct type of ' American Jew.'

" Perhaps this will have to await the days of the well developed American type in general. However, a very large percentage of the Jews of this country have recognised certain American conditions as not unfriendly and have adopted them as inevitable. To that extent, and it is not inconsiderable, they have achieved a unified outlook upon life.

" This shows itself in many hopeful ways. Less and less emphasis is being laid by thoughtful people on recent or remote European geographical loyalties. The societies based on racial unity that flourished thirty years ago are giving way to religious organisations, and religion, the ancient first-love of the Jewish people, is again assuming its important place in Israel's heart."

Chairman Daniel P. Hays: " An attachment to race—a feeling of kinship for our suffering brethren here and abroad which prompts American Jews to contribute toward the economic rehabilitation of Palestine, to sustain institutions here for the relief of the sick and unfortunate or to send money to Europe to lighten the burdens of poverty and persecution, are worthy impulses of the human heart. They may be influenced by a code of ethics which all civilised people believe in today, and if ethics on our part is the only motive power, why retain our separateness?

" Judaism is a religion, the mother of all religions. It is the spiritual legacy of the Jew and has enriched the civilisation of the world by a knowledge of God and all that makes for righteousness. We need no excuse for the observance of our religion in a land where freedom of conscience is a part of the fundamental law. We do need sorely an excuse for the maintenance of any separateness in America upon racial or ethnological grounds."

Judge Horace Stern: " The unique gift of the Jew to the world is religion, and I believe that Judaism alone constitutes the raison d'être of the Jew. I am not especially proud if a great musician happens to be a Jew, because Judaism is not a school of music, nor if a celebrated actor is a Jew, because Judaism is not a school of histrionics, nor if a famous prize fighter is a Jew, because Judaism is not a school of pugilism. I do, however, exult if a philanthropic, altruistic, spiritual, peace-loving, reverential, God-fearing man is a Jew, because those attributes and qualities are the teachings and the aim of the Jewish religion.

"Also we must ever bear in mind that we cannot live, religiously or morally speaking, upon the past glories of our race."

Edgar M. Cahn: "We are turning away our hearts and souls from the genial and warming influences of the lives and sacrifices which are our history. We no longer deserve to be called 'A Kingdom of Priests and a Holy Nation.' We are happy to be numbered with our fellow citizens as 100 per cent. Americans. We justly resent with indignation any imputation against our loyalty to our country and flag. But, now, behold the frightful discount. We are less than 50 per cent. in things Jewish and in the measure of our lives and living, as Jews, and in the observance of the Sabbath and the festivals."

Some other illuminating utterances of Jewish leaders may be added:

Dr. Julian Morgenstern: Dr. Morgenstern described reformed Judaism which, he said, was brought to America from Germany, and orthodox Judaism, which came with the East European Jewry. He said that the struggle between those two phases of Judaism was not so much over theological and ritual differences as social distinctions. He predicted that the struggle for leadership between the reform and orthodox would eventually bring forth "the American Jew."

"Forth from the strife and tumult," said Dr. Morgenstern, "born as it were upon the very field of battle, will step the victor, young and vigourous, strong, looking not backward to either German or Russian ancestry, nor cherishing suspicion or grievance against his fellow Jew of differing ancestry, but looking forward proudly to the future and dedicating himself to the sacred task of building up for himself and his children a precious heritage of truth and light, 'the American Jew.'" [64]

Mr. Louis Marshall: "I disagree totally with Mr. Zangwill's intimation that the Jews of this country should unite for political action, or that there should be such a thing as a Jewish vote in the United States. The thought cannot be tolerated that the

[64] The New York *Times,* Nov. 5, 1923.

citizens of this country should form racial or religious groups in the exercise of their civic and political functions." [65]

Dr. Samuel Schulman: " We, the non-Zionists, feel that we have been right in uncompromisingly opposing Zionism as a new philosophy of Jewish life. We were never in doubt that in rejecting modern Jewish nationalism, we were not only interpreting correctly the destiny of Israel but we were also advocating what is for the best interests of dispersed Jewry. Our thought was clear and consistent. We held that Israel today is a religious community and nothing else. And in the light of this fundamental idea all questions of organisations within Jewry must be answered and the attitude of every practical problem must be determined." . . . He denied that orthodox Judaism was ever for Zionism, as orthodox Judaism is a religion and has nothing to do with " that new secular Nationalism among the Jews, of which some of the most distinguished leaders in the Zionist movement are the exponents. . . . It is wrong to speak of Palestine as a homeland for the Jewish people or of any land as a homeland for the Jewish people. Any land can only be a home for individual Jews and Jewesses. The Jewish people, Israel, whom God called in righteousness to be a light to the nations, the Congregation of Israel, has only one home and that is the whole world." [66]

" The Jew himself has assimilated the various civilisations and cultures, of which he has been a part. In his soul is registered the progress of mankind. But the charges made against him have not changed. There is nothing new in modern anti-Semitism which in the least distinguishes it from the ancient article.

" There is nothing subtle or profound or strange about anti-Semitism which requires any special explanation, nor is it an enigma, demanding far-fetched analysis. It represents the evil in unregenerate human nature. It is a thing compact of race hatred, of mob tyranny and of religious bigotry.

" The essence of anti-Semitism consists in this unholy trinity. It is the tribal antipathy to the mass of different blood. It is the refusal of the multitude to permit a minority to dwell within it and walk the way of its own thought, and it is the bigoted deification of religious belief, which looks with horror upon those who dare to dissent from it." [67]

---

[65] *Ibid.*, Oct. 26, 1923.
[66] *Ibid.*, Nov. 5, 1923.
[67] *Ibid.*, Feb. 26, 1923.

Dr. Cyrus Adler on Dr. Solomon Schechter: " When that great man and distinguished scholar, Dr. Solomon Schechter, entered upon the Presidency of the Seminary, he declared:

" ' The religion in which the Jewish ministry should be trained must be specifically and purely Jewish, without any alloy or adulteration. Judaism must stand or fall by that which distinguishes it from other religions as well as by that which it has in common with them. . . . It permeates the whole of your life. It demands control over all your actions and interferes with your menu. It sanctifies the season, and regulates your history, both in the past and in the future. . . . Judaism is absolutely incompatible with the abandonment of the Torah. Nay, every prophet or seer must bring his imprimatur from the Torah.'

" Ten years later he said:

" ' Our work has been a hard one, considering . . . the great divisions among the people engendered by the extreme tendencies of the various parties, be they Reform or Orthodox, which could never understand a frame of mind that refused to be labelled by the names they wished to attach to it.'

" He gave as our ideal:

" ' The creation of a conservative tendency which was almost entirely absent or lay dormant in this country for a long time. Its aim was to preserve and to sustain traditional Judaism in all its integrity and by means of the spoken or written word to bring back to the consciousness of Jewry its heroic past, which must serve as a model if we were to have a glorious future, or any future at all; but, at the same time, to remain in touch with our present surroundings and modern thought, and to adopt what was the best in them and above all, to make use of modern method and system.'

" *Judaism is a way of life.* It has developed to this end a code of law and under this code there are definite and positive acts to be done. A religious Jew believes that he must act in accordance with the Jewish law." [68]

Rabbi Isaac Landman: " American Judaism, however, is the result of a religious evolution that has been in progress for more than two generations in America. It is Judaism come under the influence of American institutions and American ideals. It is Judaism released from Ghetto walls and the Ghetto spirit.

---

[68] *The Jewish Tribune,* Oct. 5, 1923, art. by Dr. Cyrus Adler, " The Story of the Seminary," p. 26.

It is Judaism that has broken through narrowing nationalism
and stifling medievalism. It is Judaism that has rediscovered
the fundamental ethical principles and the universal spiritual
ideals of the Hebrew prophets.

"It is Judaism that asks not what our fathers were and
believed and did, but what our sons will be, will believe, will
do. It is Judaism that has cast off the miraculous and the
impermanent, that rejects the elements in the Bible that were
of fugitive value and accepts only those that promulgate truths
which are compatible with reason and with science. It is the
Judaism of the age-old vision that comprehends humanity." [69]

Would Dr. Schulman " look with horror " or without reproach
on any larger acceptance by Jews of the Christian faith? Because,
back of all, there is the fundamental religious issue.[70] Honest

---

[69] *Ibid.*, Feb. 26, 1923.

[70] Sometimes, of course, the religious issue is displaced by the social or
economic issues. (See letter in *The Nation,* May 16, 1923, pp. 572 f.) Sometimes mixed with the political issues: " It is to the Christians or to those
masquerading as Christians, that your plea for social justice should be
more directly addressed, for it is only in the so-called Christian countries
of the world that the Jews are persecuted or where they are denied justice.
The non-Christian countries are more just to the Jews." (Letter from Sir
Isidore Spielmann to Dr. Isidore Singer, April 24, 1923.) Sometimes
nakedly sharp: " Anti-Semitism is a chronic aspect of Christian history.
. . . Why are the Jews the perennial devil of the piece? The answer lies
in the Christian religion itself, in the status which Christianity assigns to
the Jews and the burden it sets and binds on them. In the Christian system, then, the Jews are assigned a central and dramatic status. They are
the villains of the drama of salvation. Attitudes that Sunday Schools the
world over impart automatically to children at five may be deep buried and
forgotten at five and fifty, but they are not extirpated, nor translated. They
make a subsoil of preconceptions upon which other interests are nourished
and from which they gather strength. If you can end this teaching that the
Jews are the enemies of God and of mankind you will strike anti-Semitism
at its foundations." (*The Nation,* Feb. 28, 1923, art. by Horace M. Kallen,
" The Roots of Anti-Semitism.") But it would be easy to balance this with
Jewish utterances against Christians and against all inter-racial assimila-
tions and kinships, and one writer in the issue of *The Nation,* May 16, 1923,
declares that anti-Semitism antedated Christianity and another that Christianity " is no guiltier than its prototype, the Jewish religion, in the preaching of hate." It should be added that Jewish teachers also disavow any
opposition to intermarriage of Jews with non-Jews on racial grounds, but
declare this opposition to be wholly religious. So Rabbi Krass asserts: " All
through the ages Jews have married outside of Judaism and were thus lost
to Israel and the faith, and non-Jews married into Judaism and thus were
added to and absorbed by Israel. All these historical facts prove conclusively that there was never among the Jews any objection to intermarriage

Jews and Christians alike will try in love to show each to the other the truth which he believes has been given to him to hold and to share.

5. Our relations to Latin America. It is just as well for us in the United States and Canada to realise that Latin America does not love us and is not occupied in gazing with longing upon our prosperity and with admiration upon our blameless political righteousness. It distrusts and misbelieves our purposes. It derides our commercialism. It looks to France, not to us, for ideas and ideals. "It is evident," says Manuel Ugarte, "that nothing attracts us toward our neighbours of the North. By her origin, her education, and her spirit, South America is essentially European. We feel ourselves akin to Spain, to whom we owe our civilisation, and whose fire we carry in our blood; to France, source and origin of the thought that animates us; to England, who sends us her gold freely; to Germany, who supplies us with her manufactures; and to Italy, who gives us the arms of her sons to wrest from the soil the wealth which is to distribute itself over the world. But to the United States we are united by no ties but those of distrust and fear." Sr. Calderon calls us "the great plutocracy of the North," "The Yankee peril"; our policy toward Chile he calls "indecisive, turbid, Machiavelic." He monopolises "America" as a term of speech applied to South America, as we have monopolised it for the United States. To be unified with the North American spirit would be racial suicide, he thinks. "Where Yankees and Latin Americans intermingle, you may better observe the insoluble contradictions which divide them. The

---

merely on racial grounds. The chief reason among the Jews, as among the Catholics, for example, used against intermarriage, was religious. The admixture of alien elements always tends to weaken the faith.

"The attitude of the Jew today is still the same. We are opposed to intermarriage because we believe in our own religious mission and we feel that whatever tends to weaken that mission ought not to be encouraged. By intermarriage we understand the union of two persons of different faiths who after marriage still cling to their respective religions. . . . The minority is always in danger of being absorbed through intermarriage by the majority, and if intermarriage increased, Jews as Jews would diminish, and with the disappearance of the Jew Judaism would disappear, although many of its teachings have been incorporated in western civilisation." (New York *Times,* March 3, 1924, "Dr. Krass Advises Jews to Wed Jews.")

Anglo-Saxons are conquering America commercially and economically, but the traditions, the ideals, and the soul of these republics are hostile to them." He declares, " To save themselves from Yankee imperialism the American democracies would almost accept a German alliance, or the aid of Japanese arms; everywhere the Americans of the North are feared." He sees no real unity in the United States. He does see " the triumph of vulgarity," the increase of divorce and criminality, " plebeian brutality, excessive optimism, violent individualism, confusion, uproar, instability." It is with Europe, and not with the United States and Canada, that Latin America would identify its commercial, political, and cultural interests. " We find," he says, " practical mind, industrialism, political liberty in England; organisation and instruction in Germany; in France, inventive genius, culture, wealth, great universities, democracy. From these dominating people the New World should receive the legacy of western civilisation directly. Europe offers to the Latin-American democracies what they ask of Saxon America, which was itself formed in the schools of Europe." [71]

Dr. Alfredo L. Palacios, a distinguished Argentine educationalist, Dean of the Faculty of Juridicial and Social Sciences of the National University of La Plata, sets forth with a temperate pathos this deep feeling of distrust in Latin America:

" My attitude is frankly one of opposition toward the Pan-American movement; because I know that in a union of that sort the weak and separated peoples of South America must become the satellites and servants, the unknowing docile instruments, not of North America but of the enslaving Yankee Plutocracy.

" I believe, on the contrary, that the only salvation for these democracies of the South lies in the recognition by them of their mutual identity of race and their inevitable unity in destiny, thus bringing about a confederation of all of them to constitute a great power, like the Republic of the North, with which it might deal thus, in analogous conditions; and then a pan-Americanism would be possible and desirable which would place an incomparable barrier in the way of the irritating war-like and imperialistic pretensions of the Old World today. Unless this Confederation of

[71] Calderon, *Latin America, Its Rise and Progress*, passim.

the South is formed, the present situation as well as Pan-Americanism are both extremely dangerous for the future of South America because they incorporate the idea of the absorption, slowly but surely, of our nations, impotent and backward, by the Colossus of the North. . . . Of even more urgent interest than the important theme proposed by you, 'the advantage there would be to all nations in substituting in their present belligerent rivalries a policy of co-operation and concord,' I believe is that of the necessity there exists for the peoples of South America to unite in founding a vast Confederation which incorporates that ideal of solidarity and humane co-operation in opposition to that of rivalry and destructive struggle which Europe represents. Because I consider this as unchangeable, today, in such orientation, undermined and honeycombed by interests and forces of the past which gravitate about her like fate itself; and in the same sense, more or less, North America is heading, pushed by her all-powerful plutocrats, towards the same fatal path.

" Our Hispanic-American peoples alone are sustaining the idealism of justice and international harmony, the defense and realisation of which seems to constitute for them a mission placed upon them by destiny; for none other feels it so deeply nor finds itself free to promote it, since with us historic fatalities and interests opposed to this ideal are absent. That this splendid possibility may be realised depends upon our union, before all else; for if we continue to live apart, as we do today, we shall continue to be, successively, the irredeemable victims of North American power which perhaps may destroy forever this high aspiration." [72]

And Dr. Zeballos, of Argentina, declared, in the summer of 1923, that the United States was more unpopular than ever in South America as a result of the Pan American Conference held in Chile in the spring of 1923.[73]

---

[72] Letter Dr. Palacios, written to a friend in 1923.
[73] New York *Times*, editorial " Through South American Eyes," August 23, 1923. See press dispatch in The New York *Times*, Jan. 13, 1923: " 'Yankee imperialism' and 'North American bureaucracy' are terms used by the newspapers today in unanimously approving Mexico's refusal to participate in the Pan-American Congress at Santiago. The United States is variously described as 'a crushing giant' and 'unscrupulous potentate,' while Pan-Americanism, as interpreted by the present union, is referred to as 'a farce and comedy from which no good can come.'
" 'Under the circumstances, Mexico could do nothing but decline the invitation,' says the *Excelsior*. 'Everybody knows Pan-Americanism merely signifies continental hegemony by the United States; that the famous conferences held from time to time, ostensibly to strengthen the

The people of the United States think of themselves as so animated with the spirit of justice and good will that they cannot conceive how other people should mistrust them. But we need to see ourselves as others see us. It will " frae many a blunder free us, and foolish notion." We have a real piece of work ahead of us in working out right race relationships with our Latin American neighbours, but, once again, it can be done, and more easily than anywhere else in the world, by the old principle of justice and brotherhood.

There are elements of union to bind us together across the chasm of race. There are many of these, and they are far stronger than such writers as Calderon and Ugarte, representative though they be of the thought of Latin America, are ready to admit. Latin America and Anglo-Saxon America do already have more in common than either has with Europe as a whole. ''/hat are some of these things? (1) The principle of democracy. It is true that Latin America thinks the United States to be a plutocracy and that we think the Latin-American nations to be oligarchies, but as a matter of fact the democratic principle is inveterate in each. No Latin-American nation has ever been in danger of turning monarchy, however autocratic and prolonged its presidential dictatorship. Sr. Pezet says that without having inborn in them any of the principles of true democracy, the Latin-American nations became over night, as it were, democratic and representative republics. But there was more democracy there than Sr. Pezet allows, and the Latin-American spirit today is immovably democratic. Titles and rank and dynastic interests are alien to it. It loves freedom. It is more akin to the spirit of the United States than to the spirit of France or any European race. (2) Latin America and Anglo-Saxon America have the common characteristics which came from the struggle to tame great areas. Japan is one-third the size of Venezuela, but its population is as great as that of all South America. South America has a problem of nature subjugation more than forty-eight

---

ties of friendship and fraternity among the American republics are worth only what the White House makes them worth because at all times Yankee diplomacy is imposed on all the other countries,' the paper asserts."

times that of Japan. We have fought a good part of our battle
and have the qualities resulting from it. Latin America is just
entering a nature discipline. (3) Our political community of interest is real and fundamental. Drago and Calvo, of Argentina,
and Rio Branco and Roy Barbosa, of Brazil, have striven as
notably as our own statesmen " for the development and institution of an American international law." All the American nations
deplore and must seek together to protect themselves against the
system of state relationships and diplomacy which has plunged
Europe into the ruin and carnage of its recent war. (4) The
American nations have a common, traditional love of international peace. They have never built up great armaments or
sought to preserve peace with one another by rivalry in arming
each against the other. Before the European War it was said:
" The twenty armies of Latin America aggregate on a war footing
about 1,500,000 men. Taking the army of the United States, including the militia and volunteers, as 2,000,000, we get 3,500,000
as the total of the American military coalition. This force, hardly
capable of united action, is less than the war army of any one of
the three former leading military powers of Europe—France,
Germany, Russia." There have been wars in Latin America and
periods of revolution and anarchy and bloody dictatorship, but the
heart of all America is a heart of peace. It is a different heart
from that of the militaristic nations. (5) America is less of a
Babel than any other continent. Two languages practically cover
all America. Portuguese is, of course, different from Spanish,
but they are mutually intelligible. There are Indian dialects by
the score, but these will die away with the popular education.
English is taught throughout Latin America, and Spanish increasingly in the United States. And what is more significant, we have
more common thought by far than binds any other two continents.
(6) We are united by a common faith in and zeal for education.
(7) We are also united by a common spirit of hope. We are all
Americans. " Seldom in Spanish America does one hear any one
speak of the place his ancestors came from. . . . Seldom do
South Americans or Mexicans seem to visit Spain. . . . For
the Spanish Americans there seems to be no past at all earlier

than their own war of independence." It is true that France has
supplanted Spain, and that France means Paris, but it is not the
past of Paris that appeals. The Latin-American people are a
people of the future. They and we are moving forward together
into new things. And if we do our part the Christian ideals and
principles will determine our movement.

We have already seen how great is Latin America's own problem of race adjustment. It will help both her and us in our internal problems if we can make our inter-continental relationships right.

6. The problems of this Western World seem bright compared
with the race tangle of Europe. Those who glory in the supremacy of the white race must include in their boast its supremacy in
fratricidal strife. They realise this with heavy hearts. With
somewhat harsh language some of them describe the suicide of
Europe and its consequences: "If this great race," says Madison
Grant, "with its capacity for leadership and fighting, should
ultimately pass, with it would pass that which we call civilisation.
It would be succeeded by an unstable and bastardised population,
where worth and merit would have no inherent right to leadership
and among which a new and darker age would blot out our racial
inheritance." [74] The new population would perhaps have as clean
a parentage as the old and it would have to be possessed of rare
powers to be able to produce a darker age. But the present is
doing its best to prepare the way. And the races are still un-
awakened to their madness.

7. The immigration problems are not ours alone. Canada and
Australia share some of them with us and, so far as these problems involve relations with the races of India, they come home to
Canada as a member of the same Empire with India more even
than to us. The population of Canada of British origin in 1921
constituted 54 per cent. of the whole. Of the total population
28.96% were of English origin, 27.91% were of French, 13.36%
Scotch and 12.6% Irish. Asiatics were less than one per cent. of
the whole. In the United States, Asiatics were less than one-sixth

[74] Introduction to Stoddard's *The Rising Tide of Colour*, p. xxix f.

of one per cent. Canada has a far vaster undeveloped territory, and a greater need of labour and a greater difficulty in assimilating the labour available, and a less homogeneous population, and a lighter Anglo-Saxon proportion, and a French Catholic element almost equal to its English stock and one-half as strong as the whole British stock combined.

Australia's problem is greater still. Five million people have a continent of 2,946,691 square miles. The Northern Territory of Australia has an area of 523,620 square miles, or four times the size of France, with a population of 3,734 people. Would the argument that justified the white race in taking over America from the Indian because it could do so and needed it, justify the yellow race in taking over Australia if it needed it and could take it? If not, what but a right view of racial relationships will prevent? "Australians," says the Hon. Randolph Bedford, M.P. for Queensland, " have made racial purity their political religion." That is well. It will be well to add to the religion the element of racial justice and racial brotherhood. Australia is justified in a policy of restricted immigration if that will secure best the interests of mankind. If not, she will be neither justified in forming the policy nor capable of enforcing it.

South Africa also has the problem of Oriental race immigration. And the Allahabad *Leader* of March 11, 1923, reported an article in *New India* to the effect that the Supreme Court of the South African Union had by a vote of three judges to two confirmed the notice of the Minister of the Interior that all Asiatics were prohibited immigrants. *New India* added, " It is interesting to observe that any drunken loafer, if he has a white skin can enter, but the entry of a Tagore, of a Sastri, of a Gokhale is prohibited. Even the Christ, when He comes, as He will be, in body, an Asiatic, will be a prohibited immigrant. An act prohibiting white South Africans from entering India should be passed by the Indian Legislature."

8. The Japanese have their race issues to deal with in Korea and in China. When they took over Korea it was with the policy of political incorporation and racial amalgamation. They underestimated the spirit of the Korean people, their feeling of racial

solidarity and their will for freedom. There is an element in
Japan which would crush all this with relentless military power.
When the World War seemed to leave China at Japan's mercy the
Twenty One Demands were presented which would have subju-
gated the Chinese to Japan, almost as completely as Korea. And
the same element in Japan which would crush Korea would deal
as ruthlessly with the Chinese. But a better mind as to race rights
and relationships has come to Japan as it has come to us. It has
found its way in part into power in new policies as to Korea and
China, and it anticipates a fuller conquest. The Hon. D. Tagawa,
ex Vice-Mayor of Tokyo and member of the Japanese Diet, who
has gone to prison for his convictions and emerged as unfearing
as before, sets forth this new progress of Japanese liberalism and
the view as to its adequate sources and sanctions which underlies
these studies:

" The Japanese liberals advocate home rule for Korea, complete
restoration of Shantung to China (economic as well as political),
absolute withdrawal from Siberia, unwavering maintenance of
friendly relations with America, opening of all Cabinet posts to
civilians, universal suffrage and other similar principles.
" While, however, there are many evidences of a rising Liberal
movement in Japan, it is hard to know just how real and strong
it is. It is my own belief, true liberalism is a product of Christianity and rests on Christian foundations. It depends on vital
Christian faith for its own vitality. But the Christian movement
in Japan is still very young, and very crude and very weak. We
number scarcely more than 200,000 all told. Even so-called Christians, multitudes of them, neither understand it nor really practice
it. Not until millions of Japanese have been transformed by a
vital Christianity shall we have, in my opinion, a really strong and
a vital liberal movement.
" This is, in my humble opinion, Japan's most pressing problem.
We have indeed the forms of constitutional government and of
parliamentary institutions, but they do not as yet grow out of and
depend on the inner life of our people; they are still largely exotic.
Japan's great need is that these institutions shall become indigenous as well as effective, growing out of our own life. For
this, however, our people must more generally come under the
transforming influence of the teachings of Jesus as to God and
man, giving respect for man as man, recognising his person and

his inalienable human rights. It is upon these foundations alone that a real liberal movement must build.

"But we are not without hope. We are learning many lessons. The Christian movement is making steady growth and we are coming into even closer touch with the liberal movement in the lands, especially in England and America. As a Christian speaking to Christians, let me ask your patience, your friendships, and your co-operation." [75]

9. No area of the world is free from these issues of race. They are the questions before men's minds day and night in South Africa.[76] Before the Union the question of race relations was alive in the controversy over Chinese and Indian coolie labour and always in the problem of the native races. In Basutoland the population is almost wholly Bantu or native. In Natal it is nearly 80% with 12% more of Indians or half caste. In the Transvaal the native population is over 72%; in the Union of South Africa it is 67%; in Orange Free State it is 61%; in the Cape it is 59%. The white population is highest in Orange Free State, with 33% and lowest in Natal with 8%. These were the census figures in 1911. In the whole of British South Africa in 1904 the white population was less than one-fourth of the native or Bantu. The native is limited in his right to buy and own land. Contact with white civilisation has demoralised him.

"The South African Native Affairs Commission of 1903-5 reports gloomily on this point: 'It must apparently be accepted as an axiom that contact with what we are accustomed to regard as civilisation has a demoralising tendency as its first effect upon primitive races. It is clear that the Native year by year is becoming familiar with new forms of sexual immorality, intemperance, and dishonesty, and that his naturally imitative disposition, his virility, and escape from home and tribal influences provide a too congenial soil for the cultivation of acquired vices.' So bad, indeed, can the moral effect of a large mining centre be, that a prominent South African statesman, the Hon. John X. Merriman, in speaking of the responsibility of the white race for the Native,

---

[75] *Goodwill*, April, 1922, p. 191.
[76] *International Review of Missions,* April, 1922, art. "Native Unrest in South Africa," pp. 249, 259; *The East and the West,* Oct., 1922, art. "Coloured Races in South Africa," pp. 327-337.

referred to Johannesburg as a 'Criminal University.' . . .
Abundant evidence of the demoralising effect of life on the mines
could be adduced ; e. g.:—

"From Johannesburg, on the other hand, they (the Natives)
go back impoverished in wealth and health, and usually moral
degenerates, and from their influence flow the physical degeneration as well as the growing uneasiness among raw Natives who
have not left their kraal. It is responsible for the growing criminality, and the systematic undermining of the best traditions not
only of the Native kraals, but also of respect for the white man's
authority and loss of faith in his good intentions.' [77]

"The Native's mode of life has been largely affected by his
contact with the European. Originally a pastoralist, he has been
compelled by the enclosure of lands to occupy localities where
pastoral farming is difficult. Economic pressure has forced him
into the white man's service, where his character and mode of life
have been affected for the worse by an environment for which he
was not ready.[78]

There are also the fundamental problems of the right to own
land and the right to work. Exclusion from land ownership and
from higher occupations would be a deadly race discrimination.
"For four hundred years," says the *London Times,* "white
Europe traded in the black human beings of Africa and robbed
her of one hundred million of her people, 'transformed the face
of her social life, overthrew organised government, distorted
ancient industry, and snuffed out the lights of cultural development.' Today instead of removing labourers from Africa to
distant slavery, industry built on a new slavery approaches Africa
to deprive the natives of their land, to force them to toil and to
reap all the profit for the white world.

"A recent law of the Union of South Africa assigns nearly two
hundred and fifty million acres of the best of natives' land to a
million and a half of whites and leaves thirty-six million of acres
of swamp and marsh for four and a half million blacks. In

---

[77] From an interview in the *Cape Argus* with Mr. C. J. Levey, I. S. O.,
senior member for Tembuland in the Old Cape Parliament, at one time
C. C. and R. M. for Wodehouse and magistrate in Tembuland and the
Transkei. Quoted by Loram, p. 10.

[78] Loram, *The Education of the South African Native,* pp. 9-11.

Rhodesia over ninety million acres have been practically confiscated. In the Belgian Congo all the land was declared the property of the state." [79]

" By the Land Act of 1913 passed by white men in the Orange Free State the black man is not allowed to hire land or even to contract with a white man to plough it on half shares. He is literally a serf, landless, unable to rent land, a hired servant of the Dutchman." [80]

The Supreme Court of the Transvaal, however, recently declared invalid a legislative enactment limiting the employment of competent shiftsmen on work in mines and with machinery to white men.[81]

The reaction of such conditions on the white race is inevitable. Nature takes a sure revenge. The weaker group drags the stronger but smaller group down " like a cancerous and suffocating burden at the heart." [82] The problem for South Africa, because of numbers, is far harder than for us in America, and also because, with all its disadvantages, slavery was a school for the American Negro for which the Bantu people have had no equivalent. But, ultimately, though it be far off, the solution of South Africa's race problem is not different from our own.[83]

And India has its grave struggle over these same questions both at home and abroad. In the Kenya Colony in East Central Africa,[84] in Natal, in Guiana, the question of Indian race rights and relations is a living question. And race questions are the dominant questions in India itself. The three primary ethno-

[79] *London Times,* May 1 and April 24, 1923. Quoted in *Race Relations and the Christian Ideal,* p. 34; See Federal Council of the Churches, Research Department, *Information Service,* Jan. 12, 1924. Art. " Third Pan-African Congress."

[80] Jabavu, *The Black Problem,* p. 13.

[81] New York *Times,* Feb. 21, 1924, Editorial. " The Colour Line in South Africa."

[82] Loram, *Op. cit.,* p. 12.

[83] One of the best discussions of the race problem in Africa is the chapter entitled " The Colour Bar " in Willoughby's *Race Problems in the New Africa,* pp. 222-249.

[84] London *Spectator,* May 5, 1923, art. " The Problem of Kenya," p. 744 f.; *Current History,* Sept., 1923, art. by Llewelyn Powys, " Britain's Imperial Problem in Kenya Colony."

graphical divisions of mankind are all to be found within the area
of the Indian Empire. Most of the Indian peoples are reckoned as
belonging to the Caucasian type. The yellow race is found in the
Lesser Himalayas and furnishes an important element in the ethnology of Bengal. The Negroid type is clear in the Andaman
Islands and, some would hold, elsewhere in India. Four of the
great families of the human speech are found in India, the
Austric, the Tibeto-Chinese, the Dravidian and the Indo-
European. The Moslem conquests also brought in the Semitic
tongues, Persian and Arabic.[85] To reconcile all these racial and
linguistic strains which have ramified in the centuries, to open the
gates of organised society to the low castes, and to bind together
the Hindu and Mohammedan peoples, fictitiously united for a little
while in the Nationalist Movement under Mr. Gandhi's leadership
but now wide apart and more hostile than before,[86] to unite
Brahman and non-Brahman, and also to hold together Indian and
European in good will and confidence—what other nation has
more exacting racial problems than these?[87]

---

[85] Griswold, *Peoples and Languages of the Indian Empire.*
[86] The Allahabad *Leader,* April 2, 1923, p. 3.
[87] The Lahore *Civil and Military Gazette,* March 23, 1923. Paper by the
Earl of Ronaldshay, ex-Governor of Bengal, on " The Clash of Ideals as a
Source of Indian Unrest "; Alfred Nundy, *Indian Unrest,* 1919-20, and
Political Problems, Chs. III, IX, XV; Keir Hardie, *India,* pp. 97-107;
Allahabad *Leader,* July 9, 1922, editorial, " Untouchability and the Caste
System "; *The Missionary Review of the World,* Jan., 1923. Art., " India
in the Melting Pot "; Allahabad *Pioneer,* Sept. 16, 1923. Editorial, " Helots
in Kenya and in India "; *The Madras Mail,* April 5, 1924. Art., " Depressed Fear the Caste Hindus." For a careful study of one of the outcast
groups, see Briggs, *The Chamars.*
One of these editorials cites a " Note on the Depressed Classes in the
Madras Presidency " prepared by the Commissioner of Labour and published by the Madras Government:
" In six districts of the Madras Presidency, we are told, more than one
person in every five is theoretically not allowed to come within a distance
of 64 feet of the higher castes without pollution. The purification cere-
monies, it appears, are now generally neglected except by the most orthodox, but in some areas the restrictions are still very pronounced. A case
is described where a number of people who visited a British officer had to
go many miles round to cross a river lest they should pollute a bridge by
their presence. In 1919, an English gentleman, a pronounced Nationalist,
while driving through a municipal town was surprised when his companion,
an Indian student, asked that he might be allowed to leave the vehicle and
join him at another point. He was still more surprised when his companion explained to him that his reason for descending was that he was not

10. The race problem is offered to the Christian Church as a test and as an opportunity. On the foreign mission fields the missionaries of the Western Churches have it in their power to demonstrate in their relations with the people and in the relation of the Missions with the Native Churches the right spirit and principle of race relationships. In the Eastern lands the new Christian Churches also are called upon to illustrate the true attitude of race to race, eschewing alike all servility and all arrogance, asking nothing as a favour, and demanding nothing as a right, but doing right and deserving right. In the West the Churches which have come down with rich, merged, racial inheritances should be the leaders in race service and sympathy. Least of all should any spirit of race antipathy or injustice appear in them. They are called to lead men to pay whatever price must be paid in surrender of prejudice and of false and partial views and in the practice of brotherhood in order that they may know the truth and its freedom.

The words of two Christian men, one of whom has lived through the race problem and the other of whom sought to think it through to its central truth may well bring these studies to a close:

The first of these is one who came as an immigrant boy from Hungary, Dr. Steiner:

" I should like to point out in which direction the most valuable lessons of my experience lie. I believe they are:

" First, that racial characteristics are largely determined by environment.

---

permitted to pass through a certain street. Again, to quote the Labour Commissioner's Note: 'Theoretically all Government offices are open to persons of every class and creed, but a rich and respectable gentleman recently returned from abroad informed the writer of this Note that he was made to go outside a certain public office when it was discovered that he was of low caste. In the recent Ganjam famine it was found necessary to find work for the outcasts on a different part of the works from the other labourers. Even in the presence of actual famine, the rules of distance had to be obeyed.'

" Is it surprising when these facts are considered that Indians who are subjected to the treatment described should leave their native country in order to find careers in other lands where no implacable bar to their success in life exists? "

" Second, that race prejudice is an artificial product of the mind, induced by various influences.

" Third, that in the highest and lowest spheres of thought and activity, all races are alike.

" Fourth, that every human being, no matter what his colour, race, faith or class, has a right to earn the respect of his neighbour and his community, by virtue of what he himself is.

" Fifth, that the brotherhood of man will become an established fact as soon as each man determines to live like a brother in his relation to his fellows.

" Sixth, that Christianity has in its spirit the solution of class and race problems; but that in its practice it is lamentably far from solving them.

" Seventh, that he who wishes to enter into fellowship with the nation or race with which he lives must free himself from all isolating practices and beliefs.

" Eighth, that entrance into such a large human relationship has to be ' bought with a price ' and that it is a price worth paying; for there is no loftier human experience than that of becoming one with all mankind." [88]

The second of these two men is the late Viscount Bryce, who spent a long and honoured life defending races against wrong and promoting understanding and good will among men, and who wrote to America from the steamer on his return to England, in October, 1921 : " The most effective factor in getting rid of armaments would be to substitute for national hatred and rivalries a sense of the brotherhood of nations such as our Lord inculcated upon individual men. The idea that ' we are all members one of another ' needs to be applied to peoples." [89]

For this is the ultimate truth about the races. They are one body, of one blood.

[88] Steiner, *Against the Current*, p. 288 f.
[89] *Goodwill*, April, 1922, p. 191.

INDEX

Abel, C. W., quoted, 173.
Africa, Oriental immigration to South, 421, race problem in South, 423 f.
Agassiz, Alexander, on influence of Christianity, 252.
Alexander, Bertrand, quoted, 404 f.
Allegret, 74.
Amalgamation of races, 306-333.
Ameer Ali, Syed, 241.
American, The New York, hymn of hate against Japanese, 163.
Andrews, C. F., 160, 322.
Armenian race problem, 198 ff.
Armstrong, Gen. S. C., quoted, 362 f.
Australia, immigration problems in, 421.
Awdry. Bishop of Japan, quoted, 137 ff.

Bagehot, quoted, 12, 314.
Bahaism and race, 240.
Bantu people, a racial mixture, 34, 197.
Bashford, Bishop, quoted. 102.
Beaulieu, Leroy, quoted, 90.
Belloc, on the Jews, 72 f., 105 f.
Bevan, Edward G., quoted, 45 f.
Bhagavad Gita, 275.
Bhagavad Purana, 275.
Bickett, Mrs. B. W., quoted, 353.
Birmingham meeting of Interracial Conference, 375 f.
Boas. Franz, quoted, 39, 62, 72, 76, 98, 402.
Bolivar, quoted, 325.
Brailsford, John A., quoted, 298.
Browne, E. G., on Mohammedan racial intolerance, 240.
Browning, quoted, 132. 262.
Bryce, Lord, quoted, 62, 328 f., 364 f., 427.
Buckle, on climate, soil and race, 222.
Buddhism and race, 237 f.

Burr's *America's Race Heritage*, cited, 42.
Burroughs, Nannie Helm, quoted, 97, 109.
Burton, Sir Richard, 178, 321.
Bury, quoted, 22.

Cagots, 198.
Cahn, Edgar M., quoted, 411.
Calderon, on South American amalgamation, 326 ff., on the U. S., 415 f.
Canada, race problems in, 420 f.
Capper Marriage-Divorce Bill, 317.
Carroll, Charles, and the colour of God, 212.
Carter, T. F., letter from, 87 f.
Caste in India, 167 ff., 285 f.
Chandavarkar, Sir Narayan, 241, paper on race, 259-286.
Charleston Cotton Growers' Association, statement of, 373.
Chelmsford, Lord, quoted, 110 f., 212.
Chicago Commission on Race Relations. 378 ff.
China, harsh industrial conditions in, 174 f.
Chinese attitude to West, 56 f.
Chinese in America, 192-196.
Chinese race characteristics, 141 ff.
Chirol, Sir Valentine, quoted, 359.
Christianity and race, 148-153, 276 ff., 342-347, 427.
Cicero, quoted, 47, 49, 53.
Cleveland, Grover, 221.
Climate and race, 222 ff.
Cochran, J. B., quoted. 222.
Colour and race, 212-222, 281.
Communications and race, 228 ff.
Confucius, *Analects* of, 102.
Conklin, E. G., quoted. 16, 19, 27, 29, 40, 43, 52, 101, 304, 307 f., 315, 342.
Constructive Immigration Legislation, National Committee for, 393.

429

Rhys Davids, quoted, 238.
Richardson, quoted, 24.
Robertson, J. M., on discontent of subject races, 114 ff.
Rodebach, Georges, quoted, 226.
Rodo, Jose Enrique, quoted, 65.
Roemer's *Origin of the English People and of the English Language,* quoted, 226.
Roman view of family, 12.
Rome and its race policy, 48 ff.
Ronaldshay, Earl of, quoted, 157.
Ross, E. A., quoted, 19, 31, 123, 154, 233.
Rossiter on race composition of America, 42.
Rowell, Chester H., quoted, 291.
Rowell, N. W., quoted, 66.
Royce, Josiah, quoted, 45, 80.
Russell, Bertrand, 148, 336.
Russia, decay of economic trust in, 130.

Sarojini, Naidu, quoted, 36.
Scherer, S. A., quoted, 110.
Schreiner, Olive, quoted, 316 f.
Schulman, Samuel, quoted, 412.
Scotch-Irish animosity to English, 35, 196.
Seeley, J. R., quoted, 81.
Selborne, Lord, quoted, 255.
Semitic view of racial kinship, 11 f.
Sergi, Giuseppe, quoted, 235.
Seward, W. H., on the Chinese Coolie trade, 193.
Sex and race problems analogous, 230 ff.
Shaler, N. S., cited, 188.
Shibusawa, Baron, quoted, 398 f.
Shih, Peter, 352.
Shohl, Charles, quoted, 409 f.
Shridkar Ketkar, 168.
Singer, Isidore, quoted, 414.
Slater, T. E., quoted, 150.
Slave raid caravan, picture of, 182 f.
Slavery, 181-191, 360 f.
  in ancient times, 181.
  in Scotland, 181.
  white slavery in America, 181 f.
  in Portuguese East Africa, 185 ff.
Slessor, Mary, of Calabar, 179.
Sloane, W. M., quoted, 226.
Smith on "Language as a Link," 102, 227 f.
Smith, W. Robertson, quoted, 12.

South African Native Races Committees Report, 82, 334 f.
Southern University Commission on the Negro, 349 f.
Spaulding, C. C., quoted, 374.
Spengler, Oswald, quoted, 220.
Spielmann, Isidore, quoted, 414.
Spiller, quoted, 79, 83, 88, 304.
Stanmore, Lord, quoted, 269.
Steiner, E. A., quoted, 44, 257 f., 305 f., 427.
Stephenson, G. T., quoted, 160.
Stern, Horace, quoted, 410.
Stevens, Thaddeus, buried with Negroes, 357.
Stevenson, R. L., 266.
Stewart, James, quoted, 75 f., 176, 197, 252 f.
Stoddard, Lothron, quoted, 17, 68 f., 130 f., 159, 164 f., 225, 242, 288.
Stone's *The American Race Problem,* and other writings, quoted, 54, 71, 95, 117, 124, 154, 158, 188, 374 f.
Storrs, R. S., quoted, 67.
Student Fellowship for Life Service, Southern Conference of, 352.
Student Volunteer Convention at Indianapolis, 344 f.
Sulzberger, Mayer, 73.
Sutherland, Justice, decision on naturalization of Japanese, 394 f.
Swadeshi, 109.
Sze, Chinese Minister to the U. S., quoted, 192.

Tagore, Rabindranath, quoted, 60, 168 f., 299.
Temple, Lt. Gov. of Northern Nigeria, quoted, 302.
Temple, Sir Richard, quoted, 147.
Temps, Le, quoted, 35, 219.
Thomas, W. H., quoted, 218.
Thompson, Prof. Wm. H., *Brain and Personality,* 24.
Thomson, Joseph, quoted, 178.
Thomson, Sir Basil, on criminals, 24.
Thomson's *Outline of Service,* quoted, 32 f.
Thorndike, quoted, 21, 343, 366.
Tolstoy, 44.
Townsend, Meredith, 157.
Trotsky's *Terrorism and Communism,* 16.
Trowbridge, Stephen G., cited, 241.

Tukaram, 275.
Tuskegee Government Hospital, 220.

Uesugi Shinkichi, quoted, 59.
Uhlhorn, quoted, 244 ff.
Ugarte, Manuel, quoted, 415.

Vambery, Arminius, quoted, 297 f.
Vardaman, Senator, quoted, 332.
Venezuela difficulty, in 1895, 300.
Villa expedition, 340 f.

War, economic and racial burden of, 201 ff.
Ward, Harry F., 263.
Warne, Bishop, quoted, 37.
Washington, Booker, quoted, 93, 118, 221, 330.
Waterhouse, on assimilability of the Japanese, 392 f.
Weale, Putnam, quoted, 125, 164, 217, 222 f., 232, 242 f., 302.
Weatherford, W. D., quoted, 121, 366.
Webb, Attorney Gen. of California, on Japanese in U. S., 392.
Wee Macgregor, 287.
Wells, H. G., quoted, 31, 98, 154.

West Africa, quoted, 180.
Wheeler, Benjamin Ide, quoted, 59.
Whipple, Bishop, on our treatment of the Indians, 191 f.
Wichita Beacon, The, quoted, 40.
Wilcox, E. V., quoted, 385 f.
Wiley, Dr. Harvey, 24.
Williams, F. W., letter from, 86 f.
Williams, Mornay, quoted, 210 f., 346 f.
Winsborough, Mrs. W. C., quoted, 353.
Winston, Judge R. W., quoted, 294.
Woods, Ambassador to Japan, quoted, 129 f.
Woods, as to domination of inheritance, 17 f.
Woodward, Archdeacon H. W., quoted, 268.
Wordsworth, quoted, 262, 283.
Work, Indian Commissioner, quoted, 402.
Wu Ting Fang, quoted, 292, 313.

York, Archbishop of, quoted, 278 f.

Zeballos, quoted, 417.